Embracing Reason

This book tells a single story, in many voices, about a serious and sustained set of changes in mathematics teaching practice in a high school and how those efforts influenced and were influenced by a local university. It includes the writings and perspectives of high school students, high school teachers, preservice teacher candidates, doctoral students in mathematics education and other fields, mathematics teacher educators, and other education faculty. As a whole, this case study provides an opportunity to reflect on reform visions of mathematics for all students and the challenges inherent in the implementation of these visions in US schools. It challenges us to rethink boundaries between theory and practice and the relative roles of teachers and university faculty in educational endeavors.

Daniel Chazan, University of Maryland, College Park, Maryland

Sandra Callis, Washington Woods Middle School, Holt, Michigan

Michael Lehman, Holt High School, Holt, Michigan

T0346585

Studies in mathematical thinking and learning
Series editor: Alan H. Schoenfeld

Embracing Reason

Egalitarian Ideals and the Teaching of
High School Mathematics

Daniel Chazan, Sandra Callis, and
Michael Lehman

 Routledge
Taylor & Francis Group

NEW YORK AND LONDON

First published 2008
by Routledge
270 Madison Ave, New York, NY 10016

Simultaneously published in the UK
by Routledge
2 Park Square, Milton Park, Abingdon, Oxon OX14 4RN

Routledge is an imprint of the Taylor & Francis Group, an informa business

Transferred to Digital Printing 2009

© 2008 Taylor & Francis

Typeset in Sabon by Wearset Ltd, Boldon, Tyne and Wear

Library of Congress Cataloging in Publication Data
A catalog record for this book has been requested

ISBN10: 0-8058-6163-7 (hbk)
ISBN10: 0-415-87904-3 (pbk)
ISBN10: 1-4106-1522-7 (ebk)

ISBN13: 978-0-8058-6163-1 (hbk)
ISBN13: 978-0-415-87904-0 (pbk)
ISBN13: 978-1-4106-1522-0 (ebk)

Contents

Figures

Tables

Acknowledgments

It is not often that educators based in public schools and universities have opportunities to inquire into pressing problems of practice over long spans of time. We, the authors of the text in this volume, have been lucky. Joined by our shared interests in mathematics education, though we have been affiliated with either Holt High School or Michigan State University, we have had the chance to work collaboratively across institutional boundaries for the benefit of our students and for our own professional growth. The opportunities we have had compel us to report on our experiences to a larger public.

Indirectly, the case study presented in this book critiques many aspects of the professional organization of education in the United States: for example, the organization of high school teachers' work week with a minimum of 25 student contact hours and divisions of labor between school and university. Beyond this critical perspective, with this case study, we hope to make a convincing argument for the value of alternative arrangements. For example, in a time of societal focus on educational issues, we hope that our case study illustrates the value of professional development oriented toward an inquiring stance on daily teaching practice and organized around a substantive educational goal, in our case, promoting access to more mathematics for a wider range of students.

The work described in this volume began to take place in the summer of 1989. Over the past almost 15 years, we have all accumulated numerous professional and intellectual debts which we cannot possibly acknowledge here. In addition to our debts to the Holt Public Schools and to Michigan State University (MSU), we must acknowledge the work of a myriad of colleagues at Michigan State University and Holt High School who participated in Professional Development School (PDS) efforts, in particular Tom Davis – early on the principal of Holt High School and later the superintendent of Holt Public Schools – and Perry Lanier – on occasion the coordinator of MSU and Holt High School's PDS effort and often the coordinator of MSU's entire PDS effort.

The writing of this text has also been a long process, taken on in the midst of other pressing concerns. We began the process by collating essays previously written by various members of the project. We gratefully acknowledge the permission of Springer Science and Business Media, Elsevier Limited, Eye on Education, the National Academy of Sciences, and the Institute for Research on Teacher Learning at Michigan State University for the reprinting of the previously published essays that appear in this volume.

Support from the Spencer Foundation allowed for the development of new essays during the 1999–2000 and 2000–2001 academic years. This funding also supported a process of response to these essays. In the summer of 2000, pairs of teachers in the Holt High School mathematics department read each essay and commented on them. These responses were then collated, shaped into a dialogue form, and integrated with the essays and editorial text to create the three-part structure of this volume. Extension of the Spencer support allowed for retreats during the summer and fall of 2001 during which each of the three sections of the volume were read carefully and critiqued by the volume's authors. Our efforts received editorial and graphical support from Carolyn Shevrin, Kaustuv Roy, and Michelle Saunders, and most recently from Margaret Rogers.

Beyond these professional acknowledgements, family and friends, too numerous to mention here, have supported each of the authors in the volume. Without recognizing each of you by name, we appreciate your support for our endeavors.

Preface

From studying the structure of three high schools in the United States in the 1970s and 1980s, Phillip Cusick (1983) suggests that the keystone of the structure of those schools (one arguably still central to secondary schools in the US) is what he calls the egalitarian ideal. In his view, this ideal, which US public schools espouse whether or not they attain it, is "to provide each student with an opportunity for social, political and economic equality" (p. 1). Later, he suggests a different wording. The ideal is: "To extend the offer of education to as many people as possible regardless of their background, ambitions, or abilities" (p. 25). This book is a case study of the work of a single high school mathematics department in its efforts to take seriously this ideal in a particular place and time.

At this time, as at many others, there are many calls for substantial improvements to US schools. As a result, there are a number of trends that influence high school mathematics instruction. There are federally funded international comparative studies which analysts suggest indicate substantial room for improvement in student achievement in the United States (e.g., Schmidt *et al.*, 1999) and for fundamental changes to the nature of school curriculum in the US (Schmidt *et al.*, 1997). One comparatively new feature of recent trends is the involvement of the federal government in efforts to mandate improvement in student achievement (as codified, for example, in H.R. 1 of 2001, or the No Child Left Behind Act). This federal involvement is motivated in part by the feeling that US schools have not served minority students well. These mandates have their direct impact on high schools through increasing use of state-level, high-stakes tests as a part of the granting of high school diplomas, and in requirements for teacher qualification. More particularly, at the level of districts, there are trends to increase mathematics requirements for high school graduation (Usiskin, 2003). And, again at the national level, there have been vituperative battles, known colloquially as the Math Wars, about how to improve mathematics instruction (Jackson, 1997; Wilson, 2003). These battles have crystallized around the National Council of Teachers of Mathematics vision for the reform of school mathematics, known colloquially as the NCTM Standards (1989, 1991, 2000). These standards have come in for sharp criticism as promoting counterproductive change in mathematics classrooms, as being Fuzzy Math or the New New Math (Gardner, 1998).

At this time, it seems especially useful to portray the daily efforts of a high school mathematics department to act on its responsibilities to all of its students, to portray efforts to change and improve instruction in Algebra 1 as well as Calculus classrooms, to examine the impact of these efforts on students' experience of mathematics, and to investigate how teachers were supported in their efforts to change and improve their instruction. Though in the educational literature schools in the US there are some descriptions of attempts at school improvement through structural reform of high schools (e.g., Bensman, 2000), there are few descriptions of the attempts of *high school subject-matter departments* to sustain efforts at instructional improvement for all students (Gutiér-rez, 1996, is but one notable exception). In particular, there seem to be few descriptions that seek to link professional development for teachers with changes in instruction practices and with student achievement (NAE, 1999). Therefore, in this book, we offer a case study of the efforts of one high school mathematics department over slightly more than one decade as it grapples with what Cusick calls the egalitarian ideal.

One reason that we decided to make our work public in this way is our sense that there have been substantial changes in students' experience of mathematics at this high school. For example, during a decade in which enrollment at the high school increased by 29 percent, the number of sections of math courses taught more than doubled and the math department grew substantially (see Figure 0.1).

During this decade district requirements for graduation stayed the same; students who passed a 9th-grade math course were only required to complete one more course at the high school. Yet, in a typical year at the end of this decade, the mathematics department taught approximately 90 percent of the student body, up from approximately 54 percent in a typical year at the beginning of the decade.[1] And, all of this happened as students also took more advanced mathematics. In 1990–1991, five of the 20 sections of mathematics were Algebra 1, Pre-Algebra, or General Math; in 2001, five of the 41 sections were Algebra 1; PreAlgebra and General Math classes were no longer offered; with the exception of less than ten students a year given special exemptions by guidance staff, students do not graduate from Holt High School having only studied arithmetic (further details on course enrollment can be found in section two of this volume).[2]

	1990–1991	2000–2001	% increase
Total enrollment	930	1,143	29%
Number of math sections	20	41	105%
Approximate percentage of total enrollment taking math	$\frac{20 \times 25}{930} = 54\%$	$\frac{41 \times 25}{1,143} = 90\%$	
Number of department members: full (part)	2 (5)	7 (3)	

Figure 0.1 A comparison of math enrollments (taken from the National Academy of Education, 1999, p. 67).

Of course, such changes must not be read superficially. During the decade in question, there were nationwide trends toward students taking more mathematics (details of this phenomenon will be discussed in Part II of this volume). The population of a community does not remain unchanged during a decade; perhaps there were cohort effects at work. It would require much work to establish that particular factors were the probable causes of any change in student achievement. In the introduction, as we describe key features of our case study, that, it will become evident, is not our purpose.

School mathematics and egalitarian ideals: a focus on reason(s)

Our case study focuses on the teaching of a particular school subject matter, school mathematics. School mathematics, and indeed mathematics, has tangled relationships with egalitarian ideals. Mathematics is sometimes depicted as the quintessential subject of reason and rationality. This characterization is suggested by many commonly held views about mathematics, for example, the view that, even when people initially disagree strongly, agreement in mathematics can be attained through reasoned argument, or the view that mathematical results are not opinion. They are the way they are not because of the material world and not because of the desires or beliefs of individuals, but by necessity, by force of reason, as a result of mathematical proofs. (Though this is a common portrayal of mathematics, there are dissenting voices that characterize this common view as "dogmatism," Lakatos, 1976; "absolutism," Ernest, 1991; or "The Romance of Mathematics," Lakoff & Núñez, 2000.)

Notions of authority implicit in such common views of mathematics are, potentially, beautifully egalitarian. People are all, at least in theory, capable of establishing mathematical truths for themselves. Neither race, nor ethnicity, nor religion, nor one's mother tongue, nor social class makes any difference. Even though humanity is diverse, all those who agree to work from standard mathematical starting points (definitions, key propositions, types of argumentation) will derive the same results. Thus, in mathematics, statements can be labeled as "right" or "wrong," but such descriptions, while perhaps absolutist in Ernest's (1991) terms, are not authoritarian or doctrinal. *Anyone can establish such claims for themselves.* One does not need to take someone else's word; one does not need a big laboratory or expensive apparatus. Such notions undergird the dream of 17th-century mathematician and diplomat, Gottfried Leibniz, that mathematical arguments might some day come to replace the messy arguments of international law and create an era of peaceful resolutions to conflict (Davis & Hersh, 1986).

For proponents of egalitarian views of mathematics (for example, mathematician and author Devlin, 2000), if everyone has the "maths gene," or a propensity to do mathematical reasoning, what must be explained is why most people do not use it; few people experience mathematics in ways that support egalitarian views of the subject. Many people find mathematics difficult and frustrating. Often mathematical activity is rife with appeals to authority rather than reason (what mathematicians Davis & Hersh, 1981 call "proof by intimidation"). In school, for example, students are typically taught facts – like, pi is an irrational number – in contexts where they have few tools for reasoning. But without such tools, these facts beg important questions. For example, even when students know a definition for irrational numbers, how can they go about establishing that pi is different from a rational number, like 22/7? In a similar vein, but different curricular setting, how could students possibly establish, with what they know, that radian and degree measures of angles are incommensurable?

Mathematical authority is a general issue in school mathematics. In the press to teach students to solve problems, they are taught methods – like, invert and multiply for dividing fractions, or FOIL for multiplying binomials. Such methods for solving problems are often left unjustified. Indeed, as teacher, teacher educator, and researcher of teaching, Magdalene Lampert (1990) has argued, methods that students have learned, but which have not been justified, often function in the classroom as justification for the appropriateness of an answer, as first principles from which to reason. When an answer is justified by reference to a solution method, the validity of the method may rest solely on the authority of the teacher who introduced it.

There are other ways in which mathematics in school does not live up to the egalitarian promise of a subject based on reason. Often mathematical activity is accompanied by a sense of evaluation by others and by feelings of insecurity and anxiety. Mathematics in school is usually tracked. Often, students are grouped by their achievement – sometimes labeled "mathematical ability" – by the degree to which they say what is wrong and do what is incorrect. Tests of mathematical knowledge and skill, like the mathematics portion of the SAT, are used to determine who will and who will not have access to opportunities for advanced study. And, in advanced study, a student's hard-won mathematical results can be disparaged as trivial. As a result, many people experience mathematics as an activity that demonstrates that they cannot reason effectively and appropriately. In the extreme, such experiences result in math anxiety (in the sense of Tobias, 1993) on the part of otherwise accomplished people, let alone those who might find schooling difficult for other reasons.

Why does this happen? Why is there a gap between rhetoric about mathematics as disciplinary knowledge and people's experience of it, particularly in school? Or is it only natural that school as an institution causes a shift in disciplinary knowledge (as scholars like Thomas Popkewitz, 2004, suggest)? From the perspective of secondary school mathematics educators, there are many potential reasons. With our case study, we would like to argue for one.

One reason that rhetoric about mathematics and people's experience of school mathematics diverge has to do with a retreat from reasoning and a reliance on notions of ability to explain differences between the performances of students. As one moves from mathematics in the discipline to mathematics in school (Schwab, 1978 is an important advocate for this sort of analysis of school subjects), the egalitarian notion of each person being able to justify mathematical results for themselves is replaced by the imperative for students to learn culturally important knowledge, what others have established to be right. Similarly, definitions become already set starting points that are part of what is to be learned, and not artifacts carefully constructed in a social milieu to fit a set of proofs and understandings (as portrayed in philosopher Imre Lakatos's 1976 historical reconstruction of the development of the Descartes–Euler conjecture).

As a result of these changes in mathematics from discipline to school, important mathematical starting points and assumptions often remain hidden in school mathematics. Implicitly, students ignorant of these starting points, we suggest, begin from ones that are quite different, while some students find these starting points intuitive. Then, rather than tackle the serious difficulties involved in bringing such a clash of starting points to the surface, in order to explain differences in students' achievement, recourse is quickly and regularly made to unexamined notions of ability.

These issues do not only pertain to students. Teachers also can find themselves teaching mathematics that is accepted and deemed true, but that they cannot justify, and even might not agree with if given the chance to respond candidly. A classic example with regard to the nature of real numbers has to do with the decimal representations 0.999... and 1. Many future teachers, including mathematics majors who are intending to teach high school mathematics, do not believe that 0.999... and 1 represent the same number, and reject arguments meant to convince them that it could not be otherwise. Rather than describe these college students and future teachers as operating from an unarticulated definition of number and of equality of number (e.g., that two numbers that are different in every place of a place value system could not possibly be equal!) that conflicts with definitions of number accepted in the mathematics community, such students are often dismissed as lacking ability in mathematics. Since they are not able to accept the starting points decided upon by others, they do not have the ability to do mathematics.

Similarly, at the university level, when students are asked to reason, by producing acceptable mathematical proofs, most seem to do poorly. Mathematical proof is seen as difficult, not as the sort of reasoning that everyone can do. As a result, often university Calculus courses for non-mathematics majors, and even some courses for majors, avoid asking students to construct arguments. And, many departments offer transition or bridge courses between non-theoretical courses and the theoretical courses that are the heart of a major in mathematics. Students who are not successful in these courses are counseled out of majoring in mathematics; they do not have the ability to continue. Theoretically egalitarian notions about the nature of mathematical knowledge become a reality in which only a small number of people, the mathematically "talented," seem to be able to reason in appropriate ways.

In line with this analysis of transitions in mathematics as it moves from the discipline to school, many of the instructional changes at Holt High School involve movement toward more student reasoning and justification of results in school classrooms. (This movement is consonant with NCTM's 2000 standard on reasoning and proof throughout the school curriculum.) The expectation that students will be able to justify and explain their results permeates Michael Lehman's descriptions of the performance assessments he initiated (described in Chapter 2) as well as the modifications others have made subsequently. Similarly, such expectations play an important role in the Algebra 1 classroom vignettes described in Chapter 3. And, Marty Schnepp's presentation of a novel student proof of the product rule in Chapter 4 celebrates student justification of an important result. For us, it is this movement toward student reasoning and justification that is the key instructional move; it is this movement that is behind the variety of instructional practices described in the first section of this book.

The focus on reasoning and justification isn't for students only, however. This theme is also present in the work that Holt High School math teachers do among themselves. At Holt High School, mathematics teachers talk with each other about the mathematics they teach. They talk about how to teach this mathematics. But, they also deepen their own mathematic understandings by asking and exploring mathematical questions. They explore reasons for making different definitions (see Chapter 17) and revel in the opportunity to come to understand more deeply aspects of school mathematics that they had taken for granted. In addition to Chapter 17, this theme is found in other places throughout the text (e.g., in Chapter 16, as well as a preservice analogue in Chapter 18).

As indicated earlier, this book is a case study of the work of a single high school mathematics department and its efforts to take seriously Cusick's (1983) egalitarian ideal. The book is a retrospective account of a dozen years of collaborative work written by the participants. For us, it is about high school mathematics teaching and an egalitarian ideal, not about particular instructional practices. It is about teachers and students reasoning about mathematics and mathematics teaching. It is not a research study of a particular curriculum, or of a model for school change, or of a theory about how institutions collaborate, though readers with these interests will find grist for their mills.

The book tells a story of conversations – conversations in the classroom, as well as conversations among educators of different kinds: teachers, preservice teachers, and university-based mathematics educators. For pedagogical reasons, the mathematics educators in these conversations choose to emphasize reasoning for oneself and are unwilling to disconnect reason from judgments of right or wrong and correct or incorrect. The book is about the resulting personal growth and empowerment experienced by participants in these conversations, high school students, preservice teachers, teachers, and university faculty and doctoral students.

Chapter 1

Introduction to our case study

The case study presented in this volume does not take place in a school for a privileged elite, nor does it take place in a severely underfunded inner-city school whose building is in disrepair. The Holt Public Schools serve a 32-square-mile district with approximately 21,000 people located just south of Michigan's capital city in Ingham County. The district includes Holt, the village of Dimondale, most of Delhi Township, and small sections of southern Lansing. While the district has become increasingly suburban and is now home to some policymakers from Lansing and some Michigan State University faculty, it is still partly rural. While the district is becoming increasingly affluent, it is not one of the more affluent local districts. For example, the State Equalized Value of homes in the district usually ranks in the bottom quarter of the 12 districts in Ingham County. In the year 2000, 13 percent of students in the district were eligible for free or reduced-price lunch (see www.ses.standardandpoors.com).

From the early 1980s through the spring of 2003, Holt High School was housed in a well-maintained, one-story building. It served students in grades 10 through 12 (in the 2003–2004 school year the high school became a 9–12 school and moved to a different location). In 1989 and 1993, the school was named a State of Michigan Exemplary Secondary School and in the years 2000, 2001, and 2002, before athletic conferences were reconfigured, it won the Governor's Cup Award for the highest number of Michigan Merit Award winners in its athletic conference. Starting in 1989, it has been affiliated with Michigan State University as a Professional Development School (PDS). Enrollments in the high school gradually increased during the 1990s, for example in 2000 the high school enrolled 1,143 students. Typically, about 90 percent of the students in the school are white (89.1 percent in the year 2000 according to Standard & Poor's) and about 15 percent live in single-parent households (11 percent in the year 2000 according to Standard & Poor's). In a typical year, about 30 percent of the graduating class will go on to four-year college or university, an equal amount will go on to community college or vocational training of some kind. The remaining 40 percent of graduates go directly into the workforce or join the military. The dropout rate at the high school has decreased during the 1990s and has been between 1 and 2 percent for some time.

It is in this context that the Holt High School math department has taken on the challenge of helping a wide range of students find mathematics intellectually challenging and appealing.

Prior to beginning the first section in this three-part book, we identify three key features of our case study and then provide a quick overview of the structure of the volume.

Our goals and our own voices

One defining feature of our case study is its insider perspective. Much of what we offer is written in the words of the participants themselves, either teachers or students. Thus, our case study is centered on 20 essays authored by members of the Holt High School mathematics department, as well as faculty and graduate students at Michigan State University, some who were more direct participants in the work at Holt and others whose role was more that of observer. Two of these essays are co-authored with high school students.

This aspect of the book fits with our aims in writing the book and reflects the nature of the work of this department and its university collaborators. While external funding and a large-scale initiative involving eight schools and the university (the PDS effort described below) initially supported the collaboration between this math department and faculty and graduate students from the university, improvement of ordinary, everyday instruction at the school and the university was at the heart of this collaboration. Our collaborative work was not undertaken as a special project, or a research study on particular mechanisms for improving student achievement or for developing teachers' mathematical knowledge, rather the focus was on long-term improvement of programs at this school and university.

Though, as the essays below will indicate, there are a number of teaching practices and beliefs that we have come to value, our work has been exploratory in nature and local in scope. We sought to make improvements in local practice; thus, the central goal of our case study is *not* to argue for the adoption of these innovations on a larger scale. Indeed, our use of insider perspectives might clash with some people's notions of standards that might be used in identifying effective educational innovations. As dedicated professionals, while we paid careful attention to evidence of the successes and limitations of our classroom work, we did not design any aspect of this work as an experiment to demonstrate the effectiveness of particular innovations. Funding, when it was available to this group, was primarily deployed to support the professional development of participants and their reflection on the instructional changes undertaken, and not for the development of research projects that would demonstrate the utility of particular instructional techniques. Indeed, as a group, we are quite skeptical about the possibility of identifying practices that can be used broadly throughout the country without effectively becoming different innovations in different sites. We are skeptical about the capacity of methods and theories of teaching currently available for establishing that particular classroom innovations will have predictable outcomes. But that is another matter.

Our aim in this volume is a different one. Given the scarcity of descriptions of change in subject-matter instruction in high schools, our aim in sharing our descriptions of our experiences is to provoke others to rethink and reshape their conceptions of the possibilities for changes in high school subject-matter instruction. While we hope that some of our teaching and professional development practices will interest others who will explore their utility, as applicable, in their own settings, our aim is to provoke reconsideration of current practices, rather than to suggest particular replacements. And we hope that our portrait of some of the dilemmas and tensions that arise in seeking to rethink some aspects of secondary mathematics education will be helpful to others who are interested in similar goals.

So far, we have portrayed a situation in which a high school mathematics department has changed its instructional practices. But, in suggesting that we have come to share some points of view, it is important not to minimize differences of point of view between us; there is, of course, much about which we continue to disagree. And, it seems to us that this is an important part of our story. To bring out this aspect of our experience in this case study, a dialogue between members of the high school department follows each essay. In these dialogues, teachers point out central issues in the essay, raise questions about the positions taken in the essay, or illustrate the points made in the essay by relating their own supporting experiences. These responses add to the accounts in the essay and capture both ways in which the group has worked and differences in professional judgment which we continue to explore over time.

The points we have just made about classroom instruction, as suggested before, also hold for our efforts in professional development. The efforts of this department, as well as the efforts of colleagues in other departments in this high school, as well as colleagues in other local schools, were supported initially by a Professional Development School (PDS) relationship established with a local, state university. Just as our case study is not an assessment of particular teaching practices, neither is it a description of the outcomes of a single professional development project; the experience is far too multifaceted to be captured as a single entity. Rather, it chronicles a number of initiatives taken over time by participants in a Professional Development School (PDS) relationship between a university and a school. This relationship was a long-term one. Originally, this relationship was founded with money that was available for professional development. These funds were available for five years. Subsequently, efforts made use of other resources that the participants could muster. The relationship between the school and the university became a part of the natural mode of work in both institutions. Thus, we believe others seeking to use school–university partnerships to improve instruction in both institutions can mine our experience for insights into the development of such collaborations. But we would not suggest that our case study proves, for example, that such collaborations can predictably lead to improvements in student achievement.

The importance of teacher development

Recent legislation seeks to install highly qualified teachers in every US K–12 classroom in the relatively near future. While we appreciate the importance being placed on the initial qualifications of teachers, in this context, a key feature of our case study is the theme of continued professional growth after initial qualification. In the US, discussion of such professional growth immediately brings to mind professional development, activities that teachers undertake outside of, and away from, their classrooms and schools. By contrast, studies of teachers' professional lives in other education systems suggest that teachers work lives in other countries are structured to include avenues for professional growth that are a part of the teacher's daily work life, not a separate activity (Britton *et al.*, 2003). With the design of our case study, we hope to contribute toward an argument for policies that invest in teachers' development, perhaps through structural changes to teachers' work lives.

Among professional educators, one frequent assumption is that the knowledge, dispositions, and skills of teachers are an important component of an educational system. Building on this assumption, in order to improve a system, one might seek to enlarge its human capacity, that is, among other things, develop teachers' knowledge, dispositions, and skills (for an argument of this kind, see Cohen & Ball, 1999).

Professional Development Schools are predicated on this assumption, on the notion that the professional development of teachers leads to changes in teaching practice and ultimately to improved achievement for a wide range of students. In addition, Professional Development Schools are supposed to contribute to positive changes in teacher education and educational research (Holmes Group, 1986). With regard to teacher education, if teacher development has led to changed practice and increased student achievement, then such settings would be stronger settings for field-based components of teacher education. With regard to educational research, if teacher development has led to changed practice and increased student achievement, then the study of such examples would be of importance to educational researchers.

Yet researchers on professional development and teacher learning argue that the basic assumption that undergirds initiatives like the PDS has not been borne out by careful research studies. As argued in a National Academy of Education report to the US Department of Education's Office of Educational Research and Improvement (1999), research studies do not "connect the dots." That is, research does not bear out strong relationships between teacher development, classroom teaching practice, and student achievement. In particular, research does not document how changes in teaching practice result in positive change in student learning, nor does it show that teachers' professional development can generate changes in teaching practice that have such results. According to this report, the arrows in Figure 1.1 below are not supported by research.

Again, with our case study, in the same way we do not seek to establish that particular instructional practices have led to changes in the courses students take, we do not seek to establish that particular professional development mechanisms have led to changes in instructional practices and from there to particular student outcomes. Instead, we hope that, by providing information about teachers' instructional practices, student experience of classrooms, and teachers' professional activities, this case study argues for the plausibility of connections between these "dots."

A school–university PDS two-way relationship

Finally, as the references to the Holt High School/Michigan State University PDS initiative suggest, there is a higher-education component to this case study. Through the university's commitment to field-based

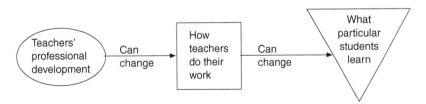

Figure 1.1 Possible effects of professional development.

teacher education and a Professional Development School (PDS) initiative (see below), university-based mathematics educators participated in this work of the high school mathematics department. In addition to an influence on the work of the high school, the participation of these university educators in the work of the Holt mathematics department provided these educators with opportunities for professional development as teachers and teacher educators and enhanced the secondary mathematics component of the teacher education program. Thus, at four points in the story, there are chapter-long interludes that focus on the higher-education components of the story.

These higher-education interludes speak about the notion of a "Professional Development School (PDS)" a term originally coined by the Holmes Group – a consortium of leading US schools of education (chaired for several years by the dean of Michigan State University's College of Education, Judith Lanier). But, the term is confusing. In the rhetoric of the Holmes Group, the Professional Development School is a new institution designed in part to breach the boundaries of theory and practice that separate universities from schools. But, in a descriptive sense, a PDS is not really a new institution. It is not like a university lab school; no new school is created. And, unlike a shortlived, focused project, it is intended to support the development of long-term, multi-faceted, and ongoing relationships. Thus, the Holmes Group's "new institution" is better described as an intense relationship between a K–12 school and a school or college of education. (For a description of a similar, long-term relationship between a school and a university, see Trubowitz & Longo, 1997.)

PDSs are "for the development of novice professionals, for continuing development of experienced professionals and *for the research and development of the teaching profession*" (Holmes Group, 1986, p. 1, italics in original). They serve this function by involving university faculty and K–12 teachers in shared work around existing aspects of their jobs, though in some cases these existing elements are supplemented. Teachers and university faculty might work together around issues of K–12 teaching. In some cases, university faculty might even teach in a K–12 school, as Daniel Chazan of MSU did at Holt High School by co-teaching Algebra 1 with Sandra Callis. They might work together on school reform, say on statewide mathematics curriculum or assessment. They might work together in preservice teacher education. For example, beyond being mentor teachers, Holt faculty like Mike Lehman, Sandy Callis, Kelly Hodges, and others outside of mathematics taught on-campus teacher education courses. And school and university faculty might work together on educational research, on projects initiated by either university or school personnel.

The stories in the four interludes indicate that the relationship between school and university was two-way. This component of the book illustrates how the work of the Holt High School mathematics department influenced and supported the development of the secondary mathematics component of MSU's five-year teacher education program. It shows that the school played a crucial role in the development of a practice-based teacher education program designed to turn out reflective practitioners eager to take on the tasks of teaching and leadership roles as teaching professionals.[1]

Our intended audiences

As is evident from the previous sections, we hope that our work will be of interest to a number of audiences: those interested in changing high school mathematics instruction, those focused on designing professional development in schools, those crafting teacher-work life policies, those seeking to connect the dots between professional development of teachers and students' experience, and those creating school/university partnerships. Readers from these audiences will find different aspects of the book most relevant to their particular interests and may choose to read the book in different orders. For example, those interested in getting the big picture first, may opt to start with Gary Sykes's essay in Chapter 21. Those focused on issues of professional development may choose to start with Part III and work their way back into Part I and II as suggested by the introductory material in the chapters they read. Those interested in preservice teacher education and teacher development may want to pay careful attention to the interludes (Chapters 5, 11, 12, and 18), as well as the chapters highlighting key aspects of the PDS relationship (Chapters 13 and 14), mentoring of intern teachers (Chapter 19), and graduate education of teachers (Chapter 20). Readers interested in the mathematics that is a part of the story may want to begin with Chapters 3, 4, 16, 17, and 18. Those most interested in instructional change might begin with Chapters 3, 4, 6, 7, 8, and 9. Those most interested in the culture of the Holt mathematics department and its view of professionalism may want to focus on Chapters 2, 3, 4, 7, 15, 17, 19, and 20.

But, regardless of the order in which the book is read and the chapters that seem most related to your interests, we urge you not to focus on only a few of the chapters. The strength of the story we are telling is in the interweaving of many strands. As mentioned earlier, rather than find bullets with suggestions for particular strategies or interventions, readers will find a complex story of the development of a professional culture and community, and its relationship to their interests.

The structure of this case study and its included texts

The case study this book examines extends over a long period of time; the work described in this book takes place over slightly more than a ten-year period. The case study is not the story of a project, some finite intervention into the life of a school. It is the story of more than a decade in the life of a mathematics department; a story in which projects have come and gone, but where there has been sustained focus on pressing problems of practice; a story in which a university has been a long-term partner with a school.

This story encompasses the work of many people; it involves the work of a group of teachers and university-based educators and their students, both high school students and preservice teachers. Actors in this story include, over time, roughly: 17 members of the Holt High School mathematics department, seven university-based mathematics educators – both doctoral students and faculty, thousands of high school students, and approximately 100 preservice teachers.

This case study describes Holt High School mathematics department's attempts to:

- make more mathematics available to a wider range of students by appealing to *all* students' intellectual capacities;
- create a collegial departmental culture – one that acknowledges rather than covers up uncertainties of teaching; and
- contribute to the teaching profession, primarily through involvement in teacher education.

In this case study, teaching is conceptualized as a professional activity, one that includes, but is not limited to, interaction inside a classroom with high school students. In this book, teaching as a professional activity also encompasses:

- a deliberative stance towards work with students that requires continual personal development and growth on the part of teachers;
- serious and sustained intellectual engagement with the subject matter one teaches;
- explicit acceptance of responsibility for determining curriculum;
- contribution to a collegial environment within one's school, district, city, and state; and
- assumption of responsibility for the direction of the profession as well (e.g., through the activity of professional organizations, participation in shaping state policy, or involvement in the education of future generations of teachers).

Thus, the story this case study seeks to tell is a complex one. In an effort to organize this complexity, the bulk of this volume is organized in three parts. The parts are titled: changes in classroom teaching practice, student experience of the curriculum, and professional growth and development. But such a partitioning of the story is to some degree arbitrary. After all, where do changes in classroom practice leave off and where does professional development begin? Teaching practice itself offers myriad opportunities for professional growth and development.

The case study begins with changes in classroom practice. Against the backdrop of standard practice in mathematics classrooms, the first section of the book illustrates the changes in classroom practice that have occurred at this high school's mathematics department over more than ten years. There were important changes in curricular orientation, the structure of classroom sessions, and the nature of assessment of students' work. These changes in classroom practice all flowed from a desire to respect the intellects of a wide range of students and to engage them in reasoning for themselves.

The second section reveals evidence of changes in students' experience of mathematics teaching and learning in this school as well as evidence of improved student achievement. The central point of this section is that changes in teaching practice made it possible to offer a wide range of students previously unavailable learning opportunities and to support them in taking up such opportunities. Course-taking changed. While a large number of students used to graduate Holt High School having only studied arithmetic, that is no longer the case. And, very few students graduate Holt High School with only one year of instruction in algebra. Most would have at least studied two years of algebra or a year of algebra and a year of geometry. These changes are directly related to changes in instructional practice and have occurred without any changes in district requirements. Indeed, it does not seem likely that simply changing district requirements without changing classroom practice would have made such changes in course-taking possible.

The final section of the book addresses issues of teachers' professional development. It identifies the particular professional development mechanisms that were salient to the Holt High School math department teachers, ones they believe influenced them to make changes in classroom practice and supported them in their efforts. There is an important theme that connects this section with the two earlier sections. In the same way text in the first section demonstrates that teachers seek to respect their students' intellect, in this section, the described professional development activities are grounded in respect for teachers' reasoning and their interests in both teaching and mathematics. This section highlights the importance of departmental culture. It suggests that, in this high school department, a professional culture developed within the departmental community. This professional culture can be illustrated by the use teachers made of a range of opportunities for professional development. These opportunities are closely tied to teaching practice and present in many schools, but are often under-utilized.

To tell this three-part story effectively, there is continual movement between the large stories that frame the case study – respect for teachers' and students' reasoning and connections between professional development, classroom practice, and student experience – and more detailed focal texts. To bring alive the experience behind the numbers, this book includes texts that bring readers into the school and that present the perspectives of teachers and students, as well as those of observers. These texts shift focus dramatically, but at the same time make the larger narrative come alive. They serve to illustrate, to elaborate, and to capture the complexity of real classroom events.

While the resulting volume speaks with many voices, it is more connected than a collection of essays loosely organized around a theme. We have organized the various texts in the volume into a whole that tells a different story in which all of the individual essays fit. Thus, within each section, each chapter includes three kinds of text: editorial framings, a focal essay, and dialogue. These chapters are not organized historically. Going backward and forward in time, the editorial framing of each chapter outlines facts relevant to the large story of the book and indicates how the focal essay fits into the book as a whole.

The focal essays are either first-person narratives from one of the participants in the project or a report of interviews with project participants. These essays are close to the ground. They directly describe experience. They are centered on aspects of the larger story that seem crucial, but need to be illuminated by first-person experience. In these essays, high school students, high school teachers, preservice teachers, or university teacher educators discuss their experience, describe their practice, or reflect on their own learning. In four of the essays, based on interviews and analysis, the author reflects on the experience of another. Four of the essays (those in italics) focus explicitly on preservice teacher education.

Finally, there is a third kind of text that illustrates the ethos of the Holt department in important ways. As the pieces for this volume were drafted, with support from the Spencer Foundation, members of the Holt mathematics department read and reacted to them by email. Starting from these initial email responses to the focal essays, short dialogues were developed for the end of each chapter. In these dialogues, members of the department point out central issues, raise questions, or illustrate the points made by relating their own experiences. Including this material in the book hopefully adds dimensions to the focal essays and encourages readers' engagement with the text.

Table 1.1 Titles of focal essays by section

Changes in classroom teaching practice	Students' experience of the curriculum	Professional growth and development
• Mathematics Performance Assessment • Starting a Functions-Based Approach to Algebra • Teacher as Course-Level Planner • Preservice Teachers as Curriculum Makers • Finding Mathematics in the World Around Us • One Teacher's Transformation in Teaching	• From an E to an A with the Help of a Graphing Calculator • Students' View of Mathematical Conversation • Developing an Interest in Mathematics • Field Experience Really Was the Best Teacher! • What Kind of Teacher Will I Be?	• Being Treated (and Treating Ourselves) as Professionals • Shared Teaching Assignments • One Transformed Teacher's Viewpoint • Teaching a Technologically supported Approach to School Algebra • Questioning Ourselves and the Authorities • Lines and Points: Aristotle v. Modern Mathematics • Becoming a Professional Teacher; Being a Mentor Teacher • Theory Is Practical!

Our case study begins in the next section with descriptions of the ways in which teaching practices in this high school mathematics department have changed from the late 1980s until the early 2000s.

Part I

Changes in classroom teaching practice

In the mid- to late 1980s, the teaching of mathematics at Holt High School was quite similar to that at many nearby high schools. Two individual teachers had earned reputations as solid practitioners and were, as a result, considered by university faculty to be good placements for student teachers. But nothing about the mathematics department as a whole made it stand out.

Ten to fifteen years later, the situation is strikingly different. Regardless of how one assesses its innovations, the Holt High School mathematics department stands out. Beyond the reputation of individual teachers, the department has become a valued site for regular placement of intern teachers from Michigan State University. Changes in the departmental culture are partially responsible for this. But, in terms of day-to-day classroom practice, teachers at Holt seem to approach the classroom differently than do their peers from other schools. Some of the innovations they've made are easily seen from a distance; others are not evident even after a classroom visit. In telling this first part of the story – that of changes in classroom practice – we'll look first at some dramatic, structural changes, then gradually bring subtler innovations and the culture of the department into focus.

Chapter 2

Assessment

How should teachers assess their students' mathematical competence at the end of units, chapters, semesters, or years? Should teachers test students by asking them to solve problems like those students have already been taught to solve in class? That will show that students have learned to do what was taught. But isn't it more important to know whether students can apply what they have learned to new and unfamiliar settings and problems? Asking students to do so on high stakes tests seems unfair, though. Furthermore, regardless of the type of problems students are asked to solve, how should they demonstrate their competence? Are individual pencil-and-paper tests the best way to assess competence? Or is it also useful to see how students articulate their understandings publicly? Finally, what role does a community play in the assessment of student learning? Is assessment solely the responsibility of schools and teachers, or is there a role for those beyond the high school to play in judging the mathematical competence of students? If mathematics is truly a discipline in which people can reason for themselves, then perhaps a larger community can be involved in the assessment of students. These issues are raised by the first Holt High School innovation outlined in this volume – the performance assessment. In this chapter's essay, Michael Lehman describes the performance exams that he pioneered and then Kelly Hodges and Kellie Huhn discuss their experiences with these exams and variations on Mike's format that they have developed.

Mathematics performance assessment

Michael F. Lehman, Holt High School

A version of this paper was originally written in 1995. Portions of the paper appeared as Lehman, M. (November, 1995). Assessing mathematics performance assessment: A continuing process, Craft Paper

95–7, East Lansing, MI: National Center for Research on Teacher Learning and Lehman, M. (1999). Group Performance Assessments, in Y. G. McCarthy (ed.), *Bringing the NCTM Standards to Life*, Larchmont, NY: Eye on Education. Mike is very grateful to members of the Holt High School Writers Club for their editing and encouragement. Members include: Larry Burgess, Jerry Gillett, Mary Gray, Bruce Kutney, and Robert Smith.

Where I came from

I have taught high school mathematics since 1977. In 1989, I started to rethink my methods. I wanted my students to be able to do more than tell back what I told them. I felt students in Algebra 2 and PreCalculus should be able to take the mathematics we studied and apply it to a wide range of situations. However, I wasn't sure what this type of student understanding looked like. If I saw it, I didn't know if I would recognize it.

I had studied a little about cooperative learning at a summer institute sponsored by MSU's Professional Development School (PDS) efforts. It sounded worthwhile and easy to implement, so I set out to try it in my classroom. I soon found that it wasn't so easy after all. I had a lot of groupwork going on, but nothing I would call cooperative learning – unless you count one student doing the first four or five problems of an assignment then cooperatively giving them to the rest of the group in exchange for the remaining problems. There was more to cooperative learning than I thought. Luckily, I had access to some excellent resources at Michigan State University and Holt High School. Together, a group of MSU faculty and Holt High School teachers started a study group on cooperative learning. We read research, discussed theory, and shared our practice. As time went on, I learned how to construct activities that led my students into high-level discussions and that better developed their understanding of the mathematics I was teaching. The problem I now faced was how to assess this type of student understanding. How could I verify that it truly existed?

First steps

My first step was to integrate writing into our studies. Students were asked to write about a problem or situation and required to explain the steps involved and why the steps made sense. For example, students might have to decide if a graph was a function or not and then explain how they knew. If they said that they used the vertical-line test, then they were asked to explain why this test worked. This type of writing not only helped me to get a better idea of what my students did or did not understand, but it also helped them. In choosing their words they had to think through the concept thoroughly. I was pleased with this approach but almost immediately realized its limitations. With 150 students per day, I would soon be out of time and wearing magnifying glasses. My next quandary: how do I gather this type of information and still have a rich family and community life outside of school?

I continued the writing in a shortened or less frequent form; then I changed my tests. I added more tasks that required students to give short explanations with their answers. This also yielded more insight into the origins of their thinking. I began to wonder if all my students were giving me their own ideas or if they were just using the ideas of other students. As time went on, I began seeing my own words come back to me. The students had learned that it was easier to ask me specific questions that they felt I might expect them to write about and then take detailed notes of my answers. If I asked the question, they had a good answer ready without much thinking on their part. So, while adding the explanations gave me some insight to my students' understanding, I still needed more information. And I wanted more from them. They, too, were struggling with what it meant to know mathematics.

The first oral exam

All these changes, combined with my continuing frustration, led me to try my first performance assessment. At the end of the year in 1991, I wanted to give my students a chance to explain orally what they knew and understood. I gave them a packet of six problems that they prepared ahead of time in cooperative learning groups. These problems were developed to cover the broad themes of the year, while getting at some of the details of the concepts. During the exam period (90 minutes in our school), my students went before a panel of three adults from the school and community and explained the problems. The panelists asked each student to explain one problem in detail. Since the students did not know ahead of time which problem they would be asked to solve and because the judges were told not to allow the students to pick, each student had to know all six problems. During these explanations the students had to detail their strategies, why they chose the method they used, any terminology involved, and how they knew their answers were correct. (I did not go over the answers before the exam.)

My variations

I have varied the process that I started in 1991. In my Algebra 2 classes, I have not only given six problems as described above, but I have also experimented with adding a piece where the judges present a new, unseen problem. During the last half-hour of the exam period the students are asked as a group to solve and explain the new problem to the judges. The judges watch for both individual contributions and how the group functions as a whole. This helps the judges see which students can think on their feet and which cannot. Understanding and solving problems in class is one thing. But being able to apply mathematics on the spot, under pressure, means students really have absorbed the mathematics being tested. Some students really shine during this part. While they may have had trouble communicating during the individual part of the exam, they can confidently articulate their understanding through the conversation presented by the group members. This variation reveals information that I didn't glean from the original form of the exam.

In my PreCalculus and Discrete Mathematics classes, my students write a major paper to go with each unit we study. These papers usually involve solving a problem given in some context, then writing about the solution. I grade and return these papers; then the students make corrections. During the performance assessment, they explain their papers to the judges. This may sound easy, but the students really concentrate on the details, reading their peers' papers and reworking their own. The exchange of ideas and the suggestions they make to each other are amazing. They talk mathematics for days without me. I become a resource for them, if needed.

Other teachers in the department have also begun to use performance exams as a regular part of their end-of-semester exams. The performance exams have become a big operation involving large numbers of classes, students, and judges. For example, for the January 2000 performance exams, the department sent out 220 letters or emails. In the end, 98 judges – including community members, preservice teachers, and visitors from other schools – participated over a three-day period. The judges interacted with 290 students in Algebra 1, Geometry, Algebra 2, Honor PreCalculus, and Honors Discrete Mathematics courses.

What I have learned

For some students, an oral exam is their first chance to be successful at a mathematics exam. Whenever I put a traditional paper-and-pencil test in front of these students they freeze. During class they seem to know what they were doing. But on a test they perform poorly. The oral exam format, however, gives them a different way to communicate what they know. The judges can help them relax and ask a few questions to get them started. Soon the students take over and do a good job of explaining what they know.

Another unexpected benefit has become apparent. Whenever I gave a traditional test and a student did poorly, usually only two people knew: the student and me. For some students having the teacher know they did poorly was something they could live with. But on the oral exam, six other people know: the three judges and their group members. My students do not tolerate this. The one certain way to avoid embarrassment is to be sure that everybody is ready. During that last week of school in June when most students have already mentally checked out, my students work very hard. They come to class and get right to work with their group, wasting very little time. In fact, I have had parents call and ask what I am doing because, much to their surprise, they had a group of students at their house on Sunday afternoon doing nothing but mathematics (and, of course, eating a lot of pizza). The change in the atmosphere of the classroom allows for a tremendous amount of learning.

With the oral exam, the students place a lot of pressure on each other to be responsible. Much of the year, they are willing to put up with someone who does not contribute. But when 20 percent of their grade depends on the performance of others in their group, they won't tolerate people who don't do their share. As with most teenagers, they can sometimes be rude to each other, so it is my job to make sure the pressure is appropriate and not degrading. At times this takes some extra work. But, for the most part, they have been working together all year and have developed functioning relationships. I think some amount of pressure from the group is constructive, provided we all observe the fine line between what is appropriate and inappropriate.

It is most important, however, that learning occurs during preparation time. I have come to view this preparation time as perhaps the most significant part of the process. I see students linking concepts they had not related earlier. I see students looking things up or asking good questions. "Mr. Lehman, I got this far and see what the results should be, but I am not sure how to verify it." Or, "Mr. Lehman, if I explain this problem using this approach, do you think the judges will understand, or should I add more details?" This is much better than in the past when they kept asking, "Mr. Lehman, is this going to be on the exam?" or "Can we use our notes on the exam?" For the first time, I have a test that gives students better control over how they will do. They know what is on the exam and understand the main element determining their grades is how much work they put into preparation.

The performance assessment also relieves me of my role as judge and jury. I become more like a coach or facilitator and my relationship with the students changes. They look to me for advice on how to present an idea, and they listen when I explain a concept or question their strategies. After the exam, they don't complain as much about their grades. Instead, they read the three sets of comments from the judges thoroughly. This, too, is a change for me. Many times I have graded tests in detail only to have a student look at the grade, then throw the test away. With a performance assessment, students seem to value and learn something from the comments. We discuss all the results, both the mathematics and the overall process. I learn from their reactions and they learn from each other's reactions, as well. If a student complains about something, usually another student will respond to it better than I can.

And my students seem to be well prepared for the next course, Pre-Calculus, which I also teach. And, our Advanced Placement Calculus teacher reports that the students coming from PreCalculus are very well prepared for the material and speed of that course.

Students' reactions

Some of my students say this type of exam is easier than a written exam, and that's fine with me. I wasn't looking to make my exams harder. According to my students, I already know how to write extremely difficult tests. What matters to me is that this exam promotes learning while providing my students with another way of showing what they know. I firmly believe this: if you truly understand mathematics you must be able to explain it symbolically, in written words, and orally.

Every year I have students come back from college and tell me how much their preparation for performance assessments has helped them. They are not afraid to give oral presentations; they know how to prepare for them and how to get their point across to an audience. These students tell me that their fellow students really worry when it comes to oral presentations or formal written papers in a mathematics or science class. This is another unexpected outcome. My students have learned useful presentation skills while studying mathematical content, and as a result feel confident in their mathematical preparation.

Community reaction

Parent reaction to these exams has been positive. Many parents have questioned me about the process, and I try to explain it at fall conferences. Once they understand, they are very supportive. For parents whose children are struggling with mathematics, the performance assessment represents a fresh opportunity. Parents understand that the traditional methods have not worked, and they welcome a new approach. In fact, parents have come in and helped the students prepare, questioning them about their work as would the judges. This gives students an idea of how ready they are and where they need more work. The parents and students usually arrange this on their own, and I only provide the time, place, and materials needed.

Concerns and issues

Do I have all the answers when it comes to assessing my students? No, and I never will. But, I am closer than I was in 1991. Difficulties still exist for which I have no answers. For one thing, coming up with problems for this type of exam is not easy. The problems I have chosen never quite seem to get at the total picture. (But then, neither does a traditional exam.) Problems should be open enough for students to show what they know without being so open that students have no idea what the problem is asking.

The consistency of the panelists is always a concern. Up to eight teams of panelists (24 individuals) work with students during a performance assessment. How can I be sure that they are consistent from one team to another? Explicit instructions to the panelists are one means of working toward consistency. But, every judge and student involved is unique; when working with people, I cannot guarantee total consistency. The only thing I can say is that when I start grading 150 exams, I know I am not totally consistent from start to finish. Therefore, I think a little variance has to be acceptable.[1]

I continue to work on the evaluation form employed by the judges. At first, I set up a rating system where the panelist rated the students on each segment of the presentation, using a scale of 1 to 5. Judges rated students on:

- their understanding of the problem;
- the appropriateness of their selected strategies;
- the accuracy of their results; and
- their communication.

Judges just added up the points, and that was the grade. I discovered, however, that this score did not always reflect what the judges thought was an appropriate overall grade. Also, sometimes the judges spent so much time trying to get the rating system to fit the grades they felt students had earned, that they did not have time to write detailed comments. And some judges felt the rating system could take the place of the comments because it was so detailed.

With the help of our district's Gifted and Talented director, I developed a new grading rubric that describes what an A, B, C, etc. would look like. Panelists are free to choose the one they feel best fits a student. I include my grading scale so judges can choose between a high A and a low A, for example, without too much difficulty. I then outline for the panelists the key categories for which I want their comments. This helps to produce comments that are truly helpful to my students and me. It also highlights the comments as the more important aspect of the assessment and de-emphasizes the grade. This is essential because I want my assessments to promote learning and not just sort students.

One big problem I face is getting enough panelists each time. I try to practice this type of assessment in all my classes at the end of the first semester and again at the end of the year. It takes a lot of time to arrange. I send out letters to our school business alliance asking for help. So far, the response has been excellent. Members of the business community find this a hands-on way to improve local education. Having Michigan State University in my backyard is another advantage. My colleagues from the university who serve as panelists enjoy the opportunity to get into a high school and to see what the students are learning. Finally, colleagues from within my school and from other districts have been very helpful. The performance assessment gives them a chance to see students in a different light and to learn about a new way to assess their learning. It's a big job arranging for enough panelists, but so is writing, giving, and grading a traditional exam. I feel it all works out.

My conclusion

From my years of experience using performance assessment, I am convinced, more than ever, of its potential to improve student levels of understanding. I continue to believe that it is an excellent alternative for those students who have trouble with traditional tests. This type of assessment, in conjunction with the more traditional evaluations I still use, has helped me gather more information about my students' understanding of mathematics. And it has also helped me to investigate what it *really* means to understand mathematics.

Alternative formats and a taxonomy of tasks

Kelly Hodges and Kellie Huhn, Holt High School

KELLIE HUHN: I did my internship with Mike and was able to see the preparation and results of the performance assessments. Since my internship, I've adopted the idea of a performance exam and have adapted Mike's performance exam format. In thinking about these exams, one very powerful aspect of the exam is the accountability that *I* face. It gives university professors, parents, community members, administrators, and other teachers a sense of what my students can do as a result of being in my class. The most helpful part of the assessment for me is hearing the judges' comments, questions, and concerns. How can I ignore a weakness in my teaching if community members are seeing it and pointing it out? I must be attentive to my teaching and how my students are learning. I've not experienced this type of conversation with community members or administrators at other times in my teaching career.

KELLY HODGES: I did a part of my ten-week student teaching, rather than a year-long internship, with Mike, though at that time he hadn't begun to use the performance assessments. I've used this sort of exam as well. Mike makes two observations about the exam that I would emphasize. First, the classroom discussions in the days leading up to the exam are of extremely high quality. Not only do students work harder than they would for a written exam, these discussions are some of the best we have all year. Second, the performance assessment changes my role from adversary to ally. The exam day in particular becomes a celebration of students' accomplishments. They generally know before the exam how hard they have worked and how well they will do. I can listen to them recount the ups and downs of their presentations without having to pass judgment on their performance. Some students have even thanked me for teaching them!

KELLIE: Yes, I've observed that there is a perceptible change in the relationship between student and teacher during exam preparation. Students look for support from the teacher, rather than expecting evaluation, and this encourages a positive rapport between teacher and student.

KELLY: Just to clarify a point, though, I wouldn't state as my primary goal that students communicate in all three of the ways that Mike identifies (symbolically, in written words, and orally). Rather, I believe that I am obligated to give students opportunities to show what they know in a variety of ways because, ultimately, I want to assess their underlying mastery of the mathematical concepts, not just their ability to communicate that understanding in the form of a classroom assessment. I do want to encourage their ability to use symbolic, written prose, and oral forms of communication, but I also want to be sure that their ability (or lack of it) to communicate skillfully in any of these forms doesn't obscure the mathematics they do or do not understand.

KELLIE: In terms of questions to use in the exams, I remember that you formalized types and categorized them into different groups.

KELLY: Yes. As Mike points out, generating good problems is one of the most difficult parts of the performance exam process. Over time, I have found that different types of tasks are needed to enact the different purposes I have for the exam. I have mainly used three types of tasks. The first is the *solve-a-problem* type. Some situation is given to the students, and they are to solve a problem, answer a question, or develop a plan by drawing on mathematics from the year. This type of exam task targets specific mathematics topics but does not reveal much about how well students understand the course as a whole or about their ability to use the mathematics on their own. The second type is the *create-a-situation*. In this type, rather than solve a problem, students generate or find an example from their own lives to illustrate a mathematical concept from the course. Usually, I ask students to generate some questions within the context they select and then answer the questions to illustrate their ability to apply the mathematics they have learned. This type of task provides better information about the students' ability to recognize and use mathematics in their lives. The third type is the *big-idea* task. Students use their course materials as a portfolio of work to illustrate an overarching theme from the course. They can focus on a strand in the course or a major concept. While this kind of task is a good measure of a student's general level of conceptual understanding, it can be difficult to elicit information about particular skills or minor topics. With this type of task, judges have found it helpful to have a list of suggested questions that probe for depth of understanding.

KELLIE: Although I like the performance assessment format, I struggle with having students judged by people who aren't specialists in mathematics and/or education. For me, it's difficult to conduct this type of exam because I can't assess individual students and see where they might be struggling. I can get information about that during the preparation process, but I'm not able to hear every student present every problem. Hearing their final presentations would help me identify areas of struggle or hear students' ideas that would, in turn, influence my planning for the next school year. As an alternative or in addition to the performance exam, I've considered conducting interviews with a sample of students throughout the year to address this issue. Another problem I see is the effect of a student's personality on his or her grade. Charismatic students may not be the best prepared, yet, because of their personalities, they may receive a higher score. While this could also happen in job interviews and elections, I still struggle with it, because I intend these performance exams as an assessment of their mathematical understanding.

KELLY: I know what you mean. Consistent judging is another concern that Mike raises and that I've tried to address. Rather than assigning judging teams to a particular group of students, I've chosen to assign teams of judges to exam questions and have students rotate from one team of judges to the next. Although it's still possible for one team of judges to be tougher than another, at least every student who answers the same problem has to meet the same standard for that problem. Also, each team of judges usually sees six to eight students present (one from each group rather than just the three to four members of a single group). The judges get a better idea of the range of student performance in the class. This helps them determine whether a student who struggles with part of a problem has done B work or D work. In general, I've found that the grades judges assign very closely match the grades I would expect to see, given a student's performance in class all year and level of preparation. Any variations from this usually fall into two types. Students who struggle on written tests but have been good participants in discussions tend to do better than usual. Students who rarely contribute in class but pass traditional written tests tend to do worse.

KELLIE: It seems okay to me that students who participate in class discussions do better in this type of assessment. If I am committed to helping students articulate mathematical ideas in their own words, then this type of assessment seems to honor the students' work towards that goal. I have some nagging questions, though. Given the dilemmas we discussed, are we really assessing what we want to assess? Is this type of test reliable and valid based on the strategies we use to evaluate standardized tests? Does it even make sense to consider the reliability and validity of this type of performance assessment?

Chapter 3

Curriculum and instructional models

The performance exams discussed in the last chapter make the work of the Holt mathematics department public. Parents, community members, teachers from other districts, teacher candidates, members of the State Department of Education, and faculty from MSU's mathematics department can all see what Holt students can do. These exams also engage people in the difficulties of assessing student learning and help communicate to others what the department values. Judges, for example, mathematicians from MSU, learn the considerations that concern Holt teachers as they assess their students' learning. And, the inclusion of judges who do not necessarily know the mathematics that students have studied concretizes the notion that everyone can reason about mathematical ideas.

In the late 1980s and early 1990s, there were broad national initiatives to increase academic standards. School districts in Michigan, partly in response to efforts of the State Department of Education, sought ways to encourage students to take more mathematics. At Holt High School, many students, especially those not in a track that prepares students for continued education after high school, were graduating without having studied any mathematics but arithmetic. Some of these students might have taken an Algebra 1 course, but were often unsuccessful.

Involvement of the community in performance exams spoke to these national initiatives, though indirectly. By making students' work public, these exams communicated the importance placed by members of the department on the study of mathematics, and as a result may also have helped signal to the community and to students the importance of studying mathematics.

But, by itself, this sort of innovation does not address issues of lower-track students and mathematics. Alongside changing the nature of assessment, a pressing issue became how to revamp mathematics courses like Algebra 1. The goal was to have students see mathematics courses as worth their attention and energy, so that they would be more likely, as a result, to succeed. Introductory algebra courses often focus on teaching students a variety of methods for solving problems involving x's and y's. Students learn to solve equations and word problems and simplify expressions. But, many students resist learning these methods. How could algebra become something that students willingly study, rather than a battleground where schools aim to increase academic standards and students resist (as described in Sedlak *et al.*, 1986)? This chapter focuses on curricular responses to this issue. How might curricular change help Algebra 1 students become more engaged with algebra? Is there a way that students could come to see school algebra as involving reasoning about something important to them?

Moving ten years ahead, in the late 1990s, the Holt mathematics department is recognized in Michigan for its commitment to teaching lower-track students challenging mathematics and for its curriculum work, particularly for its approach to Algebra. (It is this work on Algebra 1 that forms the backdrop for the focal essay in Chapter 8 by Sandy Callas and her student, Nicolas Miller.) For lack of better words, we call this a functions-based approach to algebra. (Such approaches have been advocated recently with the support of advances in graphing technology. See, for example, Heid *et al.*, 1995. For a description of this work and its connection to the NCTM Standards movement, see Chazan & Yerushalmy, 2003.). In such an approach, the intent is to have students see x's and y's as ways of communicating about relationships between quantities (quantifiable qualities of experience involving a quality, a value or potential value, and a unit of measure). In this sort of approach, instead of first meeting x as an unknown number as is commonly done in most introductory algebra courses, x's and y's are introduced to students as variables, and expressions are introduced as calculation procedures that express relationships between input and output quantities.

The subtle shift from treating x's and y's as unknowns to treating them as variables initially has a number of ramifications. Informal methods for representing change in, and accumulation of, quantities are valuable for students right from the start – such methods might include diagrams, mechanical devices, gestures, and written or spoken language (see Hall, 1990; Hall *et al.*, 1989; Koendinger & Tabachneck, 1994; Nemirovsky, 1994; Schwartz & Yerushalmy, 1995). But students must also learn to read Cartesian graphs, symbolic expressions, and tables of the values of the quantities in question (see, for example, Moschkovich *et al.*, 1993; Schoenfeld *et al.*, 1990), a task that research suggests is fraught with difficulties (e.g., Goldenberg, 1988; Janvier, 1998; Wagner, 1981).

The following essay illustrates how Holt Algebra 1 teachers change the order and content of Algebra 1 to tackle introducing lower-track students to functions and standard representations of functions. It gives a flavor of how the Algebra 1 curriculum at Holt High School has changed and of how teachers at Holt work to respect the reasoning of their students. At Holt High School, Algebra 1 begins by introducing students to functions as relationships between quantities. Students explore what quantities and relationships between quantities mean in mathematics.

Having introduced functions, that is, relationships between quantities, as the central object of study in Algebra 1, the course next looks at ways to represent these mathematical objects. With each new representation there are new aspects of relationships between quantities to notice. However, this part of the teaching of Algebra 1 at Holt is hard to describe in a purely linear way. Each teacher tends to teach this part differently. The goal is to have students comfortable with representations of function: input and output tables, procedures described in words and written with algebraic symbols, sketches of graphs, graphs where each point conveys numerical information, and written descriptions of situations ("the graph-table-symbolic rule-situation network," sometimes called the Cartesian Connection, by researchers like Moschkovich *et al.*, 1993). But classes don't work on these representations in one set sequence. Instead, each class takes its own path through this terrain. Teachers exercise their professional judgment to determine an order that is comfortable for them and responsive to their students. Of course, our presentation here is linear, after two sections investigating what functions are, the next essay describes the work on the graph-table-symbolic rule-situation network by starting with Interpreting Graphs, then Quantitative Graphs, and finally Number Recipes involving tables and literal symbols.

However, as Mike Lehman and Craig Huhn's discussion suggests, this piece does more than simply indicate a curricular approach. It also begins to show how teachers at Holt work on issues of "student motivation" by their focus on what a course is all about (although Chapter 6 is more explicit about this issue).

And, since each section of this essay is organized around a classroom conversation, it begins to illustrate the sort of instructional model used at Holt (though again more detail is to be found in Chapter 7). The teachers in the Holt mathematics department have moved from a teacher-centered, lecturing model to a problem-solving model. In this model, teachers "launch" an instructional task, students "explore" individually or in small groups, perhaps with the aid of some technology, and then there is whole class "discussion" to reflect on the exploration, discuss students' theories, and summarize what has been learned.

Finally, this essay begins to illustrate how teachers at Holt respect their lower-track students as mathematical thinkers and attempt to make curriculum responsive to their students' ideas. As a result, curricular materials are a resource; textbooks by themselves do not structure the curriculum; teachers play a larger role in determining curriculum (an issue illustrated in Chapters 4 and 5).

Starting a functions-based approach to algebra

Sandra Callis, Daniel Chazan,* Kelly Hodges, Marty Schnepp, Holt High School and Michigan State University*

This paper was originally drafted in 1995 for a special issue in the *Mathematics Teacher* on algebra. It has not appeared before in print.

The very beginning: what are functions?

What are quantities? A conversation in Sandy Callis's class

I begin Algebra 1 by asking, "What is algebra about? What are we going to study?" My answer: relationships between quantities. To investigate what I mean, we start by looking at quantities themselves.

I ask students to think about different numbers they encounter in daily life. Specifically, I ask them each to come up with five different quantities that they can get from counting and five quantities that they can get from measuring. We will also consider a third kind of quantity, one that can only be derived from counted or measured quantities by computing (using arithmetic operations). Eventually, these computed quantities are the ones we will study in detail.

Table 3.1 shows the quantities my students suggested in the fall of 1994.

Table 3.1 Students' examples of different kinds of quantities

Counting	Measuring	Computing
trees	shoe size	grade point average
plants in your yard	fish	stocks
money	height	percentage
animals	temperature	bank account
fingers	weight	prices
rooms in a house	how long your hair is	paycheck
spark plugs	pant length	gas–mileage
babies born in a day	water in a pool	miles on a trip
books	body parts	growth of a child

After students each came up with five examples for each category, we listed a subset of their ideas on the board by category. I made sure to have one example from each student in class. As we put each example in a category, we discussed it. For example, when we say we are counting money, are we really counting or are we computing? Students agreed that if we are counting the worth of money that comes in different bills, we are computing. But if we are counting how many tens, fives, and ones we have, we are counting bills. I questioned miles on a trip from the computing column, thinking that perhaps it was an example of measuring not computing. In response, the student said that when planning a trip you add up the miles between cities.

When we finished discussing the students' suggestions, I asked, "What's the difference between numbers we get from counting and numbers we get from measuring?" I was thinking that the idea of discrete versus continuous (or whole numbers versus rational numbers) would come up. I also hoped that we could talk about how the counted and measured quantities are used to develop the computed quantities. But as you will see, the conversation headed in a different direction.

Kyle thought for a minute, then raised his hand. "You don't need anything to count. You can just count in your head. When you measure something, you always have something to measure." Rachel immediately disagreed. She thought that if you were counting in your head, you were not really engaged in the act of counting. She further suggested that when measuring something one needs a tool. I asked, "What about what Kyle suggested about needing an object to measure?" Mike called out, "I don't agree with Kyle. What about time?" Rachel shot back, "Time is *something*."

While I was pleased with their engagement with my question, at this point, students were frustrated that there wasn't an easy answer. Nonetheless, they animatedly continued. It was difficult to hear what each was saying, however, because they were speaking over each other. And at times, students spoke disrespectfully to one another. For example, displeased that he wouldn't agree with her, Rachel said to Kyle, "I'll smash your face in."

While their manners suggested that we needed to work on norms for discussions, nevertheless I decided to continue. The comments about measuring time were thought-provoking. "Is time an object?" I asked following up on Kyle's idea. "How do we measure time?" Students immediately looked at the clock. I asked, "What is the clock measuring?" Someone suggested that it was measuring the space of seconds and minutes. I asked what a second and a minute were. Mike said again, " 'Time isn't anything." Rachel glared back at him. "Look at the clock!" she said. Kyle agreed with Mike, that maybe time wasn't anything, or at least that it wasn't an object.

At this point, I decided to encourage the students to think of time as a quantity that changes. I started to walk from one corner of the room out into the center. I asked, "As I'm walking, what are some quantities that are changing?" "The distance from the corner," one student called out. I pointed to the south wall. "Consider my distance from that wall. Is it changing?" "Yes," another student answered. "What else is changing?" I asked. "Your distance from that wall," Jake said as he pointed to the west wall. I started to bob up and down. "What else is changing?" "Your distance from the ceiling," students called out. "Are there any other quantities that are changing?" I asked. A student called out, "Time is going by." "How do we know?" I asked. "Because the hand on the clock is moving," someone answered.

We had gotten as far as we could that day, and the discussion disintegrated into heated individual exchanges. But I was content. We had introduced two essential ideas: first, that one quantity can vary with another (e.g., my location in the room can vary with time) and second, that one can compute quantities from other quantities that have been measured or counted. I promised that we would come back to the topic of measuring time, thinking the conversation was deeper than any I had had in the past about this topic. I wasn't sure of my own conception about time. Is time itself measured by a clock? Or is there a function implicit in our use of a clock to measure time? Is the clock really measuring something else that we identify as varying in time? In the meantime, I used the behavior that I had seen during the discussion to talk about how people can act in ways to foster respectful, constructive conversations.

Relationships between quantities as objects: a conversation in Dan Chazan's class

Through the sorts of activities that Sandy describes, students in my Algebra 1 class thought about quantities as qualities of experience, with values that may change (for example, the quantity *my weight* can change over time). They have learned to distinguish between quantities that can be directly counted or measured and those that cannot. (For example, an average score on five different tests cannot be measured or counted directly.) Now it is time to move on to relationships *between* quantities. I wanted my students to understand that people describe relationships between quantities as ways to capture their theories about how things work and what is happening in the world around them. People make arguments based on relationships between quantities that they experience.

One of my favorite activities to illustrate this point is based on a newspaper article a student brought me during the fall of 1990. My students could earn extra credit if they brought in a clipping with graphs, tables, or algebraic symbols and explained the author's argument. One student brought in the clipping shown in Figure 3.1.

The author of the introductory blurb argues that, while cars are getting more fuel-efficient, consumers seem to be driving more and using more fuel. He makes this argument by looking at both the number of miles driven by US motor vehicles and domestic fuel consumption in gallons.

The student who brought in this clip explained the author's argument as follows. We all know the number of gallons used by a car depends on the gas mileage the car gets and how far it travels. If cars are getting better gas mileage, but more gallons of gas are being used, then each car must be traveling more.

He had done a good job explaining the argument, and I gave him full extra credit. Some of the other students, however, were perturbed. They agreed that new cars were getting better gas mileage. What concerned them was that the people that they knew were all talking about driving less because the cost of gas was going up. They didn't believe the argument.

I asked if they could find a flaw in it. One of these students said that something was missing. He thought he remembered reading somewhere that cars were lasting longer and that every year many new cars are bought. It took the class a while to understand why this would make a

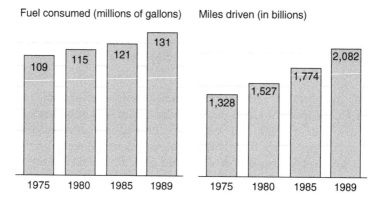

Consumption grows
Federal fuel economy laws have improved the average fuel efficiency of US vehicles. But that apparently prompted consumers to drive more and use more fuel. Here are the number of miles traveled by US motor vehicles and the number of gallons of fuel used.

Figure 3.1 A graph about fuel consumption (sources: US Environmental Protection Agency, Department of Energy and Department of Transportation and Federal Highway Administration).

difference. But then they began to understand that there might be other reasons for gasoline consumption to go up.

I like this particular article and graph because they emphasize relationships between quantities and how they are applied in reasoning. Students have to reason their way through the relationship between number of gallons used, distance traveled, and fuel efficiency. If fuel efficiency is getting higher, but the amount of fuel used is going up, what must be happening to the distance traveled? Having engaged students in this reasoning, I try to show them how the author has neglected the effect of other variables. This makes two points: identification of key variables is important (and sometimes difficult) and mathematics is often poorly applied in the media.

How do we represent relationships between quantities?

Interpreting graphs: a conversation in Marty Schnepp's class

Mathematics educators have found that many students seem to view graphs as a picture of a situation (e.g., Monk, 1992 calls this "iconic translation"). To understand this, ask a student to graph how the speed of a cyclist changes with time as the cyclist bikes over a hill. The student's graph may look like a depiction of a cross-sectional cut through the hill, rather than a graph which indicates slowing down followed by speeding up.

With an overriding goal of helping our students to develop the ability to interpret a graph qualitatively, we want them to understand that conventional graphs read from left to right and serve to represent visually the relationship between two quantities. And, we want them to be able to use the words increasing, decreasing, constant, straight, curved, and rate of change to describe the relationships between quantities depicted in a graph. To develop such facility requires that students first understand that a graph is not merely a rendering of objects in the situational context, a picture of a situation, but a means to help people picture relationships that frequently cannot be seen in other ways.

But overcoming iconic interpretations of graphs is not simple. As a matter of course, I see student responses to graphing tasks that are classic examples of renderings of objects in the given situation. Each year, I have used the problem shown in Figure 3.2 below, which we adapted from a classroom poster produced in England (Shell Centre, 1985), to surface such responses. Notice that in this problem the graphs are presented without any quantitative information. Students must employ qualities or characteristics they notice in the graph to interpret

Each morning, at the Capitol, someone has to raise the flag
to the top of the flagpole. (They pull on the rope, and the
flag rises.) Below are six possible graphs of this situation:

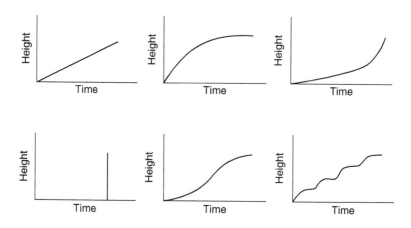

a) Explain what each of the graphs would mean for the
way in which the person raised the flag.

b) Which is the most realistic graph? Explain why.

c) Which is the least realistic graph? Explain why.

Figure 3.2 An interpreting-graphs task.

the situation. They cannot rely on information about the particular
values of the quantities. Similar problems are presented by the software
program, *Interpreting Graphs* (Dugdale & Kibbey, 1986). *The
Grapher's Sketchbook* (Yerushalmy *et al.*, 1992), another software
program, allows students to make their own qualitative graphs.

One of my classes featured an unusual number of students who could
not seem to separate the graphs from a picture of the situation. They
held to the notion that the vertical line was the best representation
for the raising of a flag and would hear nothing of the objections of
a small number of students to that graph. One student said of the second
and third graphs in the top row: "These don't make sense. Why would
the person be whipping the thing around like this?" He made a circular
swinging motion with his hand. "The stupid thing isn't a jump rope."

Another said that those two graphs showed the flag bending in the
wind. He held up a piece of paper. For the first one, he bent the upper
corner over as he raised the "flag." I was at a loss. You take a gamble
when you depend on discussion for conceptual development. My

experience has been that with discussions students move forward with a richer understanding than I have been able to foster via traditional means. This time, however, the class was clearly stuck.

The next day, several teachers from our math department got together to learn how to operate the Texas Instrument Computer Based Laboratory (CBL), which we use in conjunction with a program that employs a sound sensor to measure the distance from the sensor to an object. The program makes a distance-versus-time graph on a TI-82 calculator as the data is being collected. After gaining some experience with the set-up, I transferred the program onto an overhead TI-82 projection unit and went to the class that was having difficulty with the flag graph.

The students took the flag problem out of their folders. After a short demonstration of the CBL, I had a student volunteer stand in front of the sensor. I then asked the class to instruct her on how to walk away from the unit so that she would create a distance–time graph like the first height–time graph (the linear graph). As we worked our way through each graph, students began to see that the shape of the distance–time graph had to do with her speed as she moved away from the sensor, and not with the way she flapped her arms (or any of a variety of other things the class asked her to do). As we tackled the vertical line, several students tried a variety of movements to create this graph. One stood right at the sensor for a period of time to keep the distance zero then jumped out of the path of the sound pulses. To his dismay, the graph simply jumped to the distance of the nearest wall and continued horizontally. The vertical graph was impossible, he concluded, because it represents as he put it, "many places at the same time."

Using the CBL not only helped students move past an iconic interpretation of graphs, it showed many students how to read graphs left to right, thus helping them distinguish increasing from decreasing. Seeing the graph plotted before their eyes made for a dramatic illustration of a concept many had been struggling with for a week. It also gave me an avenue to raise the question of continuous versus discrete (why we "connect the dots"). Earlier, some students had been trying to convince their peers that we don't connect the dots on a graph solely for the purpose of making the graph easier to read. Simply changing the interval of time at which the CBL collects data gave them an opportunity to express their intuitions about continuity.

Quantitative graphs: a conversation in Kelly Hodges's class

My students come to Algebra 1 with some notion of how to plot points. This understanding can be a resource to use in concert with their qualitative understanding of graphs. But the plotting of points also brings in new issues. We want students to think about mathematical conventions related to plotting. These include the role of the zero or origin, scaling by equal intervals, relationships between the scales on each axis, whether data points should be connected or not, and choosing which variables to place on the horizontal and vertical axes.

One approach to integrating quantitative information into graphs is to start with data. For this I introduce an activity called "The Bottle Lab." (Similar problems can be found in Piccioto & Wah, 1994). I give each group of students a bucket of water, a glass container, a test tube, and a ruler. For every test tube of water added, students measure the height of the water in the bottle and record it in a table. They then make a graph of the data that they gathered while filling their bottles. Typically, they say they know how to graph data, so I let them set up and label their axes as they choose.

Each group then presents their bottle results to the class, and class members predict what the graph will look like. Based on the shape of the bottle, they can predict when the water will be rising quickly and when it will be rising slowly. Often, however, two people who correctly explain the physical change produce different graphs. Below (Figure 3.3) is my favorite bottle; it's always the one that produces the most conversation.

Figure 3.4 shows two different graphs produced by students in my class for this bottle.

The second graph, with height on the horizontal axis and volume on the vertical axis, is the one produced by the group that did the experiment. Several members of the class drew sketches that matched this graph. The rest of the class produced the first graph.

Figure 3.3 An oddly shaped bottle.

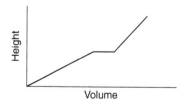
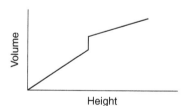

Figure 3.4 Sample student graphs.

As soon as the group presenting revealed its graph, discussion began. "That's not what I've got!" David shouted. I asked the group to describe what happened to the water level in the bottle as test tubes of water were added. Could they show on the graph how the changing height was indicated by the graph? Tim, speaking for the group, described how the water rose slowly at first (pointing to the diagonal line from the origin), then stayed level for a while as the second chamber filled (pointing to the vertical section), then rose more quickly at the end (indicating the third section). When I pressed him by asking how the vertical line indicated the level was staying the same, he used the numbers of each axis to demonstrate that from 9 to 12 test tubes full of water, the height of the water in the bottle remained at 4 centimeters.

Dwayne, however, disagreed that the graph showed that the water level stayed even. He presented the alternate version of the graph (on the left), with volume on the horizontal axis. David, seeing both graphs and listening to both students speak, declared that they were both correct, since each had demonstrated the different changes in the height. Tim agreed, adding that it was the responsibility of the reader to look carefully at how the axes are labeled and to interpret correctly.

"OK," I allowed. "Both graphs show all the data, but is one better than the other?" Beth said that the graph on the left was better, because it was easier to see the height changing if you did it that way. Angie agreed, pointing out that you couldn't expect everyone to read the labels on the axes carefully before looking at the shape. Most people agreed with this argument, except Tim, who continued to insist that for him, the graph with height along the bottom was more consistent with the way he would look at graphs. After some discussion, I convinced him of the value in agreeing on one way to do the graphs, since we would be using them to communicate with each other. Moreover, most people outside our class would also put the volume on the horizontal axis, and it would be helpful to be able to communicate easily with them as well.

I really liked this discussion. It didn't portray mathematical conventions as a sterile set of facts to be memorized, but as something established and agreed upon by people who do mathematics. In mathematics, we put volume on the horizontal axis not because there is something inherently right about it. We agreed to do it that way in order to be able to read graphs from left to right in a particular way. Economists, by way of contrast, have agreed among themselves to put the independent variable on the vertical axis. They carry on well within their community, but often redraw their graphs when communicating with those who are not economists.

Number recipes: another conversation in Marty Schnepp's class

After working with graphs, which are new for some, students feel relieved when they return to tasks that are reminiscent of arithmetic, like the number recipes in Figure 3.5 below. But these admittedly mechanical exercises provide a surprisingly rich environment for fruitful classroom discussion. Since 1992, I have reaped mathematical and pedagogical rewards from follow-up conversations with students about these exercises. Initially, I saw the activity below simply as a way to begin looking at algebra symbols as a language for describing repeated calculations. It advanced the concept that a variable is something that truly varies. After being asked to make tables for several of these recipes, my students often begin inventing their own shorthand notations to keep the words defining the procedure clear (e.g.: 9 – ##). I initially thought that this was the main purpose of these activities, to help students take such notations and see how they are related to the standard $9-x^2$.

But my students often start to look at their tables for patterns of change. If this does not happen of its own accord, I refer to question B on the worksheet (find an input that will give 0 as an output). To predict where to find 0s, students begin to pay attention to how outputs change as a result of input change. Sometimes this leads to a discussion of their difficulties with arithmetic. For example, with the rule "multiply your input by 3 and then add 2," many students decide that there is no possible answer. Some argue that at 0 the output is 2 and at –1 it is –1, so that there are no numbers in between to use as inputs. Others

> Rule 1: Multiply the input by itself and subtract the result from 9.
>
> A) Make a table with 6 inputs and outputs.
>
> B) Find an input that will give 0 as an output.
>
> C) Use your table to make a graph.
>
> D) Write a description of the graph using *increasing, decreasing, constant, straight,* and *curved.*
>
> Rule 2: Multiply your input by 2, add 2, then divide by 2.
>
> Follow the same four steps (A–D) as above.

Figure 3.5 A number recipe task.

may argue that the correct input is between 0 and −1, but that you cannot find it exactly (particularly if they are using a calculator). These conversations raise other valuable mathematical ideas like order of operations. They also provide a good setting in which to work on norms for classroom discussion.

During the fall of 1994, four key events took place as we discussed the two rules above. First, after several students finished writing their tables of values on the board, one of them looked at another's table and began to work with a calculator. He then raised his hand and said, "My table is completely wrong. I'm not sure what I did, but I'll figure it out." This was the first time that a student openly admitted a mistake in my class. This admission was of great benefit in that the student initiated an investigation into the possible causes of his wrong values. I have never been able to generate this kind of conversation intentionally. Somehow the number-recipe format presents students with incentives to explore wrong answers.

The second event came after we had resolved that student's error, ensured consistency among all tables on the board, and begun examining the second recipe. Another student called everyone's attention back to the original problem. He pointed out a mistake that we had all overlooked. We had subtracted in the opposite order of what the recipe required (x^2-9 rather than $9-x^2$). This further validated that being wrong is nothing to be embarrassed about and that we can learn from our mistakes.

As we moved on to the second rule presented in the problem, a third interesting mini-discussion developed from students' efforts to adapt familiar graphical terms "increasing" and "decreasing" to tables they had made. Two students had chosen the same inputs, only in a different order. One student's table showed the ordered pairs (5,6), (4,5), (3,4), (2,3) and (1,2); the other's showed (1,2), (2,3), (3,4), (4,5), and (5,6). As a result of displaying the tables on the board as vertical input–output columns, the two students insisted that one table would give an increasing graph and the other a decreasing one. To check this conjecture, a third student suggested graphing both on the same coordinate system. Although the two tables resulted in the same graph, this result only intensified the debate. For a portion of the class, the graph refuted the conjecture and resolved the issue. Others (the two who made the original tables in particular) insisted that "increasing" and "decreasing" meant something different for tables than they did for graphs. Although this dispute went unresolved, it illustrates students testing mathematical ideas (e.g., by graphing both tables) developed by other students.

Finally, the fourth event involved one pair of values. Students (weary from an already long discussion) were snapped back to attention when someone said, "Wait a minute! Something weird is going on here! I keep checking the answer from 7 (as an input), and I keep getting different answers! I can't figure it out!" Students computing this rule mentally tended to arrive at different outputs than students who used graphing calculators. Students spent approximately 20 minutes arguing whether an input of 7 yields an output of 15 or 8. They were typing "7*2 + 2/2" on their calculators – which results in 15. In their heads they were doing: $7*2 = 14$, $14 + 2 = 16$, $16/2 = 8$. Students made conjectures, tested them, and challenged each other's ideas.

Across these four events, the students were talking about mathematical ideas for the sake of understanding. They were comfortable with being wrong and trying to find out why. They had begun to try and convince one another with mathematical reasoning. And, they were doing all of this in a purely mathematical context (as opposed to a situated task). I knew their level of comfort and expertise would increase over time as these classroom behaviors would become a regular occurrence.

Conclusion

While this essay outlines only the very beginning of the Algebra 1 curricular story, we hope that these scenes illustrate how classroom interaction has changed. What we find most appealing about this approach to algebra is the impact that a subtle change in mathematical direction – from unknowns to variables – has on our classrooms. With an understanding of the table-graph-symbol-situation network, our students have much more to say in class discussions. There is real engagement and students insist that ideas make sense; they test their own ideas and the ideas of their peers. Our role as teachers of algebra can shift from spending most of our time telling students how to carry out manipulations for particular problem types to also helping our students understand what tasks are asking of them and evaluating solution methods they have generated.

Each episode suggests a shift away from the teacher as sole arbiter of right and wrong in the mathematics classroom:

- Sandy Callis does not tell her students how they must think about time as a quantity;
- Dan Chazan encourages students to articulate their unease with a columnist's interpretation of numerical data;
- Marty Schnepp employs CBL devices to help students understand how use of the Cartesian coordinate system to graph relationships between quantities in a situation is different from use of the picture plane to depict the situation itself; and
- Kelly Hodges, rather than simply treating conventions as arbitrary, involves her class in discussion of the purposes of mathematical conventions.

In addition, with this shift in classroom interaction, algebra no longer feels like a completely rote exercise that can only be justified as a step to further educational opportunities. Showing our students that the relationships between quantities studied in algebra are present in their experience makes a big difference in arguing for an investment of energy in studying algebra, both for students who do not see themselves continuing on to college and for those who do.

Perspectives on Holt Algebra I from the department chair and a newer teacher

Mike Lehman and Craig Huhn, Holt High School

CRAIG HUHN: This essay outlines only the very beginnings of the Algebra 1 curricular story and doesn't convey some of the details that are important farther down the line. But, as someone who teaches Algebra 1, the classroom vignettes do illustrate how classroom interaction has changed in Holt Algebra 1 classes.

MIKE LEHMAN: As department chairperson, for me, the approach to Algebra 1 that is described in this piece is a prime example of the type of education we want for all our students. I think this essay effectively demonstrates new opportunities for introducing students to the essence of algebra and some of its central ideas. For example, what I find appealing about this approach is the impact that a subtle change in mathematical direction has on our classrooms. The idea of conversations in an Algebra 1 classroom is a big change.

CRAIG: Based on my own experience in high school, Algebra felt like it was a completely rote exercise that could only be justified as a step to further educational opportunities. Now having done an internship at Holt with an opportunity to co-teach one section of Algebra 1 for a semester with a fellow intern, followed by teaching several sections of Algebra 1 since joining the department as a teacher in 1999, working with the Algebra 1 curriculum at Holt has been an important experience. This experience has helped me to see that discussing the relationships between quantities that are present in the students' experience makes a big difference in establishing the value of algebra for students who do not see themselves on a path to college.

MIKE: I agree; we want students to learn not just the manipulations of mathematics, but the reasoning behind it. I also think that describing this course in this book is a good way to make evident our growth as teachers and as a department. Through the development of this course, we in the math department have learned to use situations to bring about discussions and then the understanding of the mathematics involved.

CRAIG: As someone entering the profession, participating in this course helped set expectations for me about my teaching. From participating in this work, I'm committed to the idea that what happens in my classes should reflect the students and thus be unique each period, that I develop problems for students to work on and change handouts based on conversations that take place day-to-day in my classroom.

MIKE: This course has led the way for many of the changes we have accomplished in our department. But, when the Algebra 1 course first began to evolve I wasn't department chairman and wasn't teaching the course, so at first it didn't affect me much. I knew Dan Chazan and Sandy Callis were working on it, but it was only when I became chairman that I became more aware of what was happening and how it might affect the rest of the department. Like other members of the department, at first, I didn't really understand the goals Dan and Sandy had established for the course. I wasn't used to the emphasis on discussion and on the questioning of assumptions. Some in the department initially felt it was just a watered-down version of algebra. They didn't understand what the course was about. Once we were able to get some of the key people in the department to team-teach the course with those who had worked on it, things seemed to change. For example, from team-teaching with Sandy, I realized how powerful a course Algebra 1 had become, as compared to when I had last taught it. I came to understand that Algebra 1 at Holt is truly a course for all students, regardless of how well they have done before in math. Maybe another way to say this is that this course helped me to have a specific idea of what the NCTM Standards movement (e.g., NCTM, 2000) is really trying to say about teaching mathematics to all students. Feeling this way has allowed me as chair to be comfortable when questioned by parents about a course that proceeds without a textbook, or when parents say that this doesn't look like the algebra that they remember from school. It has also helped me advocate to the junior-high school teachers to teach this course at their building.

CRAIG: For me, even though I haven't had a year-long team-teaching experience in an Algebra 1 class, this course has also been a forum for collaborative work with other teachers in the department. As I began to teach this curriculum, there were many great worksheets and problems written by other teachers in the department and placed on the school's network. I could pull from these as I planned my classes. As an intern, I had chances to talk with Sandy Callis about her conception of how the units in the course fit together. Then the next year, I spent a lot of time working with Marty Schnepp and Tom Almeida (who were teaching other sections) on the course. As we made decisions about directions to go, we were able to talk through our rationales and evidence (that mainly Marty and Tom had from previous years). We discussed which problems seemed better at sparking students' ideas and how concepts might be better ordered for our classes.

MIKE: Turning to the essay itself, I think this essay allows us a view of how a teacher might want to proceed in an Algebra 1 course that would help students develop their understandings, while at the same time giving the teacher a better view of students' understanding of algebraic concepts. It also provides us with a view of how four teachers try to build norms in their classroom that allow students to hold discussions, make corrections in their work, and look at mathematics critically. Looking at Sandy's story about quantities, I find it interesting how the discussion went in a direction for which she was unprepared and how she was unsure of her own understanding of time. If Sandy had decided not to go in that direction and forced the students into a discussion with which she was more comfortable, would student participation and learning have been the same or less?

CRAIG: That's a thought-provoking question. I don't have a direct answer. What is interesting to me is the four different stories in the essay. From the perspective of a new teacher, as I started to teach the course, I wondered whether I would have new things to add, whether I would end up having any great stories of things my students had done that would lead me to questions about my practice like those you raised.

MIKE: With the type of teaching described in this essay and the discussions between colleagues that we have as a department, don't you think these types of questions would naturally occur?

CRAIG: Yes, I have already begun to collect such stories, stories about how students do things that teach you something as a teacher.

MIKE: Can you give me an example?

CRAIG: I have one from my first year as a teacher that may respond to your question and that also says something about how this approach plays out over the course of a year. Towards the end of the year when I was about to work with students on solving equations, I really struggled with justifying to students why in standard techniques people "add $-3x$ to both sides" (say in solving $4x + 7 = 3x - 2$). There was something unnatural about finding a magic term to operate with on both sides. It seemed so arbitrary to justify doing something just because it will get you towards a right answer.

Because of our work all year long, I had a sense that they wouldn't go for such a strategy. They had gotten to a point where they were starting to have some intuitions and weren't ready to accept anything without being clear about how and why it works. Even the phrase "both sides" seemed somewhat meaningless based on the way the classes were thinking about $f(x) = g(x)$ as just a question about the input where the outputs of $f(x)$ and $g(x)$ are equal. And I wasn't sure how they would take to the notion of actually changing the forms of the functions on each side of the equation. They had begun to see a rule, in $mx + b$ form for example, as a way to write a rule where the m and b both provide specific information about the behavior of the function. I couldn't justify to myself or imagine telling the class to just move b to the other side where the other function is. I'm not even quite sure now what it means to "get x by itself" when thinking of x as a variable quantity as opposed to an unknown.

MIKE: This makes me wonder what this has to say about us as teachers and as learners. You were obviously taught to solve symbolically in your 8th-grade Algebra 1 course.

CRAIG: I know! In class, I simply presented the task, and watched as students tried to pinpoint the exact input for the rules $11x - 9$ and $2x - 6$ that would give the exact same output. At this point in the year, students had generated strategies for getting rid of parenthesis in a rule (distribution), for simplifying rules, for recognizing what the coefficients in the different forms (y-intercept, x-intercept, and point-slope forms) tell you automatically, and how to switch between these forms. So, as a result of things we had done earlier in the year, students ended up wanting to find the x-intercept of the difference function. It made sense to them to make an equation with one function equal to zero, since some students remembered how putting a function in x-intercept form helps determine what input for that function gives an output of zero. This is what ended up on the board as a symbolic way of writing down the process students had used.

$$11x - 9 = 2x - 6$$

$$(11x - 9) - (2x - 6) = 0$$

$$1(11x + -9) + -1(2x + -6) = 0$$

$$11x + -9 + -2x + 6 = 0$$

$$9x + -3 = 0$$

$$9(x + -0.3333 \ldots) = 0$$

$$x = 0.333 \ldots$$

Without resorting to any Traditional Method provided by me, or ambient symbolic manipulation misremembered from previous coursework, the class had just proven to themselves (and to *me*) how symbols themselves could be used to solve equations, based solely on their previous knowledge and curiosity (and their own interest in finding a better way). It was also the first time that they found a circumstance where they liked using the symbols better (the first time that they were convinced that tables and graphs weren't always easier). In a class period and a half, the class was engaged in making a strategy that made sense to them given their function-based background. Best of all, they came up with it as part of a natural question in class. I guess I do believe that they pursued it more intensely because it was their ownership of the process that we used to answer the question.

MIKE: That's a great story. I think that it shows that if we can get students to think critically about mathematics, hold discussions, and examine their own work, we will have overcome a major obstacle in their understanding of algebra. Is there more you could say about what you mean when you said they were willing to pursue it more than if you had presented a method? In most mathematics classes when the teacher presents a new type of problem and asks the students to solve it, they usually know this is the sign that they are going to be getting new information and if they wait for a while the teacher will tell them how to solve it. And, as a result, they don't work hard at exploring the task.

CRAIG: I believe it's the fact that the students are following up on their ideas that makes it more engaging for them. By this point in the year, we have built a trust between us that during a discussion, as the facilitator, one of my jobs is to make sure that what we are discussing is mathematically beneficial. Also, they know that when presented with new situations, they do have the mathematical means to work them through.

MIKE: It seems to me that this is a tricky thing to have happen in a class and is also a good example of how the role as a teacher in this type of class really changes.

Chapter 4

Another kind of planning

In each of the episodes in the last piece, teachers asked students to assume some responsibility for determining the validity of their statements (Part III will focus on what led teachers to make these changes). But how can teachers ask students to take on such responsibility? In the next essay, Marty Schnepp engages the question of how teachers support student reasoning. He suggests that teachers' top-level curricular choices, for example the ordering of theorems in a Calculus course, relate to the opportunities students have to reason. Both the material in the last chapter and Marty's essay also give a sense of how the teachers at Holt plan for their teaching. Often planning for a mathematics class is conceptualized as picking lessons and activities from a textbook and/or supplementary materials. In contrast, the teachers at Holt have begun to plan by thinking about the big picture of the year as a whole. Then they work to figure out how that big picture is comprised of units. Finally, based on the big picture of the year, the particular goals of a unit, students' ideas, and interaction with colleagues, they develop activities and lessons and make decisions about the ordering of units.

One sign, at Holt, of greater teacher reflection on big-picture curricular issues has been a decreased reliance on textbooks as the spine of a mathematics curriculum. As the teachers have taken greater responsibility for the shape of the curriculum, they have become less inclined to adopt uncritically the work of textbook authors. Tinkering with canonical ordering of material in a course, as the next essay illustrates, is a second sign of attention to the big curricular picture. On the departmental level, another indication of greater involvement with curricular issues has been increased discussion of curriculum and sharing of materials and activities within the department. Teachers in the department have used a locally shared network drive to post materials. But, in a department, this sort of involvement by teachers does not of necessity only result in harmonious collaborative activity. To some degree, increased dissension about what a particular course is all about and over the degree to which different sections of the same course can diverge is another sign of teachers taking greater responsibility for curricular decisions.

In doing this sort of planning, in paying attention to the organization of instruction at the level of a year-long course and developing worksheets and activities, the teachers at Holt are taking on more than teachers usually do. Indeed, some (e.g., Lappan, 1998, when suggesting the importance of well-written and developed curricular materials) would argue that teachers' work lives are too demanding for them to take on serious responsibilities for planning the architecture of the curriculum of a course.

In contrast, in the next essay, Marty Schnepp indicates that he, as a teacher, feels it is important to take on this kind of work. He hints at why he does so by illustrating how postponing the Product Rule in his Calculus class, while it made certain differentiation problems tedious, allowed his students to understand the material in the course more deeply, and then provided an opportunity for a student to develop a novel proof justifying this result.

In discussing his piece, Sandy Callis and Kelly Hodges wonder about the importance of the feeling of "discovery" in learning and what it means to do student-centered teaching and planning. In order to have student-centered teaching, must different sections of the same course diverge? Must a teacher develop all of their materials from scratch?

Teacher as course-level planner

Marty Schnepp, Holt High School

This paper was drafted in the spring of 1998. It was originally published in 2000 under the title Proof positive: An instance of mathematical discovery in the classroom in *Mathematics in Michigan, 38(2)*, 17–20. *Mathematics in Michigan* is a publication of the Michigan Council of Teachers of Mathematics.

One March day in 1998, as I was about to prove the Product Rule in a class, something amazing happened. A student helped me see a proof for it that I'd never seen before.

I can imagine hearing your thoughts as you consider what you just read: "Wait a minute! The Product Rule in March? You must be teaching one of those watered-down Calculus classes."

I suppose I should tell you how I sequence my course before I share a classroom anecdote. Over my years as a Calculus teacher and as a student of Calculus, I've noticed great difficulty among novice analysts as they try sorting out the difference between the Chain Rule and the Product Rule. This difficulty with differentiation rules is sometimes most apparent when students are asked to anti-differentiate integrands, like $x^2\sin(x^3+1)$, that can be viewed as products of two functions.

In the standard course, in the fall, after asking students to take a number of derivatives the hard way, using the definition of the derivative, we go on to present many rules of differentiation. Likely, the first we want to hand our students is: $d/dx[f(x)+g(x)]=f'(x)+g'(x)$. We do this with very little discussion. Perhaps more for ourselves than for our students, we may present the traditional proof whose subtlety may escape our students. Having already asked our students to calculate derivatives using the definition of the derivative, why would we think this generalization about derivatives of sums would seem like a significant result to our students? Furthermore, I find that my students seem more comfortable viewing polynomials as a single function and lack the abstract sophistication to view them as the sum of monomial functions. My students don't understand why they would want to treat functions as built out of distinct addends.

As we move on to the Product Rule, even if students do see functions as the product of two functions – $h(x)=f(x)\cdot g(x)$ – it's unlikely they would think the derivative is anything other than $h'(x)=f'(x)\cdot g'(x)$. In the past, when presenting the derivative of products, I've simply made a few authoritative statements to the contrary and gone charging through the standard, but magical, proof of the Product Rule. You know the one. Start with the definition of the derivative applied to $h(x)=f(x)\cdot g(x)$, pull a "$-f(x+h)g(x)+f(x+h)g(x)$" out of thin air, and stick it into what looks (to the student) like the same proof as the Sum Rule. But now, because of the magical terms, the difference quotient can be factored to achieve the result that you (the teacher) were given as a student. Once upon a time, I honestly believed that, with some drill and practice, my students would be convinced that $h'(x)=f'(x)g(x)+f(x)g'(x)$ in the same way that I've come to believe in that result. As an experienced teacher, however, I know the standard proof doesn't convince my students. My authority as teacher persuades them to use it.

Once we throw in the Quotient Rule, Constant Multiple Rule, and the Chain Rule, the whole notion of building up theoretical tools for differentiating complicated functions has the potential to become a jumbled mess of irrelevant proofs presented by the teacher and forgotten by the students. As the year progresses, with so much to memorize, more and more of my students would typically slip up and start using $h'(x)=f'(x)\cdot g'(x)$. When we tackle various integrals of the form $\int f(x)g(x)dx$, that involve simple substitution, students incorrectly respond with things like $\int x^2 \sin(x^3 + 1)dx = 1/3x^3 \cdot -\cos(x^3 + 1) + k$. **Rather than reverse the chain rule, these students are reversing the incorrect product rule.** With so many rules, it's difficult for students to be mindful as they look for composite functions so that they can reverse the Chain Rule, that is, do simple substitution. All but the most diligent students with a natural aptitude for memorization and form recognition are unsuccessful given the limited time we typically allow them to develop proficiency as we charge through the standard list of topics and skills.

You will never hear me say things like, "some people are better at math than others;" or use terms like "gifted kids and slow kids." Whether or not a student is gifted, talented, or gifted and talented (whatever those labels mean) is a moot point. My responsibility is to see that every willing student in my class has an opportunity to learn the material in a meaningful manner. When I see a persistent obstacle to learning – like the muddling of differentiation rules – I feel it's my duty to find a better way.

In the fall of 1997, I intentionally held introduction of the Product Rule until later, when it could be connected with Integration by Parts. Ever since I realized the connection between Integration by Parts and the Product Rule, it's bothered me that Integration by Parts is taught as much as six months after the Product Rule. Because of the amount of time between these two topics, Integration by Parts is typically reduced to a procedural mandate. Despite efforts to show students where it comes from, they see little connection to the Product Rule.

Instead of the usual sequence, I chose to focus on the Chain Rule in the fall, letting the concept sit in their minds for a while. We used the Chain Rule to develop other mathematics and got used to working with integrals that required anti-differentiation related to the Chain Rule. I believe the Chain Rule is important and plays a significant role in extending mathematical theory and techniques. For example, the relationship between the derivative of inverse functions:

$$\frac{d}{dx}[f^{-1}(x)] = \frac{1}{f'(f^{-1}(x))}$$

is an easy result, given the Chain Rule, as are proofs for properties of the natural logarithm. These and many other significant topics can be approached through explorations that help build a conceptual understanding of fundamental Calculus ideas, provided the onslaught of rules and procedures that the traditional sequence of Calculus imposes from the start is tempered.

In delaying the Product Rule, I tried to front-load the course with rich, concept-developing activities. I wanted students to deeply understand rate and accumulation, differentiation and integration, and the Fundamental Theorems of Calculus before studying specific classes of functions and generalizing operations on functions as they relate to derivatives and integrals. There is a great deal of mathematics that can be done without the Product Rule.

Of course, the min–max problems I could give didn't require as much algebra. Nor could I do as much with trigonometric functions early on, and I had to be mindful of the text problems I assigned. If I wasn't careful, my students would face problems that they would find difficult or impossible to solve.

But the payoff of delaying the introduction of the Product Rule has been immeasurable. First, most of my students believe this stuff can, and should, actually make sense, and be useful. Next, their skill with the Chain Rule is better than any of the groups of students I had before I made this change. These skills included integration by reversing the Chain Rule; the ability to distinguish those integrals that require substitution from those that do not; and an understanding of the Chain Rule as a theoretical tool for expanding the types of derivatives one can compute, and not just another differentiation rule for solving textbook problems.

Well, on to my anecdote. In 1997–1998, my two AP Calculus classes eventually got to the point where they acknowledged the need to know how to differentiate the product of two functions. This need was greatest when students incorrectly anti-differentiated and wanted to use differentiation to see what was wrong with their answer. (I must admit part of the need arose from my lack of diligence in homework problem selection. I accidentally assigned some exercises that required the Product Rule.) In the fall, I was content to acknowledge examples that showed clearly that: if $h(x) = f(x)g(x)$, then $h(x) \neq f'(x) \cdot g'(x)$. When confronted with a derivative involving a product, my students had to rewrite it algebraically, so there was no product before differentiating, or they simply could not do the problem. This seemed satisfactory to my students, otherwise we would have resolved the product issue earlier.

But finally we couldn't let it ride any longer. So, I prepared to do something I had done very infrequently – to stand at the chalkboard and show them how to differentiate products by presenting to them the proof that convinces me. (As a diligent teacher, however, I admit I was uneasy about the magical step.) I could conceive of no alternative plans; so ahead I went. I had reached the step right before I was going to show them the trick. I paused to make them struggle for a bit, asking the class if they had any ideas about how to get past that point. I knew students were out there thinking things like $f(x + h)$ could be rewritten $f(x) + f(h)$, and I wanted to be sure to discuss those misconceptions. Sure enough, several variations came out, and we talked through them.

As another hand went up, I prepared to deal with a similar idea. But to my surprise, Nick simply said, "Doesn't the natural log have the property that it can change multiplication to addition? We know how to do (differentiate) addition, so can't we use that?" It took me a minute to follow his line of thinking. Having seen students randomly apply a function to an expression to force something to happen had taught me caution. Finally, I understood what he was saying:

$$h(x) = f(x) \cdot g(x)$$
$$\ln(h(x)) = \ln(f(x) \cdot g(x))$$

None of us thought to quibble that this would only work for positive values of $h(x)$ and of the product $f(x)*g(x)$ (though this difficulty can be taken care of by working with cases, because when the output of a function is negative, the derivative of the log of the opposite of the function is the derivative of the function at that point, divided by the function at that point). So, we continued on using our knowledge of the ln function:

$$\ln(h(x)) = \ln(f(x)) + \ln(g(x))$$

As Nick said, "We can differentiate that." We could because we knew the Chain Rule. As a class, we finished the proof.

$$\frac{d}{dx}[\ln(h(x))] = \frac{d}{dx}[\ln(f(x)) + \ln(g(x))]$$

$$h'(x) \cdot \frac{1}{h(x)} = f'(x) \cdot \frac{1}{f(x)} + g'(x) \cdot \frac{1}{g(x)}$$

A different student said, "we want h prime, so multiply by $h(x)$."

$$h'(x) = \left(f'(x) \cdot \frac{1}{f(x)} + g'(x) \cdot \frac{1}{g(x)} \right) \cdot h(x)$$

$$h'(x) = \left(f'(x) \cdot \frac{1}{f(x)} + g'(x) \cdot \frac{1}{g(x)} \right) \cdot f(x)g(x)$$

$$h'(x) = f'(x) \cdot g(x) + g'(x) \cdot f(x)$$

None of us had seen this argument before. My students didn't know what the outcome of differentiating a product should be. The argument was developed in a pure deductive way, a rare example of one type of true mathematical discovery. In most instances of proof in school mathematics, the result to be proven is known ahead of time and proof is a matter of analytically verifying that result.

After completing this argument, we opened our textbook to the page on which the standard proof appeared and analyzed it. The class was remarkably interested and thorough in their questioning of the work shown by the authors. This supports one of the teaching principles I try to apply: students should have an opportunity to make sense of mathematical situations before instructors show them traditionally accepted methods. I believe students learn more and analyze the mathematics of others better if they are first given a chance to probe situations with the mathematics that they already know or can create.

You may not see this anecdote as significant and you may even have seen this or a similar argument. Regardless, you have to admit that Nick's original insight is breathtaking for a high school student. You may disagree with my thesis about the importance of students having opportunities to make sense of mathematics themselves before they learn the results of others, but I am committed to this endeavor. A student thinking independently with the confidence to share a novel approach with others is heartening and to me demonstrates mathematical power. A group of students critiquing a textbook is encouraging and again demonstrates mathematical power. And the prospect of entertaining future, unexpected results that my students might derive is invigorating for me as a teacher. Nonetheless, you might feel that altering the traditional order of theorems in Calculus is unwise, or maybe even impossible. In response, I'd argue that the work of the class was possible only because I had the freedom to determine the trajectory of the course curriculum.

One unanticipated problem did arise from the success of my first class. I had no idea what to do when the next class came in to study the same topic. I certainly couldn't just do the old proof after seeing Nick's argument. I could work through the old proof and pause at the same step, hoping someone would have the same insight – but that wasn't likely. Showing them Nick's argument would be better, but it still wouldn't give the second class of students a chance to make sense of the problem for themselves. I was stuck. I talked to colleagues over the lunch break about my dilemma. I decided to have students in the second class start by reading the textbook's proof and discussing it. As it turned out, they were fairly thoughtful in questioning, discussing, and critiquing the text of the proof. This seemed a better choice than outlining and explaining every step. This way, the students were forced to think for themselves. As they discussed the proof, I candidly told them that I could see what the magic step accomplishes, but had no idea what inspired it. After they were finished picking through the old proof, I told them about Nick's idea. I gave them only his suggestion and turned them loose. Within a few minutes, they had recreated his argument.

Must teachers create curriculum? For every class?

Sandy Callis and Kelly Hodges, Holt Public Schools

SANDY CALLIS: The mathematical ideas in this essay are of great interest, and the idea of having students prepare to read a proof critically is fascinating. And, Nick's insight makes for quite a story. My interest is drawn to the questions this essay raises for me about student-centered approaches to teaching and teacher planning and our attempts to be a department that teaches in this way. In particular, there is an intriguing issue that has to do with spontaneity and discovery and their role in the classroom. In the essay, this issue was raised for me by Marty's quandary with his second class. I doubt Marty could ever again bring into play all the variables that led to Nick's suggestion that the logarithmic function would be an important step in developing the Product Rule. Does that mean that students in other classes suffer, or that in the essay Marty did not teach the second class in a student-centered manner? I do not think so. Of course, I believe in having students discover and invent. These are important ways to change what math is like for students in school. But I have come to believe that not all students need to make the same discoveries and come to understandings in the same way. They can further their understanding by sending and receiving information from other classrooms (and, as Marty illustrates, even textbooks). In this way, they are participating in a piece of the social aspect of creating mathematics, not every piece of knowledge need be generated by them as a class or by each student as an individual. Considering other students' mathematical work lays the foundation for and promotes the expectation that the reward for spontaneous discovery is serious consideration by one's peers. Coming to understand another student's proof is a great example of what in reality we do as mathematicians. In addition, pragmatically, if there is less of a premium on spontaneous discovery, classes can move along somewhat in concert and the teacher can provide some of the structure that makes meaningful and authentic mathematics learning occur in the context of real schools. I believe that mathematics is big enough to provide plenty of contexts for all students to experience the "aha" of discovery in some unpredictable and spontaneous way. But the question is whether this has to be thought of as the only way, or even the ideal way, for a class to make progress. Marty and I have discussed this in the past, and I suspect we differ. As he rightly points out, in the second class, the spontaneity of the first experience is not there for the teacher. And the experience was different for the students in the second class; students do recognize when their teacher is seeing something for the very first time!

KELLY HODGES: I'd like to think some more about the distinction between a spontaneous and unpredictable "aha" discovery and a bit of knowledge that is communicated from someone else. I certainly don't think that if one espouses constructivism as a theory of learning, it precludes one from accepting that people can and do learn from other people. I think that constructivism is more about what the learner does or doesn't do with any incoming piece of information, regardless of its source. But as one of my interns once said of her internship, "I've learned that you can't tell students anything. Or rather, you can, but it doesn't work." I think she was talking about her discovery that the quality of the telling is not the keystone to student understanding; other kinds of experiences students can have with content give teachers access to shaping student thinking in ways that telling does not. In particular, I think many of my high school students were unaware initially that mathematical knowledge could come from anywhere *besides* a textbook, or that a textbook was a representation of the mathematical understandings of some qualified person or group but that other knowledgeable parties might represent it somewhat differently. And, my students were often not skillful at taking the knowledge from a text and making it their own. It was important to me to make public the moment of discovery and the process of critiquing new knowledge in part because I wanted students to view themselves as potential producers of mathematics, and in part because that is what I thought I needed to do to make my students better consumers of other people's mathematics. These are both aspects of "student-centered" instruction, I think, and I was continually made aware of the fragility of my progress on each. In particular, if I relied too much on a scope and sequence that was convenient for me at the expense of one that connected to my students' questions, many students quickly reverted to a sit-and-get rather than an active approach to their learning. I think this issue is especially salient for high school teachers. Our students have ten-plus years of tacit or explicit messages about being mathematics students and about mathematics texts. I bet I'm not alone in wanting to ask Marty how he got his students to be so active; but I've learned that answering such a question is practically impossible and that any answer would almost certainly not be directly applicable to my teaching anyway. One of the many things I have learned from this story is that somehow it *is* possible to have a classroom in which the text plays an important but different role than sole authority for knowledge; now I need to figure out what factors contribute to the success of such an approach and whether I can gain control over them.

SANDY: Since textbooks also are a resource for teachers in their planning and help maintain direction in a school or a district, this seems like a valuable aspect of teaching for us all to figure out. I think those of us who have taught at Holt High School where we have tended to develop our own materials have to articulate more clearly our vision of student-centered instruction, so that we're not misunderstood when people read Marty's essay. I think some people might think we believe that teachers need to design all their instruction from scratch. I wouldn't agree. I think that as teachers we want to treat texts the way Marty wants his students to learn to treat texts. We don't want teachers to be curriculum technicians simply implementing what others say without trying to evaluate those ideas themselves. At the same time, in my view, student-centered instruction does not presuppose that teachers must develop curriculum for all of their classes. Similarly, I don't think that we are suggesting that different sections of the same course *must* be different, or that teachers should have the flexibility to veer off into whatever mathematical territory seems most interesting and salient at a particular time, without any constraints. If we did that, where would we be as a community of teachers in a school and a system that is trying to provide some kind of sequential, benchmarked curriculum? What would keep Algebra 1 from becoming Discrete Math?

KELLY: I agree that Algebra 1 shouldn't become Discrete Math. But, Sandy, why in this country are we so concerned about consistency within a district but not between districts or states or countries?

SANDY: I'm not saying we shouldn't be concerned about consistency across states or the country as a whole. In our district, though, I see parents and teachers struggling with the issue of how to make a rationale for teaching different students different curricula within the context of courses that share a title, like "Algebra 1" or "Algebra 2," and that build on each other. There is a general consensus in the public that a good teacher teaches the "curriculum," and if the student doesn't get it, then it's the fault of either the student, the student's circumstances, or the instructional "knowhow" of the teacher. Raising the question of whether students in a PreCalculus class even had access to the same ideas because of the students' own intervention into the direction of their Algebra 2

class certainly puts another layer of complexity on the already difficult challenge of keeping students, parents, teachers, and the public
in general convinced that what is going on in school is useful and
leads to future success.

KELLY: I'm not sure it's the case that the public would be any more convinced that what's going on in schools would lead to future success
if it were consistent, and I'm not sure that consistency alone would
even improve the situation, regardless of public opinion. I do agree
that it is much harder to *measure* student achievement or hold
anyone accountable in the traditional ways if every class is different, and that is a concern. But if what we want to do is actually
improve the state of things, perhaps putting our efforts into measuring them is counterproductive. Might it be that by constraining
instruction in ways that make it easier to measure student achievement, we sacrifice being able to improve student achievement? And,
I think consistency is a pipedream in another way. Moving beyond
the curriculum that is offered to the curriculum that is experienced
by students, regardless of the degree of similarity in the instruction
each student receives, the nature of the learning each student
experiences is different. Teachers monitor these outcomes as they
teach and then make subtle, or not so subtle, moves to influence
students' thinking. Now that I have been teaching preservice
teacher education courses, I think that part of my job as an instructor for preservice teacher interns is to help each of them figure out
how to be responsive to students within the constraints of the kinds
of schools in which they teach. From my experience with preservice
teachers, I think all teachers should assume that their students have
studied "different versions" of the preceding course. To me, planning instruction involves finding out not what students should
know, but what they actually do know, and then proceeding
accordingly. There are unique issues to bear in mind when the preceding courses vary as widely as different sections of our Algebra 2
courses at Holt used to, because in designing diagnostic questions,
or brainstorming possible student conceptions or misconceptions,
it's helpful to have an understanding of the variety of conceptual
frameworks from which students are emerging. But I found that
these differences were actually a resource for me as a teacher, in a
variety of ways. Students could learn from each other. I never considered this to be a drawback. What was your experience? Why do
you think this is a potential problem for other teachers?

SANDY: In my experiences, teachers operating as curriculum technicians
have developed a rationale for the choices they make in their classes
that doesn't have room for your way of thinking. What planning
they do arises out of the Teacher's Edition of a particular textbook

series. It's a given that the previous teacher has "covered" the previous text. Thus if instruction fails to hit its mark or the students seem confused, the teacher has a way to short-circuit the frustration and uncertainty that come from mucking around in students' misconceptions. A teacher acting as a curriculum technician, not that I'm advocating for this, simply tells the students, "You had that last year, and if you don't know it, then you need tutoring." Or else, "Well, I'm sorry your teacher last year didn't cover that chapter. I would have your parents talk to the administration about that." So the teacher him/herself doesn't have to take on the daunting task of designing activities that actually meet the students where they are with the different pieces of knowledge that we all know they will necessarily have regardless of similarities in the previous year's curriculum and instruction. I think this is a reality that needs to be addressed.

KELLY: I guess you are pushing me to think about what the ramifications of greater curricular freedom for teachers would be on a wider scale, with a range of teachers. It makes me think about the task of figuring out what students really know. One reason the task of figuring out what students really know feels so daunting is that some teachers do not feel mathematically prepared to do this work. Most of the interns in my teacher education classes come to realize the weaknesses in the mathematical preparation they've received when it comes to understanding the thrust of a curriculum. But, I think high school mathematics departments as groups and individual mathematics teachers need to challenge themselves to understand and to articulate the mathematical and pedagogical basis for their chosen curriculum and the relationship between this and the tasks and activities they use with their students, whether their choice is to closely follow a published scheme or create their own. And I think there need to be lots of opportunities for experienced teachers to work on this understanding and articulation. There have to be both means for continual learning for the experienced teachers and points of entry for new teachers. Of course, all this takes time, and time costs money and the will to invest in this sort of process for teachers. Maybe this is a copout, but I guess that part of the puzzle is for you administrators to work on!

SANDY: You are right. Now that I am an administrator, I have to provide supports and pay attention to systemic variables that need to be addressed so that the teachers I work with feel confident of their ability to tackle the challenge of responding to their students. While I've been arguing that student-centered teaching doesn't have to involve different sections following different paths or teachers writing all of their own materials, I'm not one who believes that instruction should not start where students are and that teachers cannot develop materials. As a principal, I am outraged by teachers who are not prepared to develop their own materials, when necessary, and who are not excited by chances to learn mathematics. It's just that I don't think we want to propose a model in which teachers prepare all their materials and allow each section to follow its own path in covering the curriculum, even if we sometimes did that. I found what we did challenging to do, and I think this would be quite challenging for most teachers to do for five or six periods a day. How could an individual teacher maintain such a scenario over any prolonged period, with finite time, energy, and resources? We have to be able to define student-centered teaching in a way that does not demand this sort of effort.

KELLY: I think you are right to raise questions about the model we are proposing. In my own development as a teacher, as I moved away from packaged materials, I grew more satisfied with students' engagement and understandings, but the work *was* much more demanding. Even so, it *was* more enjoyable. I was energized not only by what I thought were better results in the classroom, but also by my own learning about the mathematics I was teaching. I became a mathematics teacher in part because I so enjoyed being a mathematics learner. It was fun to be a learner of mathematics again. I think a lot of our colleagues have felt similar feelings. And, I think that Marty's story reflects some of the same sentiment. Maybe a part of the explanation for why we developed so many activities, when you and I were doing design work in our Algebra 1 and Algebra 2 classes, was that the resources for teaching algebra from a functions-based perspective were in their infancy. As we learned more about this perspective, we were excited about the potential of such a fundamental shift. But the notion that an understanding of function could come before the introduction of algebraic symbols wasn't present in any text we could find. And many of the new textbook projects are integrated materials that do not maintain the study of algebra as a separate course. This makes them hard to use in a context like Holt. And curriculum developers and researchers, as well as teachers, are still trying to figure out what a functions-based approach to algebra is. To date, there isn't a packaged curriculum that I know of that does the sort of thing we were trying to do. Even something like *Concepts in algebra* (Fey & Heid, 1999) is quite a bit different from what we ended up doing. I'm not sure how I would feel if I saw a text that really tried to do what we were trying to do. Would I want to adopt it? Over the last decade or more we have considered many possibilities for packaged curriculum, and have borrowed activities or ideas from many of them, but in the end have always decided that they don't exactly meet our needs or fit our understanding of and beliefs about the central ideas in mathematics. And, I, for one, have greatly enjoyed the challenge of developing my own understandings *and* my own materials, and sharing them with my colleagues.

Chapter 5

Interlude A

On-campus preservice assignments

Teachers at Holt High School have two sorts of students: high school students and preservice teachers from Michigan State University. So far, this section has concentrated on the Holt teachers' teaching of high school students. But, in addition to teaching mathematics to high school students, members of the Holt math department also teach future teachers about the teaching of mathematics. They actively participate in field-based teacher education – as mentor teachers for college seniors and interns, as guests in MSU teacher education classes, and sometimes as instructors of record in a teacher education class. See Figure 5.1.

In order to appreciate the work of the Holt teachers as teacher educators, in this section about classroom teaching practice, it's important to describe changes in the organization of MSU's teacher education program and in instructional practice inside the program. In the early 1990s, MSU's teacher education program was a four-year program. Students could enroll in the "standard" program, or choose an alternative, small-cohort experience. At the secondary level, regardless of this choice, there was a one-quarter-long methods course, followed by a one-quarter-long student teaching experience. Marty Schnepp and Kelly Hodges both went through this sort of program and did their student teaching at Holt High School.

When MSU moved from a quarter system to semesters, the university's College of Education recognized this shift as an opportunity to institute far-reaching changes to its teacher education programs and institute a five-year system. A significant motivation for this change was a commitment to field-based teacher education. For future secondary teachers in the standard part of the program, this move represented a huge adjustment. Under the semester system, the program would include a year-long, 11-credit methods course in a preservice teachers' subject during the senior year (including four hours a week in classrooms), followed by a year-long internship. A six-credit (over two semesters) seminar on subject-specific teaching

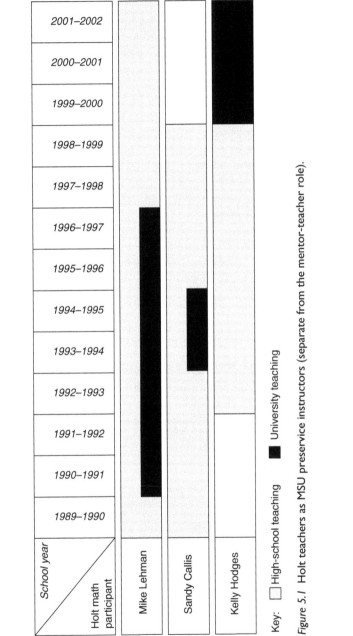

School year / Holt math participant	Mike Lehman	Sandy Callis	Kelly Hodges
2001–2002			
2000–2001			
1999–2000			
1998–1999			
1997–1998			
1996–1997			
1995–1996			
1994–1995			
1993–1994			
1992–1993			
1991–1992			
1990–1991			
1989–1990			

Key: ☐ High-school teaching ■ University teaching

Figure 5.1 Holt teachers as MSU preservice instructors (separate from the mentor-teacher role).

would accompany the internship, along with a similar seminar dealing with professional responsibilities across subject matter (see Figure 5.2).

Under the quarter system, Dan Chazan, a member of the MSU faculty, and Mike Lehman, chairman of the Holt mathematics department, had experimented with a variety of field-based ideas for teacher education, such as holding teacher education courses off-campus at Holt High School during the school day. With its expanded coursework, the five-year program provided exciting opportunities for the design of new courses and more elaborate assignments.

Planning is a central issue in preservice teacher education. Standard "methods" courses give attention to lesson-planning and unit-planning; some courses address planning on a year-long scale. But under the quarter system at MSU, mathematics teacher educators couldn't do this issue justice. With the advent of a semester-based program, that reality changed.

The last two essays, as well as the next two, address planning as an aspect of classroom teaching practice. As suggested by Chapters 3 and 6, ones about Algebra 1 at Holt High School, thoughtful

	Fall	Spring
Freshman/ Sophomore	TE 150 Reflections on Learning *and* TE 250 Human Diversity, Power and Opportunity in Social Institutions *or* CEP 240 Diverse Learners in Multicultural Perspectives	
Junior	TE 301 Learners, Learning and Teaching in Context (fall or spring)	
Senior	**TE 401 Learner Diversity and the Teaching of Subject Matter (5 credits)**	**TE 402 Designing and Studying Practice (6 credits)**
Internship	*TE 501 Internship in Teaching Diverse Learners I* TE 801 Professional Roles and Teaching Practice I **TE 802 Reflection and Inquiry in Teaching Practice I (3 credits)**	*TE 502 Internship in Teaching Diverse Learners II* TE 803 Professional Roles and Teaching Practice II **TE 804 Reflection and Inquiry in Teaching Practice II (3 credits)**

Figure 5.2 Required education classes for preservice secondary teachers in MSU's five-year education program prior to a reorganization in Fall 2002.

Note
Subject-specific courses in bold, internship in italics.

approaches to student motivation are not merely a matter of discipline in the sense of consequences and punishments, but rather of discipline in the sense of subject matter. Year-long planning can help teachers articulate to students what a course is all about. With the five-year program, it seemed important to have future teachers understand that some issues of motivation can be addressed as a whole-course planning issue, rather than as an in-the-moment response to student questions or misbehaviors or by planning "fun" or "real-world" activities. It also seemed important for preservice teachers to grasp that high-level, thematic planning on the part of the teacher can significantly help secondary students to grasp the essential thrust of a course. Finally, it also seemed important that preservice teachers challenge themselves to conceptualize curriculum, to see themselves as mathematical thinkers who can try to answer the question "What is this course all about?" These are all aspects of the work of teachers in the Holt High School mathematics department that are worthy of emulation.

But doing this sort of work with preservice teachers is controversial. Michigan State has been a national center of curriculum development in the middle grades. If this curriculum development work is valuable and important, and if teachers themselves rarely have the time or resources to develop curricula, why should the teacher preparation program involve preservice teachers, with no teaching experience, in designing course-level approaches to secondary teaching? When left to their own devices, isn't there the danger of inexperienced teachers making poor decisions? Furthermore, doesn't such a practice fly in the face of practices in countries that have been more successful in international comparisons of student achievement?

Though, as the responses to the last essay and to the next indicate a spectrum of opinion among us about these matters, there is a shared perception among us that asking questions about course-level organization is a part of the work of teaching that cannot simply be left to others, be they university-level curriculum developers, district or state coordinators, textbook authors, or national advocacy groups, to do. Inevitably, even teachers who do not think of this work as part of their domain, interpret and represent course-level themes to their students. In our educational system, we argue that it is crucial to have teachers do this sort of work explicitly and discuss it with their colleagues. Without more discussion than is now the norm, teachers cannot effectively carry out the visions of others, even when that is their goal. At the same time, we do not imagine a system in which teachers make whatever decisions they want without consultation with others and without taking responsibility for their choices. We imagine working lives for teachers in which debate and discussion of such issues among groups of educators (teachers and others) is the norm.

To show how the university involved preservice teachers in such issues, as a part of communicating expectations about what it means to teach, the following essay describes one key assignment from the 11-credit course during the senior year. Written as a letter from former MSU postdoctoral fellow and teacher educator Bill Rosenthal, now at Hunter College in New York City, it describes the kind of university instruction that preservice teachers receive and the accompanying overlap with teaching practice at Holt. This essay also provides excellent background for understanding the experiences of seniors and interns placed in the Holt High School mathematics department, a subject discussed in Part II of this volume, "Student experience of the curriculum." In their response to Bill's essay, Tom Almeida and Sean Carmody, two newer teachers in the Holt department, share their preservice experiences and their perspectives on the kind of planning they have come to do as teachers in the Holt math department.

Preservice teachers as curriculum makers

(Mr) Bill Rosenthal, Hunter College of the City of New York

This paper was written specially for this edited volume.

> Our group has been working on this BIG-Year Curriculum for about four months now. From the very start, we knew we didn't want our curriculum to be like others – not just because we wanted to be different, but because we wanted to try something new. This was really our first (and probably last) chance to plan a curriculum exactly how we wanted. We didn't have to worry about what the school principal told us we had to do, or what the school district told us to do. This was going to be *our* curriculum, so we figured we should take advantage of this and plan it how *we* wanted it.
> (Michael Fox and Todd Hecker, TE 402 Spring 1995)

To my colleagues at Holt,

I'm very aware that you've been working hard with Dan Chazan and the other MSU faculty members to establish stability and quality in the Holt High School branch office of MSU mathematics teacher education. That I've been in New York doesn't absolve me of my responsibility to concern myself with the continuity of this program. In my version of family values, family members who move away are still responsible for participating in family affairs.

Although we've kept up to some extent, I've never discussed with you an assignment that Jan Simonson and I christened the BIG-Year Curriculum (BYC). A student-created, soup-to-nuts curriculum for a year-long high school math class (even if it doesn't include all the nuts and bolts), the BYC is an idiosyncratic feature of our program that's as much a function of your department as of any other independent variable. A letter in which just one person speaks does not a discussion make. But I'm hoping that what follows initiates a genuine conversation among us about the BYC in particular and the place of student-created curriculum in mathematics teacher education in general.

Our problem, our program

Your department resolved a huge dilemma for MSU secondary mathematics, a problem plaguing every field-based teacher education enterprise. The dilemma is what I call *field-based teacher education's dirty little secret*. This secret is a conundrum that our students know well despite our reluctance as teacher educators to speak about it. Namely, the beliefs and practices that preservice teachers encounter in the field are generally at odds with what the university is teaching them to believe.

The effect your department has had on this secret is simple to state and powerful in its practicality. Namely, you've established a strong compatibility between the beliefs and practices at Holt and what MSU secondary mathematics teaches our students to believe.

The BYC is the curricular jewel in the crown of what Jan and I taught our students to believe. To understand how your department embraced the BYC project and produced the Holt solution requires a bit of background about our year-long "methods" course, particularly its goals for student learning. From the beginning, we felt it essential that each of the two semesters be *all about something* (AAS). That is, we decided that each class would feature a big idea or two as its centerpiece, a central question serving as the anchor and rudder, and/or some big picture that students should see and hear and touch from the beginning and eventually paint for themselves. Dan was influential in our thinking. His close reading of my unpublished calculus text (Rosenthal, 1989) spurred me to realize, five years after the fact, that the course for which I wrote it was AAS – that there was a mathematical story-line of which I had been unaware while writing and teaching from the book. Dan's insight inspired us to construct, with forethought, courses with a unifying story-line.

The class we designed was foundational and incorporated a good deal of mathematics. The foundations of mathematics education became the *something* of our first semester. Specifically, 401 would be all about the psychological, sociological, cultural, political, and philosophical bases of mathematics education.

402: Curriculum, curriculum, curriculum

It takes but one word to describe the *something* that TE 402 spring "methods" course would be all about: curriculum. Teachers *are* curriculum creators. Jean Clandinin and Michael Connelly (1988, 1992) have written much concerning the optimal relationship between classroom teachers and their curricula, as has Miriam Ben-Peretz. Ben-Peretz's theorem that "the creative reading of curriculum materials is conceived as freeing teachers from the tyranny of the text" (1990, p. xvi) embodies the skeptical spirit toward textbooks that Jan and I tried to impart.

Jan and I share an anti-authoritarian bent that predisposes us to distrust any mathematical master narrative. We also hatched the hypothesis that mass-produced curriculum materials are themselves a hindrance to mathematical learning. Finally, it's more than plausible that Jan's encounter with the work of the Holt math department as a participant in your department's PDS effort contributed to our story-line: teachers are curriculum creators.

Here are two quotes we frequently shared with our students. The first comes from a prominent curriculum theorist, the second from a Milwaukee public-school teacher who writes for the progressive educational journal *Rethinking Schools*.

> Unfortunately, teachers are frequently considered mere recipients of already packaged curriculum; they are viewed as implementers of curriculum, not creators. I want to acknowledge the key role teachers have in developing curriculum.
>
> (William Schubert)

> [A]s a beginning teacher I needed to see myself as a *producer*, not a consumer, of curriculum.
>
> (Bill Bigelow)

From the beginning, Jan and I made it clear to students that the meaning of curriculum was not to be reduced to a listing of topics, set of objectives, sequence of lessons and/or units, or some combination thereof. We used the following quotes with our classes to convey a sense of the possibilities inherent in the concept. The first two authors are university academics. The second two were our students. The final quote comes from a member of your own department's faculty.

> Curriculum consists of ways of engaging students in giving thought to those matters which we think important.
>
> (Eleanor Duckworth)

Curriculum is what students have the opportunity to learn.

(Gail McCutcheon)

I think of curriculum as not only what you cover, but how you cover it.... Curriculum could be thought of as the material, its presentation, and the students it is reaching.

(Eric Anderson)

Curriculum denotes what is actually being presented, but the connotation includes everything involved with the classroom ... perhaps even HOW the material is being taught.

(Kevin Tobe)

The curriculum is everything that students come in contact with from the time they enter the classroom door, even the door itself.

(Sandra Callis)

The official title of the 402 course is "Crafting teaching practice." Our view is that the crafting of teaching practice, that is, instructional planning, is identical to the making of curriculum. This equality combines a quasi-empirical theorem with a value-laden axiom. The theorem is that teachers are the *de facto* creators of the enacted curricula that students come into contact with, no matter who develops the materials we use and regardless of what school boards, superintendents, "standardistas" (Ohanian, 1999), corporate leaders, publishers, politicians, principals, and parents want our curricula to be. Teachers should exercise as much control over their own curricula as they can. But to become true curriculum creators, our preservice students would have to learn by doing, a role that finds little place in the current culture of professional teaching.

Is that all there is?

The 402 seminar of course covered more than the concept that teachers are curriculum creators. The following ideals bring the total number of story-lines for the course to four:

- Teachers should teach for relational understanding.
- Teachers should be relentless questioners, particularly of their own mathematical understandings.
- Teachers should be philosophers of mathematics.

The BYC services all these story-lines quite well. Developing a full curriculum with their peers and in accordance with our guidelines and requirements compelled our preservice students to ask mathematical questions focused on both *why* and *how*. This forced questioning brings our students into the realm of what Richard Skemp (1978) calls a *relational understanding* of mathematics – meaning "knowing both what to do and why." The BYC obliges our students to interrogate mathematics as both they themselves and others construct it. As for philosophy, we did our best to integrate issues concerning the nature, origin, and culture of mathematical knowledge.

Building a BYC

The BYC is built upon a foundation of knowing how to go about the work of creating a curriculum. Unlike the standard model of instructional planning – first designing units and planning lessons – we required our preservice students to be analysts, rather than synthesists. They start large by formulating a full and firm design of an entire year of mathematics, with a story-line, central question or two, overarching theme, and meticulously argued rationale for the value and importance of their curricular intentions. Then, and only then, are born the units, lessons, assessments, activities, and other components our preservice students see fit to include.

Schematically, the making of curriculum, i.e., planning for teaching, takes the path shown in Figure 5.3.

The making of units to be built up out of lessons or activities is a staple of preservice teacher education. Typically, however, the units are either patterned on an extant mass-produced curriculum program or are disconnected from any larger curricular context. By making our students make curriculum out of the clay of their own knowledge and experiences, we were challenging normative practice at its roots. This challenge is grounded in our belief that a teacher's primary curricular relationship is with an entire year of study rather than with lessons or units. With guidance and encouragement, students envision and create the essence of a curriculum. This curricular genome contains the program for what the curriculum is all about. Only when these genetic

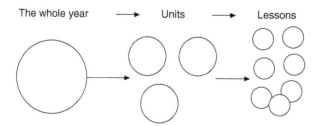

Figure 5.3 One view of planning.

instructions are sufficiently in order do they begin to differentiate their design into the curricular elements of units and lessons.

In the beginning, we communicated no more than an infinitesimal sense that the BYC needed to be AAS. In our spring 1995 syllabus, we wrote, "We are leaving to *you* the crafting of a general approach to *your* BIG-Year Curriculum. You'll be wise to consult with us as early and as frequently as you can about both your overall outlook and any and all other aspects of your work." There is a jarring inconsistency here between what Jennifer Gore (1993) calls "the pedagogy of the argument and the pedagogy being argued for" or, less technically, what we did in our teaching and what we taught our preservice students to do in theirs. The argument in our own pedagogy was that a curriculum be AAS, and we took every possible step to help students understand that "Crafting teaching practice" was all about their being curriculum creators. As for the pedagogy we wanted them to invent – how *they* would go about creating curriculum – we punted. An extremist form of teacher autonomy ("leaving to *you* the crafting of a general approach") trumped the commonsensical imperative for us to actively *teach* our students how to fashion their mathematical BIG-Year Curriculum as AAS.

The course has since evolved significantly. In addition to directing students to imbue their BYCs with a purpose, rationale, and "overarching theme," the philosophy issue is now raised by the question "What is the nature of mathematical knowledge in your BYC?" Prospective teachers must also address the psychology of mathematical learning, that is, "What does it mean for a student to understand mathematics in your BYC?" Students must also describe the history of the mathematics addressed in their BYC; how each unit serves the BYC's grand purpose; and their own understandings of the BYC's mathematical content. Jan and I had come quite a distance from leaving students to their own devices and praying that their incipient curricular-crafting knowledge would magically lead them to BYCs that were AAS. These evolutions serve to advance the process of making AAS BIG-Year Curricula happen. Better yet, the evolved BYC requirements promote not only "teachers as curriculum creators" but all the story-lines of our 402 course. These improvements illustrate how, by dictating structure, ironically, teachers can emancipate thinking and inventiveness.

"What's your rationale? What's your evidence?"

Why do we wager so much of the secondary mathematics subprogram on the BYC? What credible indicators are there that a BYC is the right course of study for an aspiring secondary mathematics educator? We have no empirical evidence of the BYC's effectiveness. Our commitment to the BYC is based on our conviction that having our preservice students conceive of themselves as creators of their own curricula is fundamental. But why? Why do we place such emphasis on teachers being curriculum creators? This question merits extensive attention.

First, let's look at the arguments against teacher involvement in curriculum development. They include the following.

1   The structure of a teacher's workday doesn't afford the time needed to create curriculum;
2   Specialists in the field of curriculum development can do a better job than classroom teachers, whose subject-matter knowledge is perhaps less thorough and whose attention is badly divided;
3   Quality curriculum materials should and can promote continued mathematical learning on the part of the teachers using them (Cohen & Ball, 1999);
4   The epidemic of student transience in low-income and minority schools compels equity-minded educators to standardize what students have the opportunity to learn.

All of these reasons can be defended as more or less legitimate, particularly the last. Our basic objection to the position that teachers shouldn't be involved in curriculum development is that mass-market curricula habitually fail to convey a sense that their mathematics is AAS. When a teacher is the author of her own curricular stories, she is continually poised to work intelligently and honestly with her students to construct answers overflowing with meaning. Teacher as curriculum creator, particularly as BYC author, enriches the mathematics in a way that teacher as curriculum implementer cannot.

Developing a BYC is not merely a matter of one's own mathematical understandings maturing and evolving. We maintain that teaching and learning are improved when teachers use their own conceptualizations as the foundation of their practice. The BYC gives students an opportunity to escape the mathematically sealed world of a textbook or series. Even the best mass-market materials portray a single mathematical point of view. There is little or no contrast, and contrast sparks creativity. Integral to any authentic curriculum creation is the gathering and critical analysis of many different mathematical sources on a given topic. What is the story-line in that algebra textbook? How does A's definition of a function compare with B's? How does the inclusion of the mean absolute deviation differentiate a statistics story from a story without that concept?

Despite some hopeful signs that commercial curriculum materials can successfully foster teacher learning (e.g., Van Zoest & Bohl, 2000), we do not hear this kind of mathematical inquiry taking place in the context of studying a lone set of materials. Why should it? What would motivate a secondary mathematics educator to go beyond mathematics that's all laid out? The solo mathematical standpoint appears to severely limit teacher teaching as well.

> The way we began was by looking at the X book. It seems to be considered a very good book by most teachers and stresses comprehension as well as skills. . . . In our limited experience, most teachers have been teaching straight from the book, moving through the units and chapters in consecutive order. Most of the teachers we've seen seem to think that since the book is written from a progressive education point of view (that is, with constructivist and critical methods in mind), they do not need to add to what the book says. Because of this, the teachers basically let the book teach the students. This is precisely what we wanted to avoid in our group.
>
> (Michael Fox and Todd Hecker, BYC, spring 1995)

Thinking of oneself as a curriculum creator underscores a teacher's sense of professionalism. If this is *my* curriculum, then *I* am responsible for the ideas my students come in contact with, for what they have the chance to learn, for everything involved with the classroom. When teachers are told it is not their business to make curriculum, it forces a limited vista of what curriculum can be, and hence of what teaching can be. I doubt that the curriculum-development industry intends teacher distance from curriculum development to mean teachers should have nothing to do with the curricula they teach. Yet the latter is what many teachers appear to hear. Teaching from one's own curriculum generates a sense of pride and ownership that cannot possibly injure self or students.

That's *our* rationale. But for years I've accepted as given curricular-creating practices at Holt High School as an instantiation in an actual, real-life secondary mathematics setting of the ideals I espouse. Let me ask. What's *your* rationale? What's *your* evidence?

The intersection of Holt mathematics and MSU secondary mathematics

To repeat the secret I mentioned earlier, the beliefs and practices that preservice teachers encounter in the field are generally at odds with what the universities are teaching them to believe. The solution that arises from the mutual collaboration between Holt and MSU suggests that compatibility can exist between the source of theory and the site of practice, so that beliefs and practice correspond with and amplify one another.

Our preservice students want an overlap between fieldwork and the university component of the course. The schism between theory and practice has plagued teacher education. Strengthening the field component is meant to repair the theory/practice divide. In the abstract, this seems obvious. In practice, conflict arises often sparked by mixed messages.

We hoped that the BYC would lay down a large overlap between the university and fieldwork. Initially, we failed. In the beginning, we attempted to forge a link by requiring our students to teach in the field from one of the units developed as part of their BYC, requiring our students to find a way to fit their lessons into the ongoing work of their placements. Fiasco is too weak a word for the results of this anti-brilliant idea, which we soon dropped, severing the BYC from fieldwork entirely and leaving us with an especially malodorous version of the secret.

Enter your department. By the time we created the BYC, you already were practicing enough of what we were preaching – not solely curriculum creation, but all four of the story-lines – to grace our theory with a coat of credibility. You were an *existence proof* that our four story-lines (a BYC, a relational understanding of mathematics, a self-questioning teaching culture, and the pedagogical importance of the philosophy of mathematics) can be realized. Let me give some examples of convergences between your curricular work and our BYC.

1   6 April 1995 was the day on which Holt secondary mathematics and MSU secondary mathematics were forever united in teacher-educational matrimony. It was on this day that Sandy Callis visited MSU to tell the story of Holt Algebra 1. From Sandy, our students heard that mathematics can have a story-line written by the teachers who teach it. Immediately after class ended, a student whose fieldwork was not at Holt ran up to me, placed her hands on my shoulders, fixed my eyes with her gaze, and beseeched, "Why didn't you do this [have Sandy visit] right away?!" Suddenly Jan and I sensed that this BYC business was not self-evident to students, and that we could, to say less than the least, benefit from some co-teaching with our friends at Holt High School.

2   Our two programs are compatible, in that each is accordant with the NCTM *Standards* while going above and beyond them. For instance, while the *Standards* make much of students debating *their* differing constructions and conjectures, they contain no hint of the importance of what our colleague (and MSU graduate student) Whitney Johnson deliciously calls "arguing with the mathematicians." In contrast, both Holt and MSU place great emphasis on developing a student's ability to challenge the assumptions and results of authorities.

3   In line with the essay before this one, here are three quotes from
    your colleague Marty Schnepp that appear in Jan's dissertation
    (Gormas, 1998). The last two stand alone. Jan prefaces the first
    with: "Based on the format of the class, (Marty) felt free to create
    curriculum based on his understanding of the concepts being
    studied and his students' sense making. As he tells it, a story of lib-
    eration emerged."

> It was amazing. I was actually in control of what was going on,
> rather than having this textbook guideline that I was chasing
> behind, trying to sort through it all.
>
> (p. 70)

> As I struggled with these classroom experiences, continued to
> collaborate with my peers, and read educational literature, I
> came to the conclusion that it was my mathematical philosophy
> that needed questioning, not my intended approach to teaching
> and learning.
>
> (p. 60)

> Looking back now, there was some conflict between figuring
> out what I was supposed to be doing with the kids in the class-
> room and the content of what I was supposed to be doing –
> pedagogy versus curriculum. I don't think I would make that
> distinction any more.
>
> (p. 76)

4   As long as we're doing quotes, here are three from seniors who did
    fieldwork at Holt.

> It seems that Sandy Callis has really looked into the concepts
> behind the math and then has really gone about trying to make
> her teaching style reflect her ideas of the meaning of math.
>
> (Benson Mitchell)

> It was a huge challenge for me to examine thoroughly the
> content and not just have an equation to plug into. It was also,
> as Eleanor Duckworth explains in her essay "Twenty-four,
> Forty-two and I Love You," an exhilarating experience to find
> that my own ideas could lead me somewhere meaningful.
>
> (Kristin Povlitz)

> At Holt High School, Kelly, my mentor teacher, told me that
> they don't have this list of things they need to teach. A group of

teachers talk about where they are now and where they want to go. They ask questions like, "Is this the direction the class wants to go? Are they interested in this now? Would it make sense to bring this up here?"

(Amy Long)

5 You create curriculum together; our students do their BYCs in groups. Credit for this connection goes entirely to you. The significance of this particular kinship stretches well beyond the obvious. Deborah W. Meier (1999–2000), one of our nation's leading educators, has recently suggested that educational standards should be set by individual schools. She believes great educational value is added when children and adolescents actively observe adults whom they trust work out vital issues, often with student participation. This type of public, local, negotiated control is one of the processes we try to live in the secondary mathematics subprogram. It is what you do in your lunchroom conversations, your open invitations to visit one another's classrooms and critique one another's teaching, and myriad additional features of life in the Holt mathematics community. *You live as we would like our students to live.*

6 Another commonality that binds our programs is *listening* as a method of teaching. What Jan says about Marty's feeling free "to create curriculum based on his understanding of the concepts being studied *and his students' sense making*" (emphasis added) permeates all that you do and all that we do. And yet this isn't evident in the BYC. We haven't required that the ideas of the high school students being taught be part of the BYC (tempered, of course by the mathematical understanding and knowledge of the BYC authors). Fortunately, some of our students have overcome our short-sightedness. Of their own initiative, they have made the acts of listening to and building upon their students' thinking forefront in their BYCs. An excellent example comes from the Before the Era of Algebraic Manipulation (BEAM) curriculum created in 1997 by Josh Minsley and Loc Tu, whom you will remember from their tenures as seniors and interns at Holt. Josh and Loc's improvement on Transition Mathematics starts with a unit designed "to assess where the students are at mathematically. What kind of misconceptions do they have in mathematics? Why do they think in that particular way? ... The most important reason that we are doing this is to learn more about what is going on in the students' heads."

We cannot, however, rely on our students' ingenuity to take care of what should be a structural, programmatic imperative to incorporate their students' thinking into curriculum. Moreover, there is an enormous difference between establishing the mathematics to be taught without consideration of high school students' conceptions and employing deliberate, systematic inquiry into mathematical thinking as a tool for selecting the mathematical content of a BIG-Year Curriculum.

The end, for now

I've recently accepted a new position that has returned me to secondary mathematics teacher education after a two-year hiatus. The conditions could hardly be more different from those of our MSU subprogram. The starkest distinction is that instead of our 11-credit, full-year marathon during the senior year, I'll be teaching a one-semester, three-credit course structurally congruent to the one that existed in MSU's old quarter system program. Faced with these less than optimal circumstances, how can I adapt the BYC? Some of you have suggested I install a modified version of the entire BYC project; others argue for developing mathematical story-lines only. Now that I've given you my thoughts about the BYC, I need yours. I am looking forward to your reply.

In solidarity,
(Mr) Bill

Should preservice teachers be encouraged to create curriculum?

Tom Almeida and Sean Carmody, Holt Schools

TOM ALMEIDA: When you were an intern, you mentioned to me that, as a senior, you had to create a full-year curriculum for a PreCalculus class. As someone who got their preservice training at another university, my first thoughts were "Holy cats! That's overkill. That's a lot of work!" But during my years at Holt, I've found out that molding your class and curriculum is a necessity. I especially appreciated the section in Bill's essay about how the curriculum that a teacher is teaching should parallel his or her own mathematical understandings.

SEAN CARMODY: When my group members and I received our assignment for our BIG-Year Curriculum (BYC) we had little idea how far we would go into the process. We began by gathering all the textbooks that we had seen or used dealing with PreCalculus and just went through the units and looked at big ideas. We also made notes about what we remembered were the big ideas and topics in our PreCalculus classes when we were high school students. I was unsure how we were going to develop a curriculum on our own that would differ significantly from the classes that we had had. In our 402 course, we had spoken a great deal about teachers creating curriculum, but I was still unsure what that meant. I was also unsure if we, as teachers, should even be creating curriculum and, if so, why. Doing the BYC taught me that it's very difficult and time-consuming to create a curriculum. There are so many questions you have to ask yourself and then answer. It was a great experience to bring the three different mathematical schemas of the members of our BYC group into this process and really identify what I truly felt mathematics was. The process was amazingly collaborative. Also, I realized how much mathematics I *didn't* know. It was perhaps the first time that I took ownership of the mathematics and developed *my* understanding of it.

TOM: The essay reflects what you are saying when it talks about how "thinking of oneself as a curriculum creator underscores a teacher's sense of professionalism." That paragraph sums up my strongest feelings about the BYC. As a teacher, I sometimes feel as though others see me as a glorified babysitter with a long vacation. When I started working on my own classes and working with other teachers on curriculum, I felt as though I was really in on something. My students could feel it too. My feeling of ownership makes my excitement contagious, and my students can key into that. Having a story-line that is moderately flexible has made me really think about what my students know, what I know, what my students need to know, and what I need to know. It's a living class. I really am forced to see it through their eyes and adapt the lessons and units for each class, sometimes for each individual.

SEAN: You're right about the sense of excitement. As we developed the PreCalculus BYC, we kept talking about how great it would be to take our class. By the time we had finished our course we had, in some sense, taken the course. We had identified our mathematical schemas and built upon them. We had done our mathematical laundry. After the BYC, I was very proud of what we had developed. I could stand behind it without any doubts. I knew why the third chapter was third and why we asked that question. I had ownership of the mathematics that I wanted my students to own. Bill's essay talks about experiencing mathematics in a different way in order to teach it differently. I had finally experienced math in the way that I wanted my students to.

TOM: Beyond the BYC itself, I find it interesting that there is a Holt impact on teacher education and that there is a much smaller difference between theory and practice for interns placed at Holt than for those in placed in other schools. I'm wondering why that is. Is it the people involved? Or does it have to do with ideas? Where I went to school, my fellow students were very focused on teaching exactly the way that they were taught in high school, while our instructors were interested in mathematics education reform. My classmates were ridiculously against the faculty, because we received so little "practical" information about teaching in our university coursework. Somehow what was being done didn't help us see the point of the change our instructors were suggesting. After reading this piece, with my 20/20 hindsight, I can see that some of our problems might have been solved with some more field experience. But I can't help but think there is more to it than just time in schools.

SEAN: Yes. I am aware that in reality some of my BYC group members were unable to implement all of the ideas we had designed in our BYC during their internship and since then in their teaching. I was very lucky to be placed at Holt as an intern and then to get hired in. It made a huge difference to begin to teach where the ideas of my teacher preparation program matched up so well with the reality of the school. But, it was not so for some others.

Chapter 6

Instructional tasks

In the last essay, Bill Rosenthal focused on having preservice teachers prepare for becoming teachers by writing a BYC, by figuring out what a year-long secondary mathematics course could be all about. The next essay returns to the context of Algebra 1 and examines how intentions at the level of the course can be concretized in tasks for students and thus address issues of student motivation in a different sort of way than fun activities or real-world problems.

As the vignettes from Algebra 1 classrooms in the second essay remind us, high school mathematics teachers work in a compulsory setting. In many situations, they teach students who are disengaged from schooling. Yet most rationales for studying mathematics are future-oriented. They are connected to future schooling and the rewards that come with it.

As mathematics teachers at Holt High School work on what their courses are all about, they have attempted to explore rationales for study that are not future-oriented. In an effort to help students see mathematics in the world around them, teachers have tried various strategies to develop present-oriented approaches. They have challenged high school students to explore quantitative rules of thumb in local workplaces, have started geometry courses by asking students to write a description of a birdhouse for a family member to sketch, and have asked Calculus students to use information on pedaling cadence from an exercise bike to compute how many times their teacher's legs must have rotated. The teachers purposely design these experiences as windows onto an understanding of what a course is all about. No matter how different these experiences, they share two goals: emphasizing the presence of mathematics in students' present and sparking student motivation.

Present-oriented approaches suggest to the students that mathematics is not as esoteric as it might first appear. Instead of seeking extraneous relevance by simply adapting problem situations by inserting local names and places, a present-oriented approach to mathematics helps students make connections between their lives and the mathematics they are learning in school. With these activities, the teachers also signal their willingness to address students' skepticism about the value of mathematics classes. In this way, they treat their students as thinkers who might have good reason for finding the offerings of a high school mathematics class unappealing, and at the same time they take such views seriously by attempting a response.

For an examination of these issues, the next essay continues to consider Algebra 1. Dan Chazan and Sandy Callis describe an activity they created for their students. Kellie Huhn and Craig Huhn discuss their use of this activity and a related activity in a geometry course that is reminiscent of some aspects of a well-known description of a reform of Euclidean geometry in the 1930s (Fawcett, 1938). Together, these texts elaborate what it means at Holt High School for a high school mathematics course to be, in Bill Rosenthal's words, All About Something (AAS).

Finding mathematics in the world around us

Daniel Chazan and Sandra Callis, Michigan State University, Holt High School

This paper was written in early 1997. It appeared in Mathematical Sciences Education Board (1998) *High school mathematics at work: Essays and examples from workplace contexts to strengthen the mathematical education of all students*. Washington, DC: National Research Council.

Teaching mathematics in the lower tracks of many high schools is a difficult assignment that many teachers avoid once they have seniority. There is an inherent tension between the high school teacher as subject-matter specialist and the disengagement from school and skepticism about academic knowledge common among lower-track students.

On the one hand, as a high school mathematics teacher one might, like Bertrand Russell, be drawn to mathematics in its pure form:

> Mathematics, rightly viewed, possesses not only truth, but supreme beauty.... Remote from human passions, remote even from the pitiful facts of nature, the generations have gradually created an ordered cosmos, where pure thought can dwell as in its natural home, and where one, at least, of our nobler impulses can escape from the dreary exile of the natural world.
>
> (Russell, 1910, p. 73)

One's students, on the other hand, may very well not have the luxury of appreciating this beauty, given their circumstances. Instead, like Jamaica Kincaid, they may be asking:

> What makes the world turn against me and all who look like me? I won nothing, I survey nothing, when I ask this question, the luxury of an answer that will fill volumes does not stretch out before me. When I ask this question, my voice is filled with despair.
>
> (Kincaid, 1996, p. 132)

Our teaching and the issues it raised for us

For two years, 1991–1992 and 1992–1993, we taught a lower-track Algebra 1 class for 10th-through 12th-grade students (for other details, see Chazan, 1996, 2000). Most of the students had failed mathematics before and many needed to pass Algebra 1 to graduate. For them, mathematics had become a charged subject; it carried a heavy burden of negative experiences. Many of our students were convinced that neither they nor their peers could be successful in mathematics.

Few of our students did well in other academic subjects and few were headed on to two- or four-year colleges. But the students differed in their affiliation to social groups within the high school. Some, called "preppies" or "jocks" by others, were active participants in school activities. Others, the so-called "smokers" or "stoners," rebelled to different degrees against school in particular and society more broadly. There were strong tensions between members of these groups (for more detail on high school students' social groups, see Eckert, 1989).

Teaching in this kind of lower-track setting gives a particular spin to the typical questions of curriculum and motivation common to most algebra classes. In our teaching, we explored many questions:

- What is it that we really want high school students, especially those who are not college-bound, to study in "algebra" and why?
- What role do algebra's manipulative skills play in a world with graphing calculators and computers? How do the manipulative skills taught in the traditional curriculum give students a new perspective on, and insight into, our world?
- Our teaching efforts depend on student investment in learning. On what grounds can we appeal, implicitly or explicitly, for their energies and effort? These students present diverse interests and talents. They are asked to learn in a tracked, compulsory setting. Many are headed to work, not college. How do we help them find value in a shared exploration of algebra?

An approach to school algebra

As a result of thinking about these questions, we wanted to avoid exhorting students to appreciate the beauty or utility of algebra. Our students were frankly skeptical of arguments based in utility. They saw few people in their community using algebra. We, too, had lost faith in the power of extrinsic rewards and punishments, like failing grades, for motivating students to study algebra. Many of our students were skeptical of the power of the high school diploma to fundamentally alter their life circumstances. They were unconcerned about failing grades. We needed different incentives. We wanted to motivate our students to care about math by helping them recognize the mathematical objects we were studying at school in the world around them. We hoped that this would help them learn to value the perspective that this mathematics might provide about their world.

To achieve this aim, we found it useful to focus on relationships between quantities as central objects of study in school algebra, what is sometimes called a functions-based approach. Here, the fundamental mathematical objects of study in school algebra are functions that can be represented by inputs and outputs (listed in tables or sketched or plotted on graphs) and calculation procedures that can be written with algebraic symbols. (Our ideas were greatly influenced by Schwartz & Yerushalmy, 1992; Yerushalmy & Schwartz, 1993.) Inspired, in part, by the following quote from Auguste Comte, we viewed these functions as mathematical representations of theories that people have developed for explaining relationships between quantities.

> In the light of previous experience, we must acknowledge the impossibility of determining, by direct measurement, most of the heights and distances we should like to know. It is this general fact which makes the science of mathematics necessary. For in renouncing the hope, in almost every case, of measuring great heights or distances directly, the human mind has had to attempt to determine them indirectly, and it is thus that philosophers were led to invent mathematics.
>
> (Quoted in Serres, 1982, p. 85)

The sponsor project

With our focus on relationships between quantities, we designed a year-long project for our students. The project asked pairs of students to find within the workplace of their community sponsor the mathematical objects we were studying in school. Students would visit their sponsor's workplace four times during the year – three after-school visits and one day-long excused absence from school. In these visits, the students would come to know the workplace and learn about their sponsor's work. Based on these visits, we would ask students to write a report describing the sponsor's workplace and answering the following questions (see Table 6.1) about the nature of the mathematical activity embedded in the workplace.

Using these questions

In order to determine how the interviews could be structured and to provide students with a model, before school started we chose to interview Sandy's husband, John Bethell. John was a coatings inspector for an engineering firm. When asked about his job, he responded, "I argue for a living." John inspects the work of contractors who paint water-towers. Since most municipalities contract with the lowest bidder when a water-tower needs to be painted, they will often hire an engineering firm to make sure the contractor works according to specification. Since the contractor has made a low bid, there are strong financial incentives for the contractor to compromise on quality in order to make a profit.

In his work John performs different kinds of inspections. For example, he has a magnetic instrument to check the thickness of the paint once it has been applied to the tower. When it gives a "thin" reading, contractors often question the technology. To argue for the reading, John uses the surface area of the tank, the number of paint cans used, the volume of paint in the can, and the percentage of this volume that evaporates to calculate the average thickness of the dry coating. Other examples from his workplace involve using different kinds of tables and measuring instruments.

Some examples of student work

When school started, students began working on their projects. Though many of the sponsors initially indicated that there were no mathematical dimensions to their work, students were often able to show sponsors places where the mathematics we were studying could be found. For example, Jackie worked with a crop and soil scientist. She was intrigued by the use of weight to count seeds. First, her sponsor would weigh a test batch of 100 seeds to generate a benchmark weight. Then, a large bin with many thousands of seeds was weighed and a computation made to indicate the number of seeds contained within that weight. No seeds were counted beyond those in the test batch.

Rebecca worked with a carpeting contractor who, to estimate costs, read the dimensions of rectangular rooms off an architect's blueprint, multiplied to find the area of the room in square feet (doing conversions where necessary), then multiplied by a cost per square foot, which

Table 6.1 Questions for the sponsor project

Measured/counted vs. computed quantities	Computing quantities	Representing quantities and relationships between quantities	Comparisons
• What quantities are measured or counted by the people you interview? • What kinds of tools are used to measure or count? • Why is it important to measure or count these quantities? • What quantities do they compute or calculate? • What kinds of tools are used to do the computing? • Why is it important to compute these quantities?	• When a quantity is computed, what information is needed and then what computations are done to get the desired result? • Are there ever different ways to compute the same thing?	• How are quantities kept track of or represented in this line of work? • Collect examples of graphs, charts, or tables that are used in the business. How is information presented to clients or to others who work in the business?	• What kinds of comparisons are made with computed quantities? • Why are these comparisons important to do? • What set of actions are set into motion as a result of this interpretation of the computations?

Table 6.2 Rebecca's table

Inputs		Outputs	
Length	Width	Area of the room	Cost for carpeting room
10	35		
20	25		
15	30		
X	Y		

depended on the type of carpet. This calculation estimated the cost of the carpet. The purpose was to prepare for the architect a bid that was as low as possible without making the job unprofitable. Rebecca used the chart shown in Table 6.2 to explain this procedure to the class.

Joe and Mick, also working in construction, found out that in laying pipes there is a "one-by-one" rule of thumb. When digging a trench for the placement of the pipe, the nonparallel sides of the trapezoidal cross-section must have a slope of one foot down for every one foot across. This ratio guarantees that the dirt in the hole will not slide down on itself. Thus, if the trapezoid must have a certain width at the bottom of the hole in order to fit the pipe, then the hole at ground level must be this width plus twice the depth of the hole. Knowing in advance how wide the hole must be avoids lengthy and costly trial and error. See Figure 6.1.

Other students found that functions were often embedded in cultural artifacts from the workplace. For example, a student who visited a doctor's office brought in the instrument shown in Figure 6.2, which predicts not only due dates for pregnant women, but average fetal weight and length as well.

Conclusion

The complexities of organizing this sort of project should not be minimized. They include arranging sponsors, securing parental permission, and addressing administrative and parental concerns about the requirement of off-campus, after-school work. But we remain encouraged by the potential of such projects to help students see mathematics in the world around them. Connecting central mathematical objects to student

Figure 6.1 The rule of thumb.

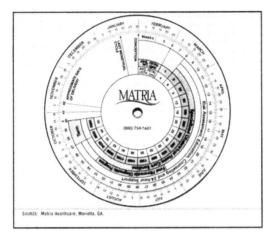

Figure 6.2 Predicting due dates (source: Matria Healthcare, Marietta, GA).

experience seems an important alternative to the use of application-based materials written by authors whose lives and social worlds may be quite different from those of students in lower-track classes.

Getting past lame justifications!

Kellie Huhn and Craig Huhn, Holt High School

KELLIE HUHN: You know, when I read the quotes from Russell and Kincaid, I realized how my thinking of mathematics education has changed from when I was an undergraduate to where I am now as an experienced teacher. At first, my goal was to create a course where students would see the beauty of mathematics, and students would learn the complexities and value of symbolism through the same traditional means that I had. Interacting with my colleagues changed these ideas. I saw that I couldn't really find applications of higher-level mathematics in my personal life. It became obvious to me that I hadn't established useful connections between my mathematics classes and the outside world. This was very unsettling, so making connections became very important to me. I couldn't justify my degree in mathematics if I couldn't apply what I knew. It only makes sense to teach mathematics – all levels of mathematics – to students with the intention that they will see throughout the year connections to their lives and to possible future careers.

CRAIG HUHN: Exactly. It makes little sense to expect students to learn if teachers justify that learning in a half-hearted, dismissive way. The traditional reasons are lame at best: "You'll need it for next year." "You need it to get into a good college." "It's going to be on the test." And so on.

KELLIE: Working at Holt has made it clear to me that my job as a teacher is to create a course that's about something worth studying, something that wouldn't need those "lame justifications," as you put it. I've taught nine different sections of Algebra 1, and each time I've used the interview part of Sandy and Dan's sponsor project. I've kept all the interviews the students have done, and I'm realizing the value now in doing so. These interviews provide material for the Algebra 2 classes that I teach. Many of the applications that students brought to class weren't linear. Our Algebra 2 course is based on the study of non-linear functions. I think these examples may have more value for students than those "written by authors whose lives and social worlds may be quite different from those of students in lower-track classes." The sisters, brothers, cousins, and neighbors of my upcoming Algebra 2 students wrote these interview summaries.

CRAIG: So, Algebra 2 can also benefit with the connections that students are seeing in the interview process. It seems like there are just as many opportunities where students could come back with ideas from geometry.

KELLIE: Well, when I first taught geometry, Sandy and I met to talk about the essential questions and the content the course should have. Sandy suggested that we use an assignment where we had students describe an object without naming it. If our geometry course was to focus on geometry as the study of shape and space, it seemed to make sense to learn about how students describe shapes. After looking at two-dimensional pictures in magazines and books, we concluded a three-dimensional object would be better. We decided to use a birdhouse that her father had made for her. Being a man-made shape, we could focus on the study of Euclidean geometry and the types of shapes studied in a high school course: cylinders, pentagons, rectangles, prisms, squares, circles, etc. In class, the students were to write a description of the birdhouse only discussing shape and size, not function. Their homework was to find someone who had not seen the birdhouse and have that person draw the birdhouse based only on the student's description. The second day of class was focused on the words students used and the difficulties that they faced when they were describing the birdhouse. As a class, we discussed the differences in interpretations between what they saw and what a friend or family member drew.

CRAIG: It sounds like a great way to start the year and to introduce students to the type of class that you are going to have. The birdhouse assignment feels different to me, though, than the one described in the essay because Dan and Sandy's sponsor project was a full-year project.

KELLIE: True, but the geometric ideas of shape, dimension, congruence, similarity, scale, measurement, proportion, and angles were at the forefront of the conversation and set the tone for the rest of the year. I remember Sandy choosing to push students on their definitions of the terms they used. She would ask them what they meant by the word circle. As students struggled to explain what they meant, they would use other words that Sandy would ask them to define. Through this questioning of terms, students developed a sense of the need for clear definitions, consensus on the meaning of terms, and the notion that some terms would remain undefined. It was apparent to students that the main difference between the drawing and the birdhouse was that one was two-dimensional and the other was three-dimensional. Through a conversation defining two-dimensions and three-dimensions, students were able to make sense of what mathematicians are thinking of when they talk about one-dimensional and zero-dimensional objects and problems of representation of mathematical ideas.

CRAIG: Earlier you reiterated what Dan and Sandy said about the interviews being an important alternative to using materials written by authors who are far removed from the students' lives. One of the things that struck me about this essay was the articulate manner in which it described the social issues in Holt Algebra 1 classes. My experience teaching in the lower-track classes has been that social issues drive every aspect of the learning environment. Conflict between students and factions of students influences their ability to work in groups and hold each other responsible. A different kind of life at home – and the life-decisions they make as a result – makes them feel even further alienated from the school environment and the importance of getting good grades. The way they view conflict resolution in their lives spills over into class, creating a power-struggle dynamic complete with intimidation, personal attacks, and withdrawal. The list goes on.

KELLIE: You've pointed out a vital issue. Reading this essay reminded me how important it is to bring some aspects of the experiences of students into the classroom. As hard as it is, I remain convinced of the importance of creating opportunities for students to make connections between their school experience and the experiences they have outside of school.

CRAIG: That seems like such a big task, but I would argue that this is one of our main challenges as professionals.

Chapter 7

Classroom roles

In 2001, Holt's performance exams and functions-based approach to Algebra 1 were widely known in Michigan. For example, requests for participation in the performance exams go out to a large number of people in the Greater Lansing area. And, others from southeastern and western Michigan often participate. But, there are other changes that, on a day-to-day basis, may be at least as important, though not as easy to characterize.

As the descriptions of Algebra 1 classes in Chapter 3 suggest, the instructional model employed in many of the Holt mathematics classes has changed dramatically. This change mirrors changes in the rhetoric of mathematics teaching in the US. In the mid-1980s, Good *et al.*'s (1983) *Active mathematics teaching* represented cutting-edge thinking about the organization of mathematics classes. In this scheme, a teacher's effectiveness was judged by how well that teacher organized the presentation of materials and subsequent student practice.

Since the publication of the first version of the NCTM *Standards* (1989, 1991, 1995), the rhetoric has changed. Many mathematics educators advocate problem-solving approaches (as reviewed in Lester, 1994) that offer a different model for the use of a class period. Rather than focus on teacher presentation and student practice, as outlined for example in the Connected Mathematics Project (Lappan *et al.*, 2002) and in work at the elementary school level (e.g., Lampert, 1990), the idea now is to structure class periods around student exploration of problems. In this instructional model, teachers launch the problem, and students explore it individually or in small groups, perhaps with the aid of some technology. A whole-class discussion follows, reflecting on the exploration, discussing student theories, and summarizing what has been learned. In these whole-class discussions, there is a focus on student reasoning and explanation for the phenomena unearthed during exploration.

Many classes in the Holt mathematics department run on this

model. What's surprising isn't the direction of the change at Holt, but rather its magnitude. In his study of teaching over the past century, Larry Cuban (1993) has argued that student-centered practices, like "launch-explore-discuss," are often advocated, but seldom carried out, especially in high schools. At Holt, however, most of the members of the mathematics department have adopted these practices as a significant component of their regular teaching practice. Not every period of every day in every mathematics class involves student exploration of a problem, but this structure is very common.

To exemplify this shift in instructional model, in the following essay, Jan Simonson describes the changes she has seen in the organization of Marty Schnepp's classroom instruction. She argues that the whole of the various changes add up to more than the sum of their parts. Using three classroom vignettes over a three-year period, Jan argues that Marty has not just adopted a number of discrete teaching practices; he has transformed his teaching. In her description, his teaching has moved from a focus on teaching students to perform skills to having them make sense of mathematics, and as a by-product of that sense-making activity, learn the skills he had focused on before. To illustrate that these changes are not limited to Marty's instruction, Mike Lehman and Marty take up Jan's observations by reflecting on changes that they have made in their teaching.

Finally, while this essay does not examine the direct effect of these changes on student learning in the particular classes described, it is important to view this text in the context of other materials in this book. In Part II, we read about shifts in student course-taking and we hear from students, including Nicolas Miller who was in a class that Marty team-taught with Sandy Callas. We propose that these aspects of our experiences are indeed linked.

One teacher's transformation in teaching

Jan Simonson, Calvin College

This paper was developed for this volume from Jan's 1998 Michigan State University dissertation, The centrality of a teacher's professional transformation in the development of mathematical power: A case study of one high school mathematics teacher.

Marty Schnepp has taught mathematics at Holt High School since 1991. He has been in Holt most of his life. He attended Holt High School as a student, student-taught in the mathematics department, then later, after three years of teaching mathematics in California, returned to Holt to teach and pursue a graduate degree. In the passages that follow I will present three lessons Marty taught over a three-year period. My intent is to show the changes he's made in his instruction.

Marty taught the first lesson in fall 1993, the second in fall 1995, and the third in spring 1996. These scenes are intended to illustrate changes in Marty's thinking and how he applies this thinking in the classroom, resulting in what I will call a transformation in his teaching practice. The following sections will present transcribed conversations from Marty's classroom, then highlight the changes in Marty's instruction that reflect changes in his thinking about instruction.

Vignette 7.1: a textbook-based Algebra I class, fall 1993

On this particular day, Marty was working with his Algebra 1 class, which was made up of 10th–12th-graders. The class was following the algebra textbook section by section. They were solving for unknown quantities in an equation and addressing questions students had about homework problems. (See problem 8 below, from McConnell *et al.*, 1990, p. 176.)

8. $1/5 = 1/80 \, y$

Marty was asked about this question while going over homework solutions and wrote the problem on the board.

(For the purposes of this piece, students are numbered as they enter conversations. This numbering system allows readers to identify when the same student is speaking in different parts of the conversation.)

M: What is the coefficient of the unknown?
Silence
M: What is the unknown?
SEVERAL STUDENTS: y
M: What is the number it is being multiplied by?
S1: One over 80.
M: What should you do to find y?
S1: Multiply by 80?
M: Yes, remember you always multiply by the reciprocal of the coefficient of the unknown. Multiply what?
A CHORUS OF STUDENTS: Both sides.
M: What do you get?
S2: 80 times one-fifth.

M: How do you do that?

Silence

M: How can we make 80 look like a fraction? Remember that if you want to somehow combine a whole number and a fraction, turn the whole number into a fraction.

S1: 80 over one.

M: Then what?

S1: You do 80 times one and one times five.

M: What do you get on the other side?

SEVERAL STUDENTS: *y*

M: What happened to the one over 80?

S2: It cancels.

M: I think what you mean is that when you multiply by 80, you get 80 over 80, which is?

A CHORUS OF STUDENTS: One.

Marty was very careful to repeat important points, rules, and skills that the students should remember in order to successfully complete problems on their own. For the students to solve for the unknown, they needed to remember the process for solving $ax = b$. Thus, after he was sure everyone knew what number represented the coefficient, Marty repeated the rule, multiply the unknown by the reciprocal of the coefficient (see the explanation below in Figure 7.1 from the text he was using).

It was obvious that he had done this quite well in the past. When he asked leading questions, such as "Multiply what?" the class responded in unison, in this case, "Both sides." Students had been taught from a previous section in the book that equivalent expressions are still equivalent, if both sides of the equation are multiplied by the same number. It was an impressive performance. It seemed that Marty's careful attention to details and slow, deliberate focus on the process of solving equations were a calm influence on his students. However, once he gave the next homework assignment, only one or two of the students worked on it (Field Notes, 9/18/93).

To solve $ax = b$ for x (when a is not zero) multiply both sides of the equation by the reciprocal of a.

In the term ax, a is called the **coefficient** of x. So to solve $ax = b$ multiply both sides by the reciprocal of the coefficient of x.

Figure 7.1 An explanation from a math textbook (source: McConnell *et al.*, 1990, p. 174).

Vignette 7.2: a functions-based Algebra I class, fall 1995

Two years later, the configuration of the students' desks has been changed from straight rows facing the board to a semicircle facing the center of the room. Marty handed out a worksheet developed by Holt mathematics teachers titled "Number Recipes #1" (Figure 7.2).

Marty invited the students to complete the worksheet collaboratively, after which they would discuss their work as a class. Some students worked in small groups, others with a partner, a couple by themselves. The students had been discussing number recipes – doing operations on a variety of inputs, resulting in different outputs.

S1: How do you want us to make the tables?
M: In whatever way makes sense to you.
S2: Why don't you just tell us the answer?
M: Because I think you guys are smart enough to think about it.
S2: Can we make up our own values for the table?
S3: But we need the values that will give us 0.
M: Will (S2's) suggestion accomplish that for you?
S2: Can you just tell us what is right?
S4: There is no one answer.
S2: Can we make up our own values?
M: That will work.

Some of the students started to make the tables by hand but soon realized it would be quicker to use a graphing calculator. Part (b), searching for inputs that would make the output 0, seemed to be a stopping point for all of the students. As they reached that point, the students seemed to diverge in their approaches. It turned out that the exact x-intercept would never appear on the calculator, since it occurred when x was

Below are two rules:

1. Take the input, multiply it by -3 and then add 2.
2. Take the input, multiply it by 5 and then take away 4.

For each rule above:

A) Make a table of 10 inputs and outputs.
B) Find any inputs which will make the output be 0.
C) Find inputs which will make the output negative.
D) Find 2 inputs which will make the output not a whole number.
E) Write down any observations you have about the rule.

Figure 7.2 Number Recipes #1.

equal to 2/3, the calculator only showing a part of this repeating decimal.

S5: Try fractions.
(Marty has her repeat her statement, but the others don't pay special attention.)
S6: We tried one and it doesn't work. We tried zero and it doesn't work. We tried negative zero and it doesn't work.
M: Do you remember what outputs you got?
S6: No. (They began looking at the output values.)
M: What else could you try?
S7: Negative two?
M: Yes, and I suggest that you expand your table to show the values so you can see if there is a pattern.

Students continue working and discussing a possible value for the x-intercept.

M: Is zero negative or positive?
S8: It's like a divider, isn't it? One way is positive and the other way is negative.

A different group has noticed something they want to share with Marty.

S9: Everything below 0.6 gives you a positive number and 0.7 and above gives you a negative.
M: Where do you think you should go looking for the number that gives you zero?
S9: I don't know.
M: Keep thinking about it – inputs below 0.6 give you a positive number and 0.7 and above give you a negative. If we were thinking about money, and everything was in cents, and if I gave you three quarters – how could you write that amount in decimals?
S9: 0.75.
M: Think about the significance of that as it relates to this problem. Think about it for a while and if you don't get anywhere, go on and come back. But don't give up on it – this is a very important idea.

Some students became very frustrated. Others began describing what was happening (identifying the interval of the input values inside of which they felt yielded an output of 0). Still others were busily narrowing the interval and at least one put the table aside and began to work on solving the problem using symbolic manipulation. The room was busy with activity, students walking across the room to talk with other students, others comparing notes with what they had tried. Some were very confident that their answer of "0.667" was close enough, others strongly disagreeing.

Class is convened as a whole group. Two students put their tables on the board. They used the values –1 to –10.

M: Take a look at your table and the table on the board. What do you notice?

S1: It goes up by three.

S3: None of the outputs are negative.

M: Question (b) asks for inputs which will make the output zero.

S10: We couldn't find any.

M: Any come up with any strategies to find it? Anyone get close?

S8: 0.1.

M: 0.1 as an input or output?

S8: Output.

M: Anyone get closer?

S11: I got 0.2, but I don't know if that is any closer.

M: What was your input?

S11: 0.6.

M: Anyone get any closer?

S9: I got 0.002.

M: What did you use as an input?

S9: 0.6666.

M: Why did you try that?

S9: Because if I used 0.67 it went too far.

S5: Try another 6.

S9: You get 0.0000002.

M: What happens when you fill up the screen?

S3: Seven zeros.

M: Anyone get any closer?

S6: –0.0001.

M: What input did you use?

S6: 0.66667.

M: Why did you think there was not a number that would do this?

S10: We tried numbers.

M: What did you do?

S10: Started with 1 and worked my way up.

M: What happened?

S10: I don't know.

M: Everyone, look at your tables and notice what happens when you go further up the number system.

S1: They go up by three every time.

M: If I were looking for zero, should I keep putting in larger numbers?

S10: No.

M: Should I look at large negative numbers?

S6: No, look in between 0 and 1.

M: (S9), can you tell us what you told me about 0.6 and 0.7?

S9: Everything 0.7 and above is negative and everything 0.6 and below is positive.

M: (Looks at the clock) Has anyone ever seen 0.6666666 when you were doing calculations?

SEVERAL STUDENTS: Yes.

M: Does anyone know a fraction that has that approximate value?

S5: Two-thirds.

(*The bell rings.*)

M: (Stopping their movement) *Remember*, the point of mathematics is not punching a number in a calculator or finding the right answer, but the thinking that goes on around it. You did some very important mathematical thinking today.

(Field Notes, 9/18/95)

The small group and whole-class discussion ended up including many fundamental mathematical ideas, including rational numbers, number sense, estimations, tabular values of linear functions, and algebraic manipulations of rules. (Marty later told me that S5 had told him, "My grandmother said if you don't know what to do in math, just undo what you did – so I subtracted 2 and divided by –3 and got 2/3.")

Comparison and contrast: some remarks

The purpose of the teaching in the first vignette seems to have been to help the students become proficient at solving a particular type of problem, a mathematical skill of sorts. Students were to learn a process presented by the textbook and teacher, practice it, and apply it with the goal of consistently obtaining the correct answer. Marty paid special attention to places students often made mistakes that might cause them future problems, such as canceling rather than noticing that dividing a number by itself is equivalent to one. He was concerned about transferring to his students the skill of performing a specific procedure.

In contrast, according to Marty, the worksheet in the second vignette gave students the chance to think about repeated calculation procedures. The procedure took on a life of its own rather than imposing –3x +2 as an abstract object right away. In Marty's view, taking time to think about this procedure gives purpose to the symbols, whereas if you go to the abstract too quickly, many students are discouraged and alienated. Later in the year, they will treat a function as an abstract object, but they are not ready for that yet.

Part (b) on this worksheet, according to Marty, is intended to "plant a seed that there are times that you are interested in a specific output." Marty viewed the problem of having a non-integer answer as a way to probe student thinking to see how they made sense of our number system. This was particularly important since these students were supposedly behind in mathematics. The students that made up this class were upper-level high school (10th–12th grades) taking introductory algebra. This question offers an opportunity for interaction and learning, forcing their sense-making to come to the forefront in a context where they are not directly answering a question about the number system. In this case, according to Marty, articulating what kinds of things fall between integers gives purpose to those kinds of numbers, while in the past, many students have not seen a purpose to, or even cared about numbers between integers.

In our conversation that followed the second class described above, Marty talked about being pleased with his students' thinking and engagement. He repeated what various students had shared in private and public conversations. In this way, he demonstrated a new interest in listening to his students' sense-making. He was beginning to think about situations he might pose the next day to challenge, guide, or encourage their investigations. During class, the students commented more than once that Mr. Schnepp never answered their questions but only asked them more questions. Though this seemed to cause them some frustration, I noticed that they did not hesitate to pursue his questions.

These two classes are different along many dimensions, from the set-up of the room to the interactions with the students. In the second lesson, Marty is no longer describing a certain process for students to memorize with the purpose of using it to find one correct answer. Although a component of the task in the second class was to find the value of x when the output is zero (the x-intercept of this function), students were not following a predetermined path in finding that value. The students determined the paths they would take, and they interacted with each other's ideas and suggestions. Marty's goal for the students, in addition to finding the x-intercept, was for them to be thinking about number patterns, and he seemed interested in all aspects of their mathematical musings. As they discussed their findings in their small groups, they were forced to articulate their thinking and defend their decisions. This form of mathematical conversation and reasoning was quite different from the pattern of conversation in the lesson focused on learning a predetermined process with the goal being to find the correct answer. In the second lesson, Marty's interaction with the students was giving them space, time to think, and encouragement to pursue their ideas as he listened closely to their thoughts. He was, however, directly involved in the whole-class discussion with most comments going directly to and through him.

Vignette 7.3: an Algebra 2 class, spring 1996

It's later the same year, spring 1996, and the students in an Algebra 2 class were investigating logarithms. While studying the graphs of logarithmic functions, they noticed that the range was all real numbers and wondered why the domain was restricted to positive real numbers. Marty decided one way to approach this question was to look at the definition in the textbook, analyze what was being said, and then critique the definition by looking at alternative restrictions. The textbook definition and graph appear in Figure 7.3 below:

The question students were considering was why the base of a logarithm had to be greater than 0 – in particular, why the base could not be negative. One conjecture was that the output (n) had to be positive, but that was shown not to be the case for inputs (values of m) between 0 and 1. If m is between 0 and 1, then n must be a negative number.

Students then began to think about the consequences of allowing bases to be negative, using –9 as a possible base. The problem of taking even roots of negative numbers (which does not result in a real number) led the class in a different direction. The conversation suggested a need for clarification of the definitions of even and odd numbers.

M: Did everyone hear what S11 just said? He said that you can raise –9 to any power, you just can't take any even root of it? [e.g., sqrt(–9)

Definition:
Let $b > 0$ and $b \neq 1$. Then n is the **logarithm of m to the base b**, written $n = \log_b m$, if and only if $b^n = m$.

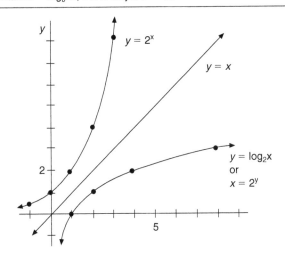

Figure 7.3 Definition and graph from a math textbook (source: from Senk et al., 1990, p. 509).

does not result in a real number, while the third root of (–9) would.]

S1: Can you repeat that?

M: You can raise –9 to any power, you just can't take any even root of it.

(Several students said they agreed.)

M: Are you agreeing only because S11 said it, or do you agree?

(Many said S11, while others said they agreed.)

S3: I want to know if it is true, *why* it is true.

S8: I always get confused when you have decimals, whether they are even or odd.

M: Say a little bit more.

S8: Like 9.6, is that even or odd?

S2: One part is even and one part is odd.

S8: Would it be even because the decimal is even?

(Lots of students talking at once.)

M: Okay, hold on. Let's take a minute to think. This is a great question, and we need to get responses, but we can't talk over each other.

S3: If we could define even and odd.

S4: Can a fraction be even or odd?

S7: It takes two halves to make a whole, never mind.

M: How does this question relate to what we were talking about?

S7: If it is odd, you can't take the square root.

S8: If you have even roots, you can't find them.

S10: Is the definition of an even number, divisible by two?

S7: So you can divide 9 by two and get 4.5, so it is even?

M: We have to get this ironed out if we are going to know what an even root is.

S7: Do you know the answer?

M: I have *an* answer in mind, but I wouldn't consider it to be *the* answer. This is what mathematicians have to do, make definitions and see what the implications are. S10 has given us a definition of even: An even number is a multiple of 2.

S10: That is what I said but not what I want to say now. I think it has to be a whole number.

M: So, tell me if this is right. An even number is a whole number multiple of 2?

S10: You also have to come out with a whole number.

M: So give me your definition of an even number.

S10: An even number is a whole number, divisible by two, that gives you a whole number [Marty begins to write on the board]. That takes care of negatives.

M: What assumption are you making when you say divisible by two? [He had not yet written, "that gives you a whole number."]

S8: You have to write, "Gives you a whole number."

M: To me, divisible by two says that.

S7: An even number is a whole number when divided by two gives you a whole number.

[Marty writes that on the board.]

S6: So decimals or fractions can't be even.

M: Is that an implication if we are going to accept this definition? So, what does that say about S10's question about decimals?

S3: They can't be even.

S4: So if we come up with a definition for odd numbers, then we will know.

M: That's a good idea, let's get a definition for odd numbers.

One noticeably different aspect of Marty's teaching in this episode is how he has dispersed the authority in his classroom among the textbook, himself, and the students. This class did not use the textbook on a regular basis, but occasionally Marty handed books out, then asked the students to read certain sections or definitions and analyze the text by writing about it or just thinking about it. This was one such occasion; in preparation for this discussion, Marty asked his students to think about the definition given in the text and be ready to talk about it.

This transcript shows Marty as more of a participant in the discussion rather than as a focal point for all student comments, as in the previous two vignettes. Here a discussion about a textbook definition of exponential functions led students to confront their understandings of even and odd numbers and eventually led to an inquiry into Peano's Axioms, one formal basis for constructing our number system. Marty didn't feel compelled to control the conversation and actually hadn't anticipated student insistence on a definition for even and odd numbers. Nor had he anticipated their questioning the bottom line of definitions, which led to the later discussion on axioms. By allowing the exponential functions to be the object of study, rather than the symbolic manipulation that would produce a predetermined answer, the students were confronted with big ideas in mathematics. Perhaps even more significant was Marty's response to a simple question that most mathematicians would call gibberish (S8: "I always get confused with decimals, whether they are even or odd"). He allowed it to become the subject of the discussion. This choice gave rise to the ensuing confrontation with unanticipated, but important mathematical ideas.

Transformation of practice: more elaborate discussion of the three vignettes

A process of transformation is not a linear process, but rather a process that precedes in fits and starts, gaining ground and losing ground. These vignettes represent changes in Marty's thinking and practice that collectively make up a transformed approach to teaching and learning. First, Marty's goal for his students' understanding has changed from learning the rules of symbolic manipulation to understanding the relationships within and between number systems and the use of symbols to model these relationships. Next, Marty has changed his view of mathematics from the content in a textbook to a discipline embedded in history and society, one socially constructed by human beings. Lastly, Marty's view of how to teach mathematics has changed from wanting to transfer his understanding of the textbook to interacting with students. By listening closely to their conceptions and designing appropriate situations, he pushes their thinking and introduces new insights. But, of course, these changes did not unfold as neatly or as cleanly as described above.

Changes in goals for student understanding

Marty's instruction and assessment before the 1993–1994 school year reflected a focus on helping his students develop what Skemp (1978) would call an instrumental understanding of mathematics. Referring to the first vignette, Marty stressed rules, without giving students the chance to work out why the rules were sensible. This is typical of school mathematics. Students are asked to memorize the process for carrying, borrowing, solving linear and quadratic equations, plugging values into area and volume formulas, writing two-column geometry proofs, etc. These processes are spelled out in the textbook, but students aren't given the supporting framework for analyzing or knowing why what they are doing works or is helpful. Traditionally, a student (like Marty no doubt was) who excels in an instrumental understanding of mathematics, not only succeeds in school mathematics, but may go on to teach mathematics.

In the spring of 1994, early on in his process of change, Marty talked about feeling rather uncomfortable at first when Sandy Callis, with whom he was team-teaching, would assign a single problem, spend a day or two or longer on it, and not necessarily assign any homework. Yet the vignette from the fall of 1995 is an example of just such an approach. The students worked on their ideas and the initial discussion during one class period. Although they had discussed less than half of the worksheet, many interesting ideas had surfaced during the small-group discussions and the whole-class discussion that would give Marty insight into their conceptions of numbers, non-integers in particular.

Before the team-teaching with Sandy, Marty thought that homework with lots of assigned problems was a way of holding students responsible for their learning. After the work with Sandy, he shared the following reflections:

I started to see that these problems [ones like Number Recipes #1 from the second vignette] had so much to them that the kids could really dig into them. They could find alternative methods of solving them and thinking about them. If they [the problems] had come out of the textbook, they [the students] could have flipped to the back and assumed there was only one correct answer. Even then [when using a text], if you talk about another way to approach it, they say it is confusing. They just want you to show them one way. With these problems, one student could talk about it graphically, another could be looking at the table. Their results could be different, or they could be the same but expressed differently. They could talk about what they were thinking and write about it.

(Marty, fall 1994)

Marty's changing view of the understanding he wanted for his students is illustrated in the second and third vignettes. In the second vignette, Marty allows students the opportunity to use any method that makes sense to them to find the x-intercept. Here the students are invited to make connections to what they know, look for patterns, and develop their own schemas to help them find an answer. Marty never gives them a procedure or rule to follow. In the third vignette, the students are thinking about the behavior of logarithmic functions, odd and even numbers, and definitions. Again, Marty's goal is the development of their collective understandings around the graph and textbook definition of logarithmic functions. He invites them to build a sensible schema without relying on either himself or the textbook as sole sources of authority or fixed procedures. Consistent with Skemp's (1978) claim about relational understandings, the students in this class remembered it two years later and referred to it in a Calculus class, even recalling the details of the conversation.

Shifts in Marty's views of mathematics

As illustrated by the first vignette, for the first five years of Marty's teaching career, he closely followed the order and content of the textbook. He later said that as he went through school, college, and the beginning years of his career, he was convinced that the mathematics *was* what was in the textbook.

I remember having the anxiety related to people being out there still creating mathematics, so the body is going to just keep getting bigger and bigger. Mathematics was just the stuff that was stored away in textbooks. That is, the stuff you had to learn if you were going to learn math. It was completely a formalist, absolutist kind of view that said that the stuff in the textbooks wasn't chosen conventions and techniques and things, but the way the world is and the way the world works. That was my conception coming out of college and for quite a while teaching.

(February, 1998)

Marty's vision of an effective mathematics teacher was one who developed and executed clear explanations of the content in textbooks. Marty's teacher education courses, and his own high school mathematics teacher when he was a high school student, left him with images of students making connections, but he saw this being a result of the teacher's clear explanations of procedures (essentially connections the teacher was making), not something initiated by or directly related to student ideas.

Deborah Schifter (1995), who researches the professional development of teachers, outlines a framework for interpreting changes in a teacher's conception of school mathematics as reforms in practice take place. In some respects, it represents a move from instrumental mathematics to relational mathematics. A summary of each stage is as follows:

> First stage: School mathematics is facts and procedures, discrete and ungrounded, learned mechanically and mechanically applied. Truth is simply incarnate in textbooks and instructor.

> Second stage: School mathematics includes students finding patterns, solving problems, and making conjectures.

> Third stage: Students follow up their ideas by investigating reasonability, generalizability, and validity.

> Fourth stage: Teaching is organized so that students confront the big ideas of the mathematics curriculum – the organizing principles of mathematics.

Marty went through similar stages in his transformation, with perhaps the addition of a fifth stage in which he gives himself and his students permission to critique existing bodies of mathematics, definitions, and school mathematics curricula. In describing Marty's changing views of school mathematics I will reference Schifter's stages.

Marty began to seriously consider the content of school mathematics, in particular introductory algebra, while sharing teaching assignments with Sandy, in the midst of being introduced to new curriculum ideas for Algebra 1. Let's consider again the first two vignettes, only this time focusing on the mathematics. In the first scene, Marty is asking the students to find the value of an unknown quantity in the linear equation, $1/5 = 1/80 \, y$. The students have been presented with a set procedure to find unknown quantities, a procedure often referred to as solving linear equations. Here Marty's conception of school mathematics is clearly in line with Schifter's first stage. Mathematics is "facts and procedures ... learned mechanically and mechanically applied." In traditional introductory algebra textbooks, the first half of the textbook is devoted to working with unknown quantities in linear situations, while in the second half the unknown becomes a variable in a function. The first half is, in many ways, a continued review of arithmetic operations with an emphasis on developing symbolic manipulation skills, presumably to go from the specific to the more general. However, when x or y, as in this case, is an unknown quantity, it is actually a very specific question, much like arithmetic problems in earlier grades.

As described earlier (e.g., Chapter 3 of this section), the approach to introductory algebra being explored at Holt is different in fundamental ways. In this approach, the unknown quantity x is treated primarily as an independent variable (rather than as a specific unknown quantity), whose changing value affects the dependent variable, y, or the output. The objective is to be able to identify attributes about the relationships between quantities that are changing. The resulting functions become the objects of study and can be studied for patterns and tendencies then classified accordingly, using rules, tables, and graphs as tools in the investigations. Thus in the second vignette, the students are working with the situation, "Take the input, multiply by -3, and then add 2," with the majority of the discussion centering around the question of which input will make the output equal to zero. In a more traditional equation-solving approach, this could have been written down as $-3x + 2 = 0$, with the directions "Solve for x." However, in this activity the goal is much different than finding this unknown value. The students end up studying the relationship and paying attention to what happens to the outputs as the inputs vary. By using tables and graphs, as well as the rule, they notice patterns and general tendencies that might transfer to other functions. In this vignette, the students are using these tools to study relationships, while exploring the mathematics and applying logical reasoning. In my view, they are becoming mathematically empowered. The mathematics in the second vignette is closer to the mathematics found in Schifter's second or third stage, where some students are finding patterns, solving problems, and making conjectures, while others are investigating the validity and reasonability of their ideas. It is also designed so that students will confront a big idea in mathematics – reasoning by continuity, consistent with Schifter's fourth stage.

Even after realizing the value of allowing students to make sense of concepts, Marty had still felt uncomfortable when students veered too far away from established mathematics. Marty describes the subsequent change in his thinking as follows:

> I started thinking [that] if I am having kids discuss [mathematical problems], then it is perfectly okay and perfectly reasonable and perfectly legal for them to come up with their own definitions, conceptions, and structures of axioms and everything else.
>
> (February, 1998)

The third vignette is a wonderful example of students coming up with their own definition, as they wrestled with the meaning of an even number. During this scenario, and in the discussion of the Product Rule in the fourth essay, Marty is allowing students to develop mathematical power. In turn, they are demonstrating the merit of his decision to organize his teaching to allow students to question and confront what Schifter refers to as "the organizing principles of mathematics" in her fourth stage.

Marty as listener

The mathematical activity in Marty's classes has changed in many ways. One of the attributes of mathematical power described in the NCTM *Standards* (1989) is the ability "to communicate about and through mathematics" (p. 1). Marty came to accept the view that mathematics is socially constructed (Ernest, 1991). Because mathematics is a human construct, Marty realizes his students' mathematical constructions are a valid and imperative aspect of their learning experience. Given this freedom, as Marty says, "they proceed 'naturally' to do mathematics." According to Marty, this happens in his classes during the conversations. This is evidenced by the conversation in the third vignette. As the students work toward a consensus, they find it necessary to define even numbers. Then the conversation produces a forum for what Marty calls "epistemological shifts and balances" amongst the students and himself. This manifestation of mathematical power is possible because Marty treats mathematics as socially constructed.

A current goal of Marty's instruction is to create situations that help students confront the big ideas of the course, while at the same time enabling them to really talk about the material and learn. To create these situations, Marty must hear and understand the students' conversations. In his transformation, Marty's vision of teaching mathematics broadened from strictly evaluative listening to include interpretive and hermeneutic listening (Davis, 1997). When he focused on explaining procedures, he only listened to hear if his students' answers were right or wrong. When Marty said he could get students to talk but didn't know what to do with what they were saying – that is the beginning of listening to interpret student understanding. As Marty began to hear and interact with his students in the process of socially constructing mathematics, his view of teaching was transformed, as is evidenced by the different sort of listening he does in the third vignette when the student says "I always get confused with decimals, whether they are even or odd." Here Marty's listening includes a deeper layer of interpretation. He listens beyond whether the student is correct or not and hears an important connection to make.

Concluding remarks

Combine the shifts in Marty's view of mathematics, learning, and his role as a teacher with the changes he has made in his practice, and you have described Marty's professional transformation. Professional transformations like this are rare and cannot be reduced to a defined set of actions or changes to practice. Instead, the fundamental components of Marty's transformation were shifts in his beliefs and in the way he thought about his work as a teacher. Those shifts, as an integral part of his changed practice, put Marty in a position to provide opportunities for his students to gain mathematical power.

The vision thing

Mike Lehman and Marty Schnepp, Holt High School

MIKE LEHMAN: I think the way Jan describes your work with students provides a good contrast between what we traditionally call mathematics teaching and what we need to do to *truly* teach mathematics to our students. In many ways, it is the type of instruction the authors of the NCTM *Standards* had in mind when the standards were first published.

MARTY SCHNEPP: I guess so. If teachers maintain static vision and look only to help students learn vocabulary and algorithms, student understanding will remain instrumental, rather than relational, as Jan discusses. Changing teaching isn't about new methods or cooperative learning or making kids write about math. It has to do with the vision that the teacher maintains. Back when I saw math in a Platonistic way – math was "God's language." It was a fixed body of information stored safely away in textbooks. I could teach it in no way other than as I was taught. I did my best to ensure that all the kids could perform the requisite skills and could use the canonical vocabulary. But so much lurked beneath the surface of my presentations and the students' canned responses. But we never got to that.

MIKE: I agree. First, we must all admit that we've faced the same situation outlined in the first vignette. We've all tried to get students to solve algebraic equations by having them perform the correct steps or by having them work the equation backwards until the x is alone. While procedurally these may be correct, we've all been asked, "When will I ever use this?" or "Why are we doing this?" Our students get so caught up in what they are learning that they lose track of the larger mathematical picture or, worse yet, they never see this picture in the first place.

MARTY: That's what I'm getting at. When I reread the first vignette, I realize it's easy to forget how superficial the learning was. Kids could learn to correctly solve $1/5 = 1/80 y$ and still have little number sense, not knowing the difference between rational, irrational, etc. Many did even internalize the existence of non-whole numbers but just played along.

MIKE: I've more than once been frustrated because students just don't seem to get procedurally orientated problems or they just don't know what to do with the answer once they get it. This is probably more evident when we try to switch our focus from just simple algebraic equations to context-based situational problems. Just the mention of doing word problems brings a grumble in most of our classrooms. The switch from solving equations to solving word problems is never easy. They just don't seem to know what to do to get the equations or what to do with the answers, either.

MARTY: The solution to these types of issues created by a teacher-centered way of teaching is to find strategies that get all the cards on the table and that make student thinking central. From team-teaching and other collaborative work, I began to see patterns of interaction that allowed kids to formulate ideas about new situations, based on their intuition and prior experience. However, I couldn't focus my search for such an approach to teaching until I understood what I was looking for. My vision of math, learning, and teaching had to evolve, and I had to articulate that vision before finding a method.

MIKE: How you translated that vision, once articulated, into the classroom is clear from the second and third vignettes. These vignettes give us two good examples of how, by changing the focus of the classroom from answers to examining ways of thinking, you changed how students interact with the mathematics. As a reader, one notices how they question each other's thinking and how they are willing to pursue their own understanding of the mathematics. Also, it's important to see that, as the teacher begins to allow this shift in the classroom, s/he can no longer come to class with a checklist of things the students will learn during the lesson. S/he must instead listen to the students, interpret their questions and ideas, and, from there, decide what's the next best step. This reminds me of help you gave me with teaching the unit circle and its relationship to the sine and cosine functions in my PreCalculus class. For years I used drawings on the chalkboard and had students repeat after me that the sine function represents the vertical distance (y coordinate) from the x axis and the cosine represents the horizontal distance (x coordinate) from the y axis, when the circle is centered at the origin. My students repeated it like the good students they were, but they never seemed to find any use for this information. And if I came back to it later in the year, I'd have to remind them of it. You suggested we try to build a model that students could look at as it was turning to help them visualize these concepts. After you and I talked for a while, we came up with a very simple device, based on a turntable, that would rotate around in a circle and that we could mark points on for the students to follow. For the introductory lesson to this unit, I simply told my students that in their groups they should watch the device turn and pick two variables, one independent, the other dependent. They were then to sketch a graph of the relationship between their two variables as the device turned and prepare an explanation why their graph represented their variables. It took the rest of class for them to complete this task. During the next two days we discussed their graphs, variable selections, and assignments, running the device to compare its motion to the graphs and deciding which motions were interesting to look at. Since the students previously had studied triangular trigonometry and knew a little about the graphs of sine and cosine, they found the graphs that looked like trigonometric waves to be the most interesting. They became curious how to make a sine wave fit the motion of the device. While this discussion took us three days to complete, I was amazed at what they knew. When I asked them to model the motion of a basketball swinging in the middle of my room or of a Ferris wheel I described, they not only knew how to proceed but also what information was necessary. If I was concerned initially about the length of time the discussion took, it more than made up for itself. A unit that normally took three to four weeks to complete was done in a week and a half. This gave me extra time to pursue more student questions as well as some topics I normally left out of the course. In this example, my students not only achieved my goals but also, in most cases, moved far beyond them. It also shows how you have not only changed the way you think about teaching but, by sharing your ideas, have changed the way others think and teach.

MARTY: Thanks, Mike. But, there is more to it than the suggestion I made. I think Jan's trying to emphasize the importance of the way a teacher thinks, that is, that my vision of math changed and, as a result, my teaching could change in significant ways.

Part II

Student experience of the curriculum

The teachers and university personnel involved in the work of the Holt department during the time of our story had a wide range of challenging responsibilities. They were involved both in making instructional change happen, and in the learning and development this required, as well as in documenting the nature and impact of these changes.

Based on documentation of the nature of the instructional change at the school, the previous section focused on how the teaching practices of the Holt math department changed during the 1990s. These changes seem quite dramatic, perhaps; as Jan Simonson just argued in the last essay of the previous section, they even constitute a transformation of mathematics teaching practices at the high school. These changes were the focus of the teacher and university actors in the story told so far. But, the purpose of these changes was to improve the experience of students. This section explores the important question of the impact of these changes on Holt High School students. Did students notice a change? Did students' experience of mathematics instruction change? Did they learn more mathematics than they might have otherwise? Did student achievement improve, particularly that of students in lower-track classes? As a result of these changes, were students more prepared for the quantitative aspects of the lives they were to lead?

As difficult as these questions are to explore, the next section tackles them. While one might want conclusively affirmative answers, as is the case in most educational endeavors, evidence that would allow definitive answers to such seemingly simple questions can be quite difficult and time-consuming to assemble. The introduction to this section begins with an examination of available quantitative information.

Did students' experience of mathematics instruction change? There are some intriguing pieces of evidence to suggest that students at Holt in the early 2000s have greater opportunities to learn more mathematics than cohorts of students in the early 1990s did, and that some students experience their mathematics courses at Holt quite differently than do many high school students in the US.

After presenting important orienting background on the organization of mathematics instruction at Holt during the 1990s, the introduction to this part will examine evidence that suggests that more students at Holt in the year 2000–2001 take more advanced mathematics than was the case in 1990–1991. The chapters in this section that follow complement the quantitative data provided in the introduction with essays that document the experiences and perspectives of particular students. These essays flesh out and complicate the simple sort of picture conjured up by the phrase "more students studying more mathematics." And, significantly, they suggest that there may be important connections between students' course-taking, their experience of mathematics classes, and the classroom practices described in the last section:

- listening carefully to students' mathematical ideas;
- asking students to justify their thinking; and
- identification of mathematical activity in students' worlds.

And yet, even this intriguing evidence must be examined carefully. During the more than a decade of time under consideration, there is some evidence from the National Assessment of Educational Progress that a similar trend of increases in advanced course-taking holds true nationwide with significantly more 12th-graders having taken Algebra 2 and fewer having taken only Algebra 1 or earlier courses (see Table 8.6 in Mitchell et al., 1999 and Table 3 in Usiskin, 2002). While the evidence for change at Holt is convincing, it is unclear whether that change is dramatically, or only slightly, different from changes experienced elsewhere during the same time period.

Before looking at the evidence that the department has collected, it is important to furnish information on the structure of the mathematics requirements that held for students in the Holt Public Schools during the period in question. During this time, Holt High School was a three-year high school (though this changed for the 2003–2004 school year), comprising grades 10–12, rather than a typical four-year high school. For mathematics, the Holt Public School District required that students pass two courses from grade 9 on. No particular content was specified for these courses and the nature of this district requirement did not change during this time period. Students who passed their 9th-grade mathematics course only needed to complete one mathematics course at the high school level. Thus, at any given time only between one-third and one-half of the enrolled students at Holt High School were required to take mathematics. (This observation is helpful in understanding changes in patterns of mathematics course-taking at Holt during this period.)

As in most public high schools in the United States, the mathematics curriculum at Holt during this period was a "layer-cake" curriculum (Kaput, 1995); at Holt, there wasn't an integrated mathematics program that would organize the study of geometry, algebra, probability, statistics, and other topics as strands in a year-long course. Instead, as is common in most parts of the US, students took courses, like Algebra 1, Algebra 2, Geometry, PreCalculus, and Calculus, sequentially, though as time went on there were some variations in the location of Geometry on occasion, Discrete Mathematics or Statistics could be taken at different times, and some students took two math courses at the same time. In the early 1990s, this layer cake had layers below Algebra 1. At that time, students entering the high school with poor achievement might enter into Practical Math or PreAlgebra.

Again, as in most districts in the US, at Holt High School during this time, mathematics was "tracked;" based on their achievement and the guidance they received from school staff at the high school and junior high school, different students received different instruction in mathematics. However, at Holt High School in the early 1990s, unlike some schools, most of this tracking was done by the title of the course students took, by their progress up the layers in the cake, and not by labeling of sections within courses. The only courses with differentiations between sections of the same course were Algebra 2 and Pre-Calculus that had honors sections and Geometry that had an Informal Geometry option early in the decade. Thus, students from different tracks could share the same Geometry class, for example (see Figure II.1). In keeping with the building's "full inclusion" policy, there were no special sections for "special education" students. (This building-wide commitment was noted by the 2001 Standard and Poor's evaluation of the district that indicated a well above average proportion of special-education students in standard coursework.)

In the early 1990s, students entered Holt High School, typically from the junior high school, somewhere in the Practical Math, PreAlgebra, Algebra 1, Geometry, Algebra 2, layer-cake curriculum. Based on their achievement in middle school and junior high school, teachers recommended students for particular courses. Students who had done very well in grades 6 and 7 were deemed ready for Algebra 1 in grade 8 and Geometry in grade 9 (an accelerated track). They were on track to complete Calculus as seniors. Students whose achievement was satisfactory through 9th grade entered the high school having completed Algebra 1 and ready to study Geometry (the standard track). Other students whose achievements in grades 6 and 7 were not considered strong might have studied Math 8 in grade 8 and Math 9 in grade 9, or perhaps a course called General Math. All of these courses involved arithmetic, particularly with negative numbers and fractions. Based on their performance at the junior high school, they would enter the high school with a recommendation that they either be placed in Practical Math or PreAlgebra or Algebra (such a placement did not easily lend itself to completing mathematics preparation for college). See Figure II.1.

Thus, even though there were not separate tracks within courses, all students enrolled in Practical Math, PreAlgebra, or Algebra 1 at the high school were in a lower track. Underlying this system of differentiated course-taking is the notion that some students are ready for algebra and others are not, and that achievement in arithmetic courses is a reliable indicator of this readiness.

These tracking decisions, primarily made at the junior high school, had important ramifications. Students entering the high school to take Practical Math could only study Algebra in high school if they successfully completed three years of mathematics at the high school. Since successful performance on the Michigan Education Assessment Program (MEAP) tests (more about them below) required at minimum some knowledge of algebra and geometry, once performance on the MEAP began to be used to endorse high school diplomas in core subjects, students in this situation would be unlikely to pass the test and receive a state-endorsed diploma. (For example, examination of the performance of students in 1997 on the proficiency test used that year and related course-taking showed that 7 percent of students enrolled in Algebra 1 at the time of the test succeeded, while 34 percent of those enrolled in Geometry did, as did 60 percent of students enrolled in Algebra 2. All the students enrolled in PreCalculus passed the test.)

And, in the early 1990s at Holt High School, changing tracks was difficult. A student entering the high school having passed Algebra 1

	Grade level	Accelerated track	Standard track	Lower track		
Senior high school	12	Calculus	PreCalculus	Algebra 2	Geometry	Algebra 1
	11	Honors PreCalculus	Algebra 2	Geometry	Algebra 1	PreAlgebra
	10	Honors Algebra 2	Geometry	Algebra	PreAlgebra	Practical Math
	9	Geometry	Algebra 1	Math 9		
Junior high school	8	Algebra 1	PreAlgebra	Math 8		

Figure Part II.1 "No failure" paths through the early 1990s' layer-cake curriculum.

and Geometry could take Calculus in their third year at the high school. Without taking two courses at one time and bypassing Geometry, a student entering to take Algebra 1 could not study Calculus. Thus, most of the students in Calculus had been tracked into an advanced mathematics course at the junior high school.

And, as mentioned before, there were special honors sections of Algebra 2 and PreCalculus. In the early 1990s, just about all of the students in Calculus classes came from these honors sections. However, at the high school, entry into these honors sections was a student's choice and did not require testing or a certain entering grade point average. When some students began to take Algebra 2 immediately after Algebra 1 (skipping Geometry), they could then also choose to switch tracks (although they would have to either take two courses to study Geometry or skip that course). In the late 1990s, the department introduced, as well, opportunities for students to achieve honors options inside sections not officially designated as honors sections. And, the availability of Statistics and Discrete Mathematics in the late 1990s also allowed some students not to study Calculus in their senior year, or to take more than one mathematics course in their senior year. So, the layer-cake picture in the late 1990s was more complicated to depict.

With all of this background, it is now possible to present information about changes in course-taking at Holt High School from the late 1980s through the early 2000s. In 1989–1990, the first year of the MSU–Holt High School PDS relationship, there were approximately 900 students at the high school and 20 sections of mathematics were taught. These 20 sections supported a department of roughly four full-time faculty, two full-time teachers and five part-timers (a full load is five 60-minute classes per day and one "preparation" period). Out of these 20 sections, there were two sections of Algebra 1, two sections of PreAlgebra, and one section of General Math (Arithmetic for those not deemed ready for PreAlgebra). There were 11 sections of either Algebra 2 or Geometry. And, finally, there were four sections of advanced mathematics (PreCalculus or Calculus). The picture was quite similar in 1990–1991 when the enrollment of the school was 930 students (See Figure II.2).

Many of the students in the PreAlgebra and General Math classes were labeled as "special-education" students. There were no "pull-out" special-education, mathematics classes; regardless of their labeling, students needed to pass to complete the district's mathematics requirement. If they passed PreAlgebra or General Math, and had received a passing grade in their 9th-grade math course, they would have completed their mathematics requirement. But, many would not pass and would repeat these courses in order to graduate; some would not graduate. Most of the approximately 80 students in these sections would not take any more advanced mathematics courses. As a result, during high school, their study of mathematics was limited primarily to arithmetic, which these students had already studied without great success from grade 1 through grade 9. A rough estimate is that approximately one-quarter of a graduating cohort at this time graduated having only studied arithmetic. Again, this course-taking would suggest that such students would perform poorly on the MEAP.

In the late 1980s and early 1990s, members of the Holt High School math department and colleagues at Michigan State, particularly Sandy Callis and Perry Lanier, were concerned about the experience of students in these lower-track courses. They initiated studies examining General Math and Practical Math courses, at both Holt High School and Holt Junior High (e.g., Kirsner & Bethell, 1992). These studies suggested that students were not engaged with mathematics, were disengaged from schooling more generally, and were failing at a high rate. There seemed to be several reasons for this failure rate, among them a lack of student interest in the continued study of arithmetic. This interpretation is captured poignantly by one student's comment that "Practical Math is practically math!" Even though mathematics content was being chosen to conform to judgments of these students' achievements in mathematics and perceptions of their abilities, it seemed that this group of students was not being well served by the department's practices.

Some of the initial PDS activities begun in 1989 focused on developing teachers' awareness of issues of student learning in lower-track classes. For example, in one PDS project in 1989–1990, some members of the department interviewed each other's students. These interviews of students in lower-track classes both indicated students' power of thought and their lack of conventional mathematical understandings.

In 1991–1992, the experience of students in lower-track classes came to a head around high failure rates in PreAlgebra. In a meeting about this issue, based on his prior work in the district, Perry Lanier, a key MSU-based participant in the Holt High School/MSU PDS effort, suggested simply eliminating the course. He thought that the students could skip PreAlgebra and take Algebra 1. He urged the department to try this and see if increased failure rates resulted. If students were equally successful – or unsuccessful – in Algebra, then perhaps Algebra was not the hurdle it was often thought to be. Maybe failure in Practical Math or PreAlgebra was not an indication that students were unprepared for Algebra. If a great many failures occurred, Perry suggested creating a second-semester section that would allow students who had failed first semester to receive extra attention as they continued to study Algebra 1. Students who attended this section and received a passing grade would receive credit for both semesters of work. This would provide students with a motivation for studying hard in the second semester after having failed the first semester.

Events played out as Perry expected. The failure rate did not increase. This experience was a powerful one in suggesting to teachers at the high school (though not yet to teachers at the junior high school) that even students who had not been successful with arithmetic could study Algebra. And, at the same time, Dan Chazan and Sandy Callis were hard at work on reconceptualizing the Algebra 1 course as described earlier in the essays in Chapters 3 and 6; attitudes and teaching practices in the department were undergoing change.

Over time, the courses offered by the department continued to change, as did students' mathematics course-taking. See Figure II.2.

Jumping forwards 11 years from 1989–1990, in 2000–2001, the official enrollment at the high school was 1,143 (as indicated at www.michigan.gov/mde), and there were 41 sections of mathematics. These 41 sections supported a department of roughly eight full-time faculty, seven full-time and three part-time.

What drove this change in the number of sections and in the size of the math department? There are clearly many influences. There have

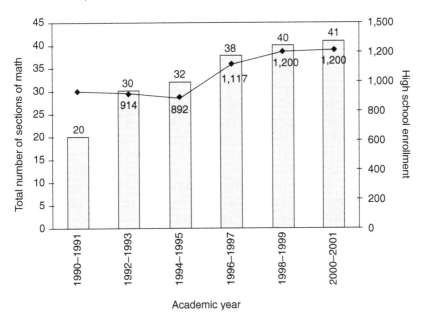

Figure Part II.2 Number of mathematics sections and high school enrollment over a decade.

been national calls for more students to take math and science. Perhaps these calls were heeded by the Holt students and their parents. And an increased student population surely accounts for some of the change in the number of sections of math courses, but certainly not all. There was an increase of roughly 30 percent in the student body. But, in a district where maximum class size has remained a constant and a part of the district's contract with teachers, a 30 percent increase in the student body cannot account for a doubling in the number of sections of mathematics courses. The percentage of students studying mathematics increased. Using a figure of 25 for average class size, in 1990–1991 500 out of 930 students were enrolled in mathematics classes, whereas in 2000–2001 1,025 out of 1,143 students were enrolled in math classes. And, in the late 1990s, some students began to "double up," to enroll in more than one math course in a given year (see for example the experiences described in Chapter 10). District requirements were not responsible for this change. These increases took place when only between one-third and one-half of the students were required by district policy to take a mathematics course in a given year.

Course-taking changed not only in absolute numbers of students studying mathematics. Inside this tracked system, students were also taking more advanced courses; they were advancing farther up the layer cake. Out of the 41 sections in 2000–2001, 15 sections were PreCalculus, Calculus, Discrete Mathematics, or AP Statistics; there were 21 sections of either Algebra 2 or Geometry, five sections of Algebra 1 and no sections of arithmetic or PreAlgebra. Special-education students were enrolling in a wide range of courses, not just the lower tracks. Almost no students were graduating having only studied arithmetic. See Figure II.3.

Looking across data from a decade, courses in arithmetic disappeared and were not offered after 1995 at the high school (though there are still a handful of students given special exemptions by counselors not to study algebra). After growing in number over the first half of the decade, by the end of the 1990s, the number of sections of Algebra 1 was in decline. Most students were now taking Algebra 1 in 8th or 9th grade at the junior high school and came into the high school prepared for more advanced coursework. Thus, the largest number of sections throughout the decade was consistently in Geometry and Algebra 2, and the number of these sections grew steadily.

While much of the attention of the Holt mathematics department has been concentrated on changing the experiences of students in lower-track classes, changes have occurred throughout the department. As Marty Schnepp's descriptions of his Calculus class attest (see Chapter 4 in this volume, as well as Chazan & Schnepp, 2002;

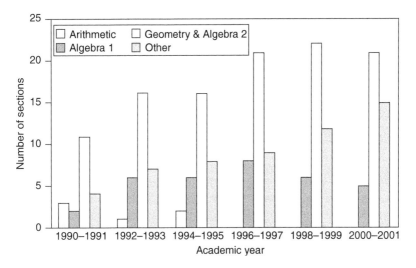

Figure Part II.3 Number of sections by type of course over a decade.

Schnepp & Chazan, 2004), there have also been changes in the experience of those students in the most advanced track, in the most advanced courses. By the end of the decade, students could study Discrete Mathematics or Advanced Placement (AP) Statistics, in addition to or instead of Advanced Placement (AP) AB Calculus. And, the advanced track has become available to a larger number of students and has become less exclusive. From 1992–1993 to 2000–2001, the population of the school rose 29 percent, from 914 to 1,143. During this same time, enrollments in AP Calculus more than doubled, swelling from 36 students to 75 students and, as a result, the number of sections of AP Calculus (this, of course, does not include the new AP Statistics and Discrete Mathematics courses) rose from one section to three sections. During this same time, the percentage of students enrolled in the course who sat for the AP exam grew as well. As a result, the number of students taking the AP Calculus exam grew tenfold, from 4 in 1992–1993 to 40 in 1999–2000. In 2000–2001, 29 sat for the AP Calculus exam, while 14 took the AP Statistics exam; in 2001–2002, these numbers were 22 and 19 respectively. While all four students in 1992–1993 scored a 5 on the AP exam, scores are now more varied, perhaps indicating that a wider range of students have come to study Calculus. Over this time period, roughly four students per year continue to receive 5s on the AP exam and a slightly higher number typically score 4s. The chart in Table II.1 below lists the AP scores of Holt High Schools students in 2000–2001 and 2001–2002.

Table Part II.1 AP scores of Holt High students in 2000–2001 and 2001–2002

Year	Exam	Score				
		5	*4*	*3*	*2*	*1*
2000–2001	Calculus	6	14	0	8	1
	Statistics	2	6	5	1	0
2001–2002	Calculus	2	8	6	6	0
	Statistics	0	6	5	7	1

Why were a greater percentage of students taking mathematics? And why were students taking more advanced courses? While it seems plausible to connect these changes with the instructional changes described in Part I, there are many other possibilities. One possibility is that these changes were simply part of a larger trend, and not a local phenomenon. There is some data to support such a hypothesis. In examining data from 1990, 1992, and 1996, the National Assessment of Education Progress finds a "trend toward students taking more advanced-level courses" (Mitchell *et al.*, 1999, p. 224) with significantly fewer 12th-grade students in 1996 not having taken Algebra yet (8 percent down from 17 percent) or only having taken Algebra 1 (23 percent down from 28 percent), and significantly more having Algebra 2 as a terminal high school course (48 percent as opposed to 43 percent) or Calculus (7 percent as opposed to 3 percent).

As a national trend, these data can be viewed as representing the choices of school administrators or of students and their parents. In the Holt context, actions of administrators made a difference. From the mid-1990s, Holt Public Schools, with support from the high school department, and sometimes with resistance from the math teachers at the junior high school, encouraged the teaching of Algebra 1 at the junior high school, and suggested an approach modeled on the one taken at the high school. Part of the push to do so may have been the impact of a larger policy environment on the Holt district administrators. But a part of the impetus may well also have been the local experience of having lower-track students at the high school engage successfully with algebra. Intriguingly, the district did not pursue such higher standards by changing its graduation requirements in mathematics, for example, requiring three years of mathematics past 9th grade for graduation.

And there are other hypotheses to consider. Were the students at Holt substantially different in 2000–2001 than they had been in the past? Throughout this span of more than a decade, the Holt district was not one of the wealthier districts in the local area, but in the late

1990s there was substantial construction of large and expensive new homes within the boundaries of the district. Yet, whatever changes in the demographics of the community there might have been, even in the late 1990s, a sizable percentage of Holt High School graduates continue not to enter institutions of higher learning upon graduation from high school. (This figure hovered around the 40 percent mark for most of the 1990s.) Upon graduation, many students from the high school go into the work world or the military. Even with many students not required to study mathematics and not heading on to further education immediately upon graduating high school, more students were studying more mathematics in 2001 than in 1991.

Setting aside causal speculations, there is quantitative and qualitative evidence that the experience of students at Holt High School, both high school students and preservice teachers, changed. Did this mean that high school students learned more mathematics? Did student achievement, particularly of lower-track students, improve? Over this time period, teachers' informal assessment of their students' progress was positive. Given all of the other demands on the project, there were no specific and targeted, comparative studies of student achievement. But, if the changes in course-taking were so dramatic, surely this should show up in achievement testing done in schools as a matter of course? If more students were taking more mathematics, shouldn't more students pass the MEAP?

Unfortunately, the data available for making historical comparisons about the performance of students in a particular school in Michigan during this time period does not allow for strong conclusions of this kind. Though Michigan has been committed to high-stakes testing and the publication of data on school achievement, during the 1990s, the nature of these tests, when and how often the tests were taken, and the schemes for reporting results of the tests all changed.

For example, in an effort to see whether changes in the Holt lower-track math courses had an impact on students' achievement on the high-stakes tests, one might want to compare students' performance on the MEAP during the 1994–1995 school year with performance from the year 2000–2001. Results available through the state and the intermediate school district indicate that in 1994–1995 75 of the 331 (22.7 percent) Holt Public Schools students who took the MEAP scored "low," while in 2000–2001 only 27 of 333 (8.1 percent) Holt High School students, based on their scores on the mathematics portion of the MEAP, will graduate with unendorsed diplomas.

Some background about testing in the State of Michigan is necessary in order to interpret this data. During the 1990s, the State of Michigan had in place the Michigan Educational Assessment Program (MEAP), an assessment program that generated data on student achievement in grades 4, 7, and 10. As part of the larger US Standards movement, towards the end of the 1990s, the state began to endorse high school diplomas. A High School Proficiency Test (HSPT), given in the 11th grade and designed to test proficiency in the four core subject areas, served to determine endorsements for Michigan high school diplomas. Students graduating from high school would only have a state-endorsed diploma in these core areas if they passed the relevant test. During the late 1990s, the two assessment programs were deemed redundant and it was decided to move the high school MEAP test into the 11th-grade year and to use it to determine endorsements in each of the four core subject areas. The 11th-grade MEAP thus became a high-stakes test for students.

As a result, the comparison of MEAP scores is not a solid one. In 1994–1995, the MEAP was not used to endorse diplomas; the stakes for students were different. The test was taken in the spring of the 10th grade and the figures reported are for first-time test-takers only, thus shedding little light on the work of a 10–12 high school. In 2000–2001, by contrast, students took the MEAP in the 11th grade, and could retake portions of the test on which they did not do well. The results report the final data for students in the class of 2001, without indicating how many times they took portions of the test. In 1994–1995, there were three categories for reporting student results, while in 2000–2001 there were four, three that allow endorsement and one that does not; the relationship between "low" in 1994–1995 and "unendorsed" in 2000–2001 is not perfectly clear. (The 1994–1995 data also include an alternative education option used by about a dozen students each year. Since achievement of these students tends to be lower, the 1994–1995 results are also not a completely accurate measure of achievement of students in the high school.)

And, in addition to all of the variables outlined above, in order to have definitive answers over more than a decade's time, one would also need to control for changes in the test itself and in the demographics of the local community. If changes in course-taking were dramatic, one might expect Holt High School mathematics scores to be dramatically out of line. This is not the case. Alternatively, one might compare achievement at Holt High School in mathematics with state norms or with a set of local schools to act as a benchmark against which to compare (such strategies can now be taken in the databases available online from the State of Michigan, reached from www.michigan.gov/mde, and Standard & Poor's School Evaluation Services, www.ses.standardandpoors.com/).[1] But, in order to make such comparisons secure, one would need a historical perspective that cannot be achieved for the time period being examined.

To identify conclusively changes in students' achievement, particularly in the lower tracks, in addition to all of the other efforts by the Holt High School mathematics department from the late 1980s until the early 2000s, the department would have had to arrange early on for the systematic collection and analysis of student data not collected as a matter of standard educational practice. Such data collection and analysis were beyond the resources available at the time.

And what of students' preparation for the quantitative aspects of their lives? Examining changes in such aspects of students' education quantitatively is beyond the capacities of the paper-and-pencil instruments currently available for student assessment.

In the rest of this section, essays will turn to qualitative examination of students' experience of instruction at Holt. Three essays on the high school students' experience each focus on a different layer of the curriculum. They present the experience of: a special-needs student in an Algebra 1 class, two students in an Algebra 2 class, and two students who ended up enrolling in advanced courses at MSU. In each case, there is a focus on a particular circumstance; the students discussed are not deemed as somehow representative. In keeping with the department's emphasis on increasing access to mathematics, there is a focus on experiences of students who have not been successful in mathematics or who are less affiliated with schooling.

After examining the experiences of high school students, the essays move on to the experiences of preservice teachers. As argued in Bill Rosenthal's essay (Chapter 5), the Holt teachers' change in classroom practices described in Part I (as well as other dimensions of the department to be described in Part III) is part of what has made Holt High School a valued placement for preservice secondary mathematics teachers. Keeping in mind that teachers at Holt teach mathematics to high school students and teach teaching to preservice teachers, this section continues to weave the story of university preservice teachers into the story of events at the high school. It includes two essays about preservice teachers' experience of their placements at Holt, alongside the three essays about high school students' experiences.

Chapter 8

Lower-track classes

Most secondary mathematics programs in the US are tracked. Students are assigned to classes based on the classes taken before and on their achievement. Classes in the secondary mathematics, layer-cake curriculum are more and less advanced; PreCalculus is more advanced than Algebra 2, which is more advanced than Algebra 1. And, the assumption is that less advanced courses are prerequisites for more advanced courses. Students who have done better move through the curriculum more quickly (one reason for saying that they have strong "abilities"); they take courses earlier than others in their age cohort.

There is an important set of pedagogical ideas implicit in this organizational structure. For example, one underlying notion is that classes that are more homogeneous with respect to achievement and background knowledge of mathematics will be better for student learning and easier to teach.

Critics of the layer-cake curriculum (like Kaput, 1995) suggest that its linear progression misrepresents mathematics. Mathematics has different areas; study of one area is not necessarily a prerequisite to study of another. Moreover, such critics also take issue with notions of ability that flow from the way mathematics is taught. They argue that mathematicians' strengths vary by area; it is a rare mathematician who is uniformly strong in a wide range of areas; matters of taste and aesthetic play an important role.

This layer-cake curriculum is challenged by the National Council of Teachers of Mathematics curricular vision for school mathematics (articulated in NCTM, 1989 and then again in NCTM, 2000). These documents, and National Science Foundation-funded projects to instantiate this vision, envision an "integrated" high school curriculum where algebra, geometry, probability and statistics, and other mathematical fields are strands in courses, rather than separate courses:

> Students develop a much richer understanding of mathematics and its applications when they can view the same phenomena

from multiple mathematical perspectives. One way to have students see mathematics in this way is to use instructional materials
that are intentionally designed to weave together different content
strands.

(p. 288)

While Holt High School's department continues to teach the
courses of the layer-cake curriculum, related to the department's
commitment to more mathematics for a wider range of students,
members of the department have begun to challenge the linear progression, prerequisites-first, component of the layer-cake curriculum.
Perry Lanier's suggestion simply to drop PreAlgebra was a push in
this direction. As a result of removing this prerequisite, there was a
wider range of prior achievement (particularly arithmetic skill) in
Algebra 1 classes. In the mid-1990s, the decision to discontinue Informal Geometry created Geometry classrooms with a wider variance in
previous achievement. In addition, teachers at the high school have
stopped treating the progression Algebra 1, Geometry, Algebra 2, Pre-
Calculus as a sacrosanct, one-course-per-year progression. Starting
in the mid-1990s, if a student expressed interest in a continued study
of algebra, teachers sometimes supported the study of Algebra 2
immediately after Algebra 1; indeed they sometimes counseled students to study in this order. Thus, Algebra 2 teachers could no longer
count on student knowledge of Geometry. Finally, Discrete Mathematics and Statistics courses were added to give students alternatives to
a continuation up the layers of the curriculum. These courses enrolled
students with a range of mathematical backgrounds.

All of these practices pushed teachers to become more comfortable
teaching classes with a wider range in student achievement, skill, and
prior knowledge (in contrast to the typical categorization of students
surfaced by Horn, in press, that is connected to the sense that many
students cannot engage with mathematics beyond arithmetic). Finally,
the exploration and development of a functions-based approach to
Algebra 1 led, initially, to Algebra 2 classes with students who had
studied Algebra 1 in different ways. And, the continuation of this
approach into Algebra 2 and PreCalculus, and an emphasis on
teachers' role in setting curriculum (as described in the Calculus class
in Chapter 4) created more diverse PreCalculus and Calculus classes
(as Kelly Hodges and Sandy Callis refer to in their response to that
essay). The diversity of students' prior knowledge in these classes
built on and reinforced a comfort at Holt with variability in students'
prior experiences and skill levels.

The next essay is written about a student's experience of success
in Algebra 1. Integrating text in Sandy Callis's voice with that of her

student, Nick Miller, it raises important issues related to the participation of a group often overlooked in discussions of increasing access to mathematics – students with diagnosed special needs. It sheds important light on how the graphing calculator represented a crucial supporting element that enabled Nick to work around his diagnosed learning disabilities and participate successfully in Algebra 1 (when introduced from the perspective of Chapter 3). While not explicitly focused on teachers, or on the question of coping with a range of student arithmetic skill in Algebra 1, this essay suggests that one reason for changes in course-taking is that technology has helped students and teachers cope with variability in students' knowledge of prerequisite skills.

In their discussion, Marty Schnepp and Dave Hildebrandt speculate about other reasons that the Algebra 1 curriculum seems to have promoted interest in mathematics among students in the lower tracks. While agreeing that graphing-calculator technology and the linked representations it provides are useful, they also suggest that an important aspect of the course is that students are encouraged to explore their own ideas.

From an E to an A with the help of a graphing calculator

Sandra Callis with Nicolas Miller, Holt Public Schools

This essay was originally published in 1998. It appeared in the February issue of *Mathematics Teacher*, pp. 118–119. This version is based on an earlier draft of the paper.

Computers and calculators have transformed mathematics education. Thinking about the high school curriculum, they support making functions a more central part of the curriculum and they support student exploration. But, their potential is not limited to these areas; they can help improve access to mathematics for a previously underserved population of American high school students, those with learning disabilities.

In this essay, my student Nicolas Miller relates his experiences in an Algebra 1 class that used computer and calculators to study functions. His comments are taken from a process of writing and talking together. As his teacher, I reflect upon Nick's situation as well. His comments are indented; mine run to the edge of the page.

My learning disability sort of slows down my learning. It makes it harder for me to catch on, harder for me to put the effort forth, to work. It sucks. The way it makes me different from others is this. People can sit down and read one thing and be able to work on a test and get 90s and 100s, where I can sit down and read a book and have to read it six or seven times before I can get 50 percent. It doesn't click for me. Things don't work out.

Nick hated Algebra 1. After the first nine weeks, he was in danger of losing his athletic eligibility because of his low algebra grades. His inattention to course content and his inability to engage in class activities were earning him a failing grade, an E (the equivalent of an F in many schools). A typical day would involve speaking to Nick at least twice about not walking round the room and disrupting class discussions. Because of Nick's poor performance in all his classes, his student advocate (the term for special educators in our building) requested that responsibility for assignments fall solely on Nick's shoulders. The advocate wanted Nick to sink or swim, based on his own decisions, and not as a result of cajoling or controlling by his teachers. As one of Nick's teachers, I decided to let him make his own decisions about whether to pass or fail, and I assumed he would take responsibility for making sure he knew class expectations.

> At the beginning of the year, I really didn't care. I wanted to pass, but I wasn't putting any effort toward it. That's how math was the year before, too. Whenever I tried, it wouldn't work out. I didn't care what happened.

Soon, I began to see a dramatic change in Nick's behavior. I assumed the change resulted in part from Nick's desire to be eligible for the wrestling team but also from the decision to give Nick more responsibility. Whatever the reason, Nick started to engage in discussions, and, at times, his contributions revealed a genuine talent for mathematics. He seemed to be comfortable when working with functions. Nick's behavior became more mature. During class he was conscientious and responsible, often helping others who were struggling. Nick ended the year with an A in the class.

> The teachers were giving me a lot of pressure and saying that, you know, "You can do better; you've just got to put forth the time." They didn't understand that I was putting forth the time and I wasn't getting any better. So I asked for time [and] ... a little less pressure. The teachers let up a little bit, and I started relaxing around the work. That's when I started playing around with the calculators and started working over the problems [like those in Chapter 3]. I started getting more interested in it, how it worked. That started to bring up my grades.

Here's an example of Nick's insights as he became more engaged in Algebra 1. The class was struggling with the question of what the slope would be for a vertical line. Nick interjected, "There is no slope." When pushed for more information, Nick replied, "Well, let's say the independent variable is time; and the dependent variable is distance. That would be like going somewhere in no time. That doesn't make any sense." (For a description of this conversation from the perspective of Marty Schnepp who was in the room, see Chapter 15.) Nick's contributions were well articulated and powerful in other instances, as well.

Because of his dramatic turnaround, I invited Nick to speak to an Algebra 1 class the following year about what had led to the changes in his own behavior and attitude and his ultimate success. This was when I first learned that it wasn't so much what we had done in giving him responsibility for his grades. What he said gave the original impetus for writing this paper. Nick stated, "It was those calculators."

> I think that once we got into using the calculators a lot, Algebra 1 became more interesting, and we got to learn that, you know, when you add certain points, you can make the graphs. On the calculators, you can see it and learn how to use it. You work out the problems at the same time, so it's like you're learning three things at once. It's better than just learning one thing at a time and then you move on. It's quicker, and that makes it easier.
>
> It wasn't just numbers, it was the whole picture. So, it's like, with numbers, you got a frame for the puzzle, you got the outside, the lines. But when you use the graphing calculators and stuff, it fills the entire picture, and you can see the entire thing clearer.

The calculator allowed Nick to explore mathematics without the direct supervision of an adult. He was struggling at this point with his relationship with authority, and he felt the need to be in control of his choices and his learning. The calculator allowed Nick to discover properties of rules, tables, and graphs independently. Because of the ease with which the calculator performed operations, Nick's particular learning disability was circumvented, and that opened up the possibility for higher levels of thinking and reasoning. He was able to tap into his talents without the frustration of computation and trying to draw lines accurately.

In some schools, students with learning disabilities are pulled out of regular mathematics classes for repeated drill and practice on basic skills, which usually consist of paper-and-pencil computation. This had happened to Nick in the past. Nick's experiences in these classes had led him to feel extremely negative about mathematics. But using technology to explore mathematical ideas made the ideas more interesting and accessible to Nick. I believe this technology holds the promise of doing so for a wide range of students.

> I'd say I'm a hell of a lot better than I used to be. I could probably work things out if you gave me a problem, if I had a calculator. Math is, like, more of a visual thing. It's more of a hands-on with numbers and graphs and things.

How important are calculators?

Dave Hildebrandt and Marty Schnepp, Holt High School

DAVE HILDEBRANDT: I think this essay touches on a lot of the things that we're trying to do with the math program at Holt. The success of students who had not been successful before, I believe, is one of our key goals. I'm thinking about students I've had in my Algebra 1 class at the high school, kids who've struggled with a traditional, structured approach. Some of these kids came in angry and frustrated, exhibiting behavior problems that interfered with their learning. They certainly wouldn't be responsive, at that time, to being spoon-fed somebody else's algorithms for solving algebraic equations step by step. Some of these students were labeled as special education; others weren't, but probably could have been. Ask them to do my stuff my way, and I'd get a belligerent response. But give them a calculator and ask them to figure something out in an interesting context, and they were capable of coming up with something.

MARTY SCHNEPP: I know what you mean. But I'm concerned that, in describing Nick's experiences, and those of others like him, we might be overemphasizing the role of the calculator. The year Nick was in Algebra 1, I joined the class second semester to team-teach with Sandy as a part of a PDS project. When I met Nick, I remember being surprised to find he had been identified as having a learning disability. I only recall seeing a kid who could piece together a connected, "big picture" explanation of just about any question that caught his interest. There were times when Nick did what Nick wanted to do, so maturity issues still arose occasionally. But, most of the time he would latch hold of an idea, work very hard to understand it, and then articulate his understanding to the rest of the class in profoundly insightful ways. His transformation from an E grade to an A grade was certainly not simply a matter of relieving his computational anxiety with a calculator. The calculator's role was enhancing his ability to simultaneously explore the tabular, graphical, and symbolic representations of functions related to situations; but I don't think that was the only thing that inspired him. Sandy let students take the time they need to explore their thinking, and I think this really helped Nick. I don't want to underestimate other things that Sandy did.

DAVE: I agree. This essay presents a student who has been frustrated with arithmetic manipulation. Nick's comments about algebra before he talks about the graphing calculator ("It doesn't click for me. Things don't work out." "I didn't care what happened.") are similar to comments I've heard from my students. Math is something "they just can't get" or that "never makes sense." Yet with the introduction of alternate forms of representations of mathematical patterns, students started to make sense for themselves of those things they just couldn't get before. A key change in the way we teach algebra is moving from teaching students' algorithms for solving problems to teaching them to use representations that they can use to solve problems.

MARTY: I think Sandy and Nick's essay is a great commentary on the possibilities of what students can do with that sort of change. I too have seen kids, not just students with learning disabilities, get turned on to math, while in a course using our Algebra 1 curriculum. Their reasons may differ from Nick's, but they somehow connect to the problems we have written and then demonstrate mathematical abilities that were previously untapped. Making students' ideas the center of instruction can open up students' minds and create a willingness to participate. Kelly Hodges has sometimes talked about feeling that students in the different tracks we have are different in how they deal with having questions about the math they are studying. In her view, students who are in lower-track classes just can't let go of questions they have, and as a result can get frustrated, if their questions are not addressed by teachers. I think Nick was that sort of kid. I imagine him sitting in a course focused on rote skills, which are difficult for him because of his disability. He has mathematical questions that bother him. But, by the time he formulates his questions, the teacher is long since off to another skill *and* isn't particularly ready to engage his question. In that kind of class, Nick would appear slow and dumb.

DAVE: I understand what you are saying about giving Nick time to develop his questions and taking time to understand what they are, but I also think that a key element of the class is thinking about patterns and that the calculators help a lot with patterns. A lot of students who haven't had a lot of success academically and don't have a lot of confidence in themselves are good at finding patterns. A lot of what goes on in our algebra classes is about finding patterns, using whatever tools we can. For students who struggle with written expression and/or calculation skills, generating a graphical or tabular representation to search for patterns sometimes represents the first step in awakening mathematical inquiry.

MARTY: Regardless of what exactly makes the difference, like Mike and Craig in their response to an earlier essay, I think this is probably the course we as a department are most proud of; much of what we have tried to do with other courses grew out of our experiences with kids like Nick in Algebra 1. I think we speak so highly of Algebra 1 because of what it allows us to see in students; we have anecdotes about interesting or complex solutions lower-track students constructed. We can all point to students who have been drawn in and ended up in PreCalculus or other advanced courses, after having gotten excited by mathematics in Algebra 1 at the high school or junior high school (like Carolyn and Ryan in one of the upcoming essays). For most of us, this course gave our first examples of students empowered by non-lecture, discussion-based instruction using the function-based materials. Personally, the language of the NCTM *Standards* came alive for me when I saw what Sandy was able to elicit from students. But, we all know the changes to the Algebra 1 and subsequent course curricula do not represent a panacea. I find my Algebra 1 classes still have a significant number of course withdraws and failing grades. Certainly not as many as I used to have lecturing straight out of a textbook, but enough that I still want to make changes to try and reach more students. I also wonder about kids who found some success with direct instruction, and who are very uncomfortable when asked to think through a problem and discuss or write about their thinking. A few of our students find this too daunting a task and shut down, and I have seen others (particularly in more advanced courses) who are angry about having to think relationally and choose not to engage in the course as much as they might have if they felt more comfortable (possibly Russ in Candy Hamilton's essay is an example of such a student). And I wonder how students like Nick will develop arithmetic and algebraic manipulation skills. My main point, though, is to suggest that maybe Nick, and perhaps Sandy, are putting too much stress on the calculator here. I think other aspects of Sandy's instruction are at least as important!

Chapter 9

Standard-track classes

As the numbers at the beginning of this section suggest, at Holt over the last decade, more students in lower-track math classes have been experiencing success, and then going on for further study. Nick's experience is the experience of a particular student; he cannot represent a range of students. Unlike Nick, many of the students in Algebra 1 do not have diagnosed learning disabilities. And, while some are strongly affiliated with school activities, like Nick with wrestling, other students in Algebra 1 are less involved in school activities and seem to care less about their grades. But, as Marty and Dave's discussion reminds us, a wide range of students have gone on from Algebra 1 to the study of further mathematics at the high school.

So far, the picture seems quite rosy. Changes in teaching practice have supported an increase in the amount of mathematics studied by students, particularly those who previously studied less. It would seem that changing teaching practices and enlarging student participation in advanced coursework would be an unalloyed gain. Yet, opening up access to advanced coursework and opening up space for student initiative inside a class can further complicate the job of teaching. Advanced coursework like Algebra 2 or PreCalculus can assume demands previously more typical of lower-track classes, like General Math or Algebra 1.

The next essay suggests that, as a wider range of students continues on to further study of mathematics, there are new tensions for students and teachers to manage in more advanced courses. Not only must teachers manage a range of skill backgrounds, but students also differ in the degree to which they connect with school and are invested in grades and homework. This may pose challenges for teachers of advanced courses used to only having students who do their homework and who are intending to go to college. As a result, over the years, there have been important debates at Holt about the practice of having "honors" sections of Algebra 2 and PreCalculus. Some teachers offer "honors" options in non-honors classes and would like to remove the special designation from honors classes, but others argue for the value of honors classes.

And there are tensions for students to manage as well. How do students deal with differences among them in commitment to academic study, or in the ways in which they like to work as students?

Researchers working with junior high schools and high schools argue that students bring very strong frames to such questions. These researchers suggest that student social groups (with names like: jocks, burnouts, smokers, nerds ...), sometimes affiliated with social class, often organize how students see themselves and others (see Eckert, 1989 for this general point). For example, at Holt, students in an Algebra 1 class described the class as predominantly "smokers," with many "preppies," a few "nerds," and one "stoner" (see Chazan, 2000, Chapter 2 for a description of this study and of the relationship of these groups to lower-track mathematics teaching). They described strong tensions between preppies and smokers.

As course-taking at Holt has changed, students, especially in classes like Algebra 2, find themselves grouped together in ways that are unfamiliar. Preppy (school-affiliated) students from the honors track may now find themselves sharing an advanced mathematics classroom with smokers, or students who are less committed to academic life. Students who affiliate with school, and who are usually cooperative with their teachers, may change their attitudes toward a class when they find themselves enrolled with students from other peer groups whom they consider academically unprepared or lacking appropriate attitudes toward homework and schooling. This can pose a daunting challenge for teachers who make classroom interaction an integral part of their teaching.

In the following essay, excerpted from a paper written for a doctoral course, Candy Hamilton, an educational psychologist, complicates the emerging picture of student experience by illustrating how students and their beliefs play an important role in the way classroom practices play out. Her essay reminds us that two students experiencing the exact same instruction may perceive things quite differently. The very practices that enable some students to participate more effectively may lead others to disengage, or may block their participation. In their discussion, Kelly Hodges and Adam Kelly take up this question, but from the perspective of the teacher. For example, as both Jill and Russ's teacher, Kelly indicates the challenges she experienced in helping them each contribute to the class environment she sought to construct.

Students' views of mathematical conversation

Candy Hamilton, Michigan State University doctoral candidate

This essay is excerpted from a paper – titled "Understanding issues of identity, belonging, and motivation in mathematical discourse" – that was given at the 1998 annual meeting of the American Educational Research Association in San Diego, CA.

This essay presents a view inside an Algebra 2 classroom at Holt High School as the teacher, Kelly Hodges, changed her teaching practice and emphasized whole-group discussion. The focus of this essay, however, is not on Kelly but on two of her students, Jill and Russ (these are pseudonyms), and how they experienced this instructional change. In particular, the essay seeks to portray differences in student involvement with the more exploratory, less conventional approach to learning that Kelly engendered and to reflect on the very different attitudes these students developed about the value of different components of whole-class discussion.

In Algebra 2, Kelly's class had been working with families of functions (e.g., linear, quadratic, exponential, rational, and others) and adding, subtracting, multiplying, and dividing functions from these families. I've chosen one lesson from which to draw examples of Jill and Russ's participation in whole-group discussion. In this lesson, students were finding that when they divided two linear functions, the resulting function sometimes had holes or gaps in its graph (see Figure 9.1).

These holes in the graphs, as the students referred to them, serve as an interesting metaphor for discontinuities in these students' experiences with mathematics. In talking about their experiences, students from Kelly's class noted that several aspects of this class were different from what they were accustomed to. They mentioned using calculators to graph functions and view their tables; not using a textbook, which most students liked because many math textbooks are dry; and doing unexpected activities, like experiments in class and writing essays. Kelly's approach, which emphasized exploration and justification of mathematics, was unlike the more customary method of copying the teacher's steps to solve routine problems, memorizing definitions and procedures, then practicing on large sets of homework problems (see Table 9.1). Of particular interest to me in students' talk were references to the messiness of class discussions and the lack of a traditional lecture–memorize pattern of learning.

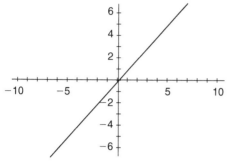

Removable discontinuity at
$x = 0$ in $f(x) = x^2/x$

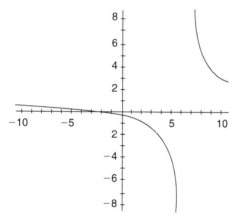

Non-removable discontinuity
at $x = 6$ in $f(x) = (x+1)/(x-6)$

Figure 9.1 Two kinds of discontinuity.

While there were many changes in Kelly's practice that students noticed, I will focus on whole-class discussions – particularly those segments where more "exploratory," in the words of Barnes (1976), or, what I like to call, "rough-draft" talk occurs. Barnes suggests that this talk, unlike the more traditional lecture or "final-draft" talk, includes hesitations, rephrasings, false starts, expressions of tentativeness, and a low level of explicitness. How do students make sense of exploratory and final-draft talk, particularly within a subject matter that has traditionally been about right answers? Why do some students participate differently in these different kinds of whole-group discussion? The two students discussed in this essay offer varying levels of participation in these two kinds of talk and contrasting conceptions of self, mathe-

Table 9.1 Discontinuities for students

Prior experience	Reform experience ("discontinuity")
Curriculum	
Standard, district-issued textbook	Teacher-developed worksheets
Hand-drawn graphs and tables	Graphing-calculator technology
Practice sets of procedures and discrete skills	Real-world, problem-centered assignments and projects
Pattern of teaching/learning	
Teacher lectures	Teacher as "guide"
Student memorizes	Students explore mathematical ideas and patterns
Conception of mathematics	
Absolutist	Social constructive
Math presented as a set of pre-determined facts & procedures; a fixed body of knowledge where "doing" math is manipulating numbers	Math viewed as "fallible, changing and like any other body of knowledge, the product of human inventiveness"
(Romberg, 1992)	(Ernest, 1991)

matics, teaching, and learning. They illustrate some of the ways in which students engaged in the mathematical activities and discourse of this classroom.

Jill: an exploratory participant

Jill comes across as bright and self-assured, though perhaps to her peers at times her self-assurance may feel like cockiness. Jill sat at the front of the class, closest to where Kelly, her teacher, often stood. As a primary participant during whole-class discussion, she, unlike some others, seemed to be paying attention the entire time. She was quite willing to speak up and did not hesitate when asked to explain something to the class. Jill was capable of getting excellent grades, but her teachers in other subjects described her as a B student. They referred to her as a "good thinker," usually the best in her class. Though she did well on tests, incomplete and missing assignments lowered her overall grades.

Jill aligned herself with others who participated in class discussions, although they were not necessarily the high achievers in the class. When the class broke into small groups, she often worked alone. It appeared she did not belong to any of the social groups in her math class. She hung out at the local convenience store during lunch with what she called the alternative group; between classes, she was generally alone. When talking about her closest friends, she referred to them (and herself) as outcasts.

Jill's ideas about learning and teaching resonated with the non-traditional teaching practices in Kelly's room. Jill enjoyed the class and praised Kelly for the ways in which she encouraged her students to explain their thinking and see math in new ways. Kelly's pedagogical style of exploration paralleled Jill's view of learning and life as self-discovery. In Jill's opinion, traditional math instruction and assessment stifled her creativity.

Speaking in class during the exploratory phase afforded Jill occasion to speak to her peers, which seemed important to her. In other classes, she had fewer such opportunities. In Algebra 2, however, her eager, strong voice was welcomed by her teacher and some, though not all, students. Jill seemed to believe that Kelly cared about her. Jill treated Kelly as a friend, someone whom she could trust and talk to on a personal level.

Jill seemed to show signs of mathematical power. Moreover, she spoke about learning algebra as enjoyable, displaying a positive attitude toward learning mathematics that math educators hope to foster in all students.

> [In this class, it was important to know] how to figure something out for yourself. [Our teacher promoted] independent learning. I got a lot of practice and ideas on how to discover something mathematically for myself, which never happened before. I had fun with it, too. I enjoyed being able to do that. Just because it's math class doesn't mean that everything has to be formulas of right and wrong. There is a little bit of work that you have to make individually.... And that is just such a great principle to teach somebody – how to figure out something for themselves ... because we're not going to have a teacher standing next to us for the rest of our lives going, "Jill, that's incorrect." It's really important to know how to check something on your own, how to draw your own conclusions, especially mathematically. I mean, you have to learn how to draw your conclusions in other classes. Why not math?

Here is an example of Jill's participation in a whole-class discussion centered on review. Note that Jill is the first to respond to the teacher's question.

KELLY: Is the [discontinuity at] 6 a removable kind or a non-removable kind?

JILL: It's non-removable.

KELLY: Removable means fixable. Could you just fill it in? Is it just a little hole that you could fill in or does it have to do with the shape of the graph?

SCOTT: It's a chunk.

JILL: It's the shape of the whole thing –

Two or more other students jump in to give an answer but Jill retains the floor.

JILL: If it's removable, you just remove, like, just a point.

KELLY: Right.

SCOTT: It's a big chunk.

JILL: Yeah, it's got to go through infinity.

In this case, even when other students attempted to deliver answers, Jill persisted in being a primary speaker. More generally, she rarely hesitated to throw out answers or give her hypotheses, and she was usually the first to volunteer an answer when others remained silent. Her persistence allowed her to prevail, even when several students attempted to speak at the same time. Jill enjoyed being able to argue her positions, and resisted attempts by classmates who tried to discourage her from participating. For example, once when Kelly posed a challenging problem to the class, there was silence until Jill announced loudly, "I have an absolutely wild guess." Immediately, another student told her, "You're not supposed to give wild guesses." She replied, "I can answer if I want to," and then proceeded to give her guess, which Kelly wrote on the board.

But this pattern of participation did not hold for all forms of class discussion. During the more "final-draft" phase, Jill tended to participate less. She may have opted out of this phase of the conversation because she was satisfied with her participation and the understanding that she achieved during exploratory talk. Or it could have been that in this phase she felt less freedom to figure things out for herself.

Russ: a final-draft participant

Russ had recently transferred to Holt High School from a strictly run, private school. Believing that attaining high grades was important, Russ viewed himself as an A student. His participation and success in honors classes, such as English and History, bore this out. Algebra 2 was a different story, though. Unlike Jill, Russ did not participate freely throughout the class period, but instead took most of his turns during the wrap-up and review phases. While Jill selected her seat up front, Russ preferred the back of the room.

During exploratory talk in whole-class discussions, his attention was sporadic. Talkative classmates easily distracted him. He normally had his worksheet out but did not often attempt to solve the problems when Kelly asked the class to graph something. Sometimes, after having had his head down for several minutes, Russ would look up and mutter something like, "What are we doing? I don't get this. I hate math." Often he would begin to copy what was on the board, but once he realized he did not understand it, he would complain and raise his hand to get Kelly's attention. If he thought Kelly's responses to his questions were insufficient, he might pout or fold his arms and put his head down. Or, he might turn to his peers; but if they could not help him, he would easily get frustrated. During small-group discussion, Russ usually worked with Brian, Jon, and Ana, but they typically had a very hard time initiating and sustaining focus.

Russ was openly critical of certain aspects of Algebra 2. He faulted Kelly for not punishing students who misbehaved and for not providing direct answers about how to solve math problems. Having been raised in a disciplined home environment and educated at strict private schools, Russ expected and wanted more order, discipline, and control on the part of his teacher.

Russ seemed to think that his Algebra 2 classmates were lazy and uninterested in good grades; listening to these students seemed to be frustrating for him. It was almost as if Russ did not see his classmates as qualified to speak about mathematical ideas. Unlike Jill, who participated wholeheartedly during exploratory talk, Russ was heard only when exploration came to a close and class talk took on more of a final-draft character. At this point, Russ's verbal participation generally took the form of asking questions to confirm procedures. More often than not, in contrast to Jill's interaction with the whole class, his comments were directed only at Kelly. Though he acknowledged and valued his own intellect and insight when solving problems, he expected the teacher to play a significant role in telling him what he needed to know.

It's interesting to note that Russ's experience in an honors American History class at Holt, where discourse among students was also emphasized, was quite different. In that setting, Russ valued and enjoyed class discussion in which students were seen as sources of knowledge and authority. Perhaps he engaged with his classmates there because, being honor students, he felt they had worthwhile contributions to make.

And yet Russ alluded several times to aspects of his classroom experience that he considered "good ideas in the making." He believed that Kelly challenged him to know more math because she demanded his understanding of the process, not just numerical answers. Russ commended the ways in which his knowledge was assessed. Writing math essays rather than just giving numerical answers appealed to his desire to understand an idea at more than a superficial level. Being able to communicate what he knew and explain to others how he came to an answer was an experience he clearly valued.

I do think that I've learned more in that area – on learning how everything connects to each other a little better. Because before it was just get the answers right, so I'd memorize the answers to things, and then the next day I wouldn't remember how I did it. This class, at least I remember *how* I did some things.

Turning to the lesson on rational functions, here is an example of Russ's participation during the review and wrap-up phases.

Russ is copying what Kelly has written on the board.

JON: What are discontinuities?

KELLY: Holes, basically. We talked about that there were two kinds. One is the kind that we're seeing right here where the graph goes like that. [Points to graph of $y_3 = (x+1)/(x-6)$.] It's coming up toward 6, on this graph. In fact, it goes like this. [Kelly traces the graph with her hand.] And right at 6 on your table there's an error.

RUSS: Oh, this is that rule thing.

KELLY: Right. Anytime you get an error, you're gonna end up with a . . . On your table, you're gonna end up with a hole in your graph. And those are the things we're calling discontinuities because as you're drawing along that graph, you have to stop and pick up your pencil and start all over again in order to make the whole graph. OK? So, we had two different kinds of those actually. One was this kind –

In this segment, Russ acknowledges the mathematical idea being reviewed. His purpose seems to be one of checking his understanding. But, as Kelly continued reviewing concepts discussed earlier, Russ grew impatient. Once he finished copying what Kelly had written on the board, he started chatting with his neighbor and then looking at a magazine.

The conversation moved from discontinuities to asymptotes. Russ began to attend as Kelly wrote "asymptote" on the board.

SUSAN: What's the definition of asymptote?

KELLY: Let's say it like this [*writing on board as she speaks*]. It's an imaginary line –

JILL: Is there a vertical one also?

KELLY: Yes. [*still writing*]

JOEY: It's the equator.

KELLY: [*talks as she writes*] the graph gets closer and closer to but can't cross –

RUSS: Why not? Wouldn't it eventually. I mean, that's sort of –

JILL: In order for it to cross that point, it has to go through infinity positive and negative. Infinity is never-ending. There is no way for it to happen.

RUSS: I've always understood that if something has got an angle that eventually it crosses the line unless it's parallel to it. This thing isn't parallel to it so then won't it cross it?

ISABEL: No, because when you have a line that's straight,

RUSS: Yeah, so . . .

ISABEL: That's diagonal, that's true. But this one curves around. Right? [*She turns to Kelly for help.*]

KELLY: This isn't a straight line. It's got a very, very slight curve in it, so every time it looks like it's coming closer to the line, it curves a little. It comes closer to the line, it curves a little, curves a little, curves a little, curves a little, and it never gets flat. It curves smaller and smaller never touching.

Because Russ was not paying attention earlier, he had missed the class discussion about curved lines and why they never crossed at the asymptote. It was at this point, when his teacher was summarizing the concept, that Russ began to pay attention and realize that he did not understand. His question about parallel lines would have fit well in an earlier exploratory phase of the discussion.

Summary

For many students, Kelly's class was discontinuous with their prior experiences of math class. Before entering this functions-based algebra classroom, these students had experienced traditional mathematics for approximately nine years. They had also developed views of learning in school. Students' ideas about subject matter, teaching, and learning form their expectations and values, which, in turn, influence their decisions about becoming involved in certain tasks (Wigfield & Eccles, 1992). Thus, when faced with changes in the curriculum, pedagogy, and assessment of mathematics in Kelly's class, students either welcomed or resisted the reform-oriented practices, depending on their epistemological beliefs and values regarding how math should be taught and learned.

Jill wanted learning to be an act of personal discovery; it makes sense that she would participate in exploratory talk where math was presented with less certainty. Jill believed that meaningful learning involved taking a journey, taking risks, forming an opinion, and not just memorizing fact. With his more conventional notions of teaching and learning mathematics, Russ participated when the math was being presented with certainty and fixedness. Russ believed that all teachers should have control – over both students and content. Meaningful learning takes place when the teacher is clear and explicit about what is to be learned.

Social relationships are also an important aspect of student experience in the classroom (see Erickson & Schultz, 1991; Eckert, 1989). In traditional math classrooms, students need only pay attention to their teacher and perhaps the textbook. In a discourse-oriented classroom, students must listen to themselves and to each other. How does this added dimension influence how students participate?

In Kelly's class, in addition to his views of how mathematics should be taught and learned, Russ's conceptions regarding the academic status of his classmates led him to see exploratory talk as inappropriate and unwelcome. In contrast, Jill's desire to relate socially and intellectually to her classmates, and her view of teaching and learning as exploratory, shaped her view of Algebra 2 as a safe and inviting learning environment, and led her to engage in exploratory talk, but to tend to withdraw during final-draft talk.

Examining these two students leads me to wonder: How can teachers help students see the importance and relevance of both exploratory and final draft talk?

Challenges of managing students' participation in classroom conversation

Kelly Hodges and Adam Kelly, Holt Public Schools

KELLY HODGES: Candy ends with a really interesting question about influencing students' views of classroom talk, one that deserves thought. But, as the teacher of this class, in addition to engaging Russ and Jill's perspectives on classroom talk, I had other immediate concerns: How do I manage what students do in my class given their perspectives on classroom talk? Candy points out that Jill has a view of learning that is personal and exploratory in nature. In classroom discourse, I attempt to highlight the personal and exploratory nature of all of mathematics. It seems like there is a good fit, but here were dilemmas for me in managing Jill's participation in what Candy calls the exploratory talk, let alone her diminished participation in final-draft talk. On the one hand, her approach to learning meshed nicely with the view of mathematics I wished to develop. Her abilities – to conjecture, to model, and to justify her claims – were traits that I wanted to foster in all of my students. Consequently, it was important to support these behaviors, even when others tried to stifle them. On the other hand, it was precisely this kind of confidence that could fuel an uncomfortable relationship for Jill with her peers. By recognizing her contributions, I ran the risk of further exacerbating the painful rejection

Jill sometimes felt at the hands of her peers. When I stifled or tempered her interactions, she would withdraw, finding no support for her own ways of knowing and learning.

ADAM KELLY: I understand. I've also struggled with the notion of "mathematical power" and how to support it. I approach new topics with the attitude that we can all discover something together. I try to create an environment where students are encouraged to offer ideas and clarify beliefs on the board or overhead. Students are told not to worry if their ideas are correct or not. They are encouraged to speak up. It seems like you are struggling with what happens when students *do* speak up.

KELLY: In Jill's case, she did little explicitly to support others in the classroom. Managing the dilemmas associated with students like Jill is complex. It requires careful balancing of many things: my goals for content and for social development; my responsibilities to individual students and the class as a whole; and my need to provide a classroom that is comfortable for students from a traditional mathematics background, yet stimulating for those open to a new kind of mathematics experience.

ADAM: I feel it is very important to hold students accountable for all aspects of the discussion of the mathematics at hand. It seems that this is a challenge with both Jill, and perhaps even more, with Russ.

KELLY: Russ was certainly a different case. He held an absolutist, right-or-wrong view of mathematics. He was very successful in traditional classes, and they meshed well with his view of learning as getting the right answers. A mathematics class not based on learning the right way to do a given set of problems caused him considerable conflict. He saw the exploratory talk as disorderly, rather than as a critical phase in developing student ability to engage in whole-class discussion. When I allow this type of interaction, he was confused about what he should be attending to and assumed this was because I lost control of the class. When he felt this way, I had to manage the resulting behavior. Candy's last selection from the class transcript, in which Russ is participating in the review, is a revealing example. I don't know how you read the tone in the transcript, but I remember at the time feeling that he was challenging my mathematical authority. By referring back to what he's "always understood," I don't think he was just checking his understanding of intersecting lines. I think he was drawing on the authority of all his previous teachers to challenge my statement that the graph could draw closer and closer to the asymptote without touching it. My response reads to me as uncharacteristically direct, even for a summing-up phase of a lesson. While I might typically have responded to this sort of question by a student by encouraging other students to try to elaborate, with Russ I felt compelled to defend myself by demonstrating that I did in fact have an answer to his challenge. I tell him directly that this "thing" isn't a straight line. I don't think my response in this case was necessarily helpful in clarifying the point for Russ, and so it was probably not very helpful in restoring his faith in my mathematical knowledge either. And although this exploratory approach had not been very effective in working with Russ, stepping away from this particular inter-action, I still believe it is an important facet of mathematics to rep-resent to students. By "giving in" and telling him an answer in this case, I feel like I justified his complaint that things would be better if I would just tell everyone how to do every problem. At the end of the year, I was sad that I had made so little progress in helping Russ explore new ways of thinking about mathematics. He left in June having changed little over the year in his acceptance of exploratory phases in mathematics. He left my class exclusively a consumer of other people's mathematics; I'm concerned that he left my class too focused on how other people think about mathematics and didn't give himself a chance to explore and come up with his own tenta-tive conclusions. Several questions arise for me. What is the best approach for a teacher of a reformed mathematics class when faced with students like Russ? Is it reasonable to say that, for some stu-dents, a less rigid, more experiential classroom is actually unsuit-able? After numerous conversations with Russ about the purpose of this shift in the nature of mathematics class, I saw little change in his willingness to engage. Is it fair on my part to ask him to fundamentally shift his view of the world in order to meet the expectations of a mathematics class?

ADAM: Important questions!

Chapter 10

Advanced coursework

The first essay in this section described Nick's experience of success in Algebra 1. This experience allowed him to proceed up the curricular layer cake. The second essay described tensions in more advanced coursework that can be exacerbated as students who have in the past been unsuccessful continue up the layer-cake curriculum. The description of Russ and Jill's experiences in this last essay alerts us to potential tensions that can be, in part, a by-product of having greater heterogeneity in advanced coursework.

The next essay picks up on one connection between the first two essays. It focuses on the experiences of two students, Carolyn and Ryan, who in middle school were not deemed as talented in mathematics. After getting excited about Algebra 1, these students took two math courses a year and as seniors were able to take Calculus at Holt High School and advanced courses in Michigan State University's mathematics department. They took semester-long courses in Abstract Algebra and Linear Algebra at Michigan State University, courses typically taken by math majors in their sophomore and junior years. Based on their interest in algebra and their willingness to work hard and to persevere in the face of the potential for poor grades in a class for which they did not have the prerequisites, they convinced a university mathematician that the prerequisites for Abstract Algebra should not be enforced. The story does not yield a simple moral; their experiences at the university were mixed and they put their mathematical studies on hold.

Carolyn and Ryan's interest in mathematics can be traced to experiencing teaching of the kind described in the first section of this book. But their story is an unusual story. These students are not meant to be representative of students in advanced coursework at Holt; many students in the advanced classes come to them having always done well in math and in school. However, this story serves to flesh out a picture of the depth of the department's commitment to providing a wider range of students with access to more mathematics and to its deliberations about what a phrase like "mathematical power" (NCTM, 2000) might mean. Perhaps it is the atypical nature of their story that allows it to pose important questions for discussion.

In this essay, Sandy Callis tracks the students' experiences in mathematics classes, while the students comment on the courses they took and how each course influenced future course-taking and their understandings of mathematics. Their comments suggest that changes in classroom practice described in the first section of the book played a role in their course-taking and the value that they came to place on mathematics (in line with the "New goals for students" articulated in NCTM, 1989, pp. 5–8).

Their comments also highlight how different areas of mathematics and different approaches to mathematics have differential appeal. Finally, their comments and Sandy's perspective on their experiences ask us to reconsider relationships between what some might call "abstract" and "contextualized" mathematics and student motivation (for related points, see Nemirovsky, 1996 and Wilensky, 1991). Intriguingly, part of what attracted Carolyn and Ryan to mathematics is not its utility in the world around us, but their understanding that mathematics has content of its own, that mathematics is "all about something," as elusive as that something may be.

In their discussion of the essay, Kellie Huhn and Marty Schnepp use both Carolyn and Ryan's willingness to pursue advanced mathematics *and* their negative feelings about their experience at the university to consider what the phrase "mathematical power" might mean. In this discussion, their dilemmas involve student curiosity and interest, as well as their knowledge of canonical mathematics.

Developing an interest in mathematics

Sandra Callis with Ryan Mosley and Carolyn Ososkie, Holt Public Schools

This essay began with Carolyn's conjecture in her Algebra 2 class. Together with Sandy Callis, she wrote up her conjecture for publication in an NCTM publication. While this first version was not published, the conversations around the writing of the first piece, together with Carolyn and Ryan's desire to study more algebra, led Sandy to develop this version with them once they had taken collegiate-level mathematics.

Mathematics department faculty members from a number of colleges (e.g., on our local scene, Hill, 2004) have expressed concern that students are not entering college with the "basic algebra facts" necessary for success in a college curriculum. For some mathematicians, the current mathematics education reforms (chiefly NCTM, 1989) are seen as partially responsible for this situation because they focus on conceptual understanding without a strong foundation on prerequisite skills, like the capacity to calculate with number and manipulate algebraic symbols. The implication is that current reforms in mathematics education will be harmful to the society at large by reducing the number of people in our society who possess a high degree of mathematical knowledge. In this essay, as someone who has worked with middle school and high school students, I offer a different perspective.

It seems to me that my colleagues who are mathematicians often view success with mathematics as solely a function of ability and previous preparation. I think this overlooks other dimensions, like students' opportunities to interact with abstract mathematics and their motivation to study mathematics. If students are to appreciate abstract mathematics as valuable and interesting, as teachers, we cannot continually postpone their interaction with abstract mathematics until they gain the seemingly necessary skills; we cannot continually ask our students to wait until they have mastered skills to do creative mathematical work. We have to give students experiences early on that will help them discover that mathematics can be of interest. If we do so, we may well help students recognize previously unidentified talents in mathematics. And, in so doing, instead of having harmed our society, we will have served our students and society well. But, there is a catch! If we engage high school students with mathematics as a practice of exploring mathematical questions and making and justifying statements about mathematical objects, students may no longer appreciate university coursework that treats mathematics as a series of skills to be mastered and not a set of questions to be explored. Such coursework may not nourish the very reasons they came to study mathematics.

For me, this argument is not a hypothetical one, but is grounded in experience. In this essay, I recount the experiences of two of my high school students, Carolyn Ososkie and Ryan Mosley. Carolyn and Ryan were denied access at the middle school level to the honors track in mathematics. At the junior high school – in Carolyn's case – and the high school – in Ryan's case, changed instructional patterns helped them both identify an interest in mathematics. In these mathematics classes, Carolyn and Ryan had a chance to think about abstract objects, operations done to these objects, and statements (conjectures or theorems) that can then be made about the interactions of these objects and operations. Carolyn and Ryan each had a chance to articulate their own statements and provide rationales for them. These instructional shifts led them to pursue an interest in mathematics, taking two mathematics courses each year in grades 10 through 12, including Abstract Algebra and Linear Algebra at Michigan State University during their senior year.

Based on a set of interviews I did with Carolyn and Ryan, starting from when Carolyn was in my Algebra 2 class and continuing through their high school years, I begin by describing some of Carolyn and Ryan's early experiences with mathematics. To give a flavor of the type of activity that engaged them, I then outline a conjecture and supporting argument prepared by Carolyn during her sophomore year in high school. Around this example, I argue that, beyond basic skills, Carolyn and Ryan learned in their junior high and high school mathematics courses how to explore and conjecture and see how mathematical facts are developed. These opportunities challenged them and allowed them access to a wider mathematical culture than high school students often have access to: how mathematicians create new strategies and persuade others that the new strategies are acceptable and warranted.

Beyond challenging us to consider the role of preparatory skills and mathematical activity, this story also raises questions about real-world contexts in mathematics education. An important aspect of the current reform movement, something we do a lot of at Holt, involves the use of problems in context, rather than mathematical problems posed solely in symbolic terms. Being able to see abstract mathematical objects in the contextualized problems tackled in class motivated Carolyn and Ryan. While at Holt we try to foster student motivation by presenting mathematical activities in context, this example illustrates that students are able to create conjectures and strategies about mathematical objects that transcend a particular context. When larger mathematical questions are worded in terms of mathematical objects (such as the example discussed below, "Where will a function and its inverse intersect?"), students gain experience with symbolic manipulation. They are learning to deal with larger mathematical issues and to practice mathematical habits of mind. The experiences of these two students illustrate that curricula designed to be accessible to all students can also nurture the abilities of students with mathematical interests.

Up through junior high

Prior to junior high school, Carolyn felt positive about mathematics.

> I always liked math, even when I was little. My dad was a math teacher for a while, and I would take his problems, some from his easy classes like Algebra 1, and I would play around with them in 4th or 5th grade.

Ryan, too, found mathematics accessible.

> Math was just kind of part of school. It was just what I did. I didn't think much about it. It was the easy part of school. Reading and writing, the English stuff, was hard for me, so math was the easy part.

Ryan's middle school experience was, as he put it, "pretty traditional stuff." He continued to do well, although he was denied access to the honors curriculum in Holt Public Schools for reasons unknown to him and undocumented by the school.

Carolyn, in contrast, struggled in middle school mathematics classes. She was unable to negotiate success in a way that would have given her access to the honors curriculum.

> I couldn't get anything above a C in sixth grade. The teacher gave us 60 problems or so to do every night. [In a situation like that], I don't give myself time to check my work and to see what the numbers mean. I don't go over my work. I just did the work to get it done. So I messed up a lot. I'd do stupid mistakes that I shouldn't have done, and I couldn't go back and check on it, because I didn't have time. So I did really bad on all my homework assignments.
>
> Seventh grade was easy. My 6th-grade teacher wouldn't let me get to a high class. She didn't think I was ready, because I got a C ... but 7th grade I did a lot better. We took a test at the beginning of the year to get into honors classes. One of my friends and I either almost passed the test or just barely passed, I'm not too sure. We weren't accepted into the honors classes because there were too many people enrolled in them.

Eighth grade continued as 7th grade had for Carolyn. She studied general mathematics concepts and found the class undemanding. Both Carolyn and Ryan experienced general mathematics as easy, and they were quite successful.

A different sort of math class

Carolyn and Ryan's experiences diverged during 9th grade at Holt Junior High School. Both took Algebra 1. But Carolyn's class, taught by Kellie Huhn, followed the functions-based approach outlined in Chapter 3, introducing her to changes in standard mathematics classroom practice. Ryan's experience remained more conventional, as he was enrolled in a traditional skills-based course. Carolyn's reaction to her experience was very favorable.

When I got into Algebra 1 last year, I found I could work on my own and look at problems differently. That's probably when I started doing my best, because I could work and teach myself so that I really understood it. I wasn't just doing the work to get it done.

Her interest in mathematics renewed, Carolyn signed up sophomore year for both Geometry and Algebra 2. I was her teacher in Algebra 2.

Ryan experienced his Algebra 1 class quite differently. He saw it as "pretty traditional" and, as always, quite easy. When it came time to sign up for high school classes, a random comment influenced his initial thinking.

When I was in junior high and we were signing up for classes, one of the teachers mentioned how some kids would take two, Geometry and Algebra 2. She wasn't talking to me; I just overheard her. She said how students were crazy that did that. She didn't understand how someone could take two math classes. So I just signed up for one.

Ryan signed up for Geometry and was assigned to a class that I taught. But after a few days of school, he decided to sign up for Algebra 2 as well.

When I got to high school the next year, I really found that after just being in my class for a day or so I wanted to take more math and not other classes, because I was enjoying it so much. I went down to the office and signed up for Algebra 2 in addition to the Geometry. In the back of my mind, I also knew that I wanted to take Calculus before leaving high school.

I taught his Algebra 2 class as well. Ryan soon discovered that he liked the Geometry much better than the Algebra.

Geometry is a lot more visual. I can picture an object easily. Talking about other dimensions was interesting. I couldn't quite visualize that but I could kind of think about what it might be like. Geometry was more real-life kinds of things, unlike algebra. Almost anything in geometry was related to something, like reflecting angles and putt-putt golf and the usefulness of triangles in construction, how triangles are rigid, the strongest shape.

Ryan was a leader in both classes. I was continually struck by how Ryan was able to generalize patterns in shapes and constructions using algebraic formulas. Although his willingness to share his ideas was hampered by his natural reticence in front of classmates, he often went to the board, drew clear representations of his ideas, and presented convincing arguments for the methods he practiced to solve problems.

Carolyn, however, preferred Algebra 2, and for very different reasons. My Algebra 2 class was reminiscent of the Algebra 1 class she had taken. But her Geometry class, which was taught by another teacher, seemed quite different to her.

> I don't really care for Geometry as much as I like Algebra this year. It's because I don't really care for learning through the book. I like trying to solve it myself and to figure it out for myself, working with the numbers. I like to try to figure out what the context means and what it has to do with the algebraic formula.
>
> In Geometry, we get homework or projects. We go over what we did the day before, if there was homework, and then we get more bookwork. The teacher usually gives us the answers and helps us out with it. Sometimes we apply information. We use CAD-key technology, so there are computers to work on, which makes the class a little different. The CAD-key helps us with some papers. The computer gives us more accurate information and numbers. It gives us an alternative to just books and papers. But we still learn the information and then use it. Like with our roofing project now, if I ever had to roof a house, that's when I'd use it. The book tells me what to do, and then I do it. I don't figure it out for myself.
>
> In Algebra, we figure things out for ourselves. For example, we were working with parabolas, and we wanted to find a certain input, an x. We had to find an inverse rule, and none of us had a way to do it. So I had to find a rule for myself, using the information I had, like where the vertex of the parabola was. Then I could put the formula in a different form, so I could get the information that I needed. But I was never told exactly how to do that. I had to figure it out myself.

Carolyn viewed algebra topics as more real-life than geometry projects; finding the vertices of parabolas seems to have more meaning for her personally than roofing.

> You would use inverses, for example, if you only have a certain budget amount. You can find out how much something's going to cost you. You would look at the opposite of that formula. You can take the cost, go through the problem backward and see how much you would actually have to use. I really do a lot of math just because I like math. I find it very interesting. The kind of stuff that

I've learned helps me deal with numbers, so that if I ever need to do any of that stuff, like bank accounts or something, the algebra will help me to think about the context as more than numbers. I can think of the quantity as more of a whole.

In Algebra 2, Carolyn was a class leader. During group activities, she daily discussed problem situations with her group mates, questioned her own understanding, and encouraged the learning of others. During whole-class discussions, Carolyn routinely made conjectures that added to the conversation and furthered the goals of the course. Unlike most of her classmates, Carolyn was also interested in providing a proof for her conjectures.

Both students spoke of their preference for Geometry or Algebra 2 by referring to its "real-life" usefulness. This is ironic, as each made a different decision and both preferred to work with mathematical abstractions rather than simply the contexts themselves.

Algebra 2: an illustration of Carolyn's attraction to the abstract

One day after Algebra 2, Carolyn ran up to me and said, "I think I have a conjecture about how to find the point where a function and its inverse intersect. I can find the exact point. I think I can prove it, too." I had to think a minute before I responded. This wasn't a conjecture that I had heard before in my previous years of teaching. Only four minutes remained until the next class period, so I suggested that Carolyn try to write something up to share with the class. Carolyn asked if she could show it to me first, before she shared it with the class. I agreed. I was very curious about Carolyn's thinking.

During the next few days of class, during whole-class discussion and while with her group, Carolyn plugged away at a TI-82 calculator. She was immersed in her thoughts, eagerly writing things down and trying out her ideas on the calculator. A few times, she checked in with me, saying things like, "I've almost got it," or, "I think I have a proof, but I don't know if it will be convincing."

This particular section of Algebra 2 had been investigating the question, "If a function and its inverse were graphed on the same set of axes, where would the two intersect?" As the teacher, I understood that graphing a function and its inverse on the same set of axes is not wise if considering the mathematics in context. If there are different quantities and units on the x- and y-axes, such a task is not sensible. From a more abstract point of view, however, the exercise has a point. I thought that if students had a chance to think about functions and their inverses by graphing them on the same axes, they would notice an important relationship; the graph of the inverse is a reflection of the original function over the line $f(x) = x$. This result may, in other mathematical circumstances students may encounter later, prove to be an important analytical tool when modeling a set of data. At this point in the term, the class had been considering linear functions exclusively. While this question wasn't focused on linear functions, most students only considered them.

After a few days of work, Carolyn presented me with the following conjecture, typed exactly as it appears in Figure 10.1.

Conjecture:

If you want to find the point in which the rule and the inverse rule intersect, you just take the y-intercept of the form,

$$7x + -48$$

and divide it by one less than the rate of change or slope.

$$-48/6 = -8$$

Then change the answer to the opposite of it. -8 becomes 8.

Write that 8 as a point (8,8), and you have the point where the rule and its inverse cross or intersect.

If you want to find the point in which they intersect with the inverse of the rule, then you divide the number in the parentheses by one less than the rate of change.

$$(x - -48)/7$$
$$-48/6 = -8$$

Then you take the opposite of your answer, 8, and write as a point: (8,8).

Proof:

This works because in an inverse rule you switch what you are doing and the table and the graph are also switched. So you need a point in which the x and y are equal. Since you need the same x and y, you need a number that goes in and comes out the same number. So you take the last number in the problem (-48) and divide it by one less than the rate of change, $-48/6 = -8$. You then take the opposite of the answer.

This works because you are dividing the -48 by 6 then multiplying by 7. Since 8 is the answer to $-48/6$ and it also becomes x, you are getting $48 + 8$. Then you add -48 or subtract 48, you are left with 8.

Figure 10.1 Carolyn's conjecture and proof.

With my two interns from Michigan State University, Tom Nikundiwe and Amy Long, I looked over her work. I understood Carolyn's conjecture, but didn't initially accept that it would work for all cases. Her proof seemed tied to the particular constants she had chosen. However, we worked with a variety of cases and finally saw the pattern that Carolyn was suggesting.

Carolyn presented her conjecture to the class. In my classes, usually a student will simply write his or her conjecture on an overhead transparency and talk about it as the class reads it on the screen. However, I felt that this conjecture was so intricate that students needed to read it and try some examples. So students were given a printed copy of the conjecture, along with the proof, to read and consider in their groups. Students ultimately understood Carolyn's conjecture and accepted it as a strategy. The proof, however, eluded most of the class.

At this point, Carolyn was unable to articulate a rationale for the usefulness of her conjecture. In Algebra 1, Carolyn had learned how to solve equations of linear functions in order to predict when a business would break even by considering revenue and costs. When encouraged to suggest an application for her conjecture, Carolyn said that it reminded her of break-even problems she had done before. But, she knew, this problem was different.

Finding the place where a function intersects the line $f(x) = x$ is extremely important for anyone exploring dynamical systems (which were not part of Carolyn's repertoire at the time). Although Carolyn's conjecture relates only to lines, many linear and non-linear functions have fixed points that are important for predicting the end behavior of a system. After her honors Discrete Mathematics course, here's what Carolyn had to say about her conjecture.

> When I first gave it to you, you told me it was something to do with dynamical systems. When I got into discrete math, I said to myself, "Oh, yeah, this is a dynamical system!" A dynamical system is a function in which the output becomes the next input. When you have a function, and you know where the function and its inverse meet, for instance (8,8) in my example above, you know that if you use 8 as the first input into the system, it results in a fixed point. It will cause the dynamical system to be a point. If you go to the smallest point above or below 8 as an input, the outputs of the dynamical system will either get really, really big or really, really small.

Senior year: Calculus, Abstract Algebra and Linear Algebra

During their junior year, Carolyn and Ryan took both honors Discrete Mathematics and PreCalculus. They teamed up in honors Discrete Mathematics, working on problems together and posing questions of their own. They decided that they would take AP Calculus during their senior year, but they also wanted more mathematics, specifically algebra.

They decided to pursue coursework at Michigan State University, which had in the past allowed students to take Calculus on campus. Carolyn contacted the Gifted and Talented Coordinator at Michigan State University in order to fulfill the documentation requirements for their dual enrollment. Then she and Ryan studied course descriptions and, because of their interest in algebra, opted for Linear Algebra and Abstract Algebra, both of which are third-year mathematics courses. They noticed that both courses required entry-level Calculus as a prerequisite, so Carolyn bought the texts for the Algebra courses, examined them, and made the argument to the MSU mathematics department chair that the courses did not really involve rigorous use of calculus.

While there was appreciation for their desire to study advanced mathematics, their argument for taking courses for which they had not taken the prerequisites was greeted with skepticism from some of the MSU mathematics department faculty members. Nonetheless, the two convinced the course instructor, a well-respected member of the faculty, to accept them and enrolled in Abstract Algebra for fall semester and Linear Algebra for spring. But classroom practices changed again in the transition from high school to university. The classroom practices that had drawn them to mathematics were not present in these university courses. Though Carolyn and Ryan stuck to their guns and successfully completed both courses, their experiences were not positive. Here's what Carolyn had to say regarding the Linear Algebra course:

> It was a lecture-based class. The teacher was saying something and doing things on the overhead. There was no discussion of any kind. You could ask questions, but it was a little intimidating. It was a rush to cover the topics. I realized that I didn't want to do that kind of math.

Ryan concurred:

> I don't like a lecture style of teaching. I have taken two math classes this year at MSU, and one of them was especially bad. If you did not understand something, it was hard to get clarity on it. . . . One

of the teachers didn't really know how to teach, at least that was my impression. He was all over the board. Sometimes it was easier to read it on your own because he would just confuse you more. I could remember more from [Algebra 2] or [Discrete Mathematics] than I could something we had just done in the MSU class.

By the end of the year, both students had decided that college mathematics was not something that they wanted to pursue any further.

Conclusion

As a group, as someone who has taught at the junior high and high school level, I wish to close with a number of ironies that arise out of curriculum work at Holt High School. First, algebra courses at Holt, designed collaboratively with faculty from MSU's College of Education, have been designed to address the special needs of students who are at academic risk because of a number of educational and social issues. As our story shows, the same classes, however, can also be rich environments for students who show academic promise. The case of Ryan and Carolyn highlights the ways in which students can develop an interest in mathematics by finding meaning in abstract mathematics that arises while solving contextual problems. For three years at Holt, these two students experienced the rewards of mathematical exploration.

Second, engaging students in creative mathematical work may, ironically, make them less willing to place themselves back into a context of learning mathematical skills to be utilized creatively only in the future. An important part of Carolyn and Ryan's experiences in the university mathematics department was a feeling of alienation from the sort of mathematical activity being offered to them. It seems ironic that, when they finally had a chance to meet professional mathematicians, the activity they were offered gave them fewer opportunities to engage mathematics creatively. Finally, it seems ironic that students in university mathematics classrooms are not having the sorts of experiences the university helps us provide to our high school students.

What is "mathematical power"? And related dilemmas of teaching

Kellie Huhn and Marty Schnepp, Holt High School

KELLIE HUHN: What these two students did was remarkable. Though it is important not to represent them as angels, there is a lot about their example that is inspiring. As captured in the story about

Carolyn's conjecture, I was always impressed by their curiosity, by their motivation and their willingness to investigate topics in a classroom setting, and by their stamina in remaining with an unsolved problem. Carolyn and Ryan really took us up on the challenges we presented them to both make sense of the mathematics they were working with and to find connections to make that mathematics more useful.

MARTY SCHNEPP: I agree on all counts. What they did was remarkable, two math courses a year for three years goes way beyond any requirements of the district; their engagement in mathematics class was impressive, yet we should not represent them as some unreal perfect children; they were a handful sometimes. For me, though, the essay about Ryan's and Carolyn's experiences isn't only about them; it shouts a question at me: "What is mathematical power?" I will avoid asking obvious rhetorical follow-up questions: Is it knowing how to execute many, many algorithms? Is it being able to demonstrate understanding? I don't see the point of asking these because it will immediately lead to the cliché response, "You need both skills and understanding;" and we would stop talking and pretend the issue is resolved.

KELLIE: I know my thinking about this question changed early in my teaching career here at Holt. Before teaching, I thought mathematical power meant the ability to perform certain algorithms, to compute using previously memorized formulas and to do what the teacher said to do. During my internship year, I would listen to students question why mathematical statements were true, struggle with articulating their ideas until they felt comfortable with mathematical terminology and symbolic notation, and make connections between different mathematical topics. After teaching for a year, I was thinking more about students; I defined a mathematically powerful student as one who could investigate mathematical topics using appropriate strategies, who would make conjectures, and who could explain why certain mathematical statements were true.

MARTY: Your definition makes sense, but I have not been able in recent years to settle on a clear idea of what it exactly looks like when students are developing mathematical power in a classroom. I feel concern both over how few topics can be covered when students investigate mathematics; and, at the same time, I feel concern over how shortlived and superficial the ideas and skills encountered in traditional classes can be. As I've written (Chazan & Schnepp, 2002), I struggle with this every February as I face questions of how to proceed in my Calculus class.

KELLIE: I understand the dilemmas you face as a teacher. For me, this question also has a personal dimension. I was overwhelmed as an intern, I would be so excited about being a part of my students' learning because I was learning so much from them. I was also outraged that my mathematical experiences to that point were so shallow that learning to question and investigate mathematical ideas came from watching my students and had not been a part of my education, including my degree in mathematics.

MARTY: I understand what you mean. After the first few times I saw kids explore mathematical objects, looking for and articulating generalizations, and seeking proof when asked to determine if their conjectures were true in all cases, some cases, etc., I began to wrestle with feelings of concern, embarrassment, excitement, anger, fear, and more. I felt embarrassed at how disengaged I had been as a student in my math classes, and how disengaged many of my students had been allowed to be while earning solid grades by simply memorizing and practicing procedures from lectures and test. Anger crept into the picture for me when for a time my knowledge of mathematics felt insufficient to attend to ideas and issues that arose when kids' inquiries raised questions I had not seen before. Anger was also a direct result of never having experienced courses that required me to stand on my own, using my own intellect and creativity. In my coursework in high school, undergrad, and graduate school, I never saw mathematics as an endeavor where people seek to explore, ask questions, make assertions, and seek arguments to verify the validity of those ideas. It was about learning preset ideas, memorizing theorems, correctly executing algorithms based on those theorems, and on occasion reproducing proofs that were shown in class. So a strong student was one who could reproduce instructed material. To change this experience for my students, though, I wonder how much weight to assign students' ability to solve problems, creatively solve problems, frame their own problems and seek valid solutions. I truly wonder about this.

KELLIE: You continue to articulate this as a dilemma you face as a teacher. It is one that feels real to me. Recently, I have been disappointed with my students' recall of mathematical ideas that we have studied in previous units or the previous semester. My immediate thought has been that I need to find ways to teach students to commit these ideas to memory. My fear, though, is that my students will then experience mathematics as you described. I don't want them to experience mathematics as I did. I don't want them to believe that a mathematically powerful student is one who can reproduce instructed material without error. But, at the same time, I want them to feel that they are responsible for the mathematical ideas we have explored and discussed.

MARTY: For me, the dilemma we are discussing has a particular flavor in advanced courses. Many of the students I have had in "honors" courses are surprisingly deficient in modes of mathematical thinking other than mastering algorithms. But I don't feel I can blame them. To be honest, in classes where "honors" is defined by the quantity of topics covered, it can be hard to tell who (if anyone) has intellectual curiosity, creativity, motivation, and understandings that are transferable to non-standard mathematical tasks. All of those things seem to be components in what mathematical power should look like. But how often are students – particularly those designated early to be "gifted" – allowed to develop, or to demonstrate, these things? I'm not being overly romantic though. Not all kids in an inquiry-based class engage at the level described for Ryan and Carolyn, and even Carolyn and Ryan did not always do so with every topic of study initiated by teachers. But I have seen so many instances of students engaging topics far deeper than I ever imagined novices could. I can't let go of what seems like a contradiction: experiences that are more comprehensive in terms of topics are often considered more advanced, despite having to remain somewhat superficial because of the quantity of topics covered. When will students who are in courses that cover a lot of material be judged by a standard of intellectual independence?

KELLIE: Those comments help me realize that I've been stereotyping honors students. Over time, I have come to think of them as unable to be curious or truly question why and how mathematics makes sense. I hadn't thought that their experience has taught them that mathematical power is memorizing facts and theorems and to reproduce them on tests. Are they making mathematical connections or memorizing the connections that teachers ask them? Do they know how to wonder and how to question mathematical content? Do they know how to investigate a question mathematically and gather enough information to convince themselves of the truth of the answer they found? Are they suspending their questions and just not bringing them to the classroom? You just helped me think about the fact that my stereotype is based on their experiences, not necessarily what they are capable of doing. I don't know what students are capable of if their experiences have taught them to hurry through mathematics and cover as many topics as possible.

MARTY: Moving back towards the other horn of my dilemma, I would be uncomfortable claiming that students emerge from inquiry-based experiences more mathematically able than those who have been exposed to a wide variety of skills and topics. What becomes of a student like Carolyn, who acquired deep understanding of polynomial functions in high school and was able to construct valid proofs of her conjectures, when she heads off to college to take classes where instructors do not assess such abilities and simply tell students what they should become proficient at? Carolyn and Ryan were clearly turned off by such an experience and I have talked to others who were as well. These students can fail to develop the skills needed to succeed, because courses failed to pique their interest.

KELLIE: I also feel uncomfortable about the type of mathematical experiences that are valued and supported at the college level, and discouraged by the ending point of the Carolyn and Ryan story. I read their lack of enjoyment in the college mathematics courses as disapproval for a course that doesn't value curiosity or inquiry. Carolyn and Ryan were motivated by their curiosity. Responsibility for assignments and investigating the mathematics fell out of their curiosity. I understand that in the short run this may seem like a negative; my hope is that we taught Carolyn and Ryan to value their own mathematical curiosity and that this will stand them in good stead in the future.

Chapter 11

Interlude B

Observation in classrooms

This section now turns to examine the experience of another kind of student at Holt High School, the student of teaching, the preservice teacher (or teacher candidate). As part of the five-year certification program at Michigan State University, preservice teachers have three field experiences. As juniors, they spend two hours a week in the schools for one semester. Seniors are in the classroom four hours a week both semesters. The fifth year follows up with a year-long internship where preservice teachers are in schools four or five days a week for the year, with a set rhythm by which they increase and decrease their teaching responsibilities. See Table 11.1.

The next essay focuses on field experience during the senior year. At this point, the preservice teachers are still college students. They are hard at work completing their majors in mathematics. Their

Table 11.1 An overview of MSU's five-year teacher preparation program

	Fall	Spring
Freshman/ Sophomore	TE 150 Reflections on Learning and TE 250 Human Diversity, Power, and Opportunity in Social Institutions Or CEP 240 Diverse Learners in Multicultural Perspectives	
Junior	TE 301 Learners, Learning, and Teaching in Context (Fall or Spring)	
Senior	TE 401 Learner Diversity and the Teaching of Subject Matter	TE 402 Designing and Studying Practice
Internship	TE 501 Internship in Teaching Diverse Learners I TE 801 Professional Roles and Teaching Practice I TE 802 Reflection and Inquiry in Teaching Practice I	TE 502 Internship in Teaching Diverse Learners II TE 803 Professional Roles and Teaching Practice II TE 804 Reflection and Inquiry in Teaching Practice II

schedules are tightly packed. Typically, they visit a local secondary classroom twice a week for two hours, often in pairs. As a result of the vagaries of scheduling, they may be seeing the same classes twice, or they may be seeing four different classes. Simultaneous with fieldwork in schools, they are enrolled in a four-hour weekly "methods" seminar. This seminar covers a range of topics. It is where the teacher candidates develop their personal philosophies of mathematics teaching, have opportunities to learn mathematics in new ways (see Chapter 18 about mathematical discussions in this class), learn to develop curricular materials (see Chapter 5 about this class and the BIG-Year Curriculum project), discuss what they see in the field, and much more.

As the year goes on, the visits to the school have different purposes. Many times seniors observe a class being taught. They may also work with small groups of students or interview a single student. They may explore the school outside of this particular classroom. And, three times a year, they teach a sequence of lessons to the same class (two or three consecutive lessons, if possible).

The next essay focuses on the experiences of one senior. Carl, a preservice teacher, was placed in one school for the first semester but then had to switch placements, moving to Holt High School for his second-semester placement. As Bill Rosenthal and Jan Simonson (Carl's seminar instructors) suggest, this shift in placement was a dramatic one for Carl. Placement in the Holt High School mathematics department helped him integrate theory and practice. From his work at Holt, he could now connect what he was learning at MSU with what could be done with high school students. In particular, he began to develop an image of what it meant to have a conversation in a secondary mathematics class, a practice promoted in his seminar but unimaginable to Carl, prior to his visits to Holt.

Carl's image of mathematics had been of a cut-and-dried subject; his image of mathematics teaching was getting students to give correct answers. Until his placement at Holt, these images made conversations in the high school mathematics classroom seem unfeasible. Placement in a high school where teachers discuss mathematical questions that arise for them from teaching (see Chapter 17 for the report of one such episode) changed his perspective on mathematics.

Bill and Jan's point is a more general one. From 1994–1995 and the start of MSU's five-year teacher certification program to 2000–2001, Holt High School served as the placement for more than 40 seniors (and seniors continue to be placed there in larger numbers as of this writing). The Holt placements allowed seniors to see in action the practices discussed on the college campus. In that way, the Holt department has eased one of the problems that vexes teacher educators – the lack of connection, or disconnect, between university coursework and observation in schools.

In their discussion, Tom Almeida and Sean Carmody interpret Carl's experience against the backdrop of their own preservice experiences. For example, Tom remembers tensions between the preservice teachers and university faculty in his teacher education program and wonders whether placement in a department like Holt High School's might have addressed these tensions.

Field experience really was the best teacher!

Jan Simonson and Bill Rosenthal, Calvin College, Hunter College

This essay is excerpted from a paper presented at the 1998 annual conference of the American Educational Research Association in San Diego, CA.

This essay examines the experience of one teacher candidate, a college senior, in a secondary mathematics methods class. This methods class is not a standard three-credit one-semester or one-quarter course. It is a year-long course that carries five credits in the fall and six in the spring. The course includes four hours a week of seminar time, as well as four hours a week of fieldwork in a school placement, as well as an additional 90 minutes of on-campus lab sessions.

In MSU's five-year, field-based teacher education program, the field experience referred to in this essay is not the equivalent of the typical student-teaching experience; it is not a preservice candidate's opportunity to learn to teach. Instead, it is a chance for teacher candidates to link their teaching methods classes with actual K–12 classrooms. The students are placed within classrooms that match their majors and intended teaching levels (middle school, junior high school, or high school), in this case high school mathematics classes. They do limited lead teaching (one to four times per semester), but are encouraged to participate in a variety of ways, including individual tutoring, participating with students in group work, curriculum decision-making discussions, assessment and evaluation of student work, interviews with students and teachers, field observations, and investigating the larger school community. The course seminar instructors provide direction to help seniors learn from their placements, and from their peers' experiences in their placements.

Within the context of this course, the particular teacher candidate we will describe was in the unique position of spending time in two different field placements, one a traditional high school, the other a Professional Development School (PDS) – Holt High School. The feedback received from this student illustrates ways in which placement with the Holt High School mathematics department during this methods course yields important experiences for MSU teacher candidates. (This is different from the value of placement at Holt High School for these teacher candidates once they have graduated as math majors and engage in a year-long internship.)

In the secondary mathematics methods course we taught, teacher candidates were encouraged to listen carefully to how students made sense of the mathematics to be taught and design curricula accordingly. The idea that listening is a method of teaching (Davis, 1997) was received, initially, with cynicism from our students. Although we modeled dialogue as a form of learning mathematics concepts, it was not part of their lived experience in mathematics classes. Our field assignments included having the teacher candidates assess a student's understanding of concepts. Most of our teacher candidates simply responded either that the students they assessed did or did not understand. Coming to know what the high school students understood or how they were understanding mathematical ideas was not easy for our students to determine and for the placements other than Holt, it was not an explicit part of their classroom field experience.

From our perspective, questioning and trying out new ways of teaching while reflecting on student learning should, ideally, become an integral part of each teacher candidate's professional identity. Realizing that many typical field experiences for teacher candidates emphasize imitation of and subservience to the supervising teacher, the Holmes Group suggests that preservice candidates' investigations of teaching and learning should build upon reflection and solving novel problems of practice (1986, p. 55). In a related vein, John Dewey (1904/1964) contrasts a traditional apprenticeship with the development of intellectual methods of teaching. In a traditional apprenticeship, a teacher candidate is trained to have a working command of class instruction and management for the sake of efficiency. The approach he favors supplies the same candidate with methods for basing instruction on knowledge of the subject matter and principles of education (pp. 313–314). The goal is for the apprenticeship to help the teacher candidate become a student of teaching. This idea is closely linked to the need to furnish field experiences for teacher candidates that are integrated with the education students' in-class learning experience.

But these notions are difficult to carry out in practice. Mathematics majors intending to be secondary mathematics teachers were successful in school; school worked for them. How can such teacher candidates be encouraged to investigate images of teaching and learning that are not a part of what Lortie (1975) calls their "apprenticeship of observation"? This is an ongoing teacher education question that challenged us as we attempted in MSU's five-year program to deliver the sort of apprenticeship into teaching envisioned by Dewey and the Holmes Group.

Our on-campus attempts to address these issues were straightforward; we tried to build on the ideas and experiences of our teacher candidates, understand their understandings, and gently lead them to extend their thinking, just as we hoped they would do for their high school mathematics students. In the mid- to late 1990s, we painstakingly designed and refined our year-long methods course to be in concordance with the principles of Dewey and the Holmes Group regarding professional practice and learning to teach for understanding. But, it became obvious that, despite our best efforts, teacher candidates had a great deal of trouble relating to the pedagogical theories we espoused and modeled, much less implementing them. Sometimes field experience reinforced preconceived notions that learning to teach is performance-oriented or that the ideas of algebra or 7th-grade mathematics are not connected, but separate skills to be perfected. We wondered how much influence our courses could have for students participating in a field experience that conformed to Dewey's traditional apprenticeship model.

It is in this context that Holt placements were beneficial for enabling our students to appreciate and assimilate less traditional ways of teaching that we wanted teacher candidates to consider. The Holt placements provided an existence proof, proving that it was possible to teach and learn in the ways we were discussing. Teacher candidates placed at Holt as seniors had a chance to take part in a paradigm that they previously had not experienced or envisioned. This experience actually mirrors the experiences of some of the teachers in the school when they were afforded the occasion to share a teaching assignment with another teacher, and to focus on developing student mathematical understandings through dialogue (see Chapter 14). Prior to the shared teaching assignment experience the teachers were confined to the visions and paradigms of their own classroom norms and procedures of transferring procedures to get right answers. They would later reflect that the experience of being in the classroom, listening to the students and participating with the teachers was instrumental in their coming to understand this kind of teaching and learning.

Carl's placements

Teacher candidates at our university have opportunities to focus on the teaching of secondary mathematics over two years of study, the second of which is a full-time post-baccalaureate internship. As mentioned earlier, during the students' senior year, the methods course is taught in conjunction with a field placement consisting of four hours per week in a secondary mathematics classroom. Most students were in the same placement all year long. Carl's case was unique; for circumstantial reasons we had to change his placement in the middle of the year. This circumstance supplied us with a superlative setting in which to examine the differential experiences of a typical senior in two different placements.

First semester, we placed Carl (a pseudonym) in a classroom where the teacher explained rules, definitions, and procedures for finding right answers, assigned problems, and then gave students chances to practice and solve the problems accordingly. Certainly, students asked questions and were free to talk with each other, but the emphasis was on reproducing the methods presented by the teacher and the textbook. During this semester Carl made observations, helped individual students, led class instruction on two occasions, and participated in conversations with his collaborating teacher.

The following semester, as a result of the change in placement, he was placed at Holt High School with Sandy Callis in an Algebra 1 class. There, the practice of his collaborating teacher allowed the direction of class discussions to be based on and sometimes driven by student ideas. Her approach made use of many elements: mathematical conversations; performance assessments, such as oral quizzes and tests, contributions to class discussions, writing and involvement in group activities, and projects; and the belief that teachers, not commercial publishers, should create curricula. Since the class was team-taught with a special-education teacher, and had an intern (in her fifth year of study), Carl had the opportunity to participate in conversations where curricular decisions were made, taking into consideration the meanings students were making and the goals of the course. He led the class in discussion on one occasion during the spring semester.

During both experiences, Carl dialogued weekly (at minimum) via email with one of the two of us, as did all of the seniors. We would frequently highlight comments and questions in Carl's emails and ask him to respond to points and problems we posed about linking the course's theoretical aspects with both his fieldwork and his own mathematical learning. This interactive journal is our principal source for the descriptions we provide below. In addition, we studied Carl's written coursework and interviewed him following both halves of his field experiences.

As the instructors of this course and of this student, our interpretations of his engagement with his placement at Holt suggest that it contributed mightily to his experience of an intellectually solid program of teacher education intertwining the wisdom of both theory and practice.

Such an achievement is one of the primary aims of university investment in professional development relationships with schools, and the placement of teacher candidates in such schools (Holmes Group, 1990, p. 48). If a teacher education program can create a positive correlation between theory and the candidate's field experience, then teacher candidates *can* learn to teach for conceptual understanding, or in this case envision this sort of teaching.

Carl's point of view

The candidate's own words capture the essence of what we learned:

> The new methods you have been teaching us didn't make sense until I went there [Holt High School].

Since we had emphasized listening to students' learning as a principal method of teaching, it seems that Carl's capacity to understand this method took a great leap forward after just one week in the new setting and continued to soar throughout the placement. Previously, he could not understand how students could carry on a conversation about mathematics – despite having himself been an avid participant in just such mathematical conversations in our on-campus classroom. One episode stands out in our minds (and Carl's) as a powerful indicant of his exponentially enhanced ability to connect our coursework with his emerging practice.

During our second interview with him (June 1997), Carl remembered an instance when he was leading the discussion in the first placement setting and students answered a question incorrectly. He remembered "something" from our course about capitalizing on incorrect answers, but nothing concrete came to him. The instructional goal in this setting was to teach students how to find right answers, so it didn't make sense to him to dwell on incorrect ones. After being placed in the Holt classroom, he reflected back and noted that the wrong answer had probably come out of some good thinking from which the class could have benefited, but he had shut it out at the time. He was amazed that students in the Holt classroom – especially those who were taking Algebra 1 in grades 10–12 (the same level as the students in the other placement) – could become so engaged in conversations about mathematics. When he had previously heard about mathematical conversation, the prospect had not struck him as feasible. He just thought it was a dream or the students had to be unique.

Carl's reflections about leading class discussion at Holt reveal his amazement. He was nervous about keeping the conversation going in the productive ways he had been observing. As it turned out:

All I needed to do was ask them what they thought, and they were off and running – telling me how they had approached the problem, agreeing and disagreeing with each other, and presenting evidence for their thinking. Now, my question is, how did they get to this point? It just isn't natural for kids that aren't necessarily college-bound to be so interested in mathematics.

This episode illustrates the differences between Carl's two field experiences. It is reasonable to attribute some of his maturation to time (the Holt placement came second) and to a newfound ability to articulate his questions and understandings. Nevertheless, Carl reported with consistency and enthusiasm that he could understand and apply our program's theories of teaching after the stimulus of events in his Holt High School classroom.

Further evidence for the importance of the Holt placement is found in the coherent and connected story-based BYC he developed for a full year of algebra. Envisioning and enacting a class in terms of a story comprising a theme, a plot, and a narrative has been central to the work of the Holt High School mathematics department and our preservice work (see earlier discussions, including Chapter 5). This curricular perspective was at the heart of Carl's conversations with Sandy Callis, his collaborating teacher at Holt. In contrast, his previous field placement featured discussions with the teacher that invariably involved only the order of presentation of textual material within a chapter and classroom management issues.

Conclusions

Teachers often report their field experience to be the most informative and influential part of their teacher education and training (e.g., Britzman, 1991; Lanier & Little, 1986). It is this sort of research that influenced MSU to provide significant field experience closely coordinated with coursework prior to student teaching, or in this case the year-long internship, and to coordinate the field experience with the methods coursework. In reflecting on Carl's experience, the placement seemed instrumental in his understanding and ability to make sense of the reform ideas being addressed in our course. Fieldwork at Holt helped Carl think about teaching and learning mathematics differently from how he himself had learned the subject. This has been our general experience of placements at Holt. When a teacher candidate is presented with differing views and ideas, field experience and the work of the mentor teacher play crucial roles in determining the student's affinity with fresh ideas – and ultimately the directions they may take in their professional lives.

As proposed by the Holmes Group (1990), the PDS is to be an institution (really a relationship between existing institutions!) that brings together schools of education and public schools for the purpose of working on issues of teaching. One task of the PDS is to question all aspects of schooling in order to capture the ideas and habits of real learning (p. 31). A similar idea is also espoused by Sharon Feiman-Nemser, one of our colleagues in Teacher Education at MSU, who says, "[A] classroom is not only a place to teach children, but a place [for teachers] to learn more about teaching and learning" (1983, p. 150). For schools to be positive learning environments for students, they must be positive learning environments for teachers as well. Teachers who are not free to construct their own activities, inquire, engage in meaningful learning, take risks, make decisions, and assess their own competence will be unable to create those possibilities for students. Our experience with Carl has shown that schools like Holt High School, where teaching is seen as a type of inquiry and creative intellectual work, serve as an invaluable model for teacher candidates to learn about teaching. This modeling gives credence and a vision for teaching that builds on students' present understandings. It can help teacher candidates move beyond the paradigm their own school experience afforded them.

Our contrasting preservice field experiences

Tom Almeida and Sean Carmody, Holt Public Schools

TOM ALMEIDA: My undergraduate experience wasn't at Michigan State University. The people in my education classes were, on the whole, very traditional and ready to make some money. Any discussion of reform of mathematics classrooms eventually turned sour. I'm saddened now, looking back, that we missed out on so much. During my student teaching, I interacted with one collaborating teacher and one university supervisor, and never with both at the same time. It felt very disconnected. Now that I've seen real collegial interaction, I'm amazed that I spent so much time and money to get so little out of my experience. I've had lengthy discussions with MSU interns since I've been at Holt High School. Most of these conversations were centered on teaching and learning, which benefited everyone involved. Probably the biggest difference between my experience as a preservice candidate and Carl's fieldwork at Holt is that I never saw an example of how to apply the theories we were exposed to on campus. I'm sure we read the same books and talked about the differences in today's classrooms, but I never saw those differences until I landed in Holt as a teacher. As I read this piece, I couldn't help thinking how well it describes what I love about my job at Holt – people sharing and helping each other to be better teachers.

SEAN CARMODY: Carl's story makes me think of my internship year and not my senior year. I had a unique experience during my internship placement at Holt. I had the opportunity throughout the year to work with three different teachers in three different classrooms and every level of student in the high school. Each one of these teachers used students' ideas to drive the course. However, each did it in a different way. I was amazed at how the students in every setting were willing and able to talk about their ideas in the course, as well as have the passion to argue about mathematics. In each of these settings I was able to plan for the course and develop both a better understanding and multiple viewpoints on how to develop an atmosphere that would encourage active student participation.

TOM: I can see what you mean because, as a teacher at Holt, I have thought more about what mathematics is and how it relates to anything and everything than I had in the previous ten years of my life. This should seem surprising, or counterintuitive, considering that during that time I received a bachelor's degree in pure mathematics and a teaching certificate. I consider myself fortunate to be here; I'm a much better teacher for coming to Holt High School.

SEAN: Over the course of my internship year, I had the opportunity to work very closely with Mike Lehman, who was my collaborating teacher. I was able to discuss with him how to plan in this environment. Besides working with Mike, I also worked very closely with other members of the department. On Wednesday mornings we would meet and discuss mathematical ideas that had been brought up in various classrooms. We also would discuss the development and substance of future courses. I worked closely with the members of the department during lunchtime as well. I could ask them questions about courses I wasn't currently teaching or bounce ideas for lessons off other members of the staff. I immediately felt like I belonged. I would stop by after school and talk with many of the staff members about issues from my class or theirs or about mathematical ideas.

TOM: I, too, have greatly enjoyed working with other teachers, interns, and university people on various aspects of a teacher's life. Especially satisfying have been the discussions about math. Our discussion this last year about the line of best fit was wonderful. Together, we dissected the purpose, meaning, and use of the correlation coefficient. I was astounded. In my previous experience at three different schools, discussion like this never happened. There simply was no time set aside for this valuable part of the teaching–learning process. I think the most significant part of my last statement is the time. Having two to three hours each week on Wednesday mornings to work things out is wonderful!

SEAN: Our dialogues definitely helped us both to make further connections between our coursework and our internship experience. Also, I felt that from our experiences in Holt we were able to bring a very different perspective back to the MSU classes we took during the internship year and share that perspective with the other interns in those courses. Our having been in Holt definitely affected our view of mathematics reform and what was possible in a classroom.

TOM: I think that more people need to be placed in a position like Carl's, where he could see for himself and choose for himself what felt best. I believe that the ideas and ideals in Holt would be accepted in most places if people had a chance to experience them for themselves.

Chapter 12

Interlude C

Student teaching/internship

Unlike the last essay, which focused on preservice teachers in their senior year, the next essay, like Sean's discussion, is from the experience of MSU interns in their postgraduate, fifth year of teacher preparation. During this year, the interns participate in an intense field-based learning experience. They are only enrolled in education courses and generally do not take on outside work, though schools are often able to find ways to pay them for work done during the internship year. During this year, they are beginning teachers more often than university students. Except for the days during which they are in their on-campus seminars, they dress in the professional garb common to their field placements. It is a year of transition.

Interns participate in their placements from the beginning of the year until MSU's graduation with their level of teaching responsibility organized to follow a general rhythm (though the exact rhythm is set in consultations between the preservice teacher, the mentor teacher, and the university field instructor). Throughout the year, they have primary responsibility for one section of their mentor teacher's load, their focus class. At points during the fall of that year, they take responsibility for two or three sections. Finally, for ten weeks in the spring, they (usually) run four of their mentor's classes. By participating in their mentor's classes throughout most of a school year (MSU's academic year ends in mid-May), and through co-teaching and co-planning (the degree to which interns and mentors co-teach and co-plan vary by placement), they are indeed the "students" of their mentor teachers. See Figure 12.1.

Throughout the year, the interns also have two three-hour seminars, which usually meet on Fridays. One of the seminars groups students by their placements and focuses on issues of teaching that can be discussed across subject matter. The second seminar, TE802–4, groups students by subject matter, but across placements.

In the following essay, the experiences of interns are examined to shed light on the type of placement Holt High School has become for

Classes lead \ Time of year	Before guided lead teaching I	Guided lead teaching I	In between guided lead teachings	Guided lead teaching II	Before lead teaching	Lead teaching (10 weeks)	Post lead teaching
5							
4							
3							
2							
1 – Focus class							

Figure 12.1 Internship rhythm of the year.

future teachers. In this piece, César Larriva, who taught in the secondary mathematics component of MSU's teacher education program from 1998 to 2001, uses notions of situated learning to suggest that interns in Holt High School's mathematics department are inducted into a different profession than that of their peers in other placements. Focusing on two strong interns, one who interned at Holt and one who did not, he finds their professional orientation to be different.

In examining the experiences of these two interns, César sought a fair comparison. The intern who is not placed at Holt is a strong student and on her way to becoming an accomplished teacher. (For an examination of some of her thinking about algebra teaching, see Chazan *et al.*, 1999.) During the internship, she is quite active in her school and attends professional conferences five times during her internship year. She is eager to improve her practice, and looks to experts to help her. The intern placed at Holt is also a strong student who is eager to improve her practice. But, her ways of being a strong intern are different. She seeks aid and guidance internally and locally, rather than from external "experts." Reflecting on these differences, César finds issues that concern him. How do teacher educators cope with differences in placement experiences and the ways in which these differences shape the kind of teachers preservice candidates become?

In their response to this essay, Kelly Hodges and Laura Kueffner discuss how their experiences at Holt have shaped their views of the profession. Sometimes the vision of the profession that they have developed puts them at odds with others who view the work of the teacher differently. They begin to work on understanding how to work productively across such differences.

What kind of teacher will I be?

César Larriva, California State Polytechnic University, Pomona

This paper was written specially for this volume. A larger paper about the study is in preparation.

From the 1998–1999 academic year through 2000–2001, I instructed Michigan State seniors and interns preparing to teach secondary mathematics. This instruction has allowed me to view several cohorts of students as they move through the multi-year program. For me, it's been fascinating to watch students' transition from a context defined primarily by mathematics coursework to one in which teaching ultimately dominates the foreground. This transition moves them from a place where mastery of mathematics is the primary focus, to one in which mathematical ideas are explored in light of pedagogy, student learning, and the role of social settings.

I did not instruct the students I will discuss here. I first encountered them while informally observing their internship-year courses, TE 802–804. Later, I interviewed them formally as part of a research study. It was during my informal observations of their cohort that I began to sense that the Holt High School interns were developing into a cohesive group with a striking public identity. I wanted to understand more about the process that contributed to this result. What was it about the Holt experience that was different, and what might this imply for the teacher education program?

And, what did the Holt placement mean for the individual preservice teachers who interned there? Classroom experience with my cohorts of seniors and interns further suggested that an internship at Holt might lead to a significantly different experience of induction into teaching. In particular, as suggested by Carl's experience in Chapter 11, differences in the ways my students engaged with the ideas of my courses seemed to relate to whether they had any experience at Holt. Also, I sensed that Holt interns as a group were at times in conflict with students in other placements.

I was familiar with certain aspects that distinguished the school. It had been a PDS for a number of years. A core group of math teachers there had been exploring alternative ways of thinking about their curriculum, and they had built weekly professional development meetings into their routine. Math teachers at Holt, as a whole, seemed stronger mathematically in relation to those at the other schools where we place our students.

I suspected, however, a more intangible difference. I began to think that being at Holt gave interns access to a unique community of practice (in the sense of Lave & Wenger, 1991). Holt might be a place where teaching mathematics and being a mathematics teacher is conceived and enacted in a markedly different way. Underlying this, perhaps, is a difference in how the teachers see themselves and understand their rights and responsibilities in relation to the practice of teaching. Indeed, Marty Schnepp's description in Chapter 4 of his efforts to improve his Calculus curriculum provides a specific example of one Holt teacher's sense of obligation. As a result of their work at Holt, our interns might also be developing a different sense of themselves as math teachers.

Learning as identity formation

There is great benefit to examining identity formation as a way of understanding the learning process, rather than as a personal trait. Using identity formation to understand learning is a notion advocated by Lave and Wenger (1991), initially researchers of apprenticeship as a mode of education, in their discussion of learning in apprenticeship situations. Wenger (1998) explains it as follows: "[Learning] is a process of becoming ... We accumulate skills and information ... in the service of an identity. It is in the formation of an identity that learning can become a source of meaningfulness ..." (p. 215).

Wenger (1998) describes identity in relation to participation in communities of practice. In his view, an individual's identity in practice cannot be reduced either to a self-image or a category imposed by others. Identity is both experienced through and results from our participation in social practices. It is fluid and cannot be located solely within or outside the individual. What an identity comes to mean depends on how an individual's participation plays out in actual practice. "The experience of identity in practice is a way of being in the world," Wenger writes (1998, p. 151). As such, identity acts as a context for experiencing the world and determining what becomes significant learning.

Barbara Rogoff, someone who writes extensively about learning as socialization, holds similar views of learning and of identity. She describes learning as a "process of transformation of participation" (1994, p. 209), and emphasizes that as we learn we change. Her view of learning is consonant with Lave and Wenger's assertion that "learning involves the construction of identities" (1991, p. 53).

Fifth year as apprenticeship

If we think of an MSU teacher candidate's fifth year as an apprenticeship, the view of identity I've just described suggests the importance of paying attention to how teacher candidates are constructing themselves and what this might tell us about the teaching practice into which they are being inducted.

This essay is drawn from interviews with two interns, Kaye and Elle, at the end of their year-long placements and with the two instructors of their TE 802–804 seminars.[1] I asked these teacher candidates to describe their field experiences and to describe themselves as mathematics teachers. In addition, I asked their instructors to describe them as seminar participants and as preservice and future teachers.

Kaye's placement was at Holt; Elle interned at another high school. Their stories reveal important differences between the Holt experience and internships at other high schools. Furthermore, there may be aspects of teaching practice at Holt that afford interns important opportunities to develop a sense of self as mathematics teachers that is quite distinct from identities fostered in other placements.

Two strong interns

Kaye and Elle's teachers considered them strong interns, and many, myself included, believe they are likely to become very good teachers. Elle's decided success as an MSU math major continued into her internship. She was diligent and proficient about her assignments in TE 802–804 and in the way she worked to participate fully in her placement site. She was familiar with a broader range of mathematical topics than most interns, and nothing in her placement shook her confidence in her own mathematical ability. Kaye, on the other hand, in her placement, sensed her own mathematical limitations, and a lack of confidence was sometimes evident. But Kaye's central strength as an intern grew from her intellectual curiosity. She recognized the value in revisiting familiar mathematical territory in order to attain deeper understanding.

These two individuals were active and energetic interns. They were extremely professional in dress, demeanor, and practice. Their involvement during their internships went beyond what our certification program requires and reflected their commitment to becoming excellent teachers. Both were well invested in teaching activity in their placement schools and interested in reform activity consistent with the vision articulated by NCTM and discussions of change in their schools. But they did this in different ways that were shaped by what they saw and did at their respective placements.

A different kind of practice

Kaye engaged in mathematics reform activity through her ongoing efforts to deepen her mathematical understandings in relation to her teaching experiences. Her means of achieving this included participating in the lunchtime conversations among teachers and interns that were already a daily ritual at Holt High School. One other math intern described Kaye as a member of the "clique." This unofficial and in some ways exclusive social group consisted of Holt math teachers, who were rethinking curriculum, and their interns. This membership offered the opportunity to be part of the ongoing, informal discussions about mathematics teaching – and mathematical ideas in general – that took place in various places around the high school building.

Kaye reports that she and her mentor "always talked" during their daily planning period, often addressing substantive mathematical issues.

> I would talk through a unit with him, and he would ask me questions, and we would start to make some connections to the different topics. I mean, he would just pose different questions and different ways to think about it so that I could think about a new way to introduce the concepts or even just think about them in order to have a better idea (in case) my students were to think about it that way.

The kind of activity Kaye describes is consonant with how mathematics teaching at Holt has been characterized.

> There is a commitment to developing personal understanding of the mathematical ideas at the core of the curriculum and using these understandings to build curriculum that is responsive to students' ideas.
>
> (Chazan, 2000, p. 161)

Indeed, one of Kaye's and Elle's TE 802–804 instructors described many of the Holt math teachers as having "a deeper mathematical understanding." They "model the continued questioning of one's mathematical understanding and what there is to be learned about the curriculum, in a way that's atypical." Further, "they're willing to challenge each other in conversation in a way that's atypical."

The nature of the conversation between Kaye and her mentor, in fact, did seem unique. Kaye describes their discussion as follows:

> He was constantly bringing physics up and motion, because calculus is based on motion. So I was always thinking about motion with him, and how that related to calculus and algebra, and how could I bring different types of motion into my classroom . . .

Kaye repeatedly emphasized her mentor's practice of exploring and making connections across topics and disciplinary boundaries.

Kaye had the guidance of a very supportive and competent mentor, one committed to improving his practice and presenting students with meaningful learning opportunities. Beyond that, Kaye had the chance to talk with teachers and interns about mathematics teaching during the department's weekly professional development meetings and ongoing lunchtime discussions. Interns also shared experiences regularly after school.

Elle and Kaye encountered very different opportunities in their placements during their internship year. Elle's description of her internship year contrasts sharply with Kaye's. Like Kaye, Elle sought to participate fully in her school's teaching community. She attended staff and department-chair meetings with her mentor teacher – who was the chair of the math department – helped her mentor organize department meetings, and established ties with another math teacher.

But the nature of the community in this department was different; despite her forms of participation, Elle felt isolated, and it frustrated her. Clearly, she established connections with people in her placement. She attended a technology conference with her mentor and spoke regularly with "one special [math] teacher" who, according to Elle, "was really interested in integrating graphing-calculator technology into his classroom teaching and writing his own unit plans – not necessarily following the text." They usually bumped into each other at lunch. "He'd throw ideas out to me about what he was doing with exponential growth in his class and I'd talk about some of the things that I was doing in my Algebra 1 [section] ..." She also had considerable interaction with the special-education teacher, a female math teacher, and her other mentor teacher in chemistry (Elle taught one section of chemistry in addition to sections of math). Her MSU field instructor visited her at the school, though somewhat infrequently. But she still felt isolated.

Elle's isolation was, in part, from her peers. She was the only math intern in her building and wished there had been other math interns assigned to her school.

> I was talking to people [i.e., interns] that were in science that also had math minors, just to try to have some communication, because it was too hard for me to try to talk to people that were at different schools. For me I think it would have been easier if I was placed at a school that also had another math intern so that I would have somebody to talk to about what was going on. I think that there were four or five [interns] at Holt....

While this suggests a problem with MSU's placement practices – perhaps interns should always be placed in bunches – the strength of

Elle's feelings of isolation suggest that the issue was not simply lack of peers. There was not enough collegial interaction among members of her host department. Unfortunately, this lack of collegial interaction is the norm in most local departments. The kinds of interactions described by Kaye are quite unique.

In addition, Elle contrasted her experience with what she had observed at Holt the previous year while she fulfilled her senior requirement for field observation.

> She [her fifth-year internship mentor] didn't plan lessons with me.... I think at Holt, the teachers spend a lot of time with their interns planning lessons and units with them, but I had to do all that on my own.

Seeking, among other things, more engagement in talk about mathematics teaching, Elle looked outside of the walls of her school and to more formal arrangements. In addition to the teaching assignments of her internship, Elle attended five teaching conferences throughout the region, as well as teacher education research seminars at MSU. She became interested in special education, volunteered as a mentor for a student considered at-risk for school failure, and became the sophomore class advisor (for pay). She also worked as a paid tutor through a school-district program for students who are homebound due to illness.

Attending conferences was her way of "making connections with people that are at different schools" and a way "to see what's happening." As a result of her experience, Elle wanted to work in "a department that likes to go to conferences and get out and see what's going on and is keeping up to date with what's happened in the mathematics education world...." Elle noted, "the one [conference] in Chicago was one that really [affected] me ... because I got to see what teachers were doing with the graphing calculator and CBL equipment, so that made a big difference in my teaching." She also shared some of these ideas about technology with her fellow math interns in a formal presentation to her TE 804 class, presumably to practice and receive feedback about something she foresaw herself doing once she was a practicing teacher.

In relation to Holt, Elle's experience acquires greater resonance. Even though she had contact with many people, she still feels that she lacked opportunities to talk about mathematics and mathematics teaching. In part, she attributes this to her placement as the sole mathematics intern in the building.

This situation stands in sharp contrast to Kaye's experience, which was marked by regular and frequent chances to observe and participate in significant discussions about mathematics and mathematics teaching. These discussions involved experienced teachers and interns in an exercise that was an essential component of the broader practice of teaching. These conversations extended the definition of teaching beyond classroom walls. Kaye was exposed to the notion that teaching is more than planning as an individual activity and enacting a plan in isolation. Before her was evidence that teaching at Holt included participation in collegial conversation of a different kind than those available to Elle. Kaye heard experienced teachers being thoughtful about the curriculum, seeking connections in the mathematics, and acting as learners. Further, Kaye had proof that the talk connected to classroom practice, "and that's a framework that I know is possible [the teaching framework she built for herself at Holt]. I'd never seen it working in a school, and I saw it working this year. . . ."

A different kind of teacher

So far, these descriptions focus on the experiences that each of the interns had. Beyond having these experiences, I believe Kaye and Elle came to see themselves in markedly different ways as teachers; they had been inducted into different visions of the profession. Certainly, Kaye and Elle expressed similar desires. Kaye talked about engaging students and colleagues; Elle spoke of motivating and inspiring students, as well as communicating with colleagues. But evidence of some significant contrasts between the two appears in the philosophy-of-teaching statements Elle and Kaye wrote for their teaching portfolios.

These philosophy statements revealed differences in how Kaye and Elle see their students in relation to the teaching of mathematics. Kaye explains the importance of "giving students the opportunities to explore complex situations with other students in order to formulate ideas" and that instructional decisions be based on developing knowledge of the students' learning.

> A teacher must be genuinely curious about student's ideas while keeping the mathematical goals in mind. A Holt High School teacher described the role of the teacher best: "You have to be able to listen to the students and in an instant decide if their idea will lead the class somewhere meaningful."

Elle's view, on the other hand, implies that mathematical content serves both as the goal and the guide for instruction.

> A teacher is a knowledgeable guide for a learner who not only shares knowledge but also attempts to develop ways of approaching the material so that students understand the content . . . I ask questions that may have more than one right answer and use these

questions to get at students' understanding of the content and not the memorization of the material.

That is, Kaye sees developing student ability to think mathematically as a goal and notes the centrality of student understanding in a teacher's decision-making. Elle sees student understanding of a set content as a central goal for instruction and believes that content guides instructional decisions.

Kaye and Elle also differed on what sort of relationships they would like to have with colleagues in their first teaching position. In describing what people discuss when they engage each other professionally, Kaye mentioned the exploration of different ways of viewing mathematics.

> With my mentor teacher alone, we were just constantly talking about the math in our curriculum and reading books on the history of mathematics and bringing that into the study of mathematics and how that related to our Algebra 2 class and how that, in turn, related to the calculus class.... And then, just talking with other interns and other teachers and the concepts that they were going to approach, they were constantly asking questions about math and exploring it with other people to see how they were thinking about it to see if they could think differently about it.

On the other hand, Elle's conception of communication with colleagues focused more on how to teach and less on thinking critically about *what* to teach.

> I need a department that's going to be talking together and saying "How did you teach this?" or "How can we get this point across to our students?"

These examples illustrate contrasts that predictably seem to exist between interns at Holt and those placed at other high schools. These examples contrast the kind of teaching practice available to interns, and, more interestingly, they contrast the kind of identity the interns were beginning to exhibit as math teachers.

Understanding the developing identities that sprang from Kaye and Elle's participation in significantly different forms of teaching practice helps illuminate how the internship site and the nature of the internship experience figure in the overall development of interns within a teacher development program. Very likely, Kaye and Elle will experience success in their teaching. But they emerged from their internships with two distinct conceptions of themselves as teachers. Kaye's view reflects her experience at Holt. It emphasizes informal professional development that is integrated into the local activity of teaching and involves others in her building, others who may know her students. Elle, placed in the more conventional setting, developed a view based on the picture of excellence she managed to construct in her school. Therefore, she sought ideas outside her immediate teaching environment and looked to experts for resources. Given the striking contrasts in their internship experiences and in their developing professional identities, it appears that Elle and Kaye were apprenticed into very different practices. Lave and Wenger's assertion that "learning involves the construction of identities" (1991, p. 53) suggests that, as a result of their apprenticeship, they learned to be different sorts of teachers.

Congruence between the field and the university classroom

I would like to close by going back to my early observation of this cohort and of the sense of the Holt interns as a group that was sometimes in conflict with students in other placements. Based on interviews with the TE 802–804 instructors and on my own experience teaching these courses, it seems that Holt interns also experience the course in notably different ways from their counterparts at other placements, especially regarding their willingness to engage with certain ideas about teaching.

The congruence that exists between the beliefs and teaching practices at Holt and our teacher education program seems to have a positive effect on how Holt interns experience our courses and the program. It also suggests, however, the less cheerful possibility that interns placed elsewhere experience a sense of discontinuity between their field and university classroom experiences. Bill Rosenthal's essay in Chapter 5 and Tom Almeida and Sean Carmody's response to Chapter 11 refer to this discontinuity (or lack of compatibility).

The social relations that developed in TE 802–804 throughout the year indicated that where interns were placed was instrumental in shaping their classroom and field experience. The Holt interns formed a cohesive group, in large part because of the scope that Holt afforded them to interact and communicate about their mathematics teaching. A small group of individuals with placements primarily in urban settings also coalesced, and, at times, clashed publicly with the Holt group during seminar discussions. (Interns in this group faced challenges that were not apparent at Holt, such as inconsistent student attendance, seemingly unmotivated students, and greater diversity in student mathematical proficiency.) The two sets of interns disagreed over their interpretations of their fieldwork, with the interns placed elsewhere convinced that the Holt interns could not possibly understand what they experienced in the field – their contexts were that different.

How do we talk with other teachers about our "Holt" experiences?

Laura Kueffner and Kelly Hodges, Holt Public Schools

LAURA KUEFFNER: I was an intern at Holt the year Kaye and Elle had their internships. I find that many of Kaye's comments are reminiscent of my own experience, and, reading about Elle's situation, I understand how it must have felt different to her. At Holt, it was a year where the five of us interns learned a vast amount in a very short time. The bond we formed was so strong that, after being gone two years teaching in another district, when I came back to Holt, I felt as if I had never left. Two of my companion interns from that year are also teaching with me now at Holt, and we are able to talk as if I had never left.

KELLY HODGES: I left my mathematics teaching position at Holt after the 1998–1999 school year. I now teach in the teacher education program at MSU and have been teaching TE 802–804. Like you, I've found that when I've visited my former colleagues, I can slip seamlessly back into their conversations about mathematics and teaching. Through discussions I've had about teaching with people from a variety of settings, I've become aware that my experience at Holt differs from that of other teachers in lots of ways. Figuring out how to represent that experience in my new role as a teacher of interns has been my latest challenge.

LAURA: I can imagine. I remember going to TE 802–804 and feeling rather ostracized at times for being an intern at Holt. The other interns felt that we had it better because we had so much help: mentor teachers to talk to, other interns to commiserate with, a community of teachers that were already used to discussing better ways to teach and form curriculum. I don't know if I ever figured out how my placement truly compared with those of other interns, but I do know that it was the toughest year of my life, even tougher than the first year of teaching. The opportunity for sharing and discussing ideas with the math department was invaluable to our learning about teaching math. It was built into the program and brought us together. But it also seemed to raise so many ideas and so many questions that it caused more work for me than seemed humanly possible. I would stay up late planning because we were constantly discussing how lessons could be made better. It really took a toll on my desire to become a teacher because I thought it would always be so much work I wouldn't have time for anything else in my life. Going to another school for a couple of years really put things into perspective for me and helped me come back with a renewed commitment to this work. César describes learning to teach as identity formation; I feel that forming one's identity is difficult no matter where or when it takes place. It has to be done individually, even when you are part of a peer group – like I was with the other Holt math interns – consisting fully of identity-forming individuals.

KELLY: Laura, I really value the perspective you can bring now as someone who has taught somewhere else after teaching at Holt. Your thoughts about the unique and individual nature of each person's teacher-identity formation help me think about how to use my own teaching experiences to instruct interns. When I first started teaching TE 802–804, many who had taught it previously cautioned me against relying too heavily on my experiences at Holt; they believed that it would contribute to a "Holt vs. the world" dynamic in the course. But I think I made a mistake my first year in avoiding any discussion about my practice. It was my teaching experience that made me a good candidate for teaching the course in the first place. As the year drew to a close, I came to realize that I *could* talk about my experience. It was just *my* experience, not the *Holt* experience. My stories are valid because they are mine.

LAURA: That's true, but I also agree with César that many differences exist between Holt and other schools. Reflecting the differences between Kaye and Elle, Holt as a whole was more concerned with discussing *what* to teach, whereas the other school I taught at was concerned with *how* to teach. But from discussions I've had with teachers from other schools, it seems that every school is unique in many ways and yet the same in others. Holt is no exception.

KELLY: Thanks. I'll definitely keep that in mind this year. Perhaps there's a way to keep the existence of any Holt clique from making other interns feel their efforts to become good teachers are somehow substandard.

LAURA: Well, during my internship year, the five of us math interns interning in the Holt math department also had a seminar, TE 801–803, that was for Holt interns across all subjects. Our classmates in that course also described the five of us as a clique. This leads me to wonder how much of our cohesiveness simply resulted from our liking to be around each other. Perhaps we would have become friends even if we weren't all placed at Holt.

KELLY: Perhaps. But I think that César is suggesting that the clique evolved because it offered you the chance to "be part of ongoing, informal discussions about mathematics teaching, and mathematics in general." Even though the classmates in your other course were interns at Holt, they couldn't share this experience with you, because they taught other subjects. You probably had other friendships with other interns because of other interests you shared, but I bet the fact that you shared this very intense, very personal type of interaction with the other Holt math interns and teachers contributed to your friendship with them.

LAURA: I can see where that would definitely steer us in the direction of being friends. I want to add, also, that we math interns did have friendships with both the other interns at Holt and other math interns in different schools. Most of the feelings about Holt math interns as a clique came out in the class discussions we had concerning curriculum and teaching, not in casual friendly conversation.

KELLY: My experience talking about my teaching at Holt is similar. People with whom I otherwise have friendly relationships seem to feel threatened by the kinds of discussions about teaching that I crave. It's been very difficult to find ways to share the essence of what I value about teaching at Holt with others in a way that is inviting, rather than off-putting. The more I think about it, the more I wonder whether it is legitimate to say that interns (or teachers) in other settings "should" attempt to enact aspects of teaching practices at Holt. Perhaps it's true, as interns in urban placements often suggest, that teachers in one setting couldn't possibly know or appreciate the realities of other settings. The particulars of our practice at Holt – the curricula we've developed, the arrangements we've made to create time to talk together – work there because of a convergence of many circumstances. This combination of factors is unlikely to exist in any other given school. So, although we often talk about our practice by using these particulars as the context, I suspect what we value about teaching at Holt is something more general and nebulous. César refers to a difference in the way Kaye and Elle describe their thinking about content knowledge. Kaye discusses the conversations she's had about her own mathematical understanding of the content she is teaching; Elle instead mentions conversations about how to teach. Whether it's true or not, it seems to me that Elle sees content as static and defined. Conversations that challenge her personal mathematical knowledge are not something she seeks from teaching colleagues. Is this a chicken-and-egg situation? In other words, is it Holt teachers' willingness to engage in these conversations that has allowed the structure to support them to develop, or is it the structures themselves that have allowed these behaviors to become commonplace? It seems to me that anyone interested in transferring our experiences to another setting would like an answer to this, but I certainly don't know.

LAURA: I would like to know too. Every time I tried to talk to a particular math teacher at my other high school about my teaching, he was only interested in the specifics of the curriculum – what worksheet came next. He didn't have the motivation to talk about personal or student mathematical knowledge. A wall developed between his idea of curriculum and mine. We couldn't collaborate unless it was around a text or something already in place. He clearly did not believe the teacher needed to take on any responsibility for creating curriculum; teachers should work with what was already given. Most of our conversations ended up focused around questions like, "How do I teach this chapter?" instead of "Why should I teach this chapter? What are my goals?" I think one of the keys to "challenging mathematical knowledge" is team-teaching. (It's also one of the only ways to transfer "Holt math.") But how is this accomplished in a school that doesn't have the money, doesn't have the resources (teachers), doesn't have a connection to a teacher education program with a year-long internship, or doesn't believe that team-teaching is worth spending time on? A young teacher would have a very hard time convincing more experienced ones to take such a big risk.

KELLY: It seems César is saying that from a teacher education program with consistent coursework and fairly consistent classmates, two interns can become different sorts of teachers. He also says that both of these interns were expected to become "successful" teachers. On the one hand, this makes sense to me. No two people will experience any teaching in quite the same way, and over the course of years the way they interpret these experiences could lead them to value different things in their teaching. Thus, they would have different teacher identities. We've all had the experience of learning things from different sorts of teachers, so the idea that different sorts of teachers could be similarly successful is not hard to accept. On the other hand, from my perspective as a teacher educator, I wonder if it's really OK for some teacher candidates to have the opportunity to wrestle with their own mathematical understandings every day in public and then plan based on the results of this work, while others do not. What exactly do we mean by "successful" for interns in such different contexts?

LAURA: And how can we say that interns who have struggled with teachers over how to teach from a textbook or some other rigid curriculum get enough perspective on teaching to become successful teachers? Figuring out new and cool ways of *telling* students information is not my idea of curriculum reform, and I don't think it's the kind of curriculum reform supported by the math education program at MSU either. How can we make sure that interns placed at other schools don't come away from their teacher preparation with such a perspective? Complaints from other interns about the relationship between their TE class work and their placements indicate they don't see TE coursework as what teaching is really about. The experience of their placement is the reality. The things they learned from their mentor teachers were the perspectives they would take away from the internship year. How much did the conversations we had in class affect their thinking about teaching and learning? I suspect not nearly as much as their experience in the field. It would so be easily pushed aside.

KELLY: As an instructor for those classes, I certainly hope this isn't true, but there seems to be some evidence it is.

Part III

Professional growth and development

The previous two sections have focused on changes in teaching practice and on the resulting experiences of the high school students and teacher candidates at the university level. These sections documented change in instructional practices and changes in student course-taking.

What led to the change in course-taking? While this change may be a part of a larger national phenomenon, the magnitude of this change seems large. There is a plausible explanation for students' course-taking that connects it with the work of the teachers outlined in Part I. In Chapter 7, Jan Simonson argued that Marty Schnepp's changes in his teaching went beyond the particular practices that he adopted; there were also important changes, indeed a transformation, in his beliefs.

This point holds more generally for the department; it is very hard to separate changes in teachers' practices from change in their espoused beliefs. Thus, changes in classroom practice also reflect shifts in the department's thinking about their students. The student experiences described in the last section reflect an important change in teachers' stance. In the words of Mike Lehman, the department chair,

> We [the Holt math department] have come to believe that instead of mathematics being for those who are gifted with the ability to do mathematics, it is for all students. It is our job to find meaningful ways to make it accessible to our students.

This shift is dramatically evident in the department's stance on algebra. The few exceptions made each year to the expectation that all students will enroll in courses that are Algebra 1 or above in the Holt layer cake only underscore the shift in the math department. Such exceptions often cause tension between the math department, which assumes that all students can learn algebra as it is taught at Holt and some members of the counseling department, who continue to view algebra as simply too difficult for some students.

This change in attitude represents a reinvigorated commitment to egalitarian ideals of mathematical reasoning. It is not simply a change of heart. It is a complicated shift that has to do with both the advocacy of individual teachers for disenfranchised students and the adoption of teaching practices that helped teachers see strengths in students traditionally perceived as weak. As teachers integrated discussion into their classrooms and practiced listening to students, what they heard often challenged their views of student abilities (see Chapter 15 for a description of an experience of Marty Schnepp's). For example, as teachers used a variety of representations in algebra, as well as calculators and computers that linked these representations, students with special needs were more successful (see Chapter 8 for example). While the changes in students' course-taking described in the introduction to the last part are complex phenomena, as the first three essays in that section suggested, it seems plausible that there is some connection between changes in teachers' beliefs and practices and changes in student course-taking.

What led to the shift in departmental stance described above? The focus of Part III shifts to teachers' experiences. This section looks at the professional development of the Holt High School mathematics department faculty. Taken together, these three sections indicate connections between teachers' professional development, their teaching practices, and students' experience (in the spirit of the National Academy of Education's (1999) desire to connect the "dots" between professional development and student achievement).

In keeping with the rest of this book, this part offers a story of professional development, a story that emphasizes principles, not a model. In particular, our story emphasizes the notion of professional development as the result of shared work, involving both university and school personnel, on important problems of practice. Though our story involves particular strategies, for example, shared teaching assignments (as emphasized in Kelly and Laura's response in Chapter 12), it does not suggest a model for how professional development might be provided to teachers, or indeed even how teachers and university educators might work together on problems of practice, once they are identified. In our view, such things are not amenable to general models, but must be tailored to the problem of practice, contextual variables, and the individuals involved.

A central challenge of this section is representation of the role and ethos of the MSU/Holt High School Professional Development School (PDS) relationship. This relationship is an important part of the story, but it is not the whole story. This section of the book testifies to an enduring connection between Holt High School and Michigan State University (MSU), only part of which can be attributed to the PDS initiative.

Since the mid-1980s, the work lives of some mathematics educators in the MSU Department of Teacher Education have been intertwined with those of the faculty in the Holt High School mathematics department. Some of this intertwining pre-dates the PDS effort. For example, in the late 1980s, Perry Lanier, a faculty member in teacher education at MSU, and Sandy Callis, then a teacher at Holt Junior High School, worked together on the experience of General Math students. Mike Lehman, then a teacher at the high school, and Bill York, then the chair of the Holt math department, were mentor teachers for an MSU teacher education program called Academic Learning. Indeed, these relationships are part of what led Holt High School to be considered a potential PDS partner. And this sort of intertwining continued. For example, as indicated earlier, university faculty and graduate students taught at the high school and high school math teachers taught in MSU's teacher education program. See Figure III.1.

Some of this intertwining of the two institutions resulted explicitly from the funding that supported a PDS relationship between the high school and the university. This section first discusses the MSU/Holt High School PDS effort. This effort was a direct and strong influence on the high school from 1989 until 1995, when its' funding was reduced. The PDS effort has been an educational reform not present in most schools, one that yielded special opportunities for teachers. For example, Mike Lehman's essay in this chapter and the essay in Chapter 14 both describe experiences that would never have happened without the special funding associated with the PDS effort.

These two essays capture an important aspect of the ethos of the PDS effort – one that is central to the argument Jan Simonson makes in Chapter 15. The rhetoric of the PDS effort focused on teachers as professionals. Rather than conceptualizing professional development as the dissemination of research results from universities to schools, the PDS effort conceptualized it as professional inquiry jointly involving university faculty and high school teachers. There was the expectation that Holt teachers and MSU faculty would carry out research and development together. Thus, in the same way that teachers at Holt seek to recognize their students' capacity for

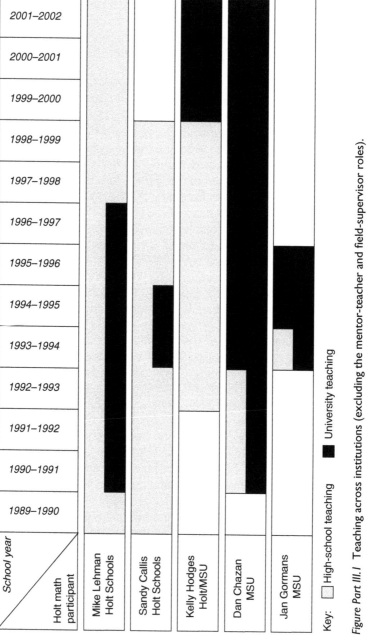

Figure Part III.1 Teaching across institutions (excluding the mentor-teacher and field-supervisor roles).

productive reasoning, the MSU/PDS effort was founded on the notion that teachers reason in important ways about their own practice. In her piece, through the eyes of one teacher, Simonson suggests that the PDS effort successfully fostered a culture of teacher professionalism and inquiry among the teachers in the high school math department.

But the professional development opportunities that support the changes described in Parts I and II are not limited to the PDS effort, nor to interaction with MSU faculty. In understanding the opportunities of Holt teachers, it is important to examine those that are more integral to everyday teaching. Some of these, like implementing curricular change and interaction with students and colleagues about the subject one teaches, involve subject matter. Others, like being a mentor teacher and continued university coursework, can be more "generic." This section will examine each of these.

Nonetheless, as this part looks at these more standard avenues for professional development, the essays suggest that the character of these opportunities is influenced strongly by the ethos of the Holt/MSU PDS effort. Teachers in the Holt mathematics department, even those who were not members of the department during the heyday of the PDS effort, approach their daily teaching, their work with interns, and their continuing education as opportunities for continued inquiry into mathematics teaching. They have worked actively to shape opportunities common in teaching towards their own goals.

Thus, the PDS effort is an important part of the professional development story in the Holt High School math department. It even seems fair to suggest that, even though since 1995 PDS funding has been limited, the money expended on the PDS effort early in the 1990s is still reaping benefits years later. These benefits continue to accrue even when some of the key participants in that effort have moved on to other endeavors, and even for members of the department who have been hired after the heyday of the PDS effort. Of course, for those who have entered since the PDS effort, these benefits may not be seen as benefits of the PDS effort, but rather as aspects of the established culture of the Holt math department. Situations like this one make evaluation of professional development initiatives quite complicated.

Once again, this section includes an interlude about on-campus activities designed for teacher candidates. But the interlude in this part has a different flavor. Some of the on-campus activities in MSU's College of Education seek to foster the very practices that the Holt math department looks for when it advertises for colleagues. Thus it is not very surprising that Holt High School has hired many of the teacher candidates who interned at the school. For these interns, their on-campus activities as part of their preservice education can also be viewed as early components of their development as teachers. As a result, Chapter 18 includes a short description of a mathematical component of the senior-level mathematics education course taken by preservice teachers.

Chapter 13

Time and respect

This section begins with the early part of the Holt/MSU PDS relationship, from 1989 to 1993. The first essay in this section by Mike Lehman, a key Holt participant in the PDS effort, delivers a retrospective account of his initial PDS experiences. Mike focuses on what it was like for him as a teacher to participate in this initiative. Before turning to Mike's essay, it seems useful to provide more background on the MSU PDS effort.

In doing so, it is helpful to distinguish between the PDS effort undertaken by MSU with a number of mid-Michigan schools, the presence of this effort inside Holt High School, and finally the particular way relationships developed inside Holt's math department. When examined from these different perspectives, there are different stories. Relationships between high school math department faculty and MSU colleagues continue to deepen over time. Relationships between faculty members in other departments at Holt and university faculty are also ongoing. But, between 1989 and the present, MSU's larger PDS effort grew, flourished, then withered. For example, by 2001, there was no office at MSU charged with administering a PDS effort.

A full-scale examination of this complex initiative is far beyond the scope of this book, but it seems useful to introduce some key features. Initially, MSU's effort to create PDS relationships began with a small number of schools (roughly ten at various times during the early stages); the plan was for MSU to have such relationships with a large number of Michigan schools. These relationships would help further school reform in Michigan, would serve MSU's teacher education needs, and would enrich educational research. Funding for this effort came from the business community, the state, and the university.

Holt High School was the only high school PDS. Like most of these PDS relationships that MSU started, the PDS initiative at Holt was a full-school effort; it did not create a school within a school; it would have an impact on the high school as a whole and its ways of working. Of course, that did not mean that every Holt faculty member participated at all times. For example, as described below by Mike Lehman, early on, teachers at the high school decided to petition the district's board of education for professional time on Wednesday mornings. The proposal was to extend the school day throughout the week and then to have students begin school at 11 a.m. on Wednesdays. Wednesday mornings would then be used for teachers' professional activity. (Indeed, this practice is still in place in 2007!) Though this action wasn't a project of the PDS effort, the idea was one that bubbled up during discussions under the PDS auspices. It represents a concrete way in which the PDS emphasis on teacher professionalism became institutionalized at Holt and influenced the whole school. Similarly, on the MSU side, the project involved the complete College of Education, not just the Department of Teacher Education (though other departments were not as involved as Teacher Education was).

Central to MSU's larger PDS effort was the notion of a project. PDS projects were most often efforts inside a single PDS. They required involvement of both university and school participants. At Holt, as a high school PDS, departments played an important role in the evolution of the PDS effort; this was not the case with the MSU's relationships with elementary schools. Initially, most of Holt High School's projects were department-sponsored. Later there were whole-school projects.

Initially, PDS schools would propose projects and budgets to the central PDS office run initially by Charles Thompson, then an MSU administrator, and Perry Lanier. This central office then examined projects and determined the budget of each school. Each school had governance structures to administer its PDS projects. At Holt, initially Perry Lanier, and then later Tom Bird and other faculty members from the Department of Teacher Education, participated in the school's PDS council. This council made important and difficult decisions about the allocation of PDS funds and directions of the PDS effort. This governance structure existed alongside the existing administrative structure of the school.

From the beginning of the PDS effort, the Holt mathematics department was an active participant. Perry Lanier, Mike Lehman, Bill York, and Sandy Callis proposed a number of projects during the early years of the PDS effort. As a result, from 1989 through 1997, MSU doctoral students (e.g., Pam Geist, Neli Wolff, Donald Dryden, Jan Simonson, and Dara Sandow) worked at Holt documenting math-department PDS projects. Most semesters, one doctoral student would work at the school on math department projects for approximately ten hours a week.

In addition to doctoral-student assistantships, the PDS effort also funded time for secondary teachers. In the mathematics department, over time, there was an evolution in how PDS release hours were used. Initially, these hours were used for meetings, writing, and other project activities, like observing in each other's classrooms, but much of the time went towards solitary work. Later on, as will be examined in Chapter 14, release hours served to free up teachers to share teaching assignments.

With this background, Mike Lehman's description of his participation in the early PDS efforts is now accessible. Following Mike's essay, Adam Kelly and Craig Huhn respond from the perspective of teachers who hired in once the PDS effort was a less direct and visible influence on the high school. For them, other aspects of the MSU/Holt partnership are more salient, like MSU's five-year teacher education program and its internship.

Being treated (and treating ourselves) as professionals

Michael F. Lehman, Holt High School

This essay was written for this volume.

The initial opportunity

In spring 1989, faculty members from the College of Education at Michigan State University approached a number of teachers at Holt High School and proposed we create a Professional Development School (PDS). As high school teachers, we didn't know exactly what that meant. We already had a long-standing relationship with MSU through our work with student teachers from the university. Many of us had been involved with an MSU teacher education program called "Academic Learning." We had helped shape some of the courses offered in Academic Learning and met with MSU personnel on a regular basis to evaluate work being done with preservice teachers.

Dr.[1] Perry Lanier from MSU, who had been a leader of Academic Learning and was going to be one of the leaders of the PDS effort, met with us that spring to discuss what a PDS was and what it might look like at Holt. Many of us had trouble envisioning this. The interaction was formal. "Just tell us what you want us to do," we told Dr. Lanier. Of course, he couldn't do that. As I have realized since, a PDS has to be developed from within, not from outside. Banking on the trust we had built with MSU and Perry over the years, we agreed to attend a two-week institute that summer. It was during the institute that we came to understand what the PDS might be about, and we became excited about the possibilities for Holt involvement. We spent much time at the institute considering how to convince other Holt staff members to participate or at least allow us to take part in the PDS effort.

Responsibility for one's own professional development

What hooked us on the PDS was the idea that we could build our own professional development program. Continually during the institute we were impressed by the quality of conversation about teaching and learning. The presenters recognized our expertise as teachers and expected us to shape our own development as professionals. It felt good to be treated as professionals with valued experience, treatment that stood in sharp contrast to the professional development we were accustomed to. Too often, professional development consisted of being given solutions to problems we didn't know we had. It was an approach that left us cold. In contrast, the professional development possibilities discussed at the 1989 summer institute were so exciting that Holt's participation the following year rose from 13 participants to 27.

I found myself energized by these conversations and was particularly intrigued by the sessions on cooperative learning. The idea of having students working together to solve a problem was nothing new, but having them work together in ways that helped them create new knowledge was. I attended every session I could on cooperative learning. But I began to notice that the presenters never featured examples from mathematics. They always used science, social studies, or language arts for their examples. When I asked why, they said they'd never thought of mathematics. They weren't sure how it would work. I discussed this with my colleagues from Holt and with some colleagues from MSU. During these discussions I realized that, if this was my question, then I should be the one to answer it. This led me to understand what all the conversations from spring were about. The goal of a PDS is to enable teachers to work to answer their own questions. From hereon out, I was convinced that the PDS concept was valuable for Holt High School.

In fall 1989, those of us who had attended the institute faced the task of convincing the rest of the teaching staff at Holt how worthwhile the PDS initiative would be. Some staff members mistrusted the university. They expected that experts from the university would come in and tell us what to do and how to teach. Many were concerned that the PDS would be another fly-by-night, short-term project: in a year or two, as soon as the university got what it wanted, it would pull out, leaving us with the consequences.

As a staff, we had many long, heated debates over these and other issues. Several things helped those who had attended the institute prevail in the end. First, we were obviously enthusiastic about the project. No matter what the detractors said, they could not dampen the excitement of the group. Second, we were ready to move forward with this. Finally, we made it clear that participation was voluntary, although teachers were welcome to join us in the PDS effort at any time. These conversations resulted in a green light for the PDS project, but we had to remain mindful of the concerns of others and work to bring them along.

Getting started: one fundamental change – making time

The nature and depth of the conversations from the summer institute were so powerful; we knew we wanted to continue them. But when, staff wondered, would these discussions take place? Under our then-current schedule, the only option was after school. We all knew that meeting after a full day of teaching would be problematic. People would be tired, and many had family or other obligations that would prevent them from participating.

As it turned out, we already had a group of teachers working on this issue. And after some of them attended the summer institute, they were increasingly motivated to find more time. They came up with a simple, unique idea. We would add five minutes to each of our classes, making our school day 30 minutes longer. This gained us two hours and 45 minutes a week. We would then end school every day at 2:35 p.m. and start four days a week at 7:45 a.m. But on Wednesdays, students wouldn't come in until 11 a.m. While our classrooms were quiet on Wednesday mornings, we the teachers would use our newly acquired time for study and discussion of professional development issues.

Since we were doing this voluntarily (not by administrative fiat!) and without extra pay, this meant the Wednesday-morning time was ours to use as we wished, particularly for discussions or projects we found appropriate. (Of course, there have been tussles from time to time between the agendas of teachers and those of administrators.) More than a decade later, the Wednesday-morning time still continues at Holt. Though we continue to argue about how best to take advantage of it, in my view, carving out time for ourselves has proven to be the biggest and most important change in my professional life since I've been at Holt. As a regular part of our week, we have time to talk with other staff members in the school. We can develop projects that we feel would improve student learning, do the necessary research, and apply the findings in our classrooms.

This approach to time was not limited to Wednesday mornings. In the early PDS activities, we scheduled time in our normal working days

– not after-school time or during family time – to work on PDS pro-jects. As part of the funding for the PDS initiative, the district deployed PDS funding to hire replacement teachers, freeing up those participating in the PDS work for an hour a day to work on related projects. This was our first encounter with this type of respect for our professionalism. We consequently developed a new attitude towards the use of our time. Since many of us valued the professional respect that was implied by this provision of time, we did not waste it. As we put our time to good use, we found that it was never enough for what we wanted to do. We became protective of it and pushed each other to use it well.

The initial startup of projects

Developing those first few PDS projects was difficult. We had never been asked to design projects that would lead to our own professional development. We were accustomed to someone in a position of higher authority telling us what kind of professional development we needed. After many long and difficult meetings, we were able to narrow down what truly interested us. As only two of us from the mathematics department had participated in the original meetings and summer insti-tute, we benefited greatly from Perry's help. As a mathematics educator, he knew a great deal about teaching and learning mathematics. He came to the meetings and served as our mentor as we developed ideas.

He also introduced us to the vast resources available at MSU and beyond. He connected us with MSU faculty members who shared our interest on many issues. To help us develop more student interaction within our classrooms, he introduced us to another MSU faculty member, Tom Bird, who taught us how students can work together in meaningful ways that enhance their understanding. Tom's guidance was important to me as I sought to introduce cooperative learning into my math classes.

Through Perry, we also connected with another valuable MSU resource: doctoral students who were willing to teach with us or for us, giving us time to work on our projects. One such student was Sandra Callis. A graduate of MSU's teacher education program, Sandy had taught at Holt Junior High for a few years before returning to MSU to work on her doctorate. During the first year of the PDS effort, while she was still a graduate student, she came back to Holt to teach a class of mine, giving me release time to work on incorporating cooperative learning and discussions in my Algebra 2 class. Before long, Sandy and I were having many conversations about teaching and learning mathe-matics. As she taught a class in my room, I found myself observing Sandy and talking with her about her approach. As it turned out, we were interested in similar issues, so I had an easily accessible model to observe. The next year, Sandy left the doctoral program and came back to teach at the high school, though at first her focus was primarily on Spanish. As projects in the math department developed, she gradually began to teach more math and finally became full-time in the department.

Pamela Geist, an MSU doctoral student hired to document PDS projects in the Holt math department, was another valuable resource from MSU. As I struggled with changing my practice, Pam would observe and document changes in my instruction. She did so in a nonjudgmental way, which made it very comfortable having her in my classroom. Pam and I soon developed a close working relationship. I could ask her about how she felt I should proceed, and she could question me on some of what I did in my class. This became an opportunity for me to study my own practice and make meaningful changes.

Looking back

In retrospect, it's hard to separate out what happened as a result of PDS from what might have happened otherwise in our school. Often it is hard to know where work on the PDS ended and the work of our department began. But, perhaps that's appropriate.

Regardless, I think some substantive changes in the mathematics department were made possible by the PDS. Probably most important are the newfound respect that has developed among those who participated in PDS projects. Sharing students, experiences, and questions about our own practice and understandings of the mathematics we teach, we have also become close friends who enjoy working and socializing together.

This type of close working relationship has benefited students at Holt beyond our expectations. The constant collaboration with MSU and the growth of relationships within our department have led to some serious curricular changes (as previously described in this book). We have changed the lower-track curriculum, while increasing the number of students taking higher-track mathematics. The latter development resulted both from the elimination of some lower-track coursework and from some changed attitudes on the part of the teaching staff. Mathematics, we now believe, is not just for those gifted with mathematical ability. Mathematics is appropriate for all students, and it is our job to find meaningful ways to make it accessible to everyone. Many changes in our classroom practices have sprung from this shift in thinking. We now encourage more discussions around the mathematics we teach. We listen more carefully to students and try to focus our teaching around their questions instead of around the next concept in the sequence. We have learned to develop concepts around situations that the students can understand and to work with, instead of around, symbol manipulation. We have come to value students' spoken contributions within the classroom and have formalized them into oral exams where students share their understanding with a panel of adults.

It would be nice to say that all members of the department share this way of thinking, and perhaps at this point we all do. But it was certainly not always the case. As indicated earlier, participation in PDS activity has been voluntary, though, of course, those of us involved in PDS activities tried to involve those who chose not to be PDS participants in our discussions and decisions. And, of course, as in any group, there were controversies. It's fair to say that those teachers have also grown professionally and are thinking differently about teaching and learning. While I would not claim the PDS as the main factor in their growth, I am comfortable saying that the atmosphere supported by the PDS effort, the atmosphere that allows teachers to think beyond traditional approaches, had an impact on their classrooms as well.

As the PDS process evolved, Holt has also grown considerably in size. The mathematics department has expanded from five members to ten, and we have hired a number of our interns to fill this need for additional teachers. In the past ten years, seven of the teachers we have hired have been interns at Holt. This has helped to develop the sense of community within our department. For these folks who were hired once the PDS effort no longer provided monetary support, PDS funding may not be salient, but I believe nonetheless that our PDS involvement continues to shape the environment in which they learned to teach and now practice their profession.

Thoughts from latecomers

Adam Kelly and Craig Huhn, Holt High School

ADAM KELLY: For the most part, I think the relationships within the Holt math department are very strong. When we discuss mathematical questions students or teachers have raised, you know how often we get teased at lunch by colleagues from other departments? We're always talking about cool ideas that students have come up with, or various contexts that we have presented, or how we can help each other further our understanding of the mathematics involved. I think we've also developed the ability to genuinely listen to each other's questions and ideas and respond to them in a patient, non-judgmental way. I know my confidence has grown so that I can present any question or idea to this group. I know my colleagues will listen, question, and attempt to help me the same way that I'm willing to help them. It is interesting to ask how this came to be.

CRAIG HUHN: We were interns together with Mike Lehman during the 1998–1999 school year, that is, roughly a decade after the initial PDS effort started. As a newcomer that year, I had no idea what it meant to be a PDS, nor was I familiar with what our Wednesday mornings were for. What *was* immediately obvious, though, is something I'm still struggling to describe. It was a feeling, an ambiance, that I had never encountered before; there was an expectation of effort, excellence, and thoughtfulness.

ADAM: It's good that you bring up Mike's name. Of course, it's possible some of our closeness stems from the fact that six of us in the math department performed our internships at Holt through MSU, five of those with Mike. We all spent *a lot* of time with him. He compelled us to consider and explain *what* and *why* we are teaching, which eventually prepared us to do the same within the department across various studies of mathematics. We get together outside of school to socialize, and I believe that our becoming true friends has helped us become more comfortable offering and sharing ideas within the workplace.

CRAIG: Our internship certainly played an important role. But it isn't the only factor. I hear about how the PDS effort has declined in participation, funding, and structure. But even if the current effort barely holds a candle to that of the past, from my perspective, the work done now during Wednesday mornings is incredibly important to me. I don't know what I missed during the height of the PDS effort. All I see now is a school that has a culture amazingly different from any other place I have been, visited, or heard about through the experiences of peers. All I see is a unique half-day, set aside every week, to work on issues of teaching and learning. All I see is a staff that has come so far working on and thinking about contemporary school issues that we are leaders at the conferences we attend. For me, the outlook of the PDS is life-changing.

ADAM: You are right to point to other aspects besides our internship. I've really enjoyed having meaningful discussions and relationships with so many individuals within the department. It's comforting to know that my colleagues will approach me with their questions, as well as listen to my inquiries. These discussions improve my capacity to talk about mathematics, which is vital to my work with students.

CRAIG: I am aware, though, that people who have been here longer feel that things are changing. Several teachers in the building now choose to use Wednesday morning as their own time, to take care of copying, grading, and the other various jobs teachers have to find time for. This is okay, since the time is voluntary, but I pick up on the feeling that a larger percentage of the staff is making this choice than before. This supports those who argue that the PDS is going downhill. PDS used to fund many projects and to provide release time for teachers to team-teach and observe their colleagues in practice. The money that used to be provided each year has dwindled to almost nothing. Apparently, we used to do more things in interdisciplinary groups to work on whole-school issues. And our department does seem different than some others. Today, there are other departments that barely work together on Wednesday mornings. But there is no denying – it's very clear those years of professional development were crucial in making Holt what it is today.

Chapter 14

Restructuring teacher work

As Mike Lehman indicates, the beginning of the PDS effort was a heady time in participant schools. Teachers felt that their expertise was being acknowledged and that their time was respected and valued. In addition, they had access to funds for project work. Similarly, university faculty interested in working with teachers in schools could find support for their efforts.

At the same time, there was a larger field of play, outside of school-level efforts. Judith Lanier, at first Dean of MSU's College of Education and President of the Holmes Group, established a coalition of funders for PDS efforts. The State of Michigan, local philanthropists, and state universities all contributed funds or resources with the hope of reforming schools in Michigan and improving teacher education and educational research. Subsequently, a new organization, the Michigan Partnership for New Education (MPNE), initially directed by Judy Lanier, was created to manage these funds and the nascent network of Professional Development Schools that would be created throughout the state. Starting in the 1993–1994 academic year, funding levels for PDS projects in existing schools increased dramatically to more than $2 million per year. These projects were supposed to have dramatic impacts on the Professional Development Schools. This was also the time during which the PDS effort was supposed to increase dramatically in size. MSU was going to develop enough PDS relationships to ensure every MSU preservice candidate a PDS placement.

Though none of the participants knew then, funding for PDS projects was about to peak. At its peak, in 1994–1995, the PDS initiative brought $208,000 to Holt High School for projects in four departments. This funding to the school provided MSU graduate students with assistantships to participate in PDS projects. On some occasions, it supplied support for faculty participation as well; but most faculty time was contributed to the effort by the university. And, the money was also employed to release teachers from teaching in order to participate in funded projects. During 1994–1995, there might have been as many as six doctoral students participating in PDS projects in different departments at Holt High School. Other doctoral students might be present at the school, as field instructors for interns placed in the department or in other capacities. At this time, the intertwining of school and university was especially evident. Teachers would see MSU faculty and doctoral students in their building on a regular basis. And, there were important venues for interaction and shared work. Individual teachers and MSU faculty members began to view each other as colleagues on matters of shared interest.

Returning to the Holt mathematics department, starting in 1993–1994 with the increase in available funds for projects, the department began to spend money on release hours for teachers. But these hours were employed differently; they were used to support the sharing of high school mathematics teaching assignments (as Sandy Callis and Dan Chazan had done in 1991–1992 and 1992–1993 with funding from the Dow-Corning Foundation). One teacher was released from teaching a section of a course and a replacement was hired or found. With this release hour, that teacher would then join another in sharing a teaching assignment in which the department was exploring an innovation in teaching. The participating teachers were expected to share what they were learning in Wednesday-morning department meetings. During the 1993–1994, 1994–1995, and 1995–1996 academic years, a majority of the department's PDS funding went to support of such arrangements. For example, in 1994–1995, $28,000 were allocated to math-department PDS projects. These funds supported three teacher release hours and one graduate student participant. Altogether, from 1993 through 1996, PDS funds supported seven shared teaching assignments.

After 1995–1996 and reductions in the levels of PDS funding, these shared teaching assignments became so important to the department that other funds were enlisted to create such arrangements. For example, Sandy Callis used her work on a professional development project for local algebra teachers funded through the provost's office at MSU to enable her to share an Algebra 1 teaching assignment with Kellie Huhn, and to share a teaching assignment in a Holt 5th-grade mathematics classroom. Similarly, Marty Schnepp used funding from Technical Education Research Center in Cambridge, Massachusetts to share a Calculus teaching assignment with Kellie Huhn. Beth Berwald and Steve Neurither used funds from a local computer manufacturer to support a shared Geometry teaching assignment. Figure 14.1 below is a complete listing of the teaching assignments shared by teachers in the Holt math department. All told, by 1996, every member of the math department in 1993 had shared at least one teaching assignment with another member of the department.

Teachers	Chazan & York	Callis & Chazan	Callis & Chazan	Hodges & Schnepp	Callis & Schnepp	Hodges & Mooney	Neurither & Schnepp	Callis & Lehman	Callis & Lehman	Larner & Schnepp	Berwald & Neurither	Callis & K. Huhn	Berwald & Neurither	Huhn & Schnepp
Class / Funder	*Algebra 1* **Dow-Corning**	*Algebra 1* **Dow-Corning**	*Algebra 1* **Dow-Corning**	*Algebra 1* **2 classes combined**	*Algebra 1* **PDS**	*Geometry* **PDS**	*Algebra 1* **PDS**	*Algebra 1* **PDS**	*Algebra 2* **PDS**	*Algebra 1* **PDS**	*Geometry* **PDS**	*Algebra 1* **MSU**	*Geometry* **CAD Firm**	*Calculus* **TERC**
School year	1990–1991	1991–1992	1992–1993		1993–1994		1994–1995			1995–1996		1996–1997	1997–1998	1998–1999

Figure 14.1 Shared teaching assignments among HHS math teachers (excluding interns): 14 over 9 years.

These shared teaching assignments are central to the ethos of the PDS effort inside the Holt mathematics department; they were a crucial mechanism for professional development. At one and the same time, they helped form the culture of inquiry into teaching that developed in the math department, and they were shaped by the ways in which the culture in the department had begun to evolve. While the university played a role as funder of these interactions, the initial model came from the interaction of a faculty member and a teacher, and some of the ideas about teaching that were being explored were initially brought to the school by university faculty; university personnel were not actively involved in these collaborations. These were collaborations among teachers.

With the shared teaching assignments, teachers could observe each other's practice firsthand as they tried out an innovation, rather than simply discuss the happenings of their separate classrooms. A host of factors influenced these shared assignments – the beliefs and personalities of the participating individuals, administrative support (versus compulsion), the role of the department chair, and general school resources and culture. We argue that four characteristics of these assignments made them valuable. Shared teaching assignments were created around identified problems of practice, involved a specific practice being tried, allowed for shared attempts at practice, and encouraged trust and reflection.

The next essay comes from an investigation of the 1994–1995 shared teaching assignments. Though the math department's PDS proposal requested $40,000 for 4.5 release hours plus three graduate students, the department was funded with $28,000 to support three release hours involving four teachers. One graduate student would document the efforts of the department. Jan Simonson, then a graduate student, and David ben-Haim, a visiting scholar, interviewed the four teachers sharing assignments that year in the fall and the spring. The teachers were then invited to write about their experience in the fall of 1995 and a meeting was held with the four of them during the spring of 1996. These data were then analyzed. Analysis of the teachers' views suggests that three dynamics explain how the shared responsibilities in the same classroom created potential for substantial professional growth. The first dynamic is the opportunity to become an observer of the students one is teaching. Rather than having to always act, teachers could take turns sitting back, watching, and reflecting on the nature of their own students' learning. The second dynamic involves the complexity of the shared experience and the need for an expanded vocabulary to discuss this kind of teaching. Sharing an experience – being able to point, rather than describe – allowed these four teachers to learn from each other in ways that were simply not possible when relying on verbal accounts to share classroom experience. The third dynamic related to the shared nature of the teachers' responsibilities. They had to arrive at decisions and act *jointly*. Team-teaching necessitated teachers working together in ways that their colleagues working solo never had to consider.

Finally, the essay hints at more long-lasting impacts of the shared teaching assignments on the culture of the Holt mathematics department. Shared teaching assignments were year-long affairs. So, while individual workdays often didn't hold enough time for reflection and planning (e.g., if the two teachers' planning periods did not match), the very length of the commitment fostered trust between partners. That trust often came into play when, almost by necessity, joint responsibility led to friction. Issues had to be worked through in order for the paired teachers to continue working productively together. An important question is whether the ties that developed between teachers throughout the experience not only helped in challenging situations but also afforded benefits that outlived the shared teaching itself. In their response to the essay, Kelly Hodges and Craig Huhn raise this question. They also point out that internships under MSU's five-year teacher preparation program have many of the characteristics of the shared teaching assignments described in this essay.

Shared teaching assignments

Daniel Chazan, David ben-Haim, and Janice Simonson with Sandra Callis, Michael Lehman, Steven Neurither, and Marty Schnepp, Michigan State University, University of Haifa, Calvin College, Holt Public Schools

This essay is excerpted from an article originally published in 1998 in *Teaching and Teacher Education*, 14(7), 687–702.

Scholarly literature on team-teaching (e.g., Geen, 1985) suggests that, to be effective, team-teaching should be organized around some defining purpose, initiated by the involved teachers, and supported by administrators and/or department heads. Many of these conditions were met in the Holt High School mathematics department.

The shared teaching assignments at Holt to be discussed below centered on a new approach to algebra, a subject that is often problematic for students. At Holt, this change of mathematical emphasis has been coupled with the teachers' desire to take responsibility for the direction of the mathematics curriculum (as discussed in Chapter 4). Rather than leave curricular decisions to textbook authors who are remote in time and space from the school, teachers have used their evolving understanding of school algebra to design their courses. Members of the Holt math department also seek to change the patterns of discourse in their algebra classrooms (as illustrated in Chapter 3). Unlike a lecture pattern, in which the teacher presents a procedure for students to learn and practice, a problem-solving orientation begins with a problem being posed, followed by student exploration and whole-group discussion. (For descriptions of problem-solving orientations toward teaching, see Lester, 1994 and National Council of Teachers of Mathematics, 1991.) And teachers (with the support of administrators) are also eager to change the nature of discourse within the department itself. In particular, in the process of adopting a new mathematical perspective on school algebra, teachers have become accustomed to questioning their own mathematical understandings. They now seek explanations for mathematics that they once took for granted. (This theme will be pursued at greater length in Chapter 17 in this section, as well as in other parts of the section.)

The 1994–1995 shared teaching assignments: arrangements between the teachers

For the 1994–1995 school year, the mathematics department wrote a Professional Development School proposal, based on previous work, calling for the participation of four teachers in three shared algebra teaching assignments. This represented half of the math department. These four teachers had previously experienced different organizational arrangements with shared responsibility for instruction. They had worked with special-education teachers, student teachers, departmental colleagues, and with a university professor. But, as Sandy Callis noted, "collaboration means different things to different people and is an extremely complex relationship to negotiate" (prepared text, fall 95).

For these team assignments, both pairs agreed to share year-long responsibility for teaching one section of Algebra 1; one pair also took responsibility for a section of Algebra 2. Team members would be present each day of class and would share the instructional tasks. Outside of class sessions, the two 1994–1995 teams had slightly different circumstances. Mike Lehman and Sandy Callis were able to schedule a common planning period, while Steve Neureither and Marty Schnepp were unable to do so. But both groups required regular, almost daily meeting time to coordinate their policies on issues such as grading, for example.

> We've been at least checking with each other almost daily. And when we have papers to grade, we will sit down and grade those together.
> (Steve, fall interview, 1994)

As a result, Steve and Marty found the lack of built-in planning time difficult.

> This meant that our collaboration time was on our common lunch and during regular meetings after school.
>
> (Steve, prepared text, fall 1995)

Though their work was joint, the teachers' contributions to the collaboration were not identical. Each team paired a teacher experienced in the new approach to algebra with one less familiar with the concept. Marty Schnepp and Sandy Callis, who had team-taught Algebra 1 in 1993–1994, agreed to help introduce the other team member to the new approach. They agreed to supply background about the overarching philosophy and direction of the concept, as well as ideas about using previously developed curriculum materials. On the Algebra 2 team, Mike and Sandy's roles were different – Mike was more familiar with the Algebra 2 curriculum, while Sandy was more familiar with the alternative view of algebra.

Though the roles of the teachers were not completely symmetrical, it is important to emphasize that opportunities to learn went in both directions. Marty and Sandy were also interested in learning from their colleagues. They hoped to participate in the further development of the curricular materials and to grow in their personal understanding of teaching algebra, particularly in the context of the Algebra 2 class. All four teachers were experienced; among them, careers ranged from 7 to 20 years. They expected to learn from the particular expertise of their colleagues (e.g., with alternative assessment) and from the wealth of their accumulated experience. In attempting to describe this dynamic, Mike wrote of his pairing with Sandy:

> Our purpose was twofold. One, to get me more acquainted with the function-based Algebra 1 curriculum and how it was taught. The second was to get Sandy acquainted with the Algebra 2 curriculum and also to begin to conceive units for this course.
>
> (prepared text, fall 1995)

Focused analysis of teacher interviews

In interviews and writing, all four teachers emphasized the power that the shared teaching assignments present as a mode of professional development. In a representative comment, Marty Schnepp wrote:

> Team-teaching has provided for me opportunities that have alleviated much of my frustration as a teacher. Traditional methods

of professional development – one-day workshops, research articles, etc. – were a large part of the frustrations I had felt as a teacher trying to improve my practice. For me, they helped foster a notion that to become an excellent teacher, I needed only see someone do it right and then copy their technique.... I know that for me and my colleagues at Holt High School teaching together on a daily basis (with the same courses and students) has helped us grow as professionals in the field of mathematics and teaching in innumerable ways. I now see good teachers as people who constantly re-evaluate their understanding of the subject, constantly struggle with activities and lessons, and who seek their colleagues as resources.

(prepared text, fall 1995)

Let's turn now to the teachers' explanations for the unique value and power of shared teaching assignments. These explanations fall into three broad categories. First, the teachers saw great benefit in being physically present in the class with another teacher. They could take turns stepping back from the action and becoming observers in their own classroom. Second, they also felt that the physical presence of two teachers created a shared experience, which allowed for the construction of mutual understandings by way of common referents. They contrasted these sorts of understandings with the misunderstandings that they felt often resulted from discussions without a common base of experience. Third, by teaching the same material to the same students at the same time, the teachers had unparalleled opportunities to collaborate in the midst of the complexities of teaching – from attempts to assess individual student understanding to decisions about course content and sequencing. The shared teaching assignment forced the teachers sooner or later to take action together; they had to reach an agreement or compromise. While tensions were associated with the need to come to joint decisions, at the same time, making joint decisions sometimes supported teachers in exploring innovations they might not have attempted on their own. These three aspects of the shared teaching assignments will be highlighted below.

Before exploring these aspects of the shared teaching, it is important to emphasize that the shared teaching assignments were structured around a new approach to school algebra, coupled with a pedagogy that allowed students to construct knowledge and develop their own understanding. In this situation, teachers were confronted with basic questions about the meaning of algebra, teaching, and learning. As high school teachers with a disciplinary focus, the teachers found this aspect personally enriching. Marty commented on this aspect in the fall and the spring:

I think that's one of the best things about team-teaching: you're getting together with other math teachers and just being able to talk about math and talk about new ideas.

(fall interview, 1994)

A lot of times where we're working after school, we'll start putting a problem together, and we'll get a little carried away and add a few more because it's fun. That's one of the neat things about the team-teaching – when you're planning together [provided] you can find the time in our schedules. It's really enjoyable, and you can get creative with problems, and I think that really shows in the class-room, too. The kids pick up on that – if you come up with a problem that they think is really interesting and unique. I think that happens more often when you're working together with someone than if you're working alone.

(spring interview, 1995)

Similarly, Mike commented,

What I like about team-teaching, number one, is the way of think-ing about the algebra, how to teach it, and stuff like that. I see my ideas changing about what content is. I'm learning a lot this year from teaming – putting content together differently.

(fall interview, 1994)

The opportunity not to act: becoming an observer in one's own classroom

Marty and Steve and Mike and Sandy found ways to step back and observe each other, rather than compete. A shared teaching assignment allowed teachers, who generally have to act and respond, to sit back and watch their partner respond to shared students in a shared class-room. The teachers highly valued this aspect of the shared assignment. For example, Marty observed that he enjoyed the chance to see another person interact with his students. Such an opportunity for reflection is rarely available to teachers: "It gives you times where you can sit back and watch your class being taught and think" (spring interview, 1995).

In both fall and spring, Mike indicated that this experience allowed him to think about the mathematical approach for himself and to see the Algebra 1 students in a different light:

Since many times I was able to take on the role of observer in the class, I was free to allow my attention to focus on the mathe-matics instead of the day-to-day operations of the classroom. This freed me up to study the mathematics, and it became very energizing to me.

(prepared text, fall 1995)

...the Algebra 1 kids can actually take a situation and talk about it and think it's true and then nine times out of ten, they'll come up with the right answer. And I don't mean that they get the number "12" and that's the right answer. But, (I mean) the right way of thinking about it, working it through. I mean, they may go off into some real harebrained thing at the beginning, but they'll come back, and they'll bring themselves back. But that was real surprising to me. Going in, I thought, this is really going to have to be watered down.

(spring interview, 1995)

Similarly, Sandy recalled a specific event from 1993–1994 when she taught with Marty. She suggests that this experience allowed her to "learn about students' capabilities" (prepared text, fall 1995).

Students had been looking at tables and graphs of linear functions while changing the slope. I remember one day sitting with the students across from Marty, who was seated with the students on the opposite side of the room facing me. He had lifted his pencil and was asking the class, "What happens if the number out in front gets larger?" Students told him that the pencil would be at a greater slant. He asked the students, "Will the pencil ever go around so that it aims this way?" As he asked this, he moved the pencil to indicate a negative slope. This caused students to pause. Someone suggested that the number would have to be negative. Marty started the pencil off where he had begun and tilted the pencil upwards and said, "What's happening to the number?" The students were saying, "Positive. Bigger. Bigger." Then he let the pencil rest pointing straight up. Students thought for a long time about this one (about 20 seconds). Then Nick said, "That's impossible." Marty asked him why. Nick suggested that the class think about the x-axis as "time" and the y-axis as "distance." He said that a line that goes straight up and down would be like going somewhere in no time. Marty glanced over at me, and our eyes widened. I think I actually fell over on the desk, saying "wow" or something. I had been concerned that the students wouldn't be able to grasp the concept and that the discussion would fall apart.

(prepared text, fall 1995)

Not having to rely solely on words: shared experience versus talk

Beyond the chance to observe someone else working with one's own students, the presence of two teachers in the room allowed paired teachers to work together outside the classroom in a different way. The teachers focused on this aspect when they reflected back on previous discussions about teaching a common course to different students.

Though proud of the collegial relationships that had developed in their department at that time, the teachers interviewed often compared conversations resulting from shared teaching favorably with departmental conversations about classes taught individually (some of which occurred during the Wednesday-morning time). In a shared teaching assignment, Sandy said: "It is the experience which gives the words meaning, rather than me just telling him [Mike]" (meeting, February 1996).

By contrast, their descriptions of previous departmental conversations highlight the difficulties inherent in having collegial discussions about teaching without opportunities for shared examination of the teaching itself. Mike reported that the shared teaching assignment had more impact on his understanding of the new approach to Algebra 1 than the conversations he had participated in during the previous three to four years.

> When Dan and Sandy and Marty had talked about it [changes in Algebra 1 instruction], I had a picture in my mind about what the classroom might look like, but it was my classroom. It was my set of norms, the way I operate a classroom. Team-teaching helped me understand how Sandy set up the norms of the class and the time spent setting up the norms. But also how she questions kids in such a way that is not threatening to them, so it's made me more aware of how I question them.
>
> (Mike, spring interview 1995)

In the teachers' views, the context of a shared teaching assignment provided supported pedagogical conversation. The pedagogical decisions undertaken in shared teaching are made with regard to a specific set of circumstances, a particular class, and particular students. Mike made this argument when comparing the shared teaching assignments with teaching the same course to different classes.

> Since we were responsible to the same set of students, we were able to plan our lessons around the students' own ideas. This is much different from teaching a common course to a different set of students. In

the latter situation, the teachers would not be able to co-plan based on questions and understandings that the students have developed, since each class would have different questions.... We both had worked together on the same lesson and taught it to the same students, so we could actually talk about the result with a common experience. This changed the whole conversation and made it go much deeper than if we had taught our individual lesson to different classes.

(prepared text, fall 1995)

Building on shared experience, the teachers constructed a different sort of vocabulary to talk about teaching and algebra. They believed that their discussions had recourse to a shared vision of the class, a shared understanding of class norms, shared referents for the mathematical language they were using, and shared observations of students' interaction with the material.

The benefit of this context is illustrated as Mike continued to talk about questioning. Mike described a dilemma faced by teachers who encourage students to share their ideas:

If a kid has a wrong answer, you're kind of like, you're stuck there ... I don't want to insult the kid and say, "You're wrong." But, on the other hand, how long do you leave a wrong answer laying out there? When is it appropriate to leave a wrong answer there?

(Mike, spring interview, 1995)

As Mike watched Sandy teach, he saw a different way of approaching this issue. For a problem about a savings account, a student had presented an input/output table with unexpected values: instead of starting at 50 and going up $5 each week, the student's table was going up $5 every five weeks. Sandy told the student that she did not understand his table of values. He did not answer right away, so she gave him time to think about it. A little later in the class she came back to him, Mike recalled.

She said, "I don't understand. I'm not understanding this piece right here." And really what she was saying was, "This isn't right," but questioning him to get him to think about it.

(Mike, spring interview, 1995)

Eventually, the student was able to explain the reason his outputs went up by fives, but not why his inputs went up by fives. Mike continued, "Finally, Sandy just said, 'Traditionally, what we do is we go, one, two, three, ...'" (spring interview, 1995). Mike found it very helpful that Sandy had allowed the student to develop his thinking, rather than just told him that he was wrong.

The ability to see the context helped Mike appreciate Sandy's action. The referent of the shared experience allowed him to see how Sandy's method for addressing incorrect answers with a student was different than his.

This benefit of the shared experience was not limited to pedagogical strategies. It also had an impact on the teacher's mathematical understanding. The shift in focus at the heart of the new approach to algebra was in many ways subtle. When outlining her frustrations with presenting the new approach to other math teachers, Sandy commented: "Because the words sound so similar, it's easy to say we do that, we do that, we do that . . ." (spring interview, 1995).

Marty identified a shared teaching assignment as a way of developing shared departmental mathematical understandings. "The thing that I see is that it gives us a common experience in mathematics so that we can have a common language to talk about it" (spring interview, 1995). He emphasized that sharing a teaching assignment also allowed him to see the curriculum as an organic response to students' ideas, rather than words or ideas taken out of the natural environment of the classroom and codified in a district guideline or a textbook. Sharing an assignment allowed him to experience the curriculum in context rather than just hear about it from an out-of-context verbal description.

> I heard Sandy talk about it [changes in curriculum], I looked through the problems and stuff, but without seeing how it played out in the classroom, I couldn't really understand the differences. And I had a lot more concerns – that the kids would be lacking certain things when they came out, because [when you look at the problems] you miss the entire discussions part of any of the problems, which is the key to when the mathematics starts coming out . . .
>
> (fall interview, 1994)

The idea that you need to witness the students doing mathematics differently was furthered emphasized by Marty:

> Until you see what goes on in the classroom . . . I don't think a person would understand otherwise. That's really pretty limited information if you are just looking at test scores or whatever. It's the change in attitude that the kids have in the classroom about math. It's what they're doing in the classroom and how they understand the material, not just if they can do problems with it. I think without team-teaching we're not going to get that point across to people, until they can actually see it and talk about it with somebody as it's happening.
>
> (fall interview, 1994)

In discussing the students' progress and understanding, Steve, who had found verbal descriptions of the class hard to understand, also mentioned the importance of what he had actually witnessed. Steve was in the unique position of teaching a section of Algebra 1 based on a textbook at the same time he was team-teaching the new approach. His experience led him to make comparisons:

> Probably the biggest thing that I carry away from the class is the fact that I think the kids generally have a better feeling about math than a textbook-driven class, just possibly because their investment in it would be in the discussions. Usually, we have some really good discussions with the class. Yesterday was an interesting one where kids were very eager to volunteer.
>
> (spring interview, 1995)

Having to decide together: joint reflection, decision-making, and action instead of individual responsibility

The teachers were not only sharing an experience in which they took turns being passive observers; they had responsibilities to act in concert. Mike and Sandy and Steve and Marty had much to say about the ways in which sharing a teaching assignment gave occasion for, and sometimes even forced, collaboration and public discussion of teaching. For example, as the department chair, Mike commented on the difference in the conversations when you are teaming versus when you are holding department meetings.

> But somehow, I really think that teaming forces you to talk about the issues that in meetings we dance around all the time. Somewhere along the line you have to talk about homework, you have to talk about content, how you present content – what is important, what is not important in the curriculum. You don't have a choice.
>
> (fall interview, 1994)

Similarly, in the spring Sandy commented on the shared, and continual, sorting out of what is going on in the class. Sharing a teaching assignment, she felt, forced one to articulate rationales for everything done with students – from disciplinary action to grading to curricular choices.

Some aspects of this sort of collaboration – even when ultimately rewarding – could be uncomfortable. In both pairings, the teachers found it important, valuable, and stressful to plan together on a regular basis. "When you team-teach ... most of the time you are going to have two opinions" (Marty, fall interview, 1994). But the teachers viewed the presence of differing opinions as valuable in reducing the isolation of teaching. Mike wrote:

> The discussion we had about content and the way we wanted to approach it were some of the most exciting conversations I have had in my career.
>
> (prepared text, fall 1995)

Of course, the presence of different views could be difficult as well.

> Teaming can be very stressful. Both partners need to be aware of the other's needs and must be able to help meet those needs. It takes a level of professionalism that is not automatic. It is not just the in-class part where in front of the students you need to put on a professional face, but in the planning where you need to allow everyone to have input and be heard. This was not always easy, but as we got used to each other's way of thinking about the mathematics and the students, we were able to use our individual strengths to make it work.
>
> (Mike Lehman, prepared text, fall 1995)

For example, early on, Mike and Sandy had quite different policies on homework. During the fall interview, when thinking about outcomes for the year, Sandy gave some indication of this tension.

> Maybe Mike and I can move more towards consensus on homework.... Maybe he'll convince me of some things that I hadn't thought of before. Maybe I'll learn some things like I have with Dan [Chazan]. And on the other hand, maybe he'll learn some things and change some ways of thinking about it.
>
> (fall interview, 1994)

Over the course of the year, as the teachers learned more about each other and developed greater trust, some of the tensions seemed to dissipate and the nature of the conversations seemed to change. All of the teachers remarked on this change in their spring interviews. For example, Marty said:

> Lately, we've been able to get a lot better reflection and a lot better discussion.... Up until now the reflections Steve and I are doing have been fairly mechanical – about how a particular thing went [or] if we should have changed the wording on something....

[Now,] we talk more about what the kids are doing as a result of this course, rather than what it is we should be doing to make the course. I think that's changed over the year.

(spring interview, 1995)

Mike commented similarly.

There's more common ground than there was before. There was a gap at the beginning of the year.... And right now I think there's more mutual respect. Or at least I should say I respect Sandy more. I understand a lot more where she's coming from. And I see her side of the issues much better than I did before.... But there are still some basic issues that we disagree on.

(spring interview, 1995)

In keeping with their favorable assessment of sharing a teaching assignment, the teachers felt it generated unique opportunities for developing trust within the department. Mike wrote:

I gained a huge amount of respect for Sandy and her ability to teach; I also sense she feels the same about me. I believe that this level of respect can only be gained though teaming. In the end, it may actually be the most important outcome as we tackle new challenges.

(prepared text, fall 1995)

At other points in the interviews, the teachers talked about the chance to take risks together that one would not take alone. They talked about the added confidence with which one could try new ideas or teaching techniques as the result of having the support of a colleague. As Sandy put it, "[you're] not out there on your own" (spring interview, 1995). She contrasted this feeling with her experience, as a curriculum innovator, of departmental meetings:

There is a huge difference between meeting to talk about curriculum and being involved daily in making decisions about what to teach and how. Then [in departmental meetings], questions of better and worse practice are always at the surface. This creates a constant friction which intensifies the burden of teaching a course.

(prepared text, fall 1995)

She illustrated the support she felt she received from sharing a teaching assignment with reference to a particular case. She was asking students questions and:

It seemed that every question was falling like lead, with students staring silently back at me.... I waited and waited, asking what seemed to me to be the next question.... After class, Marty mentioned how helpful it was to see how I stuck with the goal of having students drive the discussion.... I had felt unsuccessful. However, Marty helped me see that by insisting that students engage in order for something to happen, I had not let them off the hook.

(prepared text, fall 1995)

Mike expressed similar sentiments about the value of the support he received through teaming:

I think the most important thing teaming did for me was give me the opportunity and courage to think about the mathematics differently and to try new ways of thinking in our classrooms. It was much easier to take a chance with your students when you knew you were not in there alone. Someone else would share the burden and the whining as you tried some of these ideas.

(prepared text, fall 1995)

Mike saw these benefits as resulting from developing trust and familiarity with another person's thinking. As department chair, he thought that such trust and familiarity might aid in the development of wider collegial relations in the department.

So I think the more we can team, the more we can face the issues. Also, I think the more we can team, the more we can develop a real trust of each other.

(fall interview, 1994)

Conclusion

Compared to traditional in-service activity that happens away from the day to day of teaching, sharing teaching assignments is a slow and expensive method of professional development. But, it is close to teaching practice and as a result may, as suggested by these four teachers, have a greater impact. In talking about the impact that sharing teaching assignments had for him, Marty noted:

I was talking to one of our special ed teachers who was at an elementary school, and we were talking about teaching math differently, and she said she talked about it and talked about it and talked about it and didn't get it until she team-taught it. And I thought ... that is the conclusion we are coming to.

(fall interview, 1994)

Marty, Steve, Sandy, and Mike reported that sharing teaching assignments aided them in overcoming isolation and learning from each other. They report important changes in teacher relationships, professional development, curriculum development, and instructional practices. Through this mechanism, they claim to find themselves thinking differently about the subject matter, their colleagues, students, and themselves.

They gave three sets of reasons to explain their experience of shared teaching as professionally rewarding. They found it valuable to become observers in their own classroom, to have shared experiences of classroom interactions, and to make joint decisions. They were engaged in the joint work of teaching algebra to a particular group of students. This joint work granted them the chance to reflect, a context for sharing insights, and a task that needed to be accomplished. As a result, for them, this was a professional development opportunity like no other.

What do shared teaching assignments tell us about learning while teaching?

Kelly Hodges and Craig Huhn, Holt High School

KELLY HODGES: It is interesting to step back from teaching and think about professional development. One common criticism about team-teaching as a mechanism for professional development is that it is expensive and has a narrowly focused impact. This story is rather unique. The resources are rarely available to provide an opportunity for four teachers in one school to have the opportunity to team-teach. But, it occurs to me that an internship allows for many of the same benefits to willing mentors at essentially no cost.

CRAIG HUHN: As a matter of fact, as an intern at Holt, I had the opportunity to observe and team with a variety of teachers and experience many of the issues this essay talks about – but as a wide-eyed intern with so much to learn. We were a trio: two interns, Adam Kelly and me, and Mike Lehman, our mentor teacher. And, to round out our experience, Adam and I each also spent time with another teacher's class for one period a day. This was not a standard arrangement, but it worked well for us. As a threesome, we had ample opportunity to take part in all of the learning experiences mentioned in this essay: We challenged each other to make sense of the mathematics, and often pushed each other on issues such as "Why do we teach this?" and "How does this fit in here?" We also had several conversations weekly about what I thought a particular student meant in a particular comment or explanation, and how Adam or Mike took them. In these interactions, I became cognizant that we needed to be open and free (as well as confident in each others' abilities) to discuss questions that we had or mathematical ideas that we didn't understand (having sometimes just memorized them to get the grade in high school). Without a strong realization of this safety within the partnership, I don't think we could have accomplished much together. In general in sharing teaching, I think we must have a certain freedom to challenge each other, ask hard questions about why we teach something or teach it the way we do. And that often comes from learning about each other and our reasons for doing something.

KELLY: I understand why you emphasize the importance of trust and safety.

CRAIG: But I wonder if our situation as mentor and interns makes a difference. If our trio, instead of being a mentor and two interns, would have consisted of three experienced math teachers, the professional rewards probably would have been quite different. But in our circumstance, it was inherent that two of us had so much to learn (more than what an experienced teacher would claim to still have to learn from a colleague). We had normal intern concerns, like how to deal with different discipline issues, how the assembly schedule worked, and how to think through a unit plan. We'd have to ask Mike what he got out of being our mentor.

KELLY: We'll have to ask him. But, as someone who has been a mentor, I think that a mentor can treat the internship as an opportunity for her own professional growth [see Chapter 19 for an elaboration of this perspective]. When she does this, she not only enriches her own practice but also can illustrate, as Marty says, that "good teachers (are) people who constantly reevaluate their understanding of the subject, constantly struggle with activities and lessons, and who seek their colleagues as resources." Having an intern can give the mentor the opportunity to "sit back and watch your class being taught and think." When a mentor is undertaking a new direction in her teaching, such as a new instructional approach and/or view of mathematical content, the intern can be an asset. The opportunity to have an observer, a collaborative partner, and a person to share the work is helpful. Being responsive to the intern's questions and progress means articulating many aspects of one's practice. It also may mean delving into the mathematics behind or beyond a problem that the intern and mentor plan to use in class. I have found these conversations to be "energizing" and important for my own growth in understanding of mathematics. Some of the most exciting conversations I have had with interns have been about mathematics far beyond that which we will be teaching to our students. Not only have these conversations been important in further developing the background knowledge I draw on when evaluating students' responses in class, they are just fun! Having a partner for mathematics inquiry is a luxury that few teachers have. It isn't exactly the same, but there are definitely ways in which working with an intern is like sharing an assignment with another experienced mathematics teaching colleague. I'd like to go back to the model of sharing an assignment with an experienced teacher. I have also had the opportunity to participate in team-teaching experiences with members of the department. For the most part I would echo the points raised in the essay. However, it seems to me that the power of shared teaching assignments to increase mutual respect points out something odd here about regular teaching arrangements and what it means to be a teaching colleague. In this essay, Mike, Sandy, Marty, and Steve talk about the things they learn from each other and the specific issues on which they have a greater understanding. But, this makes it seem as if we inherently mistrust our colleagues! Do we really need something like team-teaching to build respect between colleagues? If so, why is that? It's not that my experience contradicts the experiences described in this essay. My experience is, as teachers, we assume that questions about our practice are attacks, born out of a lack of respect, rather than attempts to learn, born out of a deep respect. It makes me wonder what is it about team-teaching that turns this around and whether there are other ways to do this. And do we think that team-teaching had a larger impact on trust and respect in a department beyond the people who share an assignment? Do we have stronger mutual respect in our department now, particularly among those who have not shared a teaching assignment?

CRAIG: I see what you mean. I hadn't thought about it that way. I was focused on the benefits of this arrangement. Your question about how we think as teachers, and act as colleagues, feels connected to a question someone once asked me about my internship. It highlighted for me some of the assumptions people make about how one learns teaching. You are right; there is something strange about how we think about being colleagues in teaching. At the end of the internship, someone asked me if I felt "cheated" that I had to share my placement with another intern. I debated answering with many of the issues raised above: how powerful it is to have that many teachers in a classroom, with common experiences to talk about ("not having to rely solely on words"); getting to experience a variety of different teaching styles and philosophies; having the privilege to think about several different math classes; having a context where we have to work as a team for "joint reflection, decision-making, and action instead of individual responsibility." In fact, until that question, I hadn't even thought of my situation as having a possible negative connotation. Instead, I broke a little smile and told them, "No, I don't feel cheated," and added with a glint in my eye, "I mean, it must have been half the work, right?"

KELLY: Getting back to the text of the essay, there was something else that surprised and concerned me. Both Mike and Sandy report events that cause them to re-examine their prior assumptions about what students are capable of. In particular, the students in Algebra 1, the lower track, surprised these teachers with their ability to grapple with and comprehend sophisticated mathematical ideas. On the one hand, I applaud Mike and Sandy's willingness to admit that they had underestimated the capabilities of these students. And, it seems that team-teaching is useful if it leads to such realizations. But, on the other hand, doing the same sort of inversion that I did before, I am startled that Mike and Sandy found themselves to be underestimating student capabilities. They are both teachers whom I hold in high regard, *particularly* with respect to their expectations for students. And yet, even they found themselves underestimating students' potential for understanding mathematics. I'm wondering what this says about us when we are not team-teaching. Does team-teaching allow us to see students differently than we usually do? I guess I wonder whether Mike and Sandy would report continual surprise or delight at the extent of student capabilities even today as a result of some long-term change in the way they question and listen to students? Or is this something that happened for them primarily because of the shared teaching assignment? If so, what does that say?

CRAIG: I guess responses to these questions will depend on how you think about growth in teaching. Maybe, when we have the chance, we can all always learn about ways in which we underestimate our students.

Chapter 15

Departmental culture

After five years of continually increasing funding, the 1995–1996 PDS budget was half the expected size. Having supported PDS efforts for five years, the coalition of funders, now represented by the Michigan Partnership for New Education, did not see dramatic results in the PDS schools, nor were there as many PDSs as promised. It seemed unlikely that PDSs were going to have a substantial impact on reforming all of Michigan's schools. There are many stories outside of the scope of this volume that lie behind this perception. In the MSU part of the effort, there were simply not enough people at the university to support a dramatic increase in the number of PDSs, if a PDS was to involve a serious intertwining of the work of university and school faculty. And, some of MSU's PDS efforts, even with deep commitments from school and university faculty, ran aground on harsh realities of schools (e.g., rapid turnover among urban teachers).

Subsequently, MPNE changed its focus and began funding other educational initiatives, funding for PDS efforts at Michigan State came solely from university funds, and funding levels reduced. Activity in some PDSs continued, but MSU faculty involvement decreased, and the relationship with the university became less salient in continuing PDS schools. In the Holt math department, 1995–1996 was the last year where PDS funds supported a teacher's release hour and 1996–1997 was the last year where PDS supported graduate student involvement in the department. By the 1999–2000 academic year, funding for the PDS relationship was negligible. At Holt, the PDS council deemed funding levels were too low to continue departmental projects. Instead, resources were pooled to support professional development activity across the school. Where faculty from MSU and Holt math teachers were involved in joint work, it now became unclear whether to consider such work PDS work or not. Funding for such efforts were not from a PDS budget, but the work was often a continuation of work that had begun with PDS support, and the collegial relationships built up between school and university had certainly been supported by PDS activities.

In their response to the last essay, Kelly Hodges and Craig Huhn raised questions about the lasting impact of the trust developed among department members through shared teaching assignments. The evolution of PDS funding allows an indirect examination of this question. In the next essay written in the mid-1990s, not long after the peak of PDS funding, Jan Simonson does not take up this question directly. Instead, she comments on what she calls a professional development culture that built up inside the Holt High School mathematics department. Arguing from her in-depth study of Marty Schnepp's evolution as a teacher, she credits the Professional Development School initiative with creating circumstances that supported what she calls his transformation as a teacher (see Chapter 7). Though the shared teaching assignments described above were one of the largest particular initiatives of the PDS effort, she does not believe that the development of this culture can be traced to one particular professional development experience. More than any particular initiative, she describes the characteristics of the culture that developed at Holt that in her view supported Marty in the changes he made in teaching. In addition to shared work, she singles out teachers' opportunities to question and inquire and their propensity to engage with colleagues in conversations about mathematics (see Chapter 17 for an illustration of one such conversation). In their response to her essay, Sandy Callis and Tom Almeida focus on one important aspect of the culture that has grown up at Holt. They indicate how the culture supports the notion that high school mathematics is interesting and worthy of conversation. And, perhaps more importantly, that mathematics teachers can know their math and still have questions about the mathematics they teach, that having questions about high school mathematics is not a sign of being uneducated or poorly prepared.

One transformed teacher's viewpoint

Janice Simonson, Calvin College

This essay was adapted from Jan Simonson's dissertation. It is based on interviews that took place from 1993 through 1998.

Together, changes in the curriculum and experiences offered by the Holt High School mathematics department add up to much more than the sum of their parts. One way to describe this blend of changed curriculum and experience is to see the result as a unique professional development culture that mathematics teachers in few other high schools have the scope to enjoy, a culture influenced by the Holt High

School/MSU PDS relationship. In this essay, I will identify important components of the Holt math department professional development culture, using the experiences of one teacher, Marty Schnepp, to illustrate how one teacher perceived the sum of these changes.

The components of the culture of the Holt High School mathematics department relevant to professional development and highlighted in this essay – 1) the freedom to question; 2) opportunities to participate in shared work; and 3) ongoing dialogue – reflect the influence of the PDS effort in a variety of ways. The Holt/MSU partnership has carried out the intentions of the Holmes Group design as outlined in their publication *Tomorrow's schools: Principles for the design of Professional Development Schools* (1990). These intentions include the establishment of "a school for the development of novice professionals, for continuing development of experienced professionals, and for the research and development of the teaching profession" (Holmes Group, 1990, p. 1). Ongoing relationships – carried out as a partnership, rather than as top-down directives – have served both communities as they pursue serious inquiry related to policy, subject matters, teaching, and learning.

The transformed culture at Holt High School reflects many of the conversations held by various PDS stakeholders, both from the high school and the university, begun during the years (early 1990s) when PDS grants were a normal part of the school environment. The intention of these conversations was to develop the high school into a community of learners including students and teachers from both the high school and the universities (Holmes Group, 1990, p. 24). For example, preservice teacher education classes were held at the high school and both high school and teacher education courses were team-taught by high school teachers and college professors. The PDS-funded projects called for investigations that invited all participants to become learners and engage in the process, encouraging adults to engage in learning, as well as students (pp. 45–54). These investigations opened the door and transformed the culture in ways that made asking questions more accepted than supplying canned answers.

The PDS projects represented both theoretical as well as practical research and inquiries that spurred stimulating conversations and debates (pp. 55–66). These conversations developed into a professional dialogue that reached beyond the walls of the high school into both the local community and the international academic community. These dialogues built alliances between the high school and university, the high school mathematic department and other research institutions, and the high school mathematics teachers and university mathematics teacher educators that blurred institutional lines (pp. 67–84). The resulting professional development culture within the mathematics department at

Holt High School has unique features that frame the vision for learning and growth that permeates many of the mathematics classes at the school. This culture reflects the vision for Professional Development Schools outlined by the Holmes Group (1990).

Illustrations from the professional development opportunities of one teacher

In 1997, Marty Schnepp describes himself as a "partner in inquiry with the university," and, as a teacher, he represents a perspective that university researchers need. He also states that his interactions with Dan Chazan, the professor from Michigan State University who brought introductory algebra curricular ideas to Holt, and with a network of others that has followed, have afforded him unique opportunities to learn how others are thinking about mathematics and mathematics education. The changes that occurred in Marty's practice, as illustrated in the vignettes highlighted earlier in this book (Chapters 4 and 7), should be seen as much more than small innovations or the applications of a pre-packaged program of reform.

Initially, Marty felt out of place during his first two years teaching at Holt in 1991–1992 and 1992–1993. So many people, he observed, were "thinking deeply about education and trying out neat ideas." He wondered if he fit in and if he would ever be able to participate in similar professional activities as he was "just teaching." Marty did find his place at Holt and even brought his own influences to the culture. He became an active part of conversations that dealt with mathematics since he was very interested in developing his own understandings and identifying what it was that he wanted students to understand. Later he shared teaching assignments with Sandy Callis, who had teamed with Dan Chazan. During this time he began to break away from dependence on textbooks and experienced the freedom to follow up on his own thoughts or his students' ideas in order to design situations that would help his students compare their mathematical thinking with the accepted thinking of mathematical authorities.

Conversations about mathematics grew within the department as MSU teacher candidates were placed in larger numbers at the school. MSU teacher educators and doctoral candidates became involved in different projects, while Holt math teachers participated at various levels of the teacher education program. During this time, Dan introduced Marty to Ricardo Nemirovsky, a researcher with Technical Education Research Center (TERC), a non-profit organization in Cambridge, Massachusetts. Nemirovsky (see, for example, 1994) has worked extensively to uncover students' perceptions of mathematical ideas. He invited Marty to use a mechanical device in his classroom that connected the movement of mechanical cars with computer displays that graphed relationships and supported Marty's work with these devices. According to Marty, "the software and hardware opened up so many possibilities that I began to think of ways of thinking about and teaching the content that could not come any other ways" (interview, 1998). Dialogue continued at many levels as Marty also worked closely with another Holt teacher, Kellie Huhn (previously an MSU intern), and a mathematics-turned-education professor, Bill Rosenthal, then at MSU. Together, they developed ideas related to the high school Calculus curriculum. These experiences, and related coursework at MSU, influenced Marty's philosophy of mathematics. But these experiences are not unique to Marty, they make up parts of the culture that has evolved within this mathematics department.

Beyond the specific professional development opportunities that Marty experienced, three qualities of the culture inside the Holt math department supported Marty's professional transformation. First, teachers are invited, even expected, to question everything, including their own understandings of mathematics and the sense their students are making of it. This questioning could be described not as doubting, but as a sort of wondering. Second, teachers have the chance to take part in various kinds of shared work. And third, teachers participate in ongoing dialogue with many and varied others: among themselves, with their students, with other mathematics educators outside of their building, and with mathematicians in higher education.

Freedom to question

Let's look at the first quality: a culture that invites and expects teachers to investigate their understandings and those of their students as well as their pedagogy as a means of inquiry into learning and growing. In many schools, teachers are perceived as the people with answers, not those asking questions. They need to know the correct ways for students to get right answers, have answers for parents about a child's progress and potential, and give administrators the answers they require related to curriculum and pedagogy. Because of these expectations, teachers often end up hiding their frustrations, glossing over students who aren't learning, and informing parents rather than gleaning insight from the parents' years of experience with their child. On the other hand, in an atmosphere where questions are welcomed, students and teachers begin to relax together and investigate phenomena that would otherwise be ignored. Teachers end up modeling the type of learning they value – learning that is driven by inquiring minds, examining situations and relationships for the purposes of building a deeper understanding. This form of learning is lasting and models for students critical thinking that guides ongoing learning. The various PDS research projects and relationships established through that connection played an important role in developing a culture that values and finds time for this kind of learning and inquiring atmosphere.

In contrast, Marty shared a story with me from his second year of teaching in California right after graduation from MSU. He was in the workroom making copies, thinking about a topic that he would be introducing later that afternoon, when he ran into another math teacher. Marty asked the teacher about his approach to this topic. Later that day the assistant principal approached Marty, saying he understood that Marty was having problems with content. As Marty tells it, the culture of this school reflected a negative approach to teacher collaboration and the investigation of ideas.

According to the mathematics teachers at Holt, openness to questioning increased exponentially in 1990 when Dan Chazan joined the MSU mathematics education faculty and was given a clinical teaching position that supported teaching at Holt, alongside the existing PDS endeavor (for Dan's writing about this teaching, see Chazan, 2000). Dan was asking hard questions regarding student conceptions, and he was trying out introductory algebra ideas related to treating "x" strictly as a variable rather than an unknown. These conversations soon involved all the mathematics teachers at Holt, who eventually felt free to question their own knowledge of mathematics content, their teaching, and the understandings of their students.

Eventually, Marty began to feel comfortable verbalizing, then acting on his frustrations related to teaching mathematics.

> I got so I could control kids pretty well, and I got them to do things pretty well if they were willing to do (so). But when I started asking them to write about things and really checking to see if they really understood what they were doing, or when I went back a few weeks later to see if they could do what they used to be able to do, there was nothing there.
>
> (summer, 1996)

Marty was also frustrated with both the expectations of the textbook he was using that students read the text carefully and the low reading levels of his introductory algebra students. In the spring semester of 1993, these frustrations led him and Kelly Hodges, then a first-year teacher, to put their small classes together into the same room, identify which algebraic concepts they wanted the students to understand, and then create appropriate worksheets. Working on these sorts of issues forced them to consider their own understanding of algebra and to dig deeper into it, rather than merely accepting the algorithms, procedures, and definitions identified in the textbook as those students should memorize to get right answers.

The following year, Marty was invited to share an Algebra 1 teaching assignment with Sandy Callis as part of a PDS project extending discussions concerning functions-based algebra and a pedagogy that considered student conceptions. Marty was also teaching Algebra 1 by himself during a different class period. That period he was totally dependent on the textbook. This situation gave him the occasion to make comparisons, consider the intentions of the textbook authors in light of student conceptions, and investigate his own understandings of the mathematics.

At the time, Marty talked about feeling rather uncomfortable at first when Sandy would assign a single problem, spend a day or two on it (sometimes even longer), and not necessarily assign any homework (his discomfort is described earlier in Chapter 7). Prior to this, Marty thought that homework meant doing lots of problems and represented a way of holding students responsible for their learning. Marty noticed that in the class with Sandy students at different levels of understanding could participate equally well and stay engaged. The goal was not to work toward a single right answer but instead to give students a forum, for individual students and students in small groups, to express their understandings to the class and participate in mathematical conversations. The goal or focus was a relational understanding of the mathematics (Skemp, 1978) – knowing both what to do and why.

Marty began to question both the content of school mathematics and eventually the actual definition of algebra and mathematics.

> The course called algebra to me was teaching a bunch of techniques for solving equations and simplifying equations … an assembly line of stuff that kids had to become proficient at before they could move through the curriculum. Now I see these techniques as tools in a process of studying different kinds of patterns and relationships. It's the patterns and relationships that I see are the fundamental ideas right now.
>
> (interview, spring 1995)

In his class with Sandy, conversations among students, both in small-group and whole-class modes, took on a different dimension than he had experienced in his other algebra classes. Marty felt that at least part of this difference was related to the instructional tasks that Sandy presented the students (see Chapters 3 and 6 for examples). These problems or situations represented questions Sandy employed to push students in their thinking. They were either written by Sandy or were ones that she and Dan had used the two previous years while teaching the same course. The problems gave students something to work on and figure out. As they analyzed these situations, the students collaboratively bounced ideas off one another. Time spent presenting ideas did not have to be teacher-centered. Students would use the board to help others understand their thinking.

Marty began to question his approach to instruction. Although the problems held the students' interest, Marty noticed that Sandy's focus was on not the material but on the students. That is, Sandy listened very carefully to what they were saying and doing. And what Sandy and Marty heard (as indicated by Sandy in Chapter 14) continually amazed them: sophisticated, thoughtful responses to complex mathematical ideas. Marty contrasted the conversations from his textbook-based Algebra class with those in the functions-based class. Comments from students in the former class most often were, "How do you do this?," "I don't get this," or "What's the answer?" Students gave short, single-word answers to his questions. Beyond that, the conversations were not related to mathematics.

> Listening is a part of what I do. [Before] I did not think that it needed to be, other than listening to see if they [students] are getting it or not. I have to listen more critically now to know what they are saying, to know about when they are becoming confused or what might be an interesting thing to pick up and run with.
>
> (interview, June 1996)

In Marty's class with Sandy, the students would argue with one another or present alternative ideas. Marty was thrilled with the connections that he saw students making, for example, between tables of functions and the related algebraic expressions (or rules) that enabled them to conjecture about the behavior of the graph. As they investigated the mathematics, they were using graphs, rules, and tables as tools for a relational understanding, rather than merely as goals for an instrumental understanding.

The freedom to question many things – understandings, textbook content, the meaning of subject matter, pedagogy – provided Marty with a professional development culture, one driven by teachers' questions, frustrations, revelations, and ideas. In this culture, teachers experienced the freedom and inherent rewards for investigating hard questions, designing curricula to fit their students' understandings, taking risks, holding high expectations for students, and for using these investigations to socially construct understandings.

Opportunities to participate in shared work

The next quality that distinguishes the culture in the Holt math department is the shared nature of the work among Holt teachers, between Holt teachers and MSU faculty and students, as well as with scholars and scholarship elsewhere. Little (1990) describes something very similar when she defines joint work as follows:

> encounters among teachers that rest on shared responsibility for the work of teaching (interdependence), collective conceptions of autonomy, support for teachers' initiative and leadership with regard to professional practice, and group affiliations grounded in professional work.
>
> (p. 519)

Little identifies joint work as the type of collaboration that is most likely to affect teachers' professional development. When teachers share responsibility for their work, as they did when sharing teaching assignments at Holt, their own interactions become an integral part of their work. These teachers have similar experiences about which to reflect, and they share the intellectual risks they encounter in a less traditional classroom. Other kinds of shared work could be found in the Holt math department: work with university interns; professional development projects shared with university professors or graduate assistants; conference presentations developed by small groups of teachers; content groups (Algebra, Geometry, PreCalculus, etc.); writing projects; and seminars led and attended by teachers, mathematics educators, and mathematicians.

The sharing of teaching assignments that occurred within the Holt mathematics department was made possible through PDS grants and supported by the PDS vision requiring that research projects be documented involving various levels of reflection and follow-up. These kinds of framing helped organize and orchestrate various types of collaboration and shared work. The collaboration invited more networking and increased scope for a variety of interactions that began to define the culture at this high school, both amongst the teachers, and between the teachers and other educators.

Separate from joining classes with Kelly Hodges in the spring of 1993, Marty participated in three PDS-funded shared teaching situations – with Sandy and then later with Bruce Larner and Steve Neurither. Later, he also took advantage of funding from TERC to share a Calculus class with Kellie Huhn. Over the years, he also took a number of interns into his classroom for one hour a day; and in 1998–1999, he had a full-time intern. These shared teaching endeavors proved to be a growing experience. Having the same teachers teach the same students at the same time offered many advantages. Marty summarized his reaction to the shared teaching as follows:

> Teaching with someone gave me a common experience in mathematics so that we had a common language to develop our ideas. We could talk about what the students had said and the ideas that had surfaced and, because we were both there, we didn't have to fill in every detail or try to picture the context. Otherwise, you are hearing about someone else's experience and in your mind placing it in the context of your own classroom and practice. Team-teaching pushes you to think about your teaching and why you are doing things. It gives you time to sit back and watch your students being taught, while you listen and think. You have opportunities for someone else to tell you what they saw and were thinking while you were teaching. The greatest professional benefit that I see is that in an attempt to understand a different way of teaching or the benefits of a different curriculum, you have the opportunity to see what goes on in the classroom. Looking at test scores or professional education articles gives you rather limited information. It is the change in attitude that the kids have about mathematics, what they are doing in the classroom, and how they understand the material. . . .
>
> (interview, spring 1995)

Other types of shared work in which Marty participated include the research with Nemirovsky and the electronic/mechanical devices mentioned earlier; work with Bill Rosenthal in creating Calculus curriculum; and collaborative research with Jim Kaput, a professor at the University of Massachusetts. In January 1998 Marty, along with other high school mathematics teachers, was invited to participate in a seminar related to SimCalc, an initiative of the National Science Foundation to develop software to simulate mathematics of change. Kaput's (1995) goal of "democratizing access to big ideas" is consistent with work being done at Holt.

Marty has also played an active role in seminars involving the mathematics department at MSU, in which mathematics education, the epistemology of mathematics, and other philosophical underpinnings of the subject have been discussed. All of these activities are related to the culture of the department and connections developed at Holt in collaboration with MSU.

Through this quality of shared work, the professional development culture at Holt has addressed the isolation that teachers have historically suffered (as described by Lortie, 1975, for example). The Holt mathematics teachers have developed professional relationships that feed growth. They have partnered with mathematics educators at different levels. These teachers see themselves as part of a community that extends beyond the walls of the classroom, school, and geographic location. They are participating in this greater community and learning from it.

Ongoing dialogue

The third characteristic indicative of the culture in the Holt math department is the ongoing dialogue about mathematics and teaching mathematics. The math teachers talk about mathematics (see Chapter 17 for an illustration). This may sound very normal and what one would expect from mathematics teachers, however, based on conversations with university interns and student teachers at other high schools, it may actually be very rare. Teachers at Holt share mathematical questions with each other, share insights from students, talk about everything from basic definitions to trigonometric functions and high-order derivatives. They share student work and discuss how to use their students' conceptions to expand their own understandings and create situations that will help them extend the sense their classes are making of the mathematics.

Teachers participate in formal conversations around algebra, geometry, trigonometry, and calculus at scheduled times (after school, during the weekly professional development time, during summer vacation, or while their classes are covered by others). But informal conversations have also become prevalent as this professional development culture has developed. With the help of an internal network and database (intranet), the Holt math teachers have collected mathematical situations and problems and have begun to annotate these tasks with their students' responses and their thoughts about applications for the problems. This common ground aids the ongoing dialogue. A comment in the staff lunchroom such as, "We worked on the 'Hot Dog Vender' problem today" inevitably triggers an involved and animated discussion of the relevant mathematics. Suggestions begin to build about what the teacher or intern might follow up with the next day. Others will chime in about what they are doing in their classrooms or will change, based on the conversation.

Informal conversations also increase and take place over time beyond the department. (The discussion around the definition of a radian, written about in Chapter 17, is a good example.) This conversation became vigorous as a result of an interaction between Laura Kueffner when she was an intern at Holt and her instructor in the internship year subject-specific seminar (TE 802). Others became part of the discussion. The university seminar continued the debate, involving other interns and secondary school settings as well.

Marty has been affected by this openness and has thrived on the con-versations. Indeed he played an important role in the prehistory of the conversation about radians. According to him, one of the wonderful things about the atmosphere at Holt "is you're getting together with other math teachers and just being able to talk about math and talk about new ideas" (fall 1994). This open dialogue with students, teachers, and university personnel caused Marty to move beyond think-ing about teaching techniques and mathematical skills.

Marty made an epistemological shift in his thinking, as evidenced by the following statement.

> As I struggled with these classroom experiences, continued to collaborate with my peers, and read educational literature, I came to the conclusion that it was my mathematical philosophy that needed questioning, not my intended approach to teaching and learning.
>
> (December, 1996)

Mathematics can be understood as an existing body of knowledge on which mathematicians continue to build; it can be thought of, too, as the process of developing and analyzing these and other quantitative and spatial relationships. School mathematics (the content that students encounter in grades K–16) has traditionally been presented as an exist-ing body of knowledge. It comprises isolated skills and algorithms that students must memorize and become proficient with. Applying this knowledge in specific situations leads to the development of an instru-mental understanding. The relational understanding of mathematics that Marty began to value is dependent on a view of mathematics that is relational, where mathematics "consists of building up a conceptual structure (schema) from which its possessor can (in principle) produce an unlimited number of plans for getting from any starting point within his schema to any finishing point" (Skemp, 1978, p. 14). Marty's trans-formed philosophy of mathematics directly affected the content to be considered and the mathematical activity that went on in his classroom.

For the first five years of Marty's teaching career, he closely followed the order and content of his textbooks. He later observed that, as he went through school, college, and his early career, he was convinced that the mathematics *was* what was in the textbook.

> [Coming out of college,] mathematics was just the stuff that was stored away in textbooks. That is, the stuff you had to learn if you were going to learn math. It was completely a formalist, absolutist kind of view that said that the (concepts) in the textbooks weren't chosen conventions and techniques and things, but that is the way

the world is and that is the way the world works. That was my conception coming out of college and for quite a while teaching.

(February 1998)

The ensuing shift in Marty's view of mathematics away from something "out there to be discovered," is illustrated in this recollection of Marty's.

When I really appreciated that (my shift in thinking) was last year when an intern was sitting in on a Calculus class, and he said, "Oh my goodness, they almost discovered the derivative." No, they were doing something that is perfectly logical. They were looking at rates of change over smaller and smaller intervals, and they realized it would be a pain to keep having to do that at every single point. It would be a whole lot easier if we could generalize this in some way so that we could get a function that would do it. That is not discovering the derivative. The derivative isn't matter or some kind of energy. I don't think there is anything like that. It's not something hanging out there in space that whoever runs the universe, God or whatever, has as part of his operating principles. It is a human construction. Once the intern made his comment, that was after I read Lakatos's "Proofs and Refutations (Lakatos, 1976)," I started looking at a lot of other things. The definition of continuity – you are not saying that there is a special class of functions out there that we can do all of this wonderful mathematics on. It is "we want to get rid of all of this stuff that is hard and confusing and causes us problems, so that we can do mathematics on it." That is what the definition of continuity is all about – to kick all of the other stuff out of your conversation. That is a really different perspective on what mathematics is.

(February 1998)

This major transition in Marty's thinking afforded insight into the question that had bothered him for several years, "How do you get kids to discover what is in the textbooks?" After having spent time considering that what was in the textbooks was just a particular view of a piece of humanly constructed mathematics, Marty was thinking more about the concepts and why people had agreed to construct them in certain ways. Realizing that the process of finding a derivative is not a truth to be discovered, but instead is one way of talking about the phenomena of changing rates, represented a new perspective on mathematics. This experience helped Marty realize what he came to see as the similarities between, on the one hand, school mathematics and classroom activities and, on the other, the discipline of mathematics and its development.

Ongoing dialogues with colleagues and students, as well as graduate study, contributed greatly to Marty's arrival at this conclusion.

Realizing that his students did not have to reproduce exactly what was in the textbooks emancipated Marty. He came to rely on his own growing understanding of content and curriculum and to value student ideas that differed from convention. He offers an interesting example of his decision not to push students to textbook conclusions. As described in an earlier essay, Marty had decided to postpone study of the Product Rule in his Calculus class until late in the year, deciding to focus first on the Chain Rule in an attempt to let this concept "sit in their minds for a period of time." While dialoguing with Michal Yerushalmy, a professor from Haifa University in Israel, he began considering the ramifications of allowing students to gain a more grounded understanding of the Chain Rule. Marty was struck that Yerushalmy, a renowned mathematics educator, actually critiqued the textbook proof and shared her desire for improving the mathematical quality of those proofs. Marty felt that his questions and ideas were met with understanding and thus began a long-term conversation around making the proof sensible to students while also improving its mathematical quality. Conversations with Yerushalmy ended up playing an influential role in Marty's freedom and ultimate mathematical power as he searched his own understandings and felt at liberty to critique the canon. Marty's experience confirmed his belief that "students learn more and analyze other people's mathematics much more thoroughly if they are first given a chance to tackle situations with mathematics they already know or create new mathematics" (February 1998). This example of the effect of ongoing dialogue, including conversations beyond the school, illustrates the impact a professional development culture can have on teachers and their work.

Concluding remarks

The professional development culture within the Holt High School mathematics department is unique in many ways. The qualities described above – an atmosphere that encourages inquiring students and teachers, that supports shared work and that encourages ongoing dialogue – depict a culture that allows for and even expects growth. The professional experiences of Marty Schnepp illustrate how these qualities have supported the professional transformation that changed his thinking and practice. The culture does not merely support temporary changes, nor does it represent only a series of changed methods and techniques. Rather, it has generated a workspace that allows for epistemological shifts (in the sense of Nelson, 1995) in teacher and student thinking. In Marty's case, this adds up to a professional transformation.

He now thinks much differently about the philosophical and historical underpinnings of mathematics, the content of school mathematics, and the processes of teaching and learning.

The PDS relationship between Holt High School and Michigan State University in the early 1990s was an important catalyst for the culture that now exists in the Holt math department. The influence of this relationship is reflected in the freedom to question, shared work opportunities, and ongoing dialogue that is now a trademark of the partnership between a group of high school teachers and university educators. It is interesting that even though by the mid-1990s the PDS money was disappearing, this initiative continued to impact the culture of the Holt math department. The networking and in-depth inquiries that had been established continued to grow as former interns were hired on as full-time teachers and teachers continued to investigate their questions and participate in the larger education milieu.

Elementary mathematics + a culture of questioning = complex mathematics

Tom Almeida and Sandra Callis, Holt High School

TOM ALMEIDA: When I was in Ann Arbor, teaching from the Core Plus curriculum and from the University of Chicago series algebra text at the same time, everything was right in the text for me. All I had to do was follow the guides, and my students would be the smartest kids in the world. I was partially convinced that the power of mathematics was somewhere in those books/guides. I never had to ask questions, and I always knew how to answer those of my students. Then, I got lucky, and fell into Holt. My first year, I taught from the Chicago series and from the activities collected on the g-drive [the school's intranet]. The classes directly from the Chicago series were no more fulfilling than my previous experiences, but the classes taught using materials from the g-drive gave me that liberated feeling Marty talked about. The collegiality in Holt was a major key to my enjoyment of this course. The other teachers basically carried me through the first year, and I grew incredibly. My only reason for liking math before was that I was good at it. But in fall 1998, when I started at Holt, I found that math is really much more interesting and difficult than I had thought. Amazing! After five years of math at the collegiate level, I finally figured out my own perceptions after two months of actually teaching it from the "question everything from all sides" approach. I had never questioned anything before. I can relate to the last parts of this piece, especially the statement, "Marty was thinking more about the concepts and why people had agreed to construct them in certain ways." That's what I find my colleagues (and myself) doing every day.

SANDRA CALLIS: You're right about the complexity of even apparently obvious mathematical ideas. For me, the culture of mathematical conversation at Holt has been very supportive. I'll tell you a story about some of us struggling with different ways to think about *pi*. Five of us were headed up to the state mathematics convention to make a presentation about our Algebra 1 curriculum. We started talking about one of our teacher education graduate courses. One teacher was relating a teacher's conception that *pi* was not a concrete number that one could actually *have* in the same way that you could *have*, for example, two of something. The question was what would it mean to have *pi* apples. I sat quietly for a few moments as the conversation ensued. Everyone was talking about that teacher as if she were wrong, yet I thought I agreed with her. After a few minutes lost in my own thoughts about *pi*, I piped up, "I think I agree with that teacher." Everybody was quiet for a second. One person responded, "Can you say more about what you're thinking?" I had the sense that I was wrong, but I also knew that all the others in the group would be okay with that. In these conversations, when we get to questioning each other *ad infinitum*, we've often said something like, "Okay, I'm not one of the students; just tell me the answer." But, of course, usually nobody does. So I tried to explain. "Well, let's say you're moving on the number line to *pi*. You're going to get pretty close, but then there will be another digit added on, so you'll never really get to the exact value." Someone said, "I think you may be getting wrapped up in the decimal representation of the number." So now I had to think, "What makes a number a number, if not its numeric representation?" And, "What does the base one uses have to do with quantity?" I sat in silence for a few more minutes as the others went on to a completely different topic. After a few more minutes, I said, "I'm still struggling." A different teacher interjected this time, "Here's how I think about it. Say you draw a circle with a diameter of 1. Then you cut the circle and lay it out on a line. That would be *pi* units long." I didn't want to accept that. "But you're just defining that to be *pi*. You didn't start out with *pi* and then measure it off." She didn't respond, so I sat and thought some more. How does *pi* on a number line compare to, for example, 2? I realized that I would have to define 2 units, and then I would still have the same problem getting to 2 if I were approaching 2 by discrete numbers on the line. I didn't sort all of this out on that trip, nor have I yet. Some of my intuitive notions about numbers were challenged, and every time I have a chance, I bring the topic up with a colleague. I don't pursue this because it's part of my job as a teacher. I pursue it because it's incredibly interesting to me. As a result, I feel I'm a better teacher. My colleagues accept that I don't know everything about mathematics.

TOM: That's a fascinating story. From my first day, I felt an unbelievable amount of support. I entered into a community where immediately I felt as if my opinion on mathematics was important and where everyone can have a different perspective on how to approach a problem. As of yet, no one has told me I'm a complete idiot, or that I did it wrong. Even when I found out later that I was way off, the other teachers around me actually thought about it and made sure they and I both understood it before we moved on. I strive for this quality in my classroom. I've noticed that if the students start figuring things out for themselves, they are empowered and start to do even better things. Eventually all students start to see that they're able to critically think about a problem and figure it out one way or another. I try to create an atmosphere in my class like the one we have as a math department.

Chapter 16

Changing the math curriculum

In the last essay, Jan Simonson credits the PDS effort with an important role in shaping the culture of the Holt math department. For Jan, the culture of the Holt math department is important because it influences how teachers use professional development opportunities that come their way and indeed what they come to view as professional development opportunities. Rather than conceptualizing professional development as an activity done to teachers at a remove from their teaching, she suggests that the culture of the department orients teachers to see opportunities for professional growth in the day-to-day aspects of their teaching.

Indeed, this observation is an important theme in the rest of this section, where we examine how teachers at Holt, as a result of the professional culture in their department, take advantage of opportunities for professional growth that exist in many schools.

Chapter 13, earlier in this section, focused on how the PDS effort allowed teachers time to interact professionally. In particular, that essay examined shared teaching assignments. These assignments are a mechanism that moves the activity of professional development into the classroom. But they required special infusions of funding. There are also important professional development opportunities that are available to all teachers at all times, as they teach, without special funding. For example, important opportunities can arise from inquiry into one's own teaching. The next essay is out of the chronological sequence followed so far in this section; it goes backwards in time, to the start of the PDS effort. It illustrates an important type of teacher learning that has been prevalent at Holt during the PDS effort and since, teacher learning from curricular change that is a part of inquiry into one's own teaching. This essay will focus on teacher learning associated with the curricular change in Algebra 1 that was described in Chapters 3 and 6. The argument is that a change in curriculum can be a locus for professional growth. The likelihood that such curricular change will lead to professional growth is enhanced by a supportive teaching culture.

Reviewing some of the context of this curricular change, in the spring of 1990, the PDS initiative at Holt was under way, and teachers had identified a problem of practice. Algebra 1 in all its complexity was the issue. As Steve Neurither once commented, at this point in time, teaching Algebra 1 was like "pulling students' teeth out, through the backs of their heads." Frustration and the desire for change were present among the teachers, and this despite the use of a new, reform-minded text. Personal experiences especially with teaching lower-track algebra classes pointed to the need for change. Other indications were found through examination of student learning. In one early PDS project, a number of math teachers interviewed each other's students. These interviews indicated both students' power of thought and their lack of conventional mathematical understandings. Add to this the communal and administrative pressure to increase both test scores and the numbers of state-certified diplomas. The need for reform in mathematics education was in the air. How could teachers at Holt convince their students to engage in the study of Algebra 1?

It is important to recognize that responding to such problems of practice involves professional development. Responding to complex problems of practice is not simply a matter of changing curricula, or adopting innovations. In order to change curricula or adopt an innovation, particularly if this is being done to respond to a challenging problem of practice, teachers must learn. Of course, curricula and innovations are important resources. Awareness of a program's limitations and frustration with one's own teaching might be impetus for change, but they don't necessarily provide a way to make progress. One can still blame others and remain feeling powerless; resources necessary to support serious change may be lacking. In this case, having identified Algebra 1 as an important problem of practice, how were Holt teachers going to make progress in creating an Algebra 1 course that would be less frustrating and painful to both teachers and students?

The story of changes to the Algebra 1 curriculum involves resources from outside Holt. Starting in 1990, Dan Chazan came to Holt High School to study his own teaching of Algebra 1. He had a position in MSU's Department of Teacher Education, but the position was designed to have reduced on-campus teaching for five years to allow him to carry out research on high school mathematics teaching by teaching himself. He was interested in questions like:

- In teaching Algebra 1, what do I really want my students to learn?
- On what basis can I ask students to invest their energies in this study?

Dan brought with him both frustrations with his earlier teaching of algebra and ideas for changing school algebra (what was called a functions-based approach to algebra in Chapter 3; for more detail on his work see Chazan, 2000). This was something to try: a resource, not a solution, a set of mathematical approaches and pedagogical ideas that might help in tackling Algebra 1. Initially, these ideas were quite controversial inside the department. Would students learn what they needed to be successful in further courses? Was the Algebra 1 curriculum being covered?

But the story of the changes in Algebra 1 is not the focus here; the focus is on the teachers' professional development that resulted from changing perspective on the mathematics of Algebra 1, as a part of dealing with the problem of practice that this course represented. The next essay shifts attention to teachers' knowledge of the mathematics that they teach, another theme in this section, particularly in the next three essays.

The next essay is written by Dan Chazan, then an MSU faculty member. In this essay, however, Dan writes as a high school teacher, in particular as a teacher of Algebra 1. He writes about teachers' knowledge of the mathematics they teach by reflecting on his own experiences in teaching Algebra 1. He suggests two specific ways in which an altered approach to Algebra 1 supplied the resources for changing his teaching practices and supported his professional growth. He argues that an important connection exists between the nature of teachers' knowledge of the mathematics they teach and their capacity to create tasks for students to explore particular content. Following a functions-based approach, Dan created exploratory algebra tasks, something he argues would have been impossible for him to do with his earlier understanding of school algebra. In this context, his argument suggests that professional development, curricular change, and a rethinking of the roles played by teacher and students in the classroom are all linked. He sees the chance to rethink one's view of a curriculum one knows well, when one teaches it in a different way, as an important opportunity for professional development that can either be supported or constrained by the culture of the school as a workplace.

In the context of the Holt PDS work, the idea that a university mathematics educator could see himself learning mathematics from teaching may have been an important resource in supporting the development of a teaching culture in which discussion of mathematics is valued. But Dan's experience of learning mathematics from teaching was not unique in this setting. As Marty Schnepp and Tom Almeida's response to this essay, as well as Tom's and Sandy Callis's response to the previous essay, indicate, other teachers at Holt have experienced the teaching of a new approach to algebra as an important opportunity for professional growth. Though functions-based ideas about Algebra 1 sparked debate, as this approach to Algebra 1 spread through the department, in part through the shared teaching assignments, others began to have the experience of rethinking familiar mathematical ideas. This was exciting!

Attending to mathematical ideas is a mode of professional development that is well suited to high school mathematics teachers and teacher educators. Secondary school educators take pride in being subject-matter specialists. Separate from its particular merits and drawbacks, an approach centered on the algebraic relationships between quantities afforded an alternative view of familiar material that would prove beneficial for both school and university personnel. By its very presence, this view focused attention on the teacher's own mathematical understanding. So, even though the participants in the Algebra 1 project were subject-matter specialists, the presence of this view made all the participants into learners and explorers who were relearning school algebra. Unlike many teacher candidates who have trouble connecting the advanced study of mathematics with their future teaching, the functions-based approach enabled even those with significant professional experience to see connections between what they learned and the mathematics they taught. Seeing themselves as learners both changed their stance toward the content and undermined a view of high school mathematics as cut and dried.

Teaching a technologically supported approach to school algebra

Daniel Chazan, Michigan State University

This essay is excerpted from Chazan, D. (1999). On teachers' mathematical knowledge and student exploration: A personal story about teaching a technologically supported approach to school algebra. *International Journal for Computers in Mathematics Education, 4*(2–3), 121–149.

A preliminary story of two teaching experiences

For three years in the 1980s, I taught Algebra 1 in a private Jewish dayschool in a suburban area of the Northeastern United States. I used the revised edition of Dolciani and Wooton's (1970/1973) *Modern algebra: Structure and method* (Book One). This text builds on the work of the New Math-era School Mathematics Study Group and for a time held a large share of the Algebra 1 textbook market. For Dolciani and Wooton, expressions with x's and y's are expressions for particular numbers. Based on this view, the book focuses on topics like solving linear equations (Chapters 4 and 5), factoring quadratic trinomials (Chapter 7), and three methods for solving systems of linear equations (Chapter 11). In retrospect, underlying the book's focus on technique is a consistent story about generalizing arithmetical procedures to create algebraic ones. This generalization is supported by the notion that in both arithmetic and algebra, one is dealing with the same sorts of numbers.

While the school community was quite happy with my teaching and I enjoyed the students greatly, I was quite frustrated during these years. I was concerned that my teaching was centered on a long list of techniques, that students depended on me and on the text to tell them right from wrong, that students exercised little independent judgment, and that they did not understand what the course was all about. This last concern is similar to John Dewey's criticism that an overemphasis on curriculum often comes at the expense of the child. Dewey (1902/1990) argues that when educators forget that a subject has two aspects, "one for the scientist as a scientist; the other for the teacher as a teacher" (p. 22), there is no "motive for the learning" (p. 25). In Dewey's words, "When material is directly supplied in the form of a lesson to be learned as a lesson, the connecting links of need and aim are conspicuous for their absence there is no craving, no need, no demand" (p. 203). I was concerned that my teaching exhibited this absence.

While the textbook I was working from was well structured and rigorous in its development of algebra, and though my students were most likely college-bound and quite intent on being successful in school, I felt the course was inwardly directed to an unhealthy degree. With each topic that I taught, I could find no intrinsic justification; topics were always justified by their relationship to further chapters in the book or to further coursework. I was teaching students a course focused on numbers – mathematical objects with which I hoped they found much comfort. Yet I felt I could only justify the value of learning the algorithms I was teaching by making reference to problem types that they would encounter later in the year or in high school or college. Though my students at the time did not often question me in this way, I felt I was on quite shaky ground. I could only refer to experience that they did not have. I was teaching them methods to solve problems which they had not yet encountered and which I thought they could not understand. Furthermore, I myself could not see connections between the algorithms I was teaching them and the activity of people in the world around me. These algorithms were primarily useful in solving problems in school or on academic tests.

In addition, since I taught the same students Biblical criticism, I was disturbed to note stark differences in the nature of classroom discourse in the two subjects. In Bible class, students would debate various interpretations, critique ones that I offered, and offer their own. But in mathematics class, they rarely exercised their own judgment. They always deferred to my mathematical authority. Ironically, it was the mathematics class that felt like indoctrination, not the Bible class.

When contrasting my teaching of algebra with my experience teaching geometry at the same school, I began to concentrate on my own understanding of algebra as the source of my frustration. I had mastered the techniques taught in the algebra course and could help students solve the problems present in the algebra text, but I felt that my own understanding of the course was overly focused on technique. I could not give an overview of the course without referring to sections of the text to illustrate the kinds of problems that would be solved. I did not feel that I had the sort of conceptual understanding of the material necessary to support the sort of teaching I wanted to do.

I suspected that I was not alone in this predicament. I did not see different sorts of understandings of school algebra in the texts I reviewed and the conference presentations I attended. It seemed to me that many people sidestepped this issue in the teaching of school algebra by saying that it was not a field of mathematical study, but rather the language in which much of mathematics is written. (Lacampagne et al., 1995; Lee, 1996; National Council of Teachers of Mathematics Algebra Working Group, 1998; Usiskin, 1987). Others seemed to dismiss my frustration by suggesting that mathematics is not supposed to have the sort of meaning I was after.

In North America, interest is stirring in alternatives to the standard algebra curriculum. In part because of the availability of technology (like graphing calculators) which allows for links between input–output tables, Cartesian graphs, and algebraic symbols, one alternative is often called a "functions-based" or "technological" algebra curriculum (see for example Heid et al., 1995). Rather than organize school algebra around the continued study of numbers and concentrate on a long list of symbolic manipulations, this approach organizes introductory algebra experiences around functions, their representations, and operations on functions (see Chapters 3 and 5 for descriptions of activities in this vein with Algebra 1 students).

For three years in the 1990s, I team-taught a lower-track Algebra 1 course using an approach of this kind. I taught with Sandy Callis. Most students in our classes were not intending to go to college. To arrive in our course, many of them had failed a previous course; most had to pass ours in order to graduate (see Chazan, 1996, 2000 for more detail). The teaching at Holt was often quite difficult and our students were not shy about asking why school algebra was important. Yet I did not feel nearly as frustrated taking this approach to the curriculum as I had in my previous teaching experience. Taking a different approach to the course content, I felt better equipped to help my students understand what the course was about, how the parts of it were connected, and how algebra related to the world around them.

Making functions and their standard representations – new and less familiar mathematical objects for students – central to the course helped me grow and develop and changed my experience in a positive way. This approach helped me learn to express the problems I posed to students in ways that allowed them to understand the desired goals. At the same time, it gave them resources they could apply to solve the problems even before being taught standard methods. These standard methods could then be introduced to students as ways of solving problems they already understood. As a result of what I learned through this teaching, I felt better equipped to help students see the mathematics we were studying in the activity of people they knew, across a range of professions, vocations, and avocations. I felt on less shaky ground with respect to what Dewey calls a "motive for the learning."

To explore what it is that I learned through this teaching, in the remainder of this essay, I will focus on two issues in the introductory teaching of algebra: solving equations and helping students find algebra in the world around them.

Manipulation of symbols: solving equations

In what way did moving to this sort of technologically supported approach change my understanding of school algebra? How did my 1990s' understanding of algebra shape instruction differently than my 1980s' understanding? What was it that I learned that helped me change my teaching? I will begin to address this question by examining a particular set of symbolic manipulations usually present in a typical Algebra 1 course, but critiqued in the 1989 NCTM *Curriculum and Evaluation Standards for School Mathematics*. The summary of changes in content and emphases in the 1989 NCTM *Standards* for 9–12 mathematics suggests that decreased attention should be paid to certain traditional symbolic manipulations. Examples include "the simplification of radical expressions" and "the use of factoring to solve equations and to simplify rational expressions" (p. 127).

I find this specific recommendation fascinating; it reflects discomfort with high school algebra courses that focus solely on having students master a myriad of symbolic manipulations (Fey, 1989; Lacampagne *et al.*, 1995). It also represents an important and specific statement of values. Since calculators have symbolic capabilities and students seem to need more evidence that algebra has purpose, the authors of this Standards document indicate the specific manipulations that they find less worthy than others. These recommendations, and the general issue of symbol manipulation are one flash point between K–12 mathematics educators committed to the Standards movement and some university mathematicians. For many mathematicians, these skills are important prerequisites for successful participation on college Calculus courses.

Yet, besides calling for decreased attention to these particular manipulations, the curriculum standards give little direction to the teacher on ways to re-conceptualize the symbol manipulation work that remains in the curriculum. In attempting to capture how the view of algebra associated with a functions-based approach helps a teacher reconceptualize symbol manipulation, I have chosen to focus on solving equations.

To begin this exploration (for a more complete exploration, see Chazan, 1999), it is helpful to contrast the meaning of equations and solving equations between a standard and a functions-based approach (see Figure 16.1).

While, on the surface, these two views are different, it is initially unclear whether the differences are substantial. But it seems to me that important differences exist between the two views. To illustrate, imagine the situation of students who have not learned methods for solving equations, but who are presented with an equation and a definition of an equation, and are asked to solve the equation deploying any methods at their disposal. In suggesting this thought experiment, I am not suggesting that students must invent or discover every algorithm in

	A standard approach	A functions-based approach
What is an equation?	"a sentence about numbers" p. 24 "a pattern for the different statements – some true, some false – which you obtain by replacing each variable by the names for the different values of the variable" p. 44	A comparison of two functions that share the same domain. One seeks to find elements of the domain for which the two functions will produce the same output.
What does it mean to solve an equation of a single variable?	To find "the set consisting of the members of the domain of the variable for which an open sentence is true" p. 54	To find the values in the shared domain for which the two functions will produce the same output.

Figure 16.1 Alternative meanings for equations and the solving of equations.

school mathematics. Instead, I am trying to capture an aspect of the two approaches to algebra that seems different to me.

In my dayschool teaching, I did not give students tasks for which I had not taught an algorithm; if I had not introduced an algorithm, my assumption was that students could not solve the problem. As a result, I do not know how I would have described an unfamiliar problem to students without doing an example. Since I always taught algorithms first, I was not accustomed to describing the properties of a solution. Now I wonder about the sorts of resources my students would have had for finding numbers that would make $x^2 - 8x = 5$ a true statement. They might have chosen a number (almost randomly) and tested whether or not that particular number worked. By choosing a series of numbers they *might* have seen that they were getting closer and farther from a true statement. But they would have had no notion about the potential number of solutions. In order to work on a problem like this, I suspect my dayschool students *might* have invented a tabular representation of the sort shown in Figure 16.2.

We would not, however, have made tables of this kind before in class. We did not generally evaluate expressions for a range of different values. (Notice that this is a push in the direction of a functional approach.) And I do not know if they would have recognized that between 8 and 9 one might find a solution.

By contrast, I was regularly able to give my students at Holt problems for which they did not have an algorithm. I became practiced at describing the properties of a solution, rather than giving an example of a solution to a problem of a given type. Having access to a variety of representations and technological tools that operated on these representations somehow made this possible. The students could both understand the goal of the problem and had resources with which to tackle it. Given the same solve-an-equation type of problem (i.e., find the shared inputs that will generate equal outputs), students who have

Value of variable (x)	Resulting equation $x^2 - 8x = 5$	True/false
5	$-15 = 5$	f
6	$-12 = 5$	f
7	$-7 = 5$	f
8	$0 = 5$	f
9	$9 = 5$	f

Figure 16.2 A potential tabular representation for keeping track of a "guess and test" method for finding true statements.

been making tables and graphs of functions and who are given the functions-based definition of an equation can make a table with three familiar columns; they do not necessarily need a calculator to do this sort of work. See Table 16.1.

In analyzing such a table, my Holt students had previous experience with problems of the form: here is a function $f(x)$, say $f(x) = 3x - 2$, find the input for which the output is 0. They had experienced the capabilities of a calculator (and implicitly using arguments based on continuity) to find decimal approximations for answers involving a non-terminating decimal. I could expect them to find a solution between 8 and 9. Given their experiences with graphs, they could potentially use the graphical depiction of points of intersection to home in on that solution. They quite likely could also speculate about the number of possible solutions and perhaps search for more than one solution. Knowledge about the geometrical behavior of the graphs of particular families of functions might even allow for arguments justifying an expectation for two solutions.

These approaches seem to differ in the way they define solving an equation and the resources they lend students for solving specific types of equations before being taught an algorithm. With the functions-based approach, I was learning a different way to talk with my students about the task of solving equations; I was learning how to help them understand what the task was before they had learned methods to solve an equation.

Why study school algebra?

Dolciani and Wooton's text makes an attempt at the beginning of each chapter to state a purpose for the section, and the first chapter offers an introduction to the course as a whole. These statements often try to justify the study of school algebra. They remind me of my frustrations teaching at the dayschool. The rationale is always future-directed. Algebra is a foundation toward larger goals. It supplies techniques that can help solve interesting problems. It is not justified in and of itself. Here are some of the statements that appear:

Table 16.1 An initial table for finding shared inputs that will generate equal outputs

Valuable of variable (x)	$f(x) = x^2 - 8x$	$g(x) = 5$
5	−15	5
6	−12	5
7	−7	5
8	0	5
9	9	5

Mathematics, the language of science, is the language of dreamers who plan to achieve their dreams ... The algebra that you will learn in this course is one of the essential foundations for the theories on which space travel is based.

(Chapter 1, p. 1)

In this chapter you will study how to solve an equation by transforming it into a simpler equivalent equation. You will then be able to solve a number of interesting problems.

(Chapter 4, p. 111)

You are now ready to learn how to perform operations with expressions called polynomials. You will then use these new techniques in the solution of problems more complicated than those you have solved up to now.

(Chapter 6, p. 205)

As in the study of a language, mathematics becomes more interesting after the basic skills have been acquired. You will find this to be true in this chapter where you will study about quadratic equations and inequalities. With such open sentences you will increase your power to solve problems.

(Chapter 13, p. 495)

As you look into your own future, can you see the role mathematics may play in it? Space engineers require a knowledge of mathematics greater than that you now possess. They did not learn their mathematics as part of their jobs. They learned it in order to get their jobs. Since many occupations which are challenging require a knowledge of mathematics, you should plan to include it in your education.

(Chapter 14, p. 523)

The theme of the final chapter, that of algebra as a requirement for challenging employment, is one often employed by teachers to justify school algebra. Yet in US policy debates surrounding recent moves to ensure greater access to college by requiring algebra for graduation from high school, these rationales, which are offered by mathematicians and mathematics educators, are sometimes questioned by others. Here are some comments made following the adoption of algebra as a graduation requirement in the Washington DC school district.

Too many of us were forced to take algebra when the time and energy could have been devoted to subjects that truly were beneficial ... Would millions of high school students trudge into their algebra classes if they weren't a gate through which they were forced to pass to enter college?

(McCarthy, 20 April 1991, p. A21)

Mathematics is not just another science; it is the language through which all of science and much of management science is taught. . . . The student who closes the door on high school algebra (and so on all of mathematics) closes the door on much more. . . .

(Roberts, 27 April 1991, p. 15A)

A 1992 analysis of 1,400 jobs by the New York Department of Education found that 78 percent of them required no algebra, and only 10 percent required more than a little. . . .

(Bracey, 12 June 1992, p. C5)

Future-oriented justifications were the best that I had to offer when teaching at the dayschool, but luckily my students did not often ask this sort of question. They were all college-intending and understood that school in general and algebra in particular were stepping stones toward the futures they desired and thought they could have. My teaching at Holt was quite different. For these students, school and algebra were not outfitting them for the futures they saw available. The students Sandy Callis and I taught were quite skeptical about the value of school knowledge.

Thus, besides identifying the objects of study in algebra for myself, I felt I needed to be able to learn to find those objects of study in the worlds of my students; if not in their experience then in the experience of people whom they knew. In Dewey's terms, I needed to psychologize the subject matter, to view it "as an outgrowth of (my students') present tendencies and activities" (1902/1990, p. 203). Only then would I begin to have an answer to the question "What is algebra *all* about? Why would anyone want to know algebra?"

A typical response to the second of these questions is for the teacher to seek the relevance of school algebra to students' lives. Under Sandy's guidance, we took a different approach. Rather than assume the complete burden of generating relevance, we asked our students to share this task. We asked them to find relationships between quantities in the world around them (see Chapter 6 for descriptions of our project); we enlisted their aid in exploring connections between the mathematics studied in school and their lives. Exploration of the subject matter, in this case school algebra, became one avenue for having students share with us their experience of their world. *They* educated *us*.

Involving students in the question of relevance and the choice of relationships between quantities as the central mathematical object of school algebra have changed my response to questions about its meaning and purpose, questions I always used to dread. Since relationships between quantities are mathematical objects that my students can find in the world around them, the choice of structuring the course around these objects provides me with an alternative to looking for relevance.

Summary

When I first came to Holt to teach, I knew that I wanted my algebra class to be different than the ones I had taught at the dayschool. I didn't want the material to feel cut and dried and I didn't want to be the sole mathematical authority in the room. I wanted there to be conversations in the classroom. I wanted students to be able to have their own ideas and to exercise their own reasoning to justify conclusions and solution methods.

But, in order to make such changes in the classroom, I had to learn and grow; it wasn't simply a matter of deciding that I wanted to teach differently. I didn't know how to open up standard algebra problems for exploration. I didn't know how to talk students about what Algebra 1 might be all about.

For me, teaching a different approach to school algebra yielded important learning opportunities. Seeing familiar material from another point of view and hearing what my students had to say as I tried a new approach helped me learn. Specifically, the functions-based approach to algebra's identification of objects and the processes that can be done to these objects helped me learn to communicate with students (novice algebraists) in at least two ways. From the start of the course, it allowed me to enable students to appreciate what the course is about and how it is related to the world around them. Identification of the central objects of study was central in helping students see algebra in the world around them. This understanding also helped me learn to make algebra less mysterious by assisting students in understanding mathematical tasks in terms of the characteristics of desired solutions. This sort of understanding is precisely what I felt I was unable to give to students when teaching algebra felt like slogging through a list of disconnected techniques. With the functions-based approach, I was able to help students understand the goals of problems for which they did not have solution algorithms and to work productively on such problems.

Talking about what math is for

Marty Schnepp and Tom Almeida, Holt High School

MARTY SCHNEPP: Dan raises an issue that's very important to me. In a traditional setting students seldom, if ever, have any idea what the mathematical techniques being taught them are for, and they have no clue about the context in which these techniques were developed. I find context of development and rationale for use to be very helpful in understanding conventions and methods.

TOM ALMEIDA: Absolutely. In my class at the senior high, we attempted putting all of our algebra teaching into context – talking about relationships in the real world at the beginning of the year and then describing them mathematically by the end of the year.

MARTY: I think that's very important. Let me give you an example from calculus. Everyone's first chapter dealing with the derivative starts by introducing these things called tangents, and they set about showing how to find the slope of a tangent. Conspicuously absent is the reason anyone would ever want to know about such things. The only motivation for learning it is because the instructor says you have to, and good students know that applications will follow. The real story is that the people who developed calculus were working on rate problems, and, after graphs came into vogue, tangents to graphs became a nice way to represent what they were doing. If tangents came to represent instantaneous rates – they are a visual aid – why do we teach it as though the tangent is the important thing and rate is a secondary consideration to apply the tangent idea to? I can make a pretty strong case that playing with rate contexts first, then moving toward the abstract notion of tangent line slopes as a representation of context-based ideas, informs the learning process. Students acquire some pretty sophisticated notions of why tangents are worthwhile studying.

TOM: That makes good sense. Also, if we successfully establish context, then it would address another crucial point Dan raises in his essay – the question of justification for what we teach. I, too, have often felt that much of my justification for what my students were learning in junior high was that they would need it later. Students asked every day what the point was, and I was uncomfortable answering them.

MARTY: The best way I know to help students sense a justification for what they are doing is to help them develop mathematical power, the kind discussed in the *Standards*. The natural sequencing to make that happen is to first investigate real problems, then move to abstract mathematical technique, and finally to return to real problems. I read this approach into a quote from Maggie Lampert that I once read about "shift(ing) the locus of authority in the classroom" as a key element in reforming mathematics classes.

TOM: Shifting the locus of authority also means somehow developing joint responsibility for what happens in class. Dan's comparison between the Bible criticism class and algebra class reminded me of that hollow feeling I used to have that the burden was entirely on my shoulders as the teacher. If they didn't get the math, it was entirely my fault. Currently, as I teach from a living, changing, functions-based approach, it seems the responsibility has shifted to the students. I like that. I've always felt students should be the ones doing the work, but I hadn't realized I was getting in the way. We now have very open and heated debates about quadratics!

MARTY: We have to craft activities that target those mathematical ideas that will afford students opportunities to come to grips with the context and/or problem in a real way. Students should be able to make progress when they haven't yet been taught a technique for solving such problems. We know there's no fixed recipe for generating such problems, but just identifying this as a pedagogical goal is helpful for me. Mathematics should make sense and should be logical, so students will often come to (or at least approximate) techniques that are housed in textbooks and named in curriculum guides. But when learners look at a real question in a context they can relate to and then create and articulate a process or terminology that could be used in similar situations, that is power. It also gives one, as a teacher, a foundation from which to introduce a well-known method for solving such problems. I am convinced students learn better this way.

TOM: You know, in my school experience, I was good with numbers and patterns, so I slid through math classes. We were all bored to death. When I began to teach, I found that no matter how much energy I had, when I taught from the same perspective, I got the same reaction. "Tell me how to do it. I'll do it, and then let me sleep." What a difference now! I look forward to each day, and some of my students do, too. Many have come up to me, excited or frustrated about the day's discussion. "Isn't there an easier way?" they ask. "Can't you just show me?"

MARTY: What you are saying connects to the notion that a course should be about something, that there should be a story-line. This is what changed the Algebra 1 and Calculus classes. When Dan talks about initially seeing the Algebra course as a list of algorithms, I know what that's like every time I open the AP Calculus syllabus. I fight the urge to judge my success by how many topics I can check off the list. Why? Because I'm convinced it's far better for students if I make the course about accumulation and rate, covering techniques in the context of solving problems and answering questions about changing quantities.

TOM: Right! Teaching this way, I learn new ways to look at problems every day; I've been stunned by student ideas in front of a class more times than I care to count. I remember thinking how absolutely ingenious folks like Newton had to be. Now I know they were just looking for an answer to a problem that hadn't been solved before. I try to give my students that same experience, and occasionally it works.

MARTY: And, as you pointed out, if teachers are going to stand any chance of changing the classroom experience for students, their own understanding of mathematics must be challenged and probably changed. If mathematics for you is simply a bunch of hierarchical procedures and vocabulary, then that's what you will present to students. If this proves an ineffective way to teach (and I believe the data bear this out), then curriculum and teaching must change. But we cannot expect change to happen unless our mathematical understandings, as teachers, shift.

Chapter 17

Learning from students and colleagues

As has been mentioned earlier, the Holt mathematics teachers have a reputation within the school; they are known for talking about mathematics and being excited about doing so (sometimes to the consternation of others!). These conversations often originate from a comment a student made in class or in an issue a teacher feels as they prepare to teach a topic or share materials that they have developed. These conversations regularly take place during lunch in the teachers' lounge. Indeed for precisely this reason, the department now makes a practice of arranging for a shared lunch period. These conversations spill over outside the school, often finding their way to MSU or beyond.

Continuing with a focus on teachers' knowledge of the mathematics they teach, the next essay describes one crucial aspect of the culture of the Holt High School mathematics department – ongoing discussions of school mathematics. Such conversations are rare among teachers in schools. To some, it might seem that they are not even possible. How could school mathematics contain questions of mathematical interest to teachers? Others may not share this skepticism, but have yet to see networks of practicing teachers having such conversations as an ongoing part of their work lives. For this reason, in the next essay, Craig Huhn brings us into one such conversation, a conversation about how radians are and might be defined.

The conversation Craig narrates initially related to the notion of radians in trigonometry; it began between two teachers in the department and later came up again between an intern and a mentor. Soon, through the web of relationships that support the intern and the mentor (illustrated in Figure 17.1 below), the conversation engaged other members of the Holt High School mathematics department, the university field supervisor, the university 802–804 instructor, other mathematics interns enrolled in that course, and their mentors.

To illustrate what these mathematical conversations are like and how they relate to the work of the department, it is not sufficient to follow how an issue courses through a network of relationships.

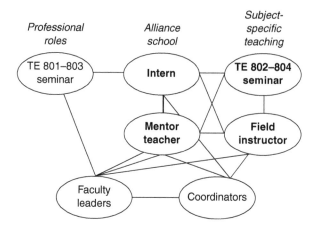

Figure 17.1 Aspects of the intern support network.

We must follow the mathematical issue as well and understand what the question was, as we follow that question through the network of collegial relations that encompass both MSU and Holt. For that reason the next essay has within it much mathematics. In their response, Dave Hildebrandt and Sean Carmody indicate that this particular conversation was not a unique phenomenon by making reference to other similar conversations in which they have participated.

Questioning ourselves and the authorities

Craig Huhn with Marty Schnepp, Sandy Callis,
Laura Kueffner, Whitney Johnson, and Dara Sandow,
Holt High School and Michigan State University

This essay was developed for this volume.

Introduction

Conversations "around the water cooler" are as common in the workplace as competitiveness and weak coffee. In a school setting, these take place in crowded hallways, neighboring rooms, and the notorious teachers' lounge. Some are similar to the conversations that happen among coworkers everywhere – why the Lions will be better with their quarterback hurt; discussion of local and national elections; how bad the roads were that morning. Others seem unique to the teaching profession – how much worse the incoming class is than in any other year; why we can't get enough subs; how could the public actually believe that the problem with public education is that teachers don't know their subject matter?

Then there are the conversations that I have been fortunate enough to have been involved in as a member of the Holt mathematics department. In my own experience, and in speaking with dozens of other teachers across the state and nation, it becomes apparent that these conversations are rare, if not nonexistent, and often consciously stifled in other districts.

These conversations are deep discussions among trusted colleagues about issues important to them and to the students. They are often impromptu. They may take place in the five minutes between classes, or may take an hour and a half after school. They can happen solely as a result of the environment that the department has created. They are addictive. Questions are honored as indications of intellectual prowess. They require mutual respect for the job that each person does and an interest to engage deeply with a colleague's question. They take place on our time. They make us better teachers.

These types of conversations seem to fall into three main categories, although they are seldom mutually exclusive. There are conversations surrounding curriculum, where we seek out colleagues who teach the same classes for questions about course storylines or connections. Over lunch one week, for example, I asked Kellie Huhn and Marty Schnepp what they thought were the most important things that we wanted our students to know after the quadratics unit in Algebra 2. There are conversations surrounding pedagogy, where we look for support and guidance from colleagues who have a similar teaching philosophy. Generally, most of them concern different issues that come up while trying to have a class discussion, or what to do about students missing class, et cetera. Between classes one day that same week, Tom Almeida and I had a conversation about how to get students into groups for the oral semester exam (see Chapter 2).

Finally, there are conversations surrounding content, where we are safe to talk to others about the mathematics we teach. One time I remember, I had stopped into Mike's room after school and asked him and his intern at the time, Brian Vessel, what to do with a student's question that came up at the end of class that day. The class had noticed that, for a table whose inputs increased by one, a function has a constant difference in outputs after the same number of differences as the highest degree of the function (they were generalizing the conjecture that a product of two "lines" has a constant change in the change). After looking at a product of three lines (a cubic in factored form) and seeing that the constant showed up after taking three differences, a student asked if we could write a rule that would find the first and second differences. My inclination was that these might be the first and second derivatives (or at least related to them), since the constant is related to the third derivative. After a few moments, the three of us had completely filled the board in his room with tables, patterns, examples, and counterexamples. Kellie Huhn saw us in there, and soon the four of us were investigating this problem until we were somewhat satisfied with what we found out (which we will leave for you to discover for yourselves). We had been learning together for well over an hour.

To illustrate these collaborative conversations among teachers that occur in our department, this essay will try to recreate the nuances of a discussion that took place during the 1998–1999 school year. The conversation described at length in this essay is an example that stands out as one of the more dynamic and unresolved discussions at that time inside the department, involving all three aspects of curriculum, pedagogy, and content. But, as suggested above, it is by no means unique to the experience of teaching at Holt. We have similar mathematical conversations on a regular basis in our efforts to best serve our students.

In recreating this conversation, the focus isn't on one particular aspect; but several. In this essay, I will try to:

- Relate how the situation arose, the discussion developed, and enthusiasm for the discussion evolved and came to involve a network of professionals, including high school mathematics teachers, interns, and university mathematics education instructors.
- Present the mathematics at issue and the arguments made. This may intrigue you and lead to your own questions, particularly if this is mathematics that you teach.
- Raise issues about teaching and show that this type of conversation – one that interweaves mathematics (what conclusions can we make here?), curriculum (why do we teach this here/this way/at all?), pedagogy (how can/should we teach this?), and professional dynamics (how can/should we interact?) – helps us grow and develop as teachers.
- Illustrate ways in which we at Holt High School, as teachers, question our own mathematical understandings (and those of the mathematics community) in our ongoing efforts to teach our students well.

I will start by offering the traditional school view of the mathematics involved, which was the question, "What is one radian?" I will then offer questions and thoughts that challenge accepted mathematical understanding. These thoughts were generated in the department and caused us to delve deeply into the issue, deconstructing all of our implanted beliefs and sifting through various perspectives, problems, and histories.

I will tell the story of this conversation about radians by having the participants speak for themselves. Marty Schnepp will share some of the questions that came up for him, and how he brought them to Sandra Callis and Mike Lehman (other teachers in the department), after school and during time set aside for professional development. During this conversation, the idea seemed to have been generated that, in order to discuss radians, radii may be used as a unit of measure. I will then pick up in 1998–1999, when Sandy's intern, Laura Kueffner, began asking questions while preparing for a trigonometry unit. I was an intern with Mike Lehman that year. The conversation spread to me (and to other fellow interns and their mentor teachers), Dara Sandow, a doctoral student and our university 802–804 mathematics education seminar instructor, and Whitney Johnson, a doctoral student in mathematics and a field instructor for MSU's Department of Teacher Education.

The mathematical issue: the radian as a privileged unit

> One radian is the measure of a central angle q that subtends (intercepts) an arc s equal in length to the radius r of the circle.
>
> (Larson *et al.*, 1997, p. 106)

This sort of definition appears in many high school and college textbooks. But, why introduce radians? Students are already familiar with degrees as a measure of angles. The standard response is that, though radians are, like degrees, a way to represent the size of an angle in trigonometry, they are preferred for simplicity in future formulas. Textbooks offer comments like, "In more advanced work in mathematics, especially in calculus, the use of degree measure for angles makes many formulas very complicated. These advanced formulas can be simplified if we measure angles with radian measure instead of degrees" (Lial and Miller, 1977, p. 63).

For example, when finding a formula for the area of a sector of a circle of radius r, setting up a proportion between the part of the circle to the whole circle makes a lot of sense. In other words, the area of the sector to that of the whole circle should be in the same proportion as the angle of the sector to the whole circle. Using degree measure for angles (which students are no doubt more comfortable with), the proportion looks like this:

$$A_{\text{sector}}: \pi r^2 = \theta: 360°$$

A cross-multiply and rearrangement later, the formula for the area of a sector becomes $A_s = (\theta \pi r^2)/360$. By contrast, using radian measure for the angle, we get A_s: $\pi r^2 = \theta$: 2π, which becomes $A_s = \theta r^2/2$, a formula that omits the inherent $\pi/180$-degree-to-radian-measure conversion factor. A similar argument can be made against measuring angles in grads, or any other possible way to measure any particular angle as a portion of the whole rotation present in a circle (whether that complete rotation is called 360°, 400 grads, 100 percent ...). Somehow, radians with 2π as their "whole" seem to be a privileged measure for angles.

This is where we begin to see a conflict with our previous notions: this privileging of radians is different from our normal approach to units. Students are familiar with formulas like $d = r*t$ or $A = \pi r^2$ and know how to work with their units. $A = \pi r^2$ is easy. For the area of a circle (not seemingly different from a formula for the area of a sector of a circle), if our radius is given as 40 microns, then the area is approximately 5026.5 square microns using the formula for area of a circle. If the radius was given as 481 kilometers, then the area of the circle, using the same formula, is about 726,842 square kilometers. Whatever unit is chosen for r, it determines the units of A. Similarly, with $d = r*t$, units must be coordinated. If one chooses a rate, it sets the units of time and distance. Sometimes conversion factors may be necessary, but the ensemble of units in the formula helps one keep track.

But these individual formulas and their use of units seem fundamentally different than $A_s = \theta r^2/2$. The formula itself works in radians; it *requires* that θ be measured in radians. So, θ, unlike the quantities in d, r, and t, cannot take on other units without overturning the formula. If the radius of a circle is 40 microns and θ is 17 degrees, the area is obviously NOT the 13,600 square microns you get with $A_s = \theta r^2/2$ (since the whole circle's area is only 5,000 square microns). How can one help students make sense of this? The following sort of monologue comes to mind:

> In order for $A_s = \theta r^2/2$ to work, you have to convert θ from degrees to radians (even though you are more comfortable with the degree measure that you know). But the units of the radius don't matter, they can stay as they are. So the radius you should keep as 40 microns, even if we can't really picture that, because that's what scale the person is working in. But we have to change 17 degrees to radians (because I said so), which is π over 180 (or, now I'm getting confused, maybe that should be 180 over π?), so that's actually 0.2967 radians. Now let's plug in the numbers, and we get 237.36. That's in microns squared. That's right, trust me.

Of course, this issue also comes up when students use calculators. I cannot think of other times when students can make a calculation correctly with a formula, and have the calculator produce an answer that is incorrect or nonsensical for the given situation. Students need to know whether they are operating in degree mode or radian mode to even use the calculator effectively, as its calculations are made with an assumption in mind; it needs to know the units of θ.

The mathematical issue continued: what are "dimensionless" measures?

There is another issue that arises with radians and with other measures of angles. Radians, like other measures of angle, are often conceptualized as dimensionless. In the ratio θ=s/r, s is the arclength cut out by the central angle theta for circle of radius r.

> Notice that the units of length for r and s cancel out and that radian measure, like degree measure, is a dimensionless number.
>
> (Thomas & Finney, 1992, from "A brief review of trigonometric functions," p. A-5)

Related to this issue of dimensionless measure, Marty Schnepp uses the following problem situation to suggest a number of questions that arise for him as a teacher who thinks about rate of change (see Figure 17.2).

The figure below represents a photographer, watching a balloon as it rises. The balloon is rising at a constant rate of 3 meters per second and the observer is 100 meters away from a point directly below the balloon. If the photographer is aiming her camera at the balloon as it rises, find the rate at which the photographer is rotating the camera to keep up with the balloon at the instant the balloon is 100 meters above the height of the camera when triangle ABC becomes an isosceles right triangle.

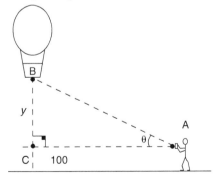

Figure 17.2 A task involving radians and dimensions.

Marty's questions focus on the changing "angle" of the camera, because it is the nature of this quantity that makes this situation problematic. In order to understand his questions, let's track the units in the question.

In this problem, one calculates the rate of change of θ to be a particular number, 0.015. If θ is a dimensionless number (meters/meters), as suggested by Thomas and Finney, then the units of the rate of change, 0.015 are meters/meters*seconds, or after "canceling" the meters, the rate of change of θ then becomes "0.015 per second" – fifteen thousandths nothings per second.

Thinking about rates of change of angles leaves Marty with the following questions:

- This result and the convention of canceling units give me pause. I have difficulty visualizing a rate of change involving nothings per second. It seems strange that we would ask students to accept such things. I would be inclined to think that many students would dismiss this result as meaningless. This would, in fact, nullify the purpose of problems like this, which is to illustrate concrete, meaningful, applications of calculus. I wonder whether we wouldn't be better off not canceling units and saying something like 0.015 meters along the ground over meters along the sight line, per second.
- It seems much easier to conceptualize an answer in terms of degrees per second or radians per second. But in what sense is radians per second, or angle per second, the same as meters along the ground over meters along the sight line, per second?

Challenging the authorities: an alternative definition/proposal

Definitions, like the one quoted from Larson *et al.* (1997), are standard in a mathematics classroom. Coming to grips with such definitions is a task for teachers and students of mathematics. First, there is what is given. Why is radian measure defined in this way? Why would anyone have chosen to define an angle measure in terms of an arclength on a unit circle? Why can a ratio between an arclength and the radius of a circle compute an angle measure? Next, there are aspects of the issue on which such definitions are silent. What are the units of such a beast? How should students think about what an angle is, when it is defined or computed in terms of arclength? As teachers, how do we get students involved with the issue, so that they can come to appreciate the intellectual work that has gone into such a definition?

It was in examining questions like these and in thinking about our students, that we began to consider an alternative view of what one radian is. Thinking about how it had seemed to make the most sense to students, some members of the department began to think of one radian as a one-radius-long arclength, measured in units of the radius of a particular circle. In this view, radians are conceptualized as a unit of arclength itself, a linear measure. They are not units with which to measure an angle. Of course, arcs with a particular arclength measured in radians would have a particular central angle associated with them. On the one hand, this definition seemed a bit peculiar. Radians become a funny sort of unit. Unlike meters with their meter "bar," there can be no "radian" bar to hold the standard forever. The size of a radian changes with the radius of the circle; this seems like saying that every circle is a unit circle when its linear components are measured in radians. On the other hand, we wondered if this definition wasn't essentially equivalent to the standard one. After all, greats like Euler had written "π is the semicircumference of the circle of which the radius$=1$, or π is the length of the arc of 180 degrees" (Fauvel & Gray, 1987, p. 449).

Over lunch, after school, in university classes, and in interactions around intern teaching, these questions gradually made their way through the intellectual community associated with the Holt High School mathematics department. The next five sections follow the evolution of the conversation from the views of five of the participants.

Initial observations from the Calculus teacher – Marty Schnepp

For me, the transformation of my current conceptualization of "radians" has its roots at a summer teacher-institute I attended at University of California San Diego (UCSD) in 1990. The instructor of a PreCalculus course brought in a display device that was basically a board with a unit circle printed on it. Affixed at the center was a rotating bar that was a diameter of the circle. At the end of the bar was attached another bar, the length of a radius, fixed to the diameter bar at one of the points of intersection with the circle (see Figure 17.3).

When the diameter bar was rotated to a given angle, the radius bar could be held perpendicular to the horizontal or vertical diameters

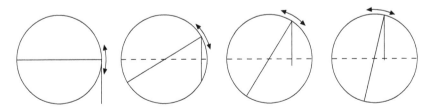

Figure 17.3 Θ at 0, $\pi/6$, $\pi/3$, $5\pi/12$ with a vertical bar of radius length.

printed on the unit circle board. The radius-length bar was marked off in tenths and hundredths. This device in effect allowed the user to rotate to one of the angles printed on the unit circle board and measure the perpendicular distance to the horizontal or vertical diameters of the circle, thus estimating the sine or cosine values of the rotated angle. As a side-note to something he was discussing in class, the instructor mentioned that the sine function could be thought of as a mapping that assigns to an angle of rotation the directed (vector) distance, perpendicular from the rotated point on the unit circle back to the horizontal diameter. I found this description of the sine function profoundly different from the typical treatment of the unit circle where points on the circle $x^2 + y^2 = 1$ are assigned the coordinates $(\cos(\theta), \sin(\theta))$, and where θ is either the degree or radian measure of the angle formed by the x-axis and a ray emanating from the center of the circle at angle θ.

I also took away from this UCSD class an image of pedagogical tools. The instructor said, "I want to give the kids some kind of visual tool for everything. They can't remember all of it, but if I approach them on the beach the next summer, I at least want them to be able to pick up a stick and draw something to help them remember." This was an intriguing notion for me.

My second year back from California, I took a class at MSU on teaching Geometry. We used the University of Chicago School Mathematics Program's (UCSMP) Macintosh version of *Geo Explorer*. After playing with this software, I realized I could simulate the device I'd seen at UCSD on the computer screen. I was teaching Calculus for the first time and was frightened to see the limits my students and I faced understanding sine, cosine, tangent, and radians when it came time to do Calculus with these objects. My students mainly seemed to think of radians as inconvenient degrees. My final project for the MSU course was to create activities where students performed computer constructions and generated tables of values for all six trig functions off unit circle diagrams using *Geo Explorer*. I based the diagrams on an article I was given at UCSD. These seemed like just the sort of pictures kids could sketch in the sand with a stick to help them remember trig ideas.

The following year, I team-taught the functions-based Algebra 1 class with Sandy. Through that experience, along with my own realization of the importance of function in calculus, I began to find a pedagogical affinity for the notion of functions as mappings. At some point, a conversation about trig developed with Sandy and Mike, both of whom were teaching PreCalculus at the time. I was motivated, as a Calculus teacher, I'm a bit ashamed to admit, by my students' lack of knowledge about radians and their limited conceptions of sine, cosine, and tangent as triangle ratios. My perception was that most students had seen the unit circle, but, to many, it was only slightly related and an annoyance.

Leery of seeming to dictate content coverage to teachers of a previous course, I nonetheless felt compelled to raise the issue. I was interested in seeing changes in students entering Calculus, and I was beginning to see the value of discussing topics with my colleagues to improve my own understanding. I did not know if the direction I was moving with re-conceptualizing trig was sound.

I don't remember how the subject was broached, but I do remember making Styrofoam circles and gluing them to poster board before bringing up the subject. I needed to make something students could use to do the activities I had created for the MSU class, but the then current IBM version of *Geo Explorer* was ineffectual and could not be used.

As conversations with colleagues progressed, radians seemed to be the focus: what the heck were they, and why did we need them in the first place? In the classroom, students saw radians as just another angle measure, with degrees being the preferred system. The typical curriculum seemed to overemphasize the relationship between degrees and radians and conversion between these two ways of measuring angles. The multiples of pi meant very little independently to my students. For my students, the multiples of pi only existed in relation to degree measure.

Being a colleague and mentor teacher – Sandy Callis

What started a change in my thinking about radians was an activity that Marty created involving string and Styrofoam discs of different sizes. Students measured around circles and collected data about the distance from points on the circle to the *x*-axis. The students weren't measuring with a protractor but rather a length of string, measured in 1/10ths of a radius. Then they made graphs of the data that they had collected.

At the same time, I was taking a class in mathematical modeling at Western Michigan University, where we used rates to come up with distances, for example, landing a lunar explorer module on the moon. The key thing was that, in this problem, it made sense to think of cosine and sine as ratios, but not in the triangular sense. Instead, they were distances of a point to an axis normalized by the size of the radius. I wondered, why wouldn't we just define them that way? If we did, then their unit could be "radians" in the sense of some fraction of a radius.

A note of clarification

From the point of view that Sandy describes, at exactly one radius along the circumference, the vertical height (found using the sine function) is approximately 0.84147, or 84.1 percent of the radius. If the radius in that circle happened to be 3 inches, then we know that the y-coordinate for that point (2.52 ... inches), as exactly as we want. A similar argument can be made with the cosine function to find that the point one radius along the circumference horizontally is 54 percent of the way from the center to the edge of the circle along the x-axis. This will always be true at that point on a circle, and, once we know the radius, we can find the scaled coordinate (in this case with radius 3 inches, the x-value of 1.62 ... inches).

More than one year after Sandy and Marty's conversation, these issues became questions for Laura Kueffner, Sandy's intern that year, as she began to prepare a unit on trigonometry.

Having to teach trig: views of the intern teacher – Laura Kueffner

Being an intern and slightly new to the kind of in-depth analysis of math that goes on at Holt, I was struggling with answering the question, why do we teach radian measure to high school students? Inherent in that question was determining the definition of radian measure. When I asked Sandy how she defined it, she said that typically mathematicians see it as a unit for angle measurement. She went on to note that it was derived from taking the length of the radius and laying it along the circumference of the circle that your angle is in. This second part made a lot of sense to me. I figured that after hearing the traditional definition for so many years and still not understanding it as well as I would have liked, why ramble on about the same traditional definition to my students? Instead, I chose to help my students think of a radian as a (non-uniform) measure of length, constant only for the circle the radius is from. We would also conceive radian measure as a way to turn all circles into the unit circle. It made more sense for me to think in this way rather than to skip all I was learning and just define radians as an angle measure. My students would make that last connection on their own, thus allowing for greater understanding than I could give them. Explaining my view of radians as a measure of length led to some interesting debate with my fellow mathematicians in MSU's College of Education, including Dara and Whitney.

Responding to an intern: perspectives of an on-campus instructor – Dara Sandow

The different conceptualizations of radian first came up for me in fall 1998. Laura Kueffner had turned in a unit overview on trig in September; it included some sample problems, several of which referred to arclength as being measured in radians, for example as shown in Figure 17.4.

We've seen that 1 radian is the arclength when 1
radius is laid along the circumference of the circle. Find
the pictured arclength(s) for each circle in centimeters.

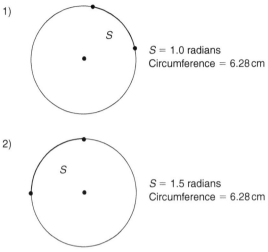

1)

$S = 1.0$ radians
Circumference $= 6.28$ cm

2)

$S = 1.5$ radians
Circumference $= 6.28$ cm

... five problems altogether

What would be your strategy for calculating an arclength
in centimeters if you know the radian measure and the
circumference?

Figure 17.4 An arclength worksheet.

In responding by email to her unit overview, towards the end of my
comments I wrote:

> One small but important point – although there's a correspondence
> between radians and arclength, a radian is an angle measure rather
> than a measure of distance; it would be good to correct that on the
> activities that are handed out to students. (That is, for a circle with
> radius 1 inch, the length of an arc corresponding to an angle of 1
> radian is 1 inch, not 1 radian.)

Laura responded to my email, and we carried out the following correspondence. (Laura's responses are shown in italics with my replies interleaved):

> *I wanted to point out my view on radian measure, sorry that I
> don't agree with your opinion that it is the measure of the degrees.*

> My opinion isn't quite that it's a measure of *degrees* – I think of
> both radians and degrees as ways to measure *angles*.

Radian measure is the measure of the arc length or circumference of a circle in my opinion. I see it this way because I consider radian measure to be the number of radians that fit around a circle when laid end to end.

A few questions –
Are the things that are being laid end-to-end really <u>radians</u>? Or are you marking off lengths that are equal to the length of the radius (and if so, where do the radians come in)? Another question is whether it makes sense to you that a given unit of measure, 1 radian, could be truly equal to different lengths depending on the radius of the circle. That is, the way you're thinking about it means that 1 radian would equal 3 cm in a circle of radius 3 cm, and 1 radian would equal 5 cm in a circle of radius 5 cm. Does it make sense to you that 3 cm = 1 radian = 5 cm?

This number is little over 6 (or two pi), hence, one radian is the length of one radius of the circle you are measuring.

This doesn't quite make sense to me. 2 pi is a constant, but the radius (and hence the circumference) can vary.

I would not describe just any right angle as being pi/2 radians. It must be a right angle within a circle and the angle measure is described by the arclength it sweeps out.

It seems to me that we can think of any angle in a plane as being a central angle in a circle (in infinitely many circles, actually, each with a different radius). Are you saying that you can only measure an angle in radians if the circle has already been identified?

I am sorry if you disagree with this but because I see it this way, I am going to teach it this way also. I am curious to hear why you might not agree with this.

I've tried to indicate some of my thinking above. I'd be happy to continue talking about this (but I'd prefer to talk than to write). There's no reason to apologize! Rather than thinking about this solely as your opinion and mine, it might be interesting to find out how other people (e.g., your CT [collaborating teacher], other interns or CTs you know, a textbook author, . . .) think about radians and why they hold the views they do. And while I don't completely agree with your ideas, I'm also not suggesting that you just toss them – I think that your ideas make a lot of sense given the way radians are typically introduced and that they can help you think about what might be confusing for students.

Laura and I subsequently met and talked some more. I was impressed by her conviction in publicly sticking to an understanding that made sense to her, instead of switching her views because her instructor disagreed with her. But I was also feeling responsible for the understanding of radian that her students were going to develop and concerned that this definition was not consistent with mainstream mathematical thought. I was at an early stage in thinking about sharing authority with students and working through what this entailed. At that point, I thought she misunderstood radians (because mathematicians think of them as an angle measure), and I was encouraging her to think why her approach might be problematic.

When I met with Laura, I learned the student task came from her mentor, Sandy, and, according to Laura, Sandy shared her concept. Prior to that, I'd assumed that these problems were ones Laura had written by herself.

The following spring, Marty Schnepp, another mentor teacher, suggested this as a topic for discussion in a session convened for interns and their mentors across all of the secondary mathematics placements. At some point in that conversation, I went up to the board to make a point about how I was thinking about radians. I marked off a 1 radian angle in a circle.

Mike Lehman then asked me how I'd determined where to mark the ray of the angle that didn't lie along the x-axis – had I thought in terms of the angle measure, or had I thought in terms of the length of one radius along the circumference? It had been the latter, and I had to think hard about why that was if I believed that radians are angle measures. One thing I thought about was the issue of commensurability; I'm pretty sure that if I'd been marking an angle the measure of which was commensurable with pi, say pi/2, then I'd have thought in terms of an angle and not an arc. I also wondered whether I'd be more comfortable with estimating radian measures if I'd had experience with protractors marked with radian measure.

Since then, I've been wondering about a number of mathematical and pedagogical issues:

- If one measures arclength in radius-lengths (rather than inches or centimeters or any other linear unit of measurement), then there's a way in which this is equivalent to inches per inch, or a linear measure per linear measure. Is that the same as the "dimensionless" measure that radians are typically taken to be?

- For those who define radians as a measure of arclength, are degrees the only way to measure angles? And similarly, is sine sometimes a function of angle measure (when the angle is measured in degrees) and sometimes a function on arclengths?
- To what extent might students' difficulties with radians arise from extended work with degrees before they're introduced to radians?
- Is it important to distinguish between how we're making sense of something and what we think best supports our students' understanding at a given point in time? For example, I can imagine thinking about radians as angle measures for myself, yet choosing to introduce them to students as a measure of arclength. If I did that, in talking with others about this, I'd want to distinguish between my own thinking and the conception presented to students.

Supporting the intern teacher and teaching trig on campus: perspectives of a field instructor – Whitney Johnson

This interaction began for me while I was helping Laura think about how she wanted to teach a trigonometry unit. She was looking through material Sandy had employed in the past and speaking with Sandy too. Sandy mentioned that radian measure could be thought of in other ways in addition to being an angular measure. It could be defined as the measure of the length of arc subtended by the angle. Also, she suggested, the sine of an angle could be thought of as the y coordinate of the point of intersection of the terminal side of the angle and a circle based at the origin (measured as a portion of the radius), regardless of the radius of the circle. At first, Laura and I were perplexed by this, and we began thinking.

I continued thinking while teaching trigonometry on campus. The collaborating teacher had given Laura the definition of one radian as an arc of length equal to one radius of the circle and thus a linear measure instead of an angular measure. The sine and cosine of this arc would be the corresponding y and x coordinate of the point where the arc ended on the circumference. This linked up with something my students on campus did. They wanted to define sine and cosine of an angle as the y and x coordinate of the intersection point of the circle of any radius and the terminal side of the angle (though it wasn't clear how they were taking the radius into account).

Concluding comments from the editor and a beginning teacher – Craig Huhn

My perspective on this conversation was as a fellow intern to Laura, also teaching trigonometry. I didn't have the history of where these thoughts had come from in Holt; all I had was the history of my own learning. It seems impossible to me now, a few years later, to distinguish my beliefs on radian measure now from how I had made sense of radians for myself prior to this episode. The evolution of thought is so intrinsic for an enveloping conversation like this, it becomes difficult to know where different thoughts may have come from and when. One thing I do know now, though, is that I have a passionate viewpoint about a mathematical topic that directly affects my teaching and the way my students will make sense of this idea.

For me today, I see one radian as simply a length equal to the length of a particular radius. I think of radians as a unit that is defined once a circle is given. In turn, this unit could be easily converted to the units you are working in – if the circle has a radius of 5 stadia, then a radian measure of 2.4 signifies to me a distance of 2.4 radiuses, where the radius is the unit standing for 5 stadia.

In the context of a traditional curriculum, it seems to me that the main goal of instruction is to be able to find the exact location (coordinates) for any position along the circumference of the circle. We could use angles in degrees or grads (or split into any random number of parts we want) to determine the coordinates of that point, or we could use radius-lengths along the circumference. Degrees are a useful measure of angle because the same degree measure works for however long the sides of the angle are (and therefore, how big a circle you have). The only other way to make a location description work for all cases of circles is to use something that changes in proportion to the size of the circle (i.e., the radius). Based on this, we can think of the sine function to be a function on the location of a point on a circle, not "sometimes a function of angle measure ... and sometimes a function on arclengths," as Dara wondered. The sine and cosine functions can give us these vertical and horizontal distances, in relation to the size of the radius.

This gives me evidence to claim that radians in this way are more mathematically correct than angle measurement. If we were to examine the question, "What is 1 degree?" it seems the only answer is 1/360th of a circle. (Think of a circle as a full angle, where the terminal side aligns itself with the initial side.) This is so is because we take as our own the convention of the ancient Sumerians, who used that number to coincide with their knowledge of the number of days in a year. Any number could have been chosen to describe a circle; 360 degrees was an invention of humanity. A radian though, as $1/(2\pi)$th of the way around, is mathematically defined. Humans had no choice in that proportion between the diameter and the circumference, and such has been constant throughout time.

This perspective on radians then could also lead to some interesting questions for students who would have to show a better understanding of a radian. I can imagine looking at a well-known point on a circle, one for which we already know the coordinates (like the one with coordinates $(0,r)$), and working backward, asking the students how many radians it is to that point. For example, if we take the top point in the circle with a radius of 3 inches, we know that the coordinates are $(0,3)$. The students should be able to tell by looking and using their previous experiences to determine right away that it is over 1 radian but less than 2, either since they can imagine a radius along the circle, or since each radian cuts off an angle of almost 60 degrees. Could students who've been given a standard definition and have had practice at converting between degrees and radians make that estimate, especially if they lacked an inherent vision of how big 1 radian is, without first converting to degrees? (This inclination to convert, Dara has suggested, is much like our instincts in the United States to convert kilometers into miles to envision an actual distance.) With the experiences of thinking about radians as arclengths, a student could reason that the top point is a quarter of the way around the circumference and so must be $\frac{1}{4}$ of 2π radians, which is about 1.57 radians, or radii, around. To check, it would be easy then to see that 1.57 times the $57.3°$ cut out by one radian is about $90°$.

Toward the beginning of the chapter, I explored what often comes right after locating points when introducing radian measure in the traditional way, the area of a sector. Now thinking of radians as arclengths along the circumference, what effect does this have? As it turns out, nothing, except it allows students an opportunity to make sense of the mathematics. The result is the same formula (I hope not surprisingly when you think about what the formula really does), and the set-up of the proportion seems just as natural (if not more so), based on the experience of thinking in terms of arcs. If a sector is described by using an arclength to determine the size – call it θ radians – then we go θ parts of the radius unit (like 3 inches, for example) to that location. The area within that slice is what we are looking for. Note that in thinking about radians this way, we have nullified the application of another formula to memorize: $s = r\theta$ (If θ. symbolizes the given radian measure, then multiplying by the length of the radius should give the absolute length of the arc in terms of the units that the radius is given in.) The proportion for area then is simply:

> area of the sector: area of the circle = arclength in terms of radii (given as θ): total radii around

or,

$$A_{sector}: \pi r^2 = \theta: 2\pi$$

and then, $A_{sector} = 0.5\theta \; r^2$ as we would expect. Thus, if thinking differently about something leads to no contradictions in one's mathematics, I don't know why we would feel the need to reject an idea simply because it doesn't match what we were taught. That just reinforces the belief that mathematics is a series of rules and definitions to memorize; an ingrained assumption that takes months as a teacher to chip away at. This has future implications far more damaging than a shifted perspective on a definition.

This conversation stands out to me as a good example of the kind of discussion that goes on in our department; it still lives in the hearts of all of us involved today. Besides the mathematical issue, which could be decried by critics simply as semantics, there is the philosophical issue of authority in mathematics and when it's all right to challenge it in your teaching. There is the pedagogical issue that Dara raises, asking if we can distinguish our personal mathematical beliefs from what we choose to teach our students. I remember Kim Dohm, a 1999–2000 Holt intern, asking a similar question: "are we martyring our students if we teach them our beliefs then send them into future math classes without the view that other teachers, who are responsible for their grade, think they should know?" There are professional issues about when and how to disagree when having a hard discussion among colleagues, while still valuing their thoughts and ideas. There are also professional issues that are deeply personal about how to ask questions and listen with the intent to understand where the other person is coming from. All of these things outside of the radian question itself repeat themselves over and over again in our conversations as we continue to improve ourselves in the role that we have made our life choice. With all of these potential issues, we still as a department believe strongly that having powerful conversations are an invaluable and ongoing part of our professional development.

Should we ever tell mathematical white lies to our students?

Dave Hildebrandt and Sean Carmody, Holt High School

DAVE HILDEBRANDT: Something that struck me when I was reading this essay was the notion that sometimes teachers keep our students from the "truth" as a matter of pedagogical expediency – it's easier to give them a limited amount of information to keep them from becoming confused, even though sometimes that information is incomplete or incorrect. It seems like there is a difference between what "true" mathematics is and what the mathematics is that at that point in time supports student understanding. In a certain sense, it seems like we often "lie" to our students. For example, I've been thinking about the development of operations on the grade-school level and the issue of closure under certain sets and operations and how it relates to the idea I mentioned above. I'm talking about the concepts that we tell kids at different grades, like "you can't subtract a bigger number from a smaller one" or "you can't divide 20 by 6 since it doesn't go into it evenly" or "you can't take the square root of a negative number." While these statements are technically true for certain domains of numbers (whole numbers, integers, and real numbers respectively) they fail under a broader context of mathematical thinking. This is where Dara's question: "Is it important to distinguish between how we're making sense of something and what we think best supports our students' understanding at a given point in time?" seems related. I think teachers use the statements I've given as examples even though they know (I hope) that the statements are inherently untrue, yet for the task at hand they serve a purpose. I just wonder about whether this sort of move really works. How often do we stifle student thinking and limit their understanding by telling them "This is how it is" in an attempt to minimize distractions or make thinking and computations easier for them rather than allow them to make sense for themselves.

SEAN CARMODY: The sorts of "white lies" you are talking about also seem to consolidate the teacher's authority with the students; the teacher or textbook allows the student to participate in a particular portion of mathematics but will let the student in on the punch-line later. While teachers may have some gains using this sort of move, this sort of move is difficult to accept when students learn the "real" way to do it. It makes mathematics seem arbitrary; at times you can do one thing, but earlier you can't.

DAVE: While we both have some difficulties with this strategy, at the same time, it seems to me that we do a similar kind of white lying with students' conjectures, if we allow incorrect ones to remain in place until they are shown to be faulty. Is there ever a time that we would allow a student to say something that was wrong and never correct them, because any contradiction wouldn't appear in any context for what they were studying in that course? I'm trying to think of an example where it's OK for a student or group of students to leave a course thinking something's true when it's not. Craig shared the following example with me from Algebra 1: Students were arguing whether 0 was positive or negative, and one student's point was that, when we write numbers, they are assumed to be positive, like 2, 6, 305, and 0. If we want to convey a negative number, we have to indicate it with the sign out front, like –2. So for her, 0 was positive, unless we wanted it to be –0. She was clear that they were the same number/amount, but if we don't write it as a negative, we are assuming it to be positive; and the reason we don't talk about it any more is because it makes no difference with this number if we do 0 or –0. To Craig as a teacher, the students that bought her argument would go out into the world proclaiming that 0 was positive; but for Craig, the fact that she was articulate and rational and trying to convince people of her thoughts was more important than "correcting" her. I think Craig's got a good point. If we can help students figure out how to intelligently come to a position, state that position, and be able to defend that position, then they should be receptive to other's opinions while at the same time requiring the same amount of rigor from another source (i.e., another teacher, a text). In other words, we should be helping students to critically analyze any information they are given.

SEAN: Based on what he wrote in this essay, I think Marty would support what you are saying. He makes a comment that suggests looking at what will work for student understanding now, rather than standing outside of the interaction and worrying about too big a picture.

DAVE: Something else that struck me from this piece was the premise that certain concepts in mathematics, ideas that might be put forth by other sources such as textbooks or teachers, can be re-examined by the teachers and students using those sources. In other words, we try and get students to think that the "authorities" don't automatically have to be right. Sean, from your experience as an Algebra 1 teacher, what do students view as "authorities" and how often do they appeal to them?

SEAN: In my Algebra 1 class there are lots of authorities that the students seem to appeal to. They seem to appeal to me, the teacher as well as others who fit that role in class (peer tutor, special-education instructors). Students also appeal to one another as authorities. Since a textbook is not used in the course it is not referred to as an authority but sometimes parents or older siblings' ideas are brought up in class. An interesting class discussion I had in my Geometry class last week shows this point very well. We were studying quadrilaterals and the students were debating whether a square was always a rectangle. In order to justify their reasoning the students looked up the definition in the text, some made drawings and arguments on their own but the students were not convinced. One student suggested that other books would have different definitions and thus yield a different result. This was interesting to me that the students saw the "authority" of the textbook as very fallible and changing. Another student was sure that I had the answer so I told him what I thought and this was very unsettling for him since it actually didn't help him make up his mind. My justification wasn't enough proof for him. This class seemed to have a very clear idea of which the authorities were as well as what would be a convincing argument in certain situations.

DAVE: Is there a difference in the way students in our more text-based classes perceive this appeal to authority? Are they more likely to accept what other people (texts) say, or are the students in the non-text-based classes also doing the same thing, but this time just assuming that what the teacher says is true? How well do we support our students' questioning of what it is that we ask them to do? Take Dara's quote on p. 271:

> I was also feeling responsible for the understanding of radian that her students were going to develop and concerned that *this definition was not consistent with mainstream mathematical thought* (italics mine). I was at an early stage in thinking about sharing authority with students and working through what this entailed.

This seems to suggest to me that we all need to struggle and learn how to play the game of relinquishing authority in an effort to establish a more legitimate authority. "Authority for authority's sake" seems to be something to avoid. But, when we emphasize having students make justifications and definitions, are we setting our students up for frustration and failure when they leave our classrooms? Here's a quote from Kim Dohm, one of my former interns: "are we martyring our students if we teach them our beliefs then send them into future math classes without the view that other teachers, who are responsible for their grade, think they should know?" Do we encourage a more open and self-constructed environment here? That is, does our own practice of asking questions and engaging in open conversations between ourselves as professionals encourage or enable us to better create that same kind of environment for our students?

SEAN: I would like to think that we do encourage a more open and self-constructing environment. One of the ways that we do that is being flexible with our curriculum to ideas that students have (conjectures as talked about above). This seems to allow students to look at their own ideas and force them to think about the ideas that other students are bringing up. I find myself in those same situations a lot of times with the students. I am trying to make sense of the students understanding of the ideas and self-constructed what it means to learn geometry in this way as opposed to memorizing the definitions and proofs that I have forgotten a long time ago. I think one model that we have to work with on how to do that is with our Wednesday-morning time or after-school planning where we talk with one another to make sense of the same ideas that the students are making sense of.

DAVE: Craig mentioned the same thing, how we use our time together to share student conjectures or misconceptions. I remember conversations about different things that we've had that really get at some basic concepts of mathematics. Kind of like the whole Euclidean–non Euclidean debate (how the majority of the geometry that gets taught in school just assumes a Euclidean stance without really getting at the details of why we would want to). Thinking about these issues forces me as a teacher to make choices in my class on a daily basis – how deep do I want students to go, and will they all be able to?

Chapter 18

Interlude D

Learning math from coursework conversation

Continuing with the theme of teachers' involvement with understanding mathematics, in the next essay, Whitney Johnson describes her rationale for doing a set of activities with seniors in MSU's teacher education program in the TE 401–402 seminar. This move to university coursework may at first feel jarring at this point. But there are two good reasons to make this shift at this time.

First, as indicated in Bill Rosenthal's first essay in Chapter 5, there are important commonalities between the practices of the Holt High School mathematics department and practices the teacher education program seeks to inculcate in teacher candidates. In particular, Whitney indicates how she intends to inculcate in teacher candidates the desire to learn to justify the propositions and methods of school mathematics and the disposition to see school mathematics as intellectually substantial and interesting. As indicated in the last essay, these are aims that teachers in the Holt department support and indeed carry out in their own work. In the context of teacher education, this involves helping teacher candidates question their own mathematical knowledge. It involves their coming to grips with how much school mathematics they take on face value, how much they cannot actually prove themselves. Examples include that pi is an irrational number or algorithms like simplifying rational expressions, where pre-service teachers can solve problems instrumentally, but have no deeper relational understanding to help their students understand what this part of mathematics is all about. When Whitney is successful in inculcating this stance in her students, it results in skepticism about some classical results (or definitions). At the same time, it has potential to make the K–12 mathematics curriculum more interesting to teacher candidates and to engage them in serious attempts to relearn more deeply the mathematics they already know.

Second, many of the current teachers in the Holt math department are graduates of MSU's five-year program. In 2001–2002, six out of the ten members of the Holt math department were recent graduates of the MSU program. Thus, for these teachers, university coursework is an early part of their professional development as teachers and is an important part of what they bring with them to the mathematics departments in which they work. In their discussion of this essay, Laura Kueffner and Craig Huhn reflect on the role that this activity played in their understandings as they went through the senior-level teacher education course at MSU and connections between this activity and their teaching at Holt.

Lines and points: Aristotle vs. modern mathematics

Whitney Johnson, Michigan State University

This essay relates to Ms. Johnson's Michigan State University dissertation, Aristotle as secondary mathematics teacher educator: Metaphors and strengths, and was written for this volume.

In his "Metaphysics" (excerpted in translation in Calinger, 1995, pp. 85–87), Aristotle meditates on the nature of the continuous and rebuts Zeno's paradoxes and the conclusion that motion is impossible. In this selection, Aristotle argues that:

> If the terms "continuous," "in contact," and "in succession" are defined as above – things being "continuous" if their extremities are one, "in contact" if their extremities are together, and "in succession" if there is nothing of their own kind intermediate between them – nothing that is continuous can be composed of indivisibles; e.g., a line cannot be composed of points, the line being continuous and the point indivisible.
>
> (p. 86, col. 1)

The example that Aristotle gives, lines and points, is a fascinating one for future high school mathematics teachers. It contradicts what they were taught as students in high school and college and what they know they will have to teach as teachers. In school mathematics, a straight line serves to represent the real-number system by creating a correspondence between points on a line and individual numbers in the real-number system. In this correspondence, there is one real number for every point on a line, and a point on the line for every real number. Thus, the school curriculum teaches that in the same way that the set of real numbers is composed of infinitely many individual numbers, the continuous real number line is composed of infinitely many individual, dimensionless, and indivisible points.

But Aristotle is not crazy; the phrase "composed of" is tricky. While we can think of the line as composed of points, can one really build the line starting from points?

One way to think about this issue is to think about lengths that can be constructed and the numbers that can be put in correspondence with them. Take the rational numbers and any given line. If we define an origin and a unit measure, we can lay off on the line all whole-number lengths and any fractional lengths. Thus, every time we measure off a given length the endpoint of that segment determines a point corresponding to the length of the segment. However, we know that all of these points do not exhaust all the points on a line because we can construct with compass and straightedge an irrational length, like the hypotenuse of a right triangle with legs both equal to 1. As the Greeks knew, this segment is incommensurable with the sides of the triangle; in our terms, laying off this segment along the line, its endpoint determines another point on the line that cannot be paired up with a rational number. So we know that there are infinitely many more points along the line, like this one, that are unaccounted for by the rational numbers.

This sort of argument suggests ways to pursue the question of whether there is a real number for every point on the line. However, it also raises the following questions whose answers will not be addressed here.

1   Does every real number have a unique point on the line?
2   If so by what process do we locate the non-constructible numbers, e.g., the cube root of 2?
3   Do the rationals and irrationals exhaust the points on the line? Could there be points whose length from the origin cannot be paired with a real number? For example, why can't the imaginary number i be put in correspondence with a point along the number line?
4   By what magic can an ensemble of zero-dimensional points come together to compose a one-dimensional line?

It is not that these questions are unanswerable in modern mathematics, but rather that these are the sorts of questions that one might take up in trying to convince oneself that Aristotle is wrong and that what we teach in school is correct, questions that are at the heart of what is now taught in university-level courses in analysis.

Since secondary teachers, in contrast to elementary-school teachers, are thought of as subject-matter specialists, in order to become secondary mathematics teachers, in addition to methods coursework, most preservice teachers complete a mathematics major, or a significant component of such a major (Holmes Group, 1986). In this essay, I hope to convey why I think it is important for the preservice secondary math teachers that I taught and who are college seniors to have a different sort of mathematical experience than they typically experience as undergraduate mathematics majors. And I will indicate of what such an experience might consist. This is not a simple task. In order to suggest why I would like math-major future teachers to have a different mathematical experience, I will draw on my own experiences as a student, tutor, and teacher of mathematics, before describing the experience that I attempted to provide my students.

Preservice secondary mathematics teachers and mathematical knowledge

As a student in university mathematics departments, a mathematics department tutor, a teacher of mathematics at the university level, and, perhaps most importantly, as an observer of a system of mathematics education, I have amassed a myriad of experiences. I have seen the pain of a wide range of college students trying to succeed, willing to do anything their instructors tell them, but failing with every attempt. I have seen how this failure convinces them that they are absolutely incapable of understanding mathematics and influences them to change their majors and life paths to avoid it. I have seen how these experiences have devastated their self-esteem and spilled over into other parts of their lives (Tobias, 1993).

Lately, I have been concentrating my efforts with college math majors who are planning to be mathematics teachers. I have seen these students, deemed successful at mathematics by their peers who are not in the sciences, pretend to know more than they actually do. At the same time, among themselves, I have seen these very same students joke and laugh about how much they don't understand the mathematics they are studying and how hard they have to work simply to pass their courses.

I wonder about how this experience affects them as future teachers. The position of such math majors is an odd position for a student to be in, knowing that they are more knowledgeable than those who could never imagine taking the courses they have taken as math majors, but feeling as if they do not understand mathematics deeply. Yet, even though they may not feel that they understand the subject matter deeply, as secondary mathematics teachers, they will be viewed by their future students and colleagues as subject-matter specialists and will be called on to represent mathematics. Please don't misunderstand me. There are students who have been pronounced successful in their coursework as mathematics majors and who believe in their success, without harboring any doubts about their control of the mathematics that they have studied. Such students are not in the odd position I describe. But I have found this group to be a very small one.

Having said this, I should note that I have not only seen, but have lived, these things. I have been both the successful and the unsuccessful student. I have been the teacher and teaching assistant who causes pain for her struggling students, while being hailed and praised by those who are succeeding. I have been the tutor who listens to students' woes, and tries to help them survive their required mathematics classes. And, after moving from a university mathematics department to a department of teacher education, I have been a field instructor who works with practicing teachers and their interns. In that role, I have observed how what the teacher and intern do with their secondary students is shaped by the university experiences of the teacher and the intern. And I have been a course instructor in teacher education. It is in this context that I have explored possible alternative mathematical experiences for future teachers.

Undergraduate mathematics education: few opportunities to make connections and many unanswered questions

I consider myself to be a survivor of my preparation in mathematics. My bachelor and master's degrees are both in mathematics. Although the experiences in my bachelor's degree moved me to study for a master's, they were quite stifling to me as a thinker and as someone who wanted to possess and develop my own mathematical ideas. It wasn't that my professors took control of my thinking. It was more that some important things were missing. Throughout these experiences, I had few opportunities to understand how what I was learning was connected. And many of the questions that I had were left unanswered. Yet, unlike many of my peers, I continued actively to think about mathematics and at times, when alone, to do mathematics in ways that were sensible and aesthetically pleasing to me. It is in this regard that I consider myself a survivor of my mathematical preparation. I managed to survive my education and continue to do mathematics. The obstacles before me – the demeanor of my professors in class, their lack of patience in office hours, the lecture structure of their classes, their lack of interest in my own thinking about crucial mathematical ideas – led me to a posture of outwardly conforming to their way of doing mathematics, while inwardly chafing at how I was being asked to learn.

I recall from my undergraduate experience my first course in Analysis; I subsequently took other analysis courses as a master's student. Analysis, at least in the places that I've studied, is one of the courses that weeds out math majors. It is a hurdle that keeps some from being successful mathematics majors and becoming teachers. Even for those who jump over this hurdle, their GPAs may have been bruised as a result. Analysis is also where math majors might learn about the underpinnings of the real-number system and why the relationship between lines and points is supposed to mirror the relationship between real numbers and the real-number system.

Where I studied, Analysis was one of the first "theoretical" courses in which the focus is on proving theorems, rather than simply solving problems. There was an important change in classroom practice. Prior courses, particularly in the Calculus sequence, emphasized procedural aspects of problem-solving, while in Analysis there were few mechanical procedures to do. Unlike my experience of prior courses, in order to be successful in Analysis, it was necessary to pay close attention to the definitions and theorems, and learn how to prove statements. There seemed to be a consensus amongst my professors, as well as the junior and senior math majors, that this was the course where students begin to study mathematics, not that we discussed what mathematics is and what it means to study it.

The following quote from an undergraduate analysis text suggests that my experiences were not unique. In *Mathematical analysis: An introduction* (Scott & Tims, 1966), the authors state that the purpose of their book is "to widen and deepen his [the student's] understanding of the fundamental notions on which they [mathematical results, theorems etc.] rest, and to clarify the logical connections between them" (p. 1). When discussing limits they write

> the reader will almost certainly have had some manipulative practice with "limits", and very likely will have used the theorems of 5.2.4 without question; but this is a different thing from understanding what the definition of a limit is, from knowing how the theorems may be proved from that definition and from realizing that such proofs are desirable
>
> (p. 1).

Here is how this issue came up for me in my first course in Analysis. After a number of preliminaries, we began to use the definition of convergence to prove that sequences had limits. At the time, this seemed illogical to me. In Calculus classes, we had computed the limits for many of the sequences we looked at in the Analysis class. And we had made use of these limits, but now somehow it seemed as if we had been reckless in Calculus. On the other hand, our capacity to compute limits was recognized in Analysis, because whenever we began a proof it wasn't necessary to first compute the limit, the professor always gave the limit to us.

There are important subtleties here. At the time, I did not understand why it was necessary to prove that a sequence for which one has calculated a limit indeed has a limit; I did not see a difference between calculating that a particular number is a good candidate for the limit of a sequence and proving that the limit of a sequence indeed exists. And without a good understanding of the definition of convergence, our proofs seemed funny, consisting of finding a way to compute N as a function of epsilon.[1] It was not clear to me at the time why this constituted a proof that the limit existed. As I indicated earlier, the nature of this course was different from ones I had taken in the past, but none of these differences were stated or clarified. The fact that the professor paid no attention to the differences in the nature of the mathematics courses made learning the material a difficult chore.

An interpretation of the post-Calculus transition

In *Human information processing: An introduction to psychology* (1977), Lindsay and Norman suggest that the process of understanding in humans beyond the child stage

> develops as new concepts are assimilated mainly on the basis of analogies with what is already known. The main problem lies in incorporating the new concept into the existing structure. When the relation is established, all the previous experience is automatically included into a fuller interpretation and understanding of new situations.
>
> (p. 438)

They go on to say that

> if the received information is in obvious contradiction with previous experience, his or her conceptual structure, which constructed such a complicated system of interrelations, stands against any revision. And thus an adult prefers to reject inconsistent information or change its meaning rather than rebuild the system of his or her convictions.
>
> (p. 439)

Lindsay's statements certainly apply to my experience with analysis. There certainly were many new concepts facing me. What I knew upon entering the course was all that I had to rely on. The professor did not succeed in establishing a relation to this prior information. I was operating under the assumption that such connections were present, but I wasn't able to create them for myself at that time.

In prior courses it was possible and very often the goal to learn and master procedures. This emphasis, I thought, would continue into Analysis and other courses as well. Since the material wasn't presented in a way that allowed me to make connections, in order to have some success, I had to find the procedural aspects of the course and master them. I did this successfully in Analysis and in other coursework as an undergraduate major. But it left me dissatisfied, and with average grades. After completing my bachelor's degree I still had a great desire to understand more about mathematics. I wasn't bitter about my prior experiences but I felt that they weren't sufficient in some way. I could function as a successful student of mathematics but I didn't know what mathematics was about; I sought a more unified understanding.

From my peers' experiences as undergraduates, as well as those of undergraduates I have taught, I think my experience is not idiosyncratic; I believe many preservice teacher math majors have similar experiences. In coming to learn the mathematics beyond calculus there is a fundamental change in the type of material that is studied; it is vastly different than anything that has come before. Frustration with this change begins to create a new attitude towards knowledge and learning. The behaviors that develop set in and are not challenged by the students but are instead expected. In each math course you begin to look for a set of operations to solve particular types of problems. You don't expect that a rationale will be given for a course. You don't expect to understand the entire course; you only expect to pass. You no longer expect that the material in one course will be connected to any others that you have taken.

Knowing that many math majors experience advanced mathematics courses in the ways I did, I think it would be beneficial for senior math majors intending to teach to have a different type of mathematical experience. I would like them to begin to join their passion and interest in the subject (which some of them still possess and which might be (re-)awakened in others) with their collegiate study of mathematics. I believe that this is important, not only for them personally, but for them in light of the impact that they will have on their future students. If they cannot come to see that mathematics has room for the ideas and thoughts of individuals, they will teach their students as they were taught. And the cycle of passive student learning will remain unbroken.

The question then became how to help them to develop a passion for the subject and to connect that with their collegiate study of mathematics. When thinking about this goal, I imagined an experience that would allow future teachers to do mathematics "freely." By this I mean an experience in which students could ask any question that occurred to them, one in which members of a class could begin connecting, not new mathematical material, but the mathematics they had already learned. I imagined an experience that could strengthen future teachers' conceptual understandings of the structure of mathematics. And I wondered about how to get at ideas about the real-number system.

An experience for preservice secondary mathematics teachers

For three years I taught Michigan State University senior-level preservice secondary mathematics teachers. As I expected, there was a lot of variety among the students in terms of their understandings of mathematics. Some knew more facts than others; some had a deeper understanding of what occurred in the courses that they had taken than others. But overall no one could complete the sentence, Analysis (or any other course) is the study of _____, and its purpose or connection to the discipline of mathematics is _____ in any other way than listing the operations and theorems that they proved in the course.

For example, uniformly my students felt that Analysis was hard. Here are some of their reasons for this assessment:

1 Professors don't recognize how new it is to us.
2 They can't get the ideas across to us.
3 They don't explain it to us in a real way.

And, here is what they thought Analysis was all about:

1 There are no great revelations; it's just about cleaning up details.
2 You learn why you do a derivative.
3 Analysis frees you from having to worry about proofs.

Knowing that Analysis is one of the walls math majors hit while earning their degree made it seem useful to work with the future teachers on their understanding of the real-number system and its representation by the real line. Although I knew the type of experience that I wanted to create for the seniors I wasn't quite sure how to create it. With the support of others in the secondary mathematics component of the teacher education program, I decided to use a portion of the translated text from Aristotle's "Metaphysics" (1068b–1069a) described earlier.

Although one might question the choice to introduce a text to the seniors in which the mathematics is outdated, I chose to do just this. I had read the text in a doctoral seminar I had taken. For me, the article brought to the forefront of my thinking the relationship between the real numbers, the real line, and the nature of the real-number system. I was also amazed by the effect that it had on other students in the class. I knew that Aristotle's writing is dense, and expected the preservice students would struggle with it. But it was in this very struggle with Aristotle's point of view that I hoped that they would begin to examine their own thinking about the relationship between points and lines, and of the nature of the real-number system. I expected that my students would believe that lines are made out of points. The fact that Aristotle contradicts this claim might get the students to question actively their own mathematical knowledge. I thought this text might engage their curiosity and also challenge their mathematical beliefs. Furthermore, in working through Aristotle's argument, it is necessary to have a firm understanding of his terms and the definitions he gives them. The compactness of the writing and the nesting of the definitions require that readers bring other knowledge to the text. I believed that this process of interpreting the text would offer them the scope to begin to question their thinking.

More specifically, the pictorial representation of the real-number system as a line made of points is built on a number of key assumptions, for example, that:

- There is a bijection (one to one onto mapping) between the set of points and the real numbers.
- The points are ordered by their position on the line.

But, these assumptions must be integrated with what math majors learn in Analysis. In Analysis, majors learn that the real numbers are uncountable which suggest that they cannot be put in an order that would allow them to be counted off (put in a one-to-one relationship with the counting numbers). How can the points on the number line be uncountable but ordered? This question connects to a series of other questions. If the real numbers can be ordered, what lies adjacent to π? If there is no such point, how is it that we can definitely locate π or any other irrational length of the line? These questions and others like them were the type that I hoped the seniors would begin to ask themselves as they read the text.

Over three years, I read this selection with three different cohorts of seniors. The transcripts in this essay come from the 1999–2000 academic year. During this year there was one class period solely dedicated to the discussion of the article. However, that discussion continued alongside other discussions for the remainder of the year. For the discussion that I will report below, I had given the students the text a session before and simply asked them to try and summarize Aristotle's argument. When we met again, I asked for initial responses to the reading and their experiences in reading it. The emotional response to the reading was negative; they found Aristotle's prose and argument hard to understand. At the same time, their engagement with the task of interpreting Aristotle was high. Students actively participated in a discussion with little direction from me.

We began by discussing Aristotle's terms. As we moved through the terms individually the students refined or checked their thinking about the prior terms to ensure that the argument as a whole held together. They moved in and out of the text using some examples that were mathematical and some that were not. It was not long before they began to question the nature of the numbers on the real line. The students arrived at the notion that Aristotle is arguing that lines are not composed of points and also that this is the opposite to what they have been taught.

In the section of the conversation that I present, two students are active, though others participate. We join it as Baron is trying to understand the definition of contiguous. He uses an example of the students in the room holding hands and says that that would make them contiguous. He then argues that the integers are not contiguous because, although they succeed one another, there are many other numbers in between them so that they aren't touching and therefore are not continuous. Bothered by the human analogy Schroeder poses another; integers are like blocks. This one is also unsatisfactory. As they struggle with finding a representation for Aristotle's argument, they are inherently concerned with the real numbers and the relationship between the numbers as they sit on the real line.

SCHROEDER: (interrupts) well think – what if you think of integers of like as like blocks like one like there's a block that's 1,2,3, . . . you just stick them together . . .
[*Inaudible background discusison*]
BARON: Integers aren't blocks though.
CB: They aren't humans either. But you could represent them by blocks.
[*Inaudible background discusison*]
BARON: Well he's [Aristotle's] not even talking about the integers. We're just, I mean we're applying all sorts of integers as analogy that we're all applying, but he's not talking about that.
SCHROEDER: Yeah.
BARON: I mean he does in certain points, but it's not, he's not looking at himself, it's just an analogy.
SCHROEDER: So you think that integers are not contiguous then?
BARON: No, because there's some, there's things of other classes that I can shove between them.
ANDY: So is there a number line that is contiguous?
BARON: The real?
ANDY: The real line is contiguous only?

At this point, the discussion is about the representation of sets of numbers on the number line. They have decided that the real numbers, as opposed to the rational numbers or integers, are the only set of numbers where numbers outside of the set are not interspersed among them along the number line. (This assumes for example that complex numbers cannot be represented along the number line.) But there is still a lot of dissatisfaction. Schroeder doesn't feel that they are being true to Aristotle's argument.

SCHROEDER: We're using the word "between" an awful lot here. And he doesn't use the word "between," he uses the word "touch." So that's where I [Baron: Right] so.

PAM: Because if two things touch they're not [*inaudible*].

SCHROEDER: He says the extremes that are together touch, so what's the extreme of an integer? That's what I want, that's what I'm asking.

BARON: That's why they can't touch.

SCHROEDER: Because why?

BARON: They don't have an extreme. So they can't touch. So they're not contiguous.

(*Everyone speaks at once*).

R: I don't want to disagree with you but I don't know how....

SCHROEDER: ... What's the extreme of a real number?

[*Inaudible background discusison*]

ANDY: ... But what, that's the thing, what's the extreme of ... then there's no number line that can that's contiguous then.

BARON: I'm happy with that.

A very shortlived resolution has been reached. It appears the consensus is that there is no set of numbers that are contiguous in Aristotle's sense of the term, of touching and not having others of a different class interspersed among them. However this doesn't last for long. Although Schroeder participated in taking Baron to the conclusion that no set of numbers is contiguous he is still bothered. He remarks "I don't know that I agree with that, I mean, with all that we've said yeah, sure, but I don't know if I." And moment's later Andy demands an example of a line that's continuous. A little later Baron again states that nothing is continuous and Patty expresses her discomfort with that, although she can't explain why. They are now back into a deep discussion about the numbers on the real line. The problem is that they have a sense that the real numbers are continuous. But they are now convinced through Aristotle's argument that the real numbers aren't contiguous. But, according to Aristotle's definitions, in order to be continuous a set needs to first be contiguous.

BARON: But are you, I mean, there's a lot of words that we use in math that don't that have like different meanings based on the context, so how do you know that this definition of continuous applies to the real numbers?

SCHROEDER: No, it doesn't. I –

BARON: I mean, they might be continuous in a different sense of the word, like in the limit sense of the word.

SCHROEDER: I know, I just, I just think that it would be nice if the word continuous, I mean it seems like it brings a nice picture to mind if you, it would be nice if we could all, we could just, this model that he's talking about would apply to the real numbers. But I guess it doesn't it's (unclear) in between.

Throughout the discussion Baron and Schroeder provide an interesting contrast in interacting with the document and discussion. While others are still puzzling over the differences between the real numbers and the real line, what it means for either of those to be continuous, and how Aristotle fits in, Baron comments:

> Because it's easier to have a totally different setup. Like we were talking and looking at what he knows. And so what we know now is a lot different than what he knew at the time he wrote this. So –

Not accepting this, the class demands that Baron prove that the real numbers are continuous without specifying the sense in which they mean the term. He asks for their definition of continuity and then he says:

> Well, isn't – if you're talking about like a, the real numbers being continuous, wouldn't that mean that every point is a limit point? That's pretty much what continuous means to real numbers, right? We're not talking about like a function being continuous, and that has like epsilon delta definition, but if you're just talking about real line being continuous, it's that every point is a limit point, right?

No one questions this statement or makes any comments. With that it appears that for Baron the case is closed even though he doesn't seem fully to understand his own statement.

Schroeder on the other hand is in a different place. He agrees with Baron that the ideas of the past no longer hold today. But he appears to be very willing to use this discussion to first understand the ideas of the past and then to improve his understanding of the present.

> I don't know, I, I, I think, I thought I was hearing like different, a bunch of different things, and I, I was just thinking that we've all been exposed to the definition of continuity so many times that I, I, why don't we just use that definition instead of (unclear)

No one offers a current definition of continuity for Schroeder. Instead CB says.

Yeah, I don't know. I gotta. 'Cause all the continuous definitions I've seen have all been about functions. Never about financial numbers, whether from one to two is continuous.

For him it appears that there is nowhere else to go. His understandings aren't allowing him to continue along this line of thinking. Continuing to push his own thinking, Schroeder goes on to say:

SCHROEDER: No, I think, I think what, at least what, what I want to say the real numbers are continuous for whatever reason, I don't know. But, and I'm thinking that maybe, there's another, another word that I want to say instead of continuous. But I guess since I'm probably the only one that's thinking that, no one else would call it something else.

[*One long targeted comment excised*]

SCHROEDER: That's what I'm thinking, too, but I was just wondering if there's a mathematical term that's different from continuous that would describe that property of real numbers. That's what I was asking. I don't know. Seems like there should be. Probably is.

Making sense of my attempt to use Aristotle in mathematics teacher education

In reflecting back on the conversations about the real numbers that I had with students by reading the selection from Aristotle, I offer three observations. First, the article did indeed prompt students to begin questioning the mathematics that they had learned. Even though my students often initially complained about Aristotle and his style of writing, they not only vigorously participated in these conversations but, later on in the year, they would also incorporate portions of those discussions into those of other articles and events from their placement in classrooms.

Second, the conversations affirmed my suspicions that my undergraduate experiences are common ones for preservice teachers. Many preservice candidates leave their mathematics courses without having a relational understanding of the material taught. They learn something, but they aren't getting the wider and deeper understanding of the fundamental notions that Scott and Tims (1966) refer to. In any case, it seems that the students still have many unanswered questions and they make many assumptions about the nature of the real numbers.

Finally, as I think about these seniors, the creation of courses able to transform them as learners and thinkers, and thus make them more critical teachers, appears a daunting task. The problem is quite complex. And for students, its resolution depends on how their mathematical preparation plays out with many factors – their disposition towards mathematics, their image of themselves as thinkers, their image of what a mathematics teacher should be, their ability to empathize with their future students and their desire to make the path for those students as enjoyable as possible, and their willingness to revisit and re-learn the mathematics from their undergraduate programs.

From a program perspective it would be wise for us to consider some of the decisions that are made in setting the requirements for a secondary mathematics certification, for instance, the suggestion of the Holmes Group (1986) that earning a degree in a discipline will give one sufficient background in the subject to be able to teach it. From my work with seniors it became apparent that many students in mathematics programs receive little more than exposure to the mathematical ideas. But understanding an idea for oneself and explaining it to someone else requires much more. This works demonstrates the struggle the seniors had in both of these areas. Instead of simply requiring prospective students to earn a degree in mathematics we should consider changing the curriculum for secondary mathematics teachers so that they don't have to go back and re-learn material but can instead have fruitful experiences the first time through. One possibility for accomplishing this could be to redesign some of the current courses that students have to take within their major and making these courses more inclusive of the students' thinking. Another possibility is to create other courses for these students that would allow access to the questions behind the mathematics that they are learning and would allow them to learn the mathematics while pursuing answers to these and their own questions.

A chance to disagree about math

Laura Kueffner and Craig Huhn, Holt High School

CRAIG HUHN: As one of the students that took TE 401 and 402 with Whitney, this article was of special interest to me. At that point in my own education, I hadn't interned yet, and was finishing up my undergraduate BA degree in Mathematics. Based on what I know now, and what I have come to understand since then, at that point in my life I had a long way to go before coming to many of the mathematical and educational commitments I now hold passionately. I was still more of a student and less of an educator. I thought that good math teaching was to make sure students had a good time and wanted to be there, then they would be open to learning. To accomplish that, I just had to tell students how to think and give them my knowledge of how it all connects. I also didn't realize how the math classes above Calculus could have anything to do with teaching high school. Based on what I have retained and the understanding I am now lacking, it is clear to me that I didn't try to make sense of the mathematics for myself. I was still trying to do what I had to do to get through the final math classes with a decent grade. As I read Whitney's struggles to make sense of her Analysis course, I was struck with this memory. Her description sounded eerily similar to my experience when I took the course (a few years later). Only in her case, she tried to make sense of the material for herself, while I simply tried to memorize enough stuff to get through. Like Whitney speculates, I came in with a "mathematical structure," but no idea that mathematics could be any different than how I had experienced it. Was your perspective coming into your senior year similar?

LAURA KUEFFNER: I remember at some point during that year coming to the realization that I had developed certain "math class survival" techniques and that these mostly consisted of memorizing material. Of course most texts are based on the student being able to digest the material and commit it to their brain as though reading equals understanding. Until I took 401–402 and was forced to think about what I truly understood about math and not just regurgitate words I had read, I didn't realize what I had such a problem with in some of my higher math classes. I think the key idea that I needed to learn about learning is that teacher "telling" does not equal student learning. The statement you made earlier, "I thought that good math teaching was to make sure students had a good time and wanted to be there, then they would be open to learning;" and "to accomplish that, I just *TELL* students how to think and give them my knowledge of how it all connects," touches on this. I do think it is important to make students feel comfortable and motivated (let's not forget Maslow's Hierarchy from our early TE course) and that as a teacher I will be imparting my own knowledge of mathematics to my students; but again the key idea and the point I think you're trying to make is that telling (or reading) doesn't equal learning. It seems a simple thing to realize but I hadn't really thought about it until the TE 401–402 class.

CRAIG: I certainly hadn't. And even for me, I didn't get it during the class, when Whitney had us read and discuss the Aristotle article. I knew I enjoyed debating and trying to make sense of it, but I didn't understand that it was supposed to be a model for us to see how our future students can experience mathematics. I didn't know why we were doing it.

LAURA: The Aristotle article did an excellent job of opening my eyes to thinking about what I really understood about mathematics and that just reading (or telling) does not equal comprehension. It's not an article that you can just read through and commit to memory and get the full effect or understanding that Aristotle was going for. It seemed a very confusing article to read. I wasn't sure what the terms meant, let alone the purpose of the article. In class, Whitney made sure we spent time discussing these things. The discussion forced me to think about the definitions of terms and the conventional meaning of points and lines. I remember that we did not all have the same definitions in mind for even simple things like points and lines. And the fact that we were all about to graduate with math degrees felt disconcerting. I started to think about how the class discussion was helping us all learn math more effectively than any "math" class we took. Did you have this experience while studying the Aristotle article?

CRAIG: I remember just thinking that it was cool that we have a room full of math majors that couldn't agree on some of the most basic cornerstones of mathematics. I was immediately struck with how exciting that concept could be, because when I began the teacher-prep program, I intended to teach history, my minor, because I wanted to have debates and discussions in my class. This was the first time anything like that had happened to me about mathematics. It wasn't just an argument about what was right; people were engaging in an intellectual dialogue about math, and it didn't seem we could come to a reasoned consensus about anything. One thing that really is a strong memory about this process was how angry and frustrated a lot of classmates were. I remember several classmates withdrawing from the conversation completely. Whether it was because they were out of their comfort level (not having the right answer), frustrated by not being heard, wondering what the point was, etc., I don't know. Outside of class, I remember people expressing frustration that Whitney wasn't giving us the answer. They were angry that she would let us debate and argue for so long instead of just telling us. Unlike those classmates, I enjoyed the experience, but I was in no better place in understanding the big picture.

LAURA: Yeah, I remember the attitudes that some people had. It was really frustrating for us to understand why Whitney wanted to spend so much time on this article when at times it felt like we weren't getting anywhere. I really enjoyed it though when everyone got into the conversation. I find it interesting how much complaining went on before class but then during class many participated. Maybe I am mis-remembering, did many people participate?

CRAIG: I seem to recall a strong majority taking the floor most often, while others observed. I wonder what it was that made it so frustrating to many of our classmates? It makes me realize how being taken slightly outside of our comfort level could really be a beneficial, educational experience, even though we lacked the big picture and it was frustrating to many. I don't think I could have understood what it would be like to experience math as a discipline that could be debated over, rather than the "black-and-white" "right-or-wrong" perspective that many people have.

LAURA: Comparing that class to the ones I now teach, a lot more makes sense to me about my students' attitudes. Our dialogue challenges me to rethink my outlook on what my students are thinking right now about the discussions we have in the classes I'm teaching now.

Chapter 19

Participation in teacher education

As Laura and Craig just commented in response to Whitney's essay about the experience with Aristotle on the nature of lines and its implications for the real-number line, there are important commonalities between their coursework in the teacher education program and the mathematical practices of the Holt math department. Thus, when Holt hires graduates of MSU's teacher education program, that program contributes to the mathematical culture of the department as well.

MSU's program also contributes to professional development in the Holt math department by supporting no-cost, shared teaching assignments similar to those once sponsored by the PDS effort (the year-long internships for preservice teacher preparation candidates). Since six out of the ten members of the department have done internships at Holt, even though the last shared teaching assignment funded by the PDS initiative was in 1995–1996, many current math department members have actually taught together for a full year. Indeed, since some interns are placed with more than one teacher, when one adds to the 15 shared teaching assignments depicted in the figure in Chapter 14 the internships of teachers who were subsequently hired in the department, one generates ten or more year-long, shared teaching assignments inside the department. See Figure 19.1.

The presence of these shared teaching assignments is important, as emphasized in Chapter 14, because of the trust they established inside the department. This trust, in turn, plays an important role in nurturing the department's internal culture.

Of course, these internships, and the shared teaching assignments they support, are important venues for professional development for the interns and have an impact on the Holt department through the hiring of these interns as teachers. But, based on the tradition of PDS-funded, shared teaching assignments, Holt teachers have often interpreted their work with interns as an important avenue for their own professional development. In the next essay, implicitly writing to an

Mentor teacher	1987	1991	1993–1994	1994–1995	1995–1996	1996–1997	1997–1998	1998–1999	1999–2000	2000–2001	2001–2002	2002–2003	2003–2004	2004–2005
(intern)	*Marty Schnepp*	*Kelly Hodges*												
Bill York	Was eligible	*	Retired											
Mike Lehman			Dave Hildebrandt	*	Kellie (B) Huhn	*	*	Craig Huhn/ Adam Kelly	Sean Carmody	0.5 (to finish in 2003–2004)	**	**	1.5 (one finishes from 2000–2001)	*
Sandy Callis				*	*	*	**	Laura Kueffner	Left LHS					
Marty Schnepp			Became eligible					*	Left LHS					
Kelly Hodges					Became eligible	*	*	*	*	*	*	*	*	*
Dave Hildebrandt								Became eligible						
Kellie Huhn										Became eligible	*	*	*	*
Craig Huhn													* Didn't finish	*
Laura Kueffner													*	
Sean Carmody														Became eligible
Total # of interns	N/A		1	2	2	3	4	5	2	1.5	4	4	4.5 +0.5	4

Named interns became teachers in the dept, asterisks indicate employed elsewhere; italics indicate one quarter student teaching, rather than full-year internship

Figure 19.1 Internships in the Holt mathematics department: 37.5 year-long internships from 1993–1994 to 2004–2005.

audience of fellow teachers, Kelly Hodges reflects on what she has learned from being a mentor teacher. She also indicates how the decision to be a mentor teacher, and the ways in which she enacts this role, both reflect her notions of professionalism. In her view, to be a professional teacher is to be committed to the profession writ large, not just to one's immediate students, and thus to engage in teacher preparation.

Others in the Holt department share this commitment of Kelly's. In fact, members of the department have committed themselves to contributing to mathematics education in a variety of ways, including: making presentations at state and national conferences of mathematics teachers; running state-wide inservice projects; participating in the research of MSU doctoral candidates; writing for publication in journals and books; taking leadership roles in the Michigan Council of Teachers of Mathematics; and becoming a site for a research and development project on using moving devices in the teaching of Calculus and PreCalculus. Consistent with their views of teaching as presenting opportunities for professional growth, the Holt teachers see these commitments as being important professional contributions, and as providing chances for personal and professional growth, as well.

Being a mentor teacher is a particularly interesting example of this sort of commitment. Mentors contribute to the education of future teachers, and are at the same time enriched themselves. In their discussion of this essay, Dave Hildebrandt and Sandy Callis discuss the professional growth that they experienced as mentor teachers. They also mention their involvement with the field experiences of juniors and seniors in MSU's teacher education program.

Becoming a professional teacher; being a mentor teacher

Kelly Hodges, Holt High School

This essay was written for this volume.

When comparing teaching with other professions, such as law or medicine, it is often considered a less ambitious or prestigious field. In particular, teaching has a shorter training period and a seemingly smaller specialized body of knowledge. Some might even argue that teachers are merely technicians who follow an established curriculum and lesson format – guidelines that are set by others. In my experience, however, teaching is never this straightforward.

Each day as a teacher, I make hundreds of decisions. I do not make these decisions by following set rules. My commitments, standards, and goals as a teacher are part of the basis for these decisions, and they are influenced by the school in which I work, the classes that I teach, and even by my own view of my purpose and charge as a teacher. Equally important to my decision-making are the students I teach. I must consider their background knowledge, perceptions, and goals in order to create a classroom that will maximize the potential for student learning. Because all these factors affect the choices I make, I often find myself faced with dilemmas in which no course of action presents itself as an obvious choice superior to all others on every possible dimension. Quite often I must in an instant weigh many various factors and decide what to do. Because of my responsibility to do much more than follow an established set of rules, I think teaching is much more than just a technical occupation.

Although I worked hard to learn as much as I could about being a teacher during my teacher education program, I don't think I appreciated that I would need to make so many decisions on a daily basis. Early on, I found I was not always making the best decisions when trying to manage the dilemmas I faced in teaching; sometimes I was even unaware that a decision needed to be made. For a while, I felt I might not be teacher material. But then I realized, to get better at making these decisions, I just needed to learn even more. To avoid making bad decisions, I found I needed to develop a more professional approach to teaching.

What is a professional teacher?

To me, being a professional teacher is not necessarily associated with the style in which one teaches or the amount of teaching experience one has. I think mostly of certain beliefs, attitudes, or habits of mind that help teachers weigh all the necessary variables and make the best possible decisions regarding the students entrusted to them. Some of these beliefs, attitudes, and habits have been central to my development as a professional in teaching.

The belief that I am in continual need of improvement is central to my stance as a professional teacher. For many teachers, their teaching practice is a reflection of their personal selves. To them, admitting that they are in need of improvement would mean accepting that they are unsuccessful people whose personalities are not suited to teaching. In contrast, I have found it helpful to distinguish my actions as a teacher from my self, to view teaching as a role I play. Making this distinction, I can examine my teacher role more easily, be critical of it, and change it without feeling threatened or defensive, because my actions as a teacher are not identical to who I am as a person. Of course, by saying this,

I don't mean to imply that my personality doesn't influence the type of teacher I choose to be. Nor do I mean to say that I can control everything that students perceive about me. But I can choose to appear calm or excited in response to a student's comment. I can choose to be warm or distant. I can choose to look angered, disappointed, or unruffled by students' behavior. Not only do I have more options available to me when I willingly craft my teacher persona, I am also buffered from students' responses to it. If something I do results in students being angered or frustrated, I can simply choose to do it differently next time, rather than feeling powerless to change. By distinguishing my teacher role from my person, I can both accept that I am in need of improvement and feel capable of improving.

So much knowledge exists among members of the teaching profession that one person could not hope to know it all. In the process of attempting to improve my practice, I see it as my responsibility to draw from this collective body of knowledge. I read a variety of publications and attend conferences and seminars. I'm hoping not only to improve my repertoire of skills in carrying out lessons but also to clarify my view of school's purpose and broaden my understanding of my students. I seek out opportunities to talk with other teachers about teaching or even to watch them teach. I have found it helpful to ask questions aimed at understanding their perspective and to suspend judgment on what I see and hear until I understand their perspective. All of these things help me access the knowledge of other teaching professionals.

Being professional also means adopting a learner's standpoint about my own teaching. Each day, after I've taught, I reflect back on what happened. I try to understand how students experienced the class. I identify things I liked and things I disliked. I pose questions to myself about what happened and think about ways to get answers to these questions. I view my experience in class as yet another source from which I can get information about improving as a teacher.

Since I rely so heavily on the knowledge and experience of other teachers, I feel obligated to contribute to the public body of knowledge about teaching as well. I do this in a variety of ways, from writing about my teaching to offering ideas when talking with colleagues. While I hope to be a resource for others, I also expect others will scrutinize my ideas. In this sense, even in sharing what I know with others, I am gaining the chance to improve my teaching practice.

There are many other aspects of professional teaching. These include facets of the teacher's interaction with students, the relationships she develops with colleagues, and her attitudes about her purpose and responsibilities. The development of these things, however, depends on the teacher's view of her capacity to learn, her use of available resources, and her sense of obligation to the growth of other teachers.

Teacher education as a professional obligation

One of the most important parts of my work as a professional teacher is participation in preservice teacher education. Mentoring an intern teacher gives me the opportunity to contribute to the professional growth of another teacher, as well as to gain a resource in that new teacher for my own professional development. Because of this, it has been central to my continual attempts to improve my practice.

Like most other professional activities, mentoring an intern asks of me both courage and hard work. As a mentor, I am not only baring every aspect of my teaching practice to the scrutiny of another adult, I am also accepting responsibility for the actions of the intern in my classroom. I have to take extra time to meet with the intern as well as to explain or write down many aspects of my practice that are second nature.

The rewards of mentoring are considerable. By helping the intern grow, I am contributing to educational quality for the intern's future students. Through the growth I experience as a teacher myself, I also improve the quality of instruction I can give to my own future students.

I began my involvement in teacher education during my second year of teaching. My reason for becoming involved didn't have anything to do with the expertise I thought I could give to intern teachers. It was an attempt to repay a debt to my own teacher preparation. One of the most helpful parts of my education was the opportunity to observe another teacher in a classroom. The teacher whom I observed was certainly not the best teacher I had ever met. But it was the first chance I had had to be in a classroom where I was imagining being the teacher rather than trying to perform as a student. I saw things I liked, things I disliked, and things I didn't understand. From this experience I gleaned ideas about what I wanted to do as a teacher, those I didn't want to do, and questions that I needed to pursue. Most significantly, I learned it was important to watch a teacher who didn't necessarily teach the way I thought I wanted to teach, in order to challenge my assumptions about teaching. So, initially, I invited teacher education students into my classroom with the idea that they would see things they didn't like or understand, because I was unsatisfied with aspects of my teaching, as well. I just wanted to give them a place to go watch someone teach.

Now, as an experienced mentor teacher, I have additional reasons for working with interns. It frustrates me to try talking about teaching with someone who does not share the professional stance I have described. I want to help new teachers develop this stance because of the scope it gives them to improve their practice. Being a mentor teacher is also a way to become acquainted with another professional teacher. Having an intern teacher in my classroom gives me a collaborative teaching partner. Being questioned by another teacher helps me grow by forcing me to clarify my rationale or justify my actions. The chance to watch someone else teach lets me think about what I'm seeing without having to respond immediately as I do when I am teaching. In these and other ways, having an intern teacher represents a valuable resource in improving my own practice. Through being a mentor teacher, I am improving my own practice and contributing to the growth of other teachers, thus widening the circle of students whose education I can positively affect.

What interns need to learn

The most important thing I want interns to learn is that teaching is a profession. Like most people, interns are most familiar with the technical aspects of a teacher's work. They are most concerned with learning the best strategies and ideas for communicating their content and managing student behavior. There is no one best way to teach, however, because so many variables affect the learning process. Since teaching is so complex, the teaching profession has a shared body of knowledge that cannot be transmitted in full from expert to novice. In order to make good decisions about teaching their students, interns must learn right away to relinquish the idea that best teaching practices exist and that these are all that need to be learned. They need to learn that being a professional means fulfilling an obligation to intelligently apply the collective knowledge that teachers share to make decisions in the best interest of their students.

Prior to the internship, intern teachers have accessed this collective knowledge through reading and discussion, field observation, and reflection. They have not had much experience of actually being the teacher. They often believe that, if they could just get some experience in the classroom, they will become expert teachers. Although experience in the classroom is important, experience alone does not make one an expert. Interns need to recognize the importance of reading, observing, thinking, and talking in teachers' professional lives. When focusing solely on the classroom, teachers cannot access the knowledge of others in the profession. Because of this isolation, collaboration is a central part of the professional lives of teachers.

The internship is an apprenticeship in collaboration. The interaction between the mentor and the intern is the first professional collaborative relationship in teaching the intern will have, and through it the intern should be taught how to engage in collaboration. I think it is also important that the mentor model similar relationships with other colleagues so that the intern can see that collaboration is not unique to the mentor–intern relationship. Interns must understand that professional teachers seek out such relationships throughout their careers.

Through collaboration, teachers both contribute to and draw from each other's practice. Interns should have opportunities to do both these things. They must learn to access the collective knowledge of teachers, and they must learn how to develop and share contributions to the profession.

The internship is a collaborative setting, not just a tutorial. Teacher preparation is not merely training, in the sense of transferring skills and knowledge from expert to novice. Certainly interns do acquire skills and knowledge from the mentor. But I want interns to become discriminating in the skills and knowledge they embrace. I want them to consider the many variables that contribute to the success of any teaching episode. Since the best teaching depends on the students one teaches and the community in which one works, interns cannot become replicas of the mentor teacher. They need to leave the internship with the ability to adapt to a new setting. They need to understand that I do not expect them to be just like me.

It is important to me that interns learn early in the internship that they do not have to agree with everything I say, but that they do need to think about it. They need to suspend judgment about an idea until they have worked hard to understand my rationale. They should be able to articulate my position. Only then can they make a decision about whether or when they might incorporate the idea into their practice.

One issue about which interns often want to disagree with me is the use of extrinsic rewards for student performance and behavior. All teachers are confined within a system of extrinsic rewards in the grades we must give. But the reward of good grades does not motivate all students. Some students are aware of the ultimate subjectivity of grades and are consequently turned off from engaging in school because of a rebellion against the meritocracy built around school performance. In my teaching, I strive to remove extrinsic systems of reward. By focusing on the intrinsic rewards of intellectual pursuit, I believe I can create students who will persevere in the face of the seemingly senseless aspects of extrinsic reward systems. They will be much less likely to withdraw in the future, provided they find something personally rewarding about which to learn.

I know, however, that some students have not responded to this approach. An intern may argue that an elaborate system of extrinsic rewards might hook these students into participating. Some may later be able to appreciate the intrinsic rewards once they start participating. Others may not, but at least they might be achieving better grades and attaining the cultural capital associated with school success. The intern might ultimately choose to take this approach in some or all cases. But since I have made a commitment to eliminating extrinsic rewards, while we are together, they must at least try to understand my perspective.

They may never agree with it, but they will be better able to understand the implications of their own choice on this issue.

Over time, I want interns to develop a habit of curiosity about the teaching practice they see, especially when they don't understand it or don't like it. I have two goals in mind when I demand this intellectual stance from interns. My first is to teach them how to be good colleagues who listen and learn from fellow teachers. My second is to prepare them to be discriminating in their application of teaching ideas. I want them to understand that every teacher action conveys something about that teacher's goals, standards, or commitments.

Because all teacher actions are perceived as a reflection of the teacher's philosophy, a teacher cannot take the stance that it is acceptable to do things in the classroom without thinking about them. I want interns to learn that considering the purpose and rationale for including each action in their teaching and the implications of its inclusion are part of being a professional teacher. Teachers are public servants, not private practitioners. They are accountable for the things they do with students and the way they choose to spend students' time. They will have to respond to administrative, parental, community, and student critiques of everything from the way they assign grades or choose lessons to the language they use with students and the behavioral norms they establish and enforce. If they are challenged on something and have no justification for their actions, they will appear insensitive or even ignorant. They will not appear professional.

As in the example of extrinsic rewards, there is rarely one right way to teach that will work for all students at all times. Interns have to understand that diversity in approach is not necessarily a bad thing. Diversity without a good rationale, though, is unprofessional. Throughout the internship, the intern should be continually questioning the motivation behind my actions. Through my explanations, I will both contribute to the intern's development and clarify my own philosophy. When the intern is then asked to explain his own reasoning or philosophy, he is not being criticized for his novice status but is instead being included in the conversation of professional teachers.

Although interns will undoubtedly be the recipients of quite a bit of knowledge about teaching during the internship, they also need to learn how to contribute to the professional growth of others. They can do this by asking questions, which forces other teachers to examine their goals and reasoning. This can help teachers clarify their rationale or perhaps even change their practice entirely. In addition, interns have plenty of valuable knowledge to draw on despite their limited teaching experience. For example, no one enters teaching unfamiliar with the dynamics of a classroom. Throughout their years of schooling, interns have experienced many different classrooms and have learned much about what makes a classroom effective for them. Interns do need to be aware that the students they teach will not all experience school in this same way. But they also must understand that they already have a lot of knowledge to draw on and to contribute.

I often learn from interns, and I don't think I'm alone in this. Sometimes I learn directly; for example, an intern may show me how to use new software. Sometimes they create new activities from their experiences, which I add to my repertoire. But I also learn from them in subtler ways. Sometimes, when I let an intern make mistakes or do things I don't think will work, I learn that they do. For example, one intern struggled early in the year with understanding what students meant by their comments during discussion. We worked on getting him to control his urge to respond immediately and to take the time to understand what students were trying to say before he responded. As he worked on this, he did improve in his responses, but the class would often continue the discussion on their own as he thought and listened. The time that he waited before responding sometimes became uncomfortably long for me. What I learned, though, was that it wasn't uncomfortably long to him. In watching him, I found that often students were able to accomplish some consensus on the discussion topic without a teacher's facilitation. I learned that, even while I might understand what they are saying, even though I realize what is confusing or unclear, often they are able to work through it themselves. I shouldn't always deny them the opportunity. In this case, the students learned what to do when they were confused or frustrated. They learned that as a group they could accomplish more than they could individually. They saw that everyone could potentially contribute to the resolution, even if their ideas were not clear at first.

In cases like this, when I'm aware that I've learned something from an intern, I let him or her know about it. Sometimes interns are unaware of the significance of what they've done or said. Talking about how their work has affected me helps interns understand the importance of sharing their work with others. It also illustrates that even experienced teachers still have things to learn.

When interns learn that they are responsible for more than a repertoire of skills, they are well on their way to becoming professional teachers. By developing the habits of justifying their own actions and questioning the actions of others, they are poised to engage in productive collaborative relationships. Through these relationships they will be able to fulfill their obligations to draw from and contribute to their colleagues' knowledge about teaching. As a mentor teacher, I focus on modeling and nurturing these behaviors in interns.

Obstacles to professionalism in interns

Although the internship is an ideal time to learn about professionalism and collaboration, there are features that make it difficult for interns to think of themselves as professionals.

The collegial relationship between the mentor and the intern is not a symmetrical one. Clearly, the mentor teacher has more experience. It is expected that the intern will be drawing on the mentor's knowledge and experience more heavily than the mentor will draw on the intern's. Interns often feel that they do not have anything significant to contribute to the mentor. More notably, though, the mentor is responsible for passing judgment on the intern's performance at the conclusion of the internship. Interns are often hesitant to disagree with, or even question, the mentor, for fear of damaging the relationship, perceiving their careers to be at stake.

Another difficulty is my dual responsibility as a mentor teacher to the intern and as a teacher to my high school students. It is important to let the intern experiment and to experience failure, but I also want my students to experience the best possible teaching. Since the students' learning is ultimately my responsibility, I have veto power over anything that the intern plans. In this way, the internship is unlike other collegial relationships. The arrangement provides some safety for the intern because the mentor is responsible for what the intern does and for fixing things the intern cannot. But it can also inhibit the development of professionalism in the intern. The intern may resort to mimicking the mentor to avoid having his ideas rejected. In doing so, he avoids both contributing ideas as a professional and critically examining the mentor's practice.

The intern may also mimic the mentor simply because there is so much to think about in teaching. It is difficult for interns to defend all of their decisions early on because the experience is so new. Many situations arise which they have not anticipated, and they are not practiced at using their theoretical philosophies and goals to inform the decisions they make. All interns struggle with this early in the internship, but some become so paralyzed by the fear of doing something wrong that they are unable to continue teaching. They think that being professional means knowing what to do all the time. They don't realize that it just means always trying to understand the implications of what we do and trying to do better next time.

As a mentor, then, I find it important to think purposefully about strategies to adopt with interns. I have to be artful in creating experiences that not only help them learn their responsibilities as professional teachers but that actively work to overcome the obstacles to professionalism inherent in the mentor–intern relationship. These experiences, along with the modeling that I provide as a professional teacher myself, are necessary to fulfill my professional obligation to teacher education.

Guiding interns' professional development

Despite the obstacles, the internship is in many significant ways well suited to developing professionalism in intern teachers. One of the most important features of the internship is its length. Because interns have an entire year in which to develop, we have time to work on the intern's practice in more ways than putting the intern in front of students.

Early in the year, before interns ever try to design their own lessons, they work with me on improving my practice. This is important for helping interns see that I am not the final authority on teaching because my practice is still changing and growing. I continually try to improve my practice, and I bring interns on that journey with me. They need to learn how to exist as teachers who have sound rationales but who are changing and learning.

Something I work on every year is trying to teach students how to participate appropriately in a class discussion. Before the school year begins, I show interns examples of things I've tried: rubrics for grading student participation on a daily basis; specially designed lessons for addressing how to be a good group member and a good discussion participant; strategies for managing who speaks when in a discussion, such as keeping a written list of the order in which hands are raised. I talk about what I was trying to accomplish and why I think the ideas needed to be abandoned, revised, or limited to certain circumstances. We work together to think of other things to try. We meet with other colleagues to solicit ideas and suggestions. When the year begins, the intern watches as I try the new ideas. Then we evaluate how they went. I draw heavily on the intern's observations of how the students were responding, whether the goals are being met, and what other issues are arising. I talk about what I liked as well as what I didn't like. I bring the intern along as I share stories of my efforts with other colleagues. Then I decide what to do next – always talking about what my rationale is and how the evidence we have gained has influenced my decision. By participating in my attempts to improve my practice, interns learn about the process of reflection in improving teaching practice and the value of involving colleagues in the process. The experience helps them see how we will work together on their practice later in the year. I especially want them to see that, after drawing on all available resources, the teacher professional must be the final authority in deciding what to do next.

Once the intern begins teaching lessons, we work on his practice in the same way. I help him develop questions about his own teaching and think about what he has tried so far and how he feels about it. We brainstorm ideas together. Then I let the intern choose what to try next. I observe what students are doing and saying and sometimes informally interview students to get information about the impact of an intern's teaching. When we meet again to discuss effort, I help the intern think about what he saw and heard and offer anything else that I noticed. Then the intern decides whether to continue to pursue the question or leave it for a while and move on to something else. There are always plenty of things to work on. Although I will inevitably need to intervene on a few occasions during the year, for the most part, interns need to practice being in control of their own professional development.

In short, then, before improving the intern's teaching, I help the intern *learn how* to learn how to teach. Once they begin teaching, they need to know what to do when they are faced with a classroom episode they don't like. It is much more difficult for an intern to learn this while simultaneously dealing with the emotional impact of being less than successful. By beginning with an issue in my teaching, they can learn strategies for improving teaching practice without an emotional investment. Also, I think this structure helps an intern learn that, as a professional, he is responsible for growing as a teacher. Interns need to see that they will always be in need of improvement. They need to see that this kind of work is the daily business of professional teaching.

To help interns learn to have these conversations beyond the internship year, I purposely send them to other colleagues in my school to look for answers to some of their questions about their practice. They may observe another teacher or they may talk at length. In a sense, the intern is apprenticed to the entire school, not just to me. This helps the intern to appreciate the diversity of perspective among experienced professional teachers. It also allows the intern to practice initiating professional conversations outside the mentor–intern relationship. I also specifically encourage them to share their skills, learning activities they create, or observations they have with other colleagues in the school. The teaching practice at our school has been enriched many times by the contributions of interns.

Because we are not only able to converse as professional colleagues but to teach together as well, the internship is also suited to helping the intern learn how to look for chances to grow as a teacher while actually teaching. Often, both the intern and I teach during the same lesson. This allows both of us to work on our own teaching at the same time, as well as watch and listen for the other. For example, in our Algebra 2 class, we continually push students to think about how to know that what one is claiming is true. One day, as an intern was teaching this particular class, students started to respond in ways that I had never heard from them before. They spontaneously began to say things about needing to show that a statement is true for all numbers and that examples aren't enough, even if they are cleverly chosen. I appreciated that this was different from what Algebra 2 students usually said, and I wanted to see how far I could get students to go with this idea. I interjected into the conversation and contributed considerably to the next few lessons. The intern also added things along the way, for example, some new notation the students found helpful. Together we invented a way of teaching the idea of proof in Algebra 2.

This example is important for two reasons. Even though I had taught the course many times, I was still learning how to teach it better. We changed our plans because I saw a way to improve what we were doing. I was able to model that I was still improving. Also, I was able to model that I could learn a lot about my own teaching by watching someone else teach. The things the intern did in the classroom allowed some new ideas to come out, which inspired me to develop a new approach. As a professional, these opportunities are rare, which makes them all the more valuable. I want interns to appreciate that, as professionals, they should continue to seek out opportunities to be in classrooms with another teacher. The features of the internship that contribute to the intern's learning are features of nurturing professional relationships for all teachers.

By modeling my approach to working on my own teaching, by encouraging interns to work with other teachers, and by taking full advantage of the assets the internship brings to each of us, I hope to instill in the intern the desire to be a truly professional teacher. When interns feel this obligation and are prepared with strategies to develop their own professional identities, I have fulfilled my professional obligations as well.

Conclusion

Teaching is perceived as less demanding than other professional careers. It also has a less prestigious position in our society. Teachers are less autonomous from supervision or control. But like those in medical and legal positions, teachers provide a specialized and vital service to every member of society, and they are trusted. In order to maintain the trust of those they serve, I think teachers have certain obligations to uphold, just as do those in the medical or legal professions. Teachers are obligated to continue to improve themselves, and they are obligated to aid in the improvement of other teachers. Because of these obligations and the knowledge needed in order to meet them, I think teaching is a professional career.

A teaching internship is an initiation into the teaching profession. It is not the conclusion of a teacher's education; it is the beginning.

During the internship, interns will gain classroom experience, but they should also come to understand their responsibilities as professionals. Over the course of the year, the mentor teacher has the opportunity to shape this process, supporting the growth of another professional teacher.

By not merely passing on skills to the intern but instead focusing on the collaborative relationship, the mentor teaches the intern that collaboration is a critical component of professional development. It is important that the intern not only learns from the collaboration but has the chance to help the mentor learn as well. In this way, the intern learns that the benefits of collaboration should be sought well beyond the internship year. They learn that, even as novices, they are capable of contributing to the growth of other teachers. And even as veterans, they will be in need of colleagues who can support their continued improvement.

In addition, teachers who mentor an intern teacher gain a valuable resource for their own teaching. Not only do they gain a collaborative partner for the course of the internship, they gain another professional colleague who can be a resource throughout their career. They also fulfill their professional obligation to enrich the education of all students through the nurturing of other professional teachers.

The hard work of being a mentor teacher

Dave Hildebrandt and Sandra Callis, Holt High School

DAVE HILDEBRANDT: I thought Kelly's piece on her beliefs about what constitutes a professional teacher points out one aspect of professional collaboration that often gets overlooked – the collaboration between mentor and intern. Kelly makes some good observations about the importance of communicating with other professionals as a means of reflecting on one's own practice and that this ongoing reflection on oneself as a teacher is integral to the change process that enables us to become better educators. So many of us, in all content areas here at Holt, expect our students to express ideas, to listen to the ideas of other students, to react to those ideas, and to absorb reactions of others. We expect them to process this information to either revise or restate their original ideas. But we often forget that this description of the learning process, and the demand it also puts on learners, also describes our own professional development as well.

SANDRA CALLIS: I agree. As a mentor, I was often forced to examine my own beliefs about what went into a well-crafted lesson. For example, how much do I allow students to struggle with the mathematical content? How do I establish norms for engaging in the struggle? When students sat silently or spoke inappropriately, I have often cajoled or reacted strongly. Having an intern in the class has given me the space to see that students can sit silently for a long period, then come up with penetrating insights.

DAVE: The sheer amount of time spent together in a mentor–intern relation creates tremendous opportunity for this type of professional collaboration. I think some teachers overlook this as a source of development for the simple reason that they don't think they have anything to learn from an intern or pre-intern student. They see the process as being one-way. But what they forget is that any conversation between two or more people, if conducted openly and intelligently, should result in a mediated interpretation of concepts. The end product is a redefinition on all sides of how each individual perceives the concepts being discussed.

SANDY: Having an intern made me realize what a learning community is and how to put the beliefs and arguments of every participant on the line.

DAVE: In the past few years, I've had the opportunity to work with a few MSU juniors, a number of MSU seniors, and a handful of MSU interns. On each of those occasions I have had to describe what it is I do in the classroom. And each time, I not only had to think for myself how to describe what I do, but I also had to justify to a certain extent *why* I do what I do. Over the past few years I've discovered that some of the practices I had been following without much thought – that I had been mentally justifying – didn't sound as good when I attempted to express them to someone else. Sometimes we get so caught up in the day-to-day aspects of our job that we forget to question or examine our own practice. With the presence of an intern, it is exactly the day-to-day aspects that get questioned. Everything we do, everything we take for granted is open for examination under the fresh eyes of the intern.

SANDY: That brings up a crucial point for me. Mentoring an intern is also hard work. On the one hand, the mentor is wholly responsible for the quality of educational experience that her students are getting; on the other hand, she is committed to making room for the intern to try out different ideas and experiment. When I look at an idea for a lesson brought by the intern, I may see some flaws and insufficiencies, but only the actual lesson will tell what will work and what won't. Sometimes the worst-crafted lessons turn out to be the best learning opportunities. At the same time, I have to consider that students may experience frustration or may misunderstand the concept. The mentor teacher is caught in between competing teaching responsibilities. And the dilemma plays out daily; the stress is unbelievable.

DAVE: That's a very important point. Also, as Kelly mentioned, it's important for the intern to feel empowered to take chances and create something new, to see if it works or doesn't. So many times we ourselves are hesitant to try something new, to rock the boat. Having an intern helps free me up to take chances and to ask them to take chances. Once the intern begins to relax and teach more, the relationship changes to more of a team-teaching one. This is where true collaboration can take off. The mentor and intern should take the time that gets freed up to investigate new lessons and fresh approaches, to document student performance and analyze what works and what doesn't with two pairs of eyes. Having interns assess and critique my performance, and getting them to realize that I need to learn and change just as they do, is a point Kelly made and that I agree with. It is important for the intern to take full advantage of this collaborative experience.

Chapter 20

Graduate study

Kelly Hodges's essay on aspects of professional development that come with being a mentor teacher, and Dave Hildebrandt and Sandy Callis's response, like the other essays in this section, focused on professional development that is quite close to the classroom. This section of the book, perhaps surprisingly, given its focus on professional development, has not described workshops or conferences that happen at a remove from the classroom. The last essay in this section shifts focus to professional development that occurs far from the classroom. However, rather than conferences or workshops, this essay reflects on graduate study as professional development.

As in other states, public school teachers in Michigan must continue to study while teaching. Early in their career, the amount of study they must complete in order to maintain their certification leads just about all teachers to complete a master's degree and move up their district's pay scale. Like the university's need for field placements for its teacher candidates' practice teaching, teachers' needs for continuing education units (CEUs) may represent another place where university and school might meet.

Yet, this meeting place of school and university is often more about credentials than about substance. Teachers accuse colleges of education of preoccupation with theory and a lack of attention to practice. On the other hand, to university faculty, these accusations smack of anti-intellectualism. It is a rare occasion where teachers find their work at universities intellectually fulfilling and of practical use.

In the next essay, Marty Schnepp voices a minority view on relationships between theory and practice (similar to that raised by Dewey, 1990; Schwab, 1978; Karmiloff-Smith & Inhelder, 1977). Rather than dichotomize experience into the theoretical and the practical, from the perspective of a practicing teacher, he indicates how and when the theoretical has influenced and shaped his teaching practice (the practice described in Chapters 3, 4, and 7, as well as Schnepp & Nemirovsky, 2001; Chazan & Schnepp, 2002; and Schnepp & Chazan,

2004). In describing his professional evolution as a teacher, he high-lights his preservice teacher education, as well as three master's-level courses in education. This university coursework shaped in important ways his views of learning, knowledge, school curricula, and mathematics as a discipline. In pointing to these influences on his teaching practice, he suggests an alternative image for how university and school can connect in the professional development of teachers. Dave Hildebrandt and Kellie Huhn take up the discussion by indicating their interest in similarly "theoretical" issues and the impact that this interest has had on their teaching practice as teachers.

Theory is practical!

Marty Schnepp, Holt High School

This essay was written for this volume.

Few people reach a political opinion by deduction from an abstract system of philosophy; most feel their way into the opinions they hold, often contradictory ones, and are hardly aware of the forces within and without that drive them (Packer, 2000, p. 7).

What Packer (2000) says about political opinion could well be said about opinions in nearly all other pursuits. In particular, Packer's comment resonates for me as a teacher. Over my career, I have spent a significant amount of time sitting in workshops where formulaic approaches to instructional practices were presented. Cooperative Learning, Socratic Seminar, Reciprocal Teaching, and Cross-Curricular Writing are examples of the topics of these sessions. More time was frittered away in conference work sessions where manipulatives, allegedly fun problems, or semi-curricular recreations (like origami and kite-building) were demonstrated. In the early stages of my career, inspired by such workshops, I might have added a group assignment to the week's lesson, a writing task, or maybe taken a day away from the curriculum to let students build paper polyhedra. Taking bits and pieces from workshops helped me feel my way as to what worked in the classroom. Over time my instructional practice became fragmented by incongruent lesson formats and activities. It is my experience that conference-style workshops focus only on teaching techniques and implicitly encourage assimilation of their themes into one's teaching repertoire without deliberation on how the method or activity fits one's educational philosophy.

A more productive avenue for professional development for me has been teacher education courses where education was studied as a discipline. Post-modern literary criticism, Dewey's aesthetics, definitions of curriculum, the purpose of school, and the philosophy of mathematics were some of the seemingly esoteric subjects discussed in my graduate courses. I found thinking about these abstract notions to be exceedingly practical. In my experience, educational theory and philosophy have been vehicles for improving my teaching, giving it a focus, and minimizing contradictions among my goals and actions in the classroom. Personally, I would much rather discuss "the transcendental signifiers that are operational in the discourse-practices of advocates of standards-based reform" (paraphrased topic of conversation from TE 870 – "Curriculum Development and Deliberation" taught by Cleo Cherryholmes, now an MSU faculty member emeritus) than sit through a lecture on Cooperative Learning, a workshop titled "Origami for Your Math Class," or a sales pitch disguised as a conference put on by the publisher of a new textbook series. Somewhere along the path of my recent studies I read, "there is nothing more practical than a sound theory;" this has become my personal mantra.

How I teach now: social constructivist math teaching

The math department at Holt, and its MSU partner mathematics educators, encourages curricular variation and pedagogical exploration. My colleagues and I discuss the results of our teaching in light of related educational literature, the implications of constructivist learning theory to instruction and assessment, and study mathematical content together. Collaboration sustains a high level of accountability and has reshaped our expectations for teaching as professionals. We are all curriculum writers, researchers, and mathematicians.

At Holt I have taken part in the development of curricula for courses in which students explore mathematical ideas that grow out of tangible problem contexts. The foundation for this curriculum is based upon the relationships between changing quantities, that is, functions. With this as background, collaboration with peers, researchers, and teacher educators, and my graduate coursework have motivated me to analyze the ways I work with students in my classroom via intensive study of theory and philosophy.

My current thinking about instructional practice compels me to begin each new area of study with a common, everyday type of problem context, one that is realistic and within the range of experience my students would likely have. I often use computer-driven mechanical devices, for example, toy cars or a bicycle rider that will move in relation to function rules and graphs that can be manipulated to alter the motion (Schnepp & Nemirovsky, 2001). Although the problem contexts I select must be amenable to my students, the questions I pose are ones for which students have been taught no previous algorithm for answering. Reasonable progress must be possible with previously known mathematics. Early in the year, students are typically arranged in groups, presented with a context and asked questions. They discuss their ideas. I listen. I want to hear students formulate arguments, refute arguments, support arguments, and raise new questions. Students write, discuss, calculate, and make presentations, all the while defining and refining terminology. New mathematics grows out of the discussion of students' attempts to work toward answers to my questions and others that arise as they work.

We move on to discuss new functions to see how previous conclusions and methods play out in those situations. As the school year progresses, we compare students' conclusions to those outlined in texts or to historical constructs presented by me. Sharing thoughts (subjective ideas) with others for the purpose of analysis, critique, or conjecture-testing provides the mechanism for objectification or refutation; this leads to more discussion, thought, and (in theory) better understanding of the mathematics. Learning stems from social interaction and so I believe the label social constructivist teaching applies.

This approach makes it explicit that development of linked meaning is valued, and it seeks to make it unavoidable. Another thread running through this pedagogy is that misconceptions about the previous knowledge are confronted daily as students try to make use of old mathematics in new contexts. Conceptual change happens naturally as a part of this instructional paradigm; it is explicit and difficult to avoid. The dynamics of classroom discourse are fascinating for me and, most importantly, empowering for students.

I approach my teaching and curriculum endeavors with a goal of minimizing occasions when students and their ideas play a subordinate role with little or no idea where the mathematics we are discussing came from or why we are discussing it in the first place. I want my students to develop inquiring habits of mind that will help make new situations accessible at some level. Cooperative groups, class discussions, and assigned writing tasks are strategies that fit this way of working with students because they all promote articulation and clarification of student thinking.

In contrast, traditional pedagogy, with its direct instruction of algorithms followed by drill and practice, followed by word problems that are obvious applications of the algorithm, can hide lack of understanding about the contexts of applications and the algorithms themselves and promote an intellectual dependence on the instructor. It is the very nature of algorithms and mathematical systems to allow one to strip away details and move toward a mechanistic mode of operation. If the curriculum of mathematics courses consists only of those algorithms, it is possible, if not probable, that many students comprehend little while being taught skills to achieve answers that match those at the back of the textbooks. What I am describing is very much like what mathematician-turned-mathematics educator, Alan Schoenfeld, found in one classroom he studied:

> almost everything that took place in the classroom went as intended – both in terms of the curriculum and in terms of the quality of instruction. The class was well managed and well taught, and the students did well on standardized performance measures. Seen from this perspective, the class was quite successful. Yet from another perspective, the class was an important illustrative failure. There were significant ways in which, from a mathematician's point of view, having taken the course may have done the students as much harm as good. Despite gaining proficiency at certain kinds of procedures, the students gained at best a fragmented sense of the subject matter and understood few if any of the connections that tie together the procedures that they have studied. More importantly, the students developed perspectives regarding the nature of mathematics that were not only inaccurate, but were likely to impede their acquisition and use of other mathematical knowledge.
>
> (Schoenfeld, 1988, p. 145)

Moving away from the traditional instructional models I experienced as a student and learning to thoughtfully integrate new strategies and new problem contexts was no simple task. It was a complicated process that involved much theoretical learning, not one- or two-day workshops and inservices. In what follows, I will discuss three key ways in which theory has informed and shifted my practice.

Constructivist models of learning and student experience

To start to illustrate how the theoretical has had important implications for my teaching practice, I will go back to my initial training. In the 1980s, while enrolled in Michigan State University's undergraduate education program, I was introduced to learning theories that portray learning as a process of analyzing and assimilating new ideas by comparison to previous experiences. I recall readings from Piaget and others as an introduction to these so-called constructivist learning theories. These theories pervaded all courses and the analysis of content for the purpose of lesson design. So omnipresent was this view of learning that there was a tendency to take it for granted and not give it due consideration. Thus, constructivist ideas were established in my subconscious, but a firm grasp of them remained out of reach for some time because of my inexperience and inattention. Instructional technique was primarily what I gleaned from the program as I tried to make sense of the profession. In my science methods courses, the conceptual change model was exhibited as *the* instructional paradigm (Watson & Konick, 1990). A teaching prescription was given: units should begin with exercises intended to help students clearly articulate pre-existing conceptions of the topic to be studied; those activities should be followed with experiments in which students experience empirical challenges to their pre-existing conceptions; the correct conception is then explained. This lesson format was supposed to force students to restructure their personal understanding and align their thinking with accepted academic conceptions.

This approach felt right when used in the Physics courses I taught during my first few years after college. To start a unit on gravitation for example, I would drop a sheet of notebook paper and a textbook side by side in front of the class, asking students to then write about their observation and try to explain what they saw. Most would have said the book fell faster and did so because it weighed more (as I expected). I would have set to work changing their conceptions through a series of labs, demonstrations, readings, and lectures. This approach did not feel right in my mathematics classes. To start a unit on circular functions, following an example of another teacher, I would ask students to make a table of values for sine and cosine functions using calculator outputs, graph the ordered pairs, and describe any patterns or relationships they observed. The conceptual change model did not work because students only made observations regarding the graphs. There were no real conceptions to change. All I could do was to forge ahead with the proscribed skills, giving names like period to characteristics they observed like the repeating pattern of outputs, and explain what I knew of the sine function. Not realizing what was going wrong, but seeing misconceptions forming after I had shown students how to do problems, I began to simply lecture first, and then challenge their interpretations of what I said. This was the pattern of instruction I settled into for the first three or four years of my career.

I moved back to Holt during my fourth year of teaching. I heard colleagues discussing teaching and learning in terms of constructivist theory. They and MSU collaborators were deliberate and explicit about planning opportunities in the classroom for students to construct linked meaning of new mathematics to previous experiences. Team-teaching with Sandy Callis gave me my first glimpse of a professional working toward teaching practices that grew out of a belief about how people learn. She and others in the department began to challenge habitual ways of working with students in an almost uncompromising effort to stay true to constructivist ideals. As I came to understand constructivist learning theory as being distinct from other ways of viewing knowledge transfer to students, I began to see contradictions among the things I was asking students to do, the goals held for the lessons I planned, and what students were able to do as a result of my lessons. I will share two insights resulting from analysis of my early teaching practice to illustrate contradictions that impeded learning.

The first insight that helped to refine my understanding of constructed meaning was a simple idea: students must first have some conception in order to have a misconception. In my math classes, while attempting to utilize the conceptual change model, I was often trying to elicit pre-existing conceptions of things the students had never before experienced. For example, students had *no* conceptions of the sine function when circular functions were first introduced. Students would ask: "Why does it go up and down?" But they could not construct even an intuitive response to this question, let alone an analytical one. In Physics, when students asked: "Why does a book fall faster than a sheet of paper?" Having held and dropped books and paper, they have mental images of those experiences to draw on. Not so with a mathematical object they were encountering for the first time. Often my introductory activities were of little benefit, but took valuable time.

After working with other educators who sought to align their teaching methodology with their accepted theory of learning, a second insight emerged. In undergraduate education, I was taught to make concept maps showing links between skills and concepts as I planned an instructional unit. I understood that linking concepts was a part of constructivist teaching and so I based my lectures on my linked understanding. Unwittingly, my connections became as much a part of the content as the general skills and mathematical ideas. I was not allowing students to construct meaning, I was simply adding to the list of things that they had to learn. Students not only had to try and make sense of the content, they also had to try to understand my way of understanding the content. A more informed consideration of constructivist learning theory made it clear that a learner constructs meaning for new information based on prior experience – his or her own, not mine.

The format of starting each new unit of study with problem contexts within students' sphere of experience with new questions about these contexts beyond their prior experience, with no new instruction, grew out of these and other insights. Allowing students the chance to form conceptions and consider new content in relation to their understanding of old content or empirical observations fits with constructivist psychological models as I now understand them. Listening to how a community of students approaches the questions posed in one of these introductory activities gives me a chance to structure lectures or short presentations of formal mathematics in ways that link or build off students' ideas, thereby being mindful of the second insight.

The path I followed to this point in my teaching career has convinced me that the constructivist learning models I misunderstood in my early teacher training are important to consider for classroom practice and curriculum development. I believe that people make sense of the world by connecting new knowledge to previous knowledge and that teachers should create learning activities taking this into account.

Covering the curriculum and philosophy of mathematics

At Holt, my colleagues and I began to experiment with an approach to teaching that involved students in groups exploring everyday situations in an effort to answer mathematical questions for which they had no algorithm for solving. Student groups would share the results of their effort with the whole class and the class would discuss the work after the presentation. Exploration of everyday situations felt like a much better starting point than what I had previously used. I saw improvement in student learning as I became more proficient at leading discussions and writing problem contexts. Students seemed more engaged. And I saw constructivist ideas become operational in my pedagogy. Without a set process to follow, students were required to read the situation, reflect on their experience with such situations in everyday life, and draw on previous mathematical experiences in their pursuit of answers. As they discussed proposed solutions, misconceptions surfaced and were challenged. Student conversation seemed to reveal linked meanings that students constructed. However, I found that a significant degree of tension still existed as I considered my classroom practice (elaborated in Chazan & Schnepp, 2002). One aspect of that discomfort relates to coverage of course curriculum (particularly in my AP Calculus classes); constructivist teaching takes more time. It can make checking off each and every topic on lengthy syllabi difficult. But what I truly had to come to terms with was the realization and resolution of a conflict between my philosophy of mathematics and how open-ended student exploration plays out in the classroom.

Having grasped that learning through constructed meaning implies that students assimilate new information filtered through personal experiences – not that I was supposed to show them connections – I was in a position to better understand the approach my Holt High School mathematics department colleagues were taking in the early stages of our reform. Yet when I first watched and listened as students created their own understandings and methods, I found that these were often different from those the problem context and questions were designed to elicit. It took several years for me to understand why students constructed alternative methods and not the ones I intended them to discover. As my responsibilities came to include curriculum-writing (as described in Chapter 4), I found certain aspects of my thinking about education were underdeveloped and in need of challenging. My conceptions of mathematics itself were not in line with these new teaching methods.

Early in my career at Holt, I would have said that the major objective of our curriculum work was to design situations that would allow students to discover mathematics imbedded in (relatively) real-life contexts. I believed that students could reach conclusions via various paths (based on their prior experience), but that the end result was independent of the person making sense of the mathematics contained in the situation. Although tacit, I held an absolutist philosophical position with a bent toward Platonism, toward maintaining "that the objects and structures of mathematics have a real existence independent of humanity, and that doing mathematics is the process of discovering the pre-existing relationships" (Ernest, 1991, p. 29). I believed that carefully chosen problem contexts contained a mathematical essence. The mathematics was there, just waiting for the thoughtful student to extract it and generalize its use to other settings.

An example from Algebra 1 serves to illustrate how this philosophy was in conflict with the teaching practices I wished to adopt and why I eventually rejected it:

> At the beginning of the week, Susan goes to the gas station to fill up her car. Her odometer reads 57,500 miles. At the end of the week, she fills up again. Now the odometer reads 57,750 miles. It takes 8 gallons to fill the tank. If she has a 12-gallon tank, and had not filled up the second time, what would her odometer have read when she ran out of gas?

To me, this problem had slope written all over it. I theorized that gas mileage is a common quantity that all students recognize; as students endeavor to answer the question, it seemed certain that a natural transition into a study of rate of change would evolve. I was comfortable knowing that different students would get to the conclusion of the slope algorithm in different ways, but I truly believed that $(y_2-y_1)/(x_2-x_1)$ was an inherent part of this task.

From situations like this I learned how subtle the implications of constructivist psychology could be. In the gas mileage example, students with good proportional reasoning can answer any question about the situation without calculating anything close to $(y_2-y_1)/(x_2-x_1)$.

An articulate student can make a clear case and convince peers to approach these problems without any rate computations. For example: 8 is 2/3 of 12 therefore, Susan travels 1/2 of 250 miles more on the last part of the tank; 1/2 of 250 is 125, so Susan could drive 250 + 125 or 375 miles on the entire tank.

The mathematics that appears inherent in the problem is often recognizable to me only because of my training. It will not always appear to a novice, even in a rudimentary form. The training to which I am referring is in part my study of advanced mathematics. But primarily I believe that my teacher training is what fostered Platonistic sentiments. Tools I was taught for planning teaching units such as concept-mapping instilled a habit of examining my own understanding with the goal of knowing a topic deeply before constructing lessons. In my curriculum work, understanding my own way of understanding the content was followed by a search for problem situations that exemplified my understanding of the concept. The problems I chose did not have a mathematical essence, but characteristics that fit my personal understanding of the concept. This made them appear to have some essential idea imbedded in them.

Prior to this realization, when students developed alternative approaches to my situations (as in the gas mileage question), I did not lose my resolve. I would instead go in search of another situation. I believed that it was the situation or the questions that I was asking that prevented students from finding the mathematical essence. The tasks I gave became more structured and directed. I found myself trying to expedite mathematical discovery in other ways. Analyses of class discussions showed that I often nurtured comments from students who put forth ideas that could be shaped into the purpose I had set. I found myself (and my students) caught in an artificial game of discovery. I posed problems; if they discovered what I wanted them to find, we would move on. If not, they would get another problem to explore, and, once a conversation could be guided in the direction I wanted, we would move on. Students were justified in their exasperated request, "Why don't you just tell us the answer?" Realizing this, I again questioned constructivist ideals. Yet I could not dismiss them because it was clear that students were constructing meaning and valid solutions to the problems I posed.

As I struggled with the issue of an artificial quest to discover math, I coincidentally enrolled in a class taught by a postdoctoral fellow at MSU, mathematician and mathematics educator, Bill Rosenthal. The course was called "Exploring Mathematical Ways of Knowing." It had a significant impact on my thinking about mathematics philosophy and introduced mathematical epistemology. This study motivated a supposition that it was my mathematics philosophy that needed questioning, not my theory of learning or intended approach to teaching. In the

Algebra 1 example, slope is a convention. It is a useful human abstraction that has been adopted by the mathematics community. It does not have an absolute existence in some universal realm independent of people as I, a former Platonist, once believed (and could only articulate after studying various philosophical schools found in Ernest, 1991).

My questioning and eventual rejection of the absolute nature of mathematics was firmly established after I began reading Imre Lakatos' (1976) *Proofs and refutations* and was introduced to Paul Ernest's work in this class.

> It can be seen that at the heart of Lakatos' philosophy of mathematics is a theory of the genesis of mathematical knowledge. This is a theory of mathematical practice, and hence a theory of the history of mathematics. Lakatos is not offering a psychological theory of mathematical creation or discovery.... His focus is instead on the process which transforms private creations into accepted public mathematical knowledge, a process which centrally involves criticism and reformulation.
>
> (Ernest, 1991, p. 37)

In the years that followed my introduction to Lakatos and Ernest, I have read a great deal more about philosophy in mathematics, science, and education. Popper, Wittgenstein, Derrida, Foucault, Dewey, Cherryholmes, and others have added to, and altered, my personal philosophical positions. Now, as I study mathematics from textbooks, I see definitions that have been rigidly stated for the purpose of allowing a proof of a related theorem. I see theorems whose validity is dependent on tailor-made definitions. Definitions evolve as much to remove counterexamples and to preserve axiomatic structure as to support intuition. I now see algorithms that are not *the* way to approach a computation, but one way to approach a computation. I now conceive of the content that I teach as mathematical, cultural constructs, not absolute truths.

From the mathematical histories with which I am acquainted, I can only settle on a quasi-empirical account for the genesis of mathematical systems and techniques, and a social account of their formalization. I cite as examples: Lakatos's characterization of the history of Euler's formula for polyhedra, $V - E + F = 2$; the work of Hilbert and others that grew out of a critique of Euclid's geometry; and the many accounts of the development of calculus. Be it a several-century evolution of a field, or the work that goes into the publication of a single textbook, a great deal of thought and deliberation is hidden behind the summation an author presents in a text. Awareness of this complexity has implications for teachers and students as they together attempt to ascertain the mathematics within a text.

In my view, a social constructivist philosophy of mathematics is inconsistent with pedagogy that seeks to inspire discovery of mathematical absolutes. As Judah Schwartz asserts, "for the most part, the mathematics we teach in primary and secondary schools is the mathematics already made by other people" (Schwartz, 1997, p. 95). Once I came to see mathematics as the by-product of quasi-empirical, social processes, it became clear that students could not discover the results of other people's conversations. The contexts leading to the genesis of mathematical ideas and the refutations that forced decisions during the formalization and acceptance phase of canonical mathematical systems are not present in textbooks. I do not have the time to exhume the historical record for each topic and theorem my students are required to understand. Nor do I have class time for such presentation.

Given the complex background underlying the math taught in school, I began to wonder if I should even attempt to help my students appreciate and build understanding of the subtle connections that underlie the mathematics we study together. I know many math educators and math professors, parents, standardized test proponents, and others who feel it is a waste of time to teach for understanding. As long as students can execute the skills, many who have a stake in mathematics education are happy. I felt overwhelmed by my initial conclusions regarding the consequences of a social constructivist philosophy and the criticism being leveled against math-reform efforts that coincided with my discord. "Why bother?" I began to ask myself and, for a time, my teaching regressed strictly to lecture, followed by drill-and-practice exercises. My conscience, however, could not tolerate the student attrition that resulted from my return to traditional pedagogy.

One unit on differentiation rules was enough to remind me how direct instruction often casts a veil over students' true level of understanding. After careful presentation of algorithms and reading a textbook section that provided examples, most students had the ability to match their answers to exercises in the back of the textbook. But, as I discussed exercises with students as they practiced, it was clear that, despite their ability to execute procedures correctly, few carefully considered the ideas underlying the algorithms. The few became fewer with each passing lesson. If I told them when to use a technique they were fine, but most were not able to use techniques without guidance or to talk about how ideas were related.

Students' alternative conceptions, curriculum theory, and textual meaning

In the midst of what amounted to mental turmoil, I enrolled in another course at MSU called "Curriculum and Its Social Context." On the first day, the MSU faculty member who taught the course, Wanda May, asked each member of the class to write a personal definition of curriculum and a short essay about a personal vision of the purpose of school. Throughout the semester, she introduced various curriculum perspectives (or philosophies). Schubert's curriculum paradigms: empirical/analytic, hermeneutic, and critical praxis are examples of distinctions made in the course (Schubert, 1986). As a result of this study and discussions, I watched my personal curriculum definition, educational philosophy, and teaching evolve to find a focus.

I developed an affinity for a critical praxis perspective. The writers with whom I most agreed were those who promote education as an empowering and transformative experience, conceptualizing knowledge as "cultural capital" (see, for example, Cherryholmes, 1988, p. 64). I now believe I should aspire to find a curriculum that supports development of a deep knowledge base and habits of mind that will allow individuals to successfully navigate the field of mathematics, leaving them with serviceable knowledge.

> Novices and the ignorant deserve a good-faith introduction to socially accepted, systematic, authoritative knowledge, because this knowledge and the structure it promotes are the world, for the time being, of teachers, students and everyone else. . . . A place to begin, then, is with coherent stories or sets of ideas that provide students with information and knowledge that subsequently can be expanded, explicated, criticized, and deconstructed.
>
> (Cherryholmes, 1988, p. 69)

At the conclusion of this course, I was at a crossroads. I felt compelled to find a way to do a better job of helping my students learn and to improve the quality of the mathematics they took away from my classroom. And, although what I was learning to do at Holt felt the most promising of all the approaches I had seen, the discovery issue was still problematic.

In my final master's degree course, "Curriculum Development and Deliberation," the MSU faculty member who taught the course, Cleo Cherryholmes, introduced post-modern literary criticism, post-structural criticism, and pragmatic philosophy as tools with which to analyze curricular issues. Another look at the teaching I saw developing at Holt through these lenses helped to resolve my cognitive conflict and further focus my teaching methodology. Constructivist psychology, social constructivist philosophy of mathematics, and a praxis view of curriculum were synthesized. I saw an opportunity to use the alternative approaches and definitions students adopted as the beginning of "coherent stories or sets of ideas" described by Cherryholmes in the quote above. Students' own story-lines can serve as cultural capital, granting a degree of authority that permits knowledgeable analysis and critique of the constructs of formal mathematics.

After reading Cherryholmes, Derrida, Foucault, and others, my rationale for constructivist teaching no longer rested solely on constructivist learning theory. After thinking about the social and linguistic practices within the culture of the academic discipline of mathematics, I came to reject textbooks and lectures as viable foundations for my instructional practice.

In textbooks, expert mathematicians have written summaries of mathematical histories primarily from a foundationalist perspective. Lectures tend to be organized in a like manner: starting with definitions, axioms, etc. and progressing to theorems and algorithms. Yet what mathematicians treat as the foundation of an evolved theory is the result of quasi-empirical and social processes. In a standard account of a mathematical field, the context of the mathematical genesis is usually disregarded; key difficulties that played a role in the theoretical evolution are stripped away; initial attempts at formulation and subsequent refutations are ignored. All that remains is a formal abstract system, full of idiosyncratic symbols that are described by an intricately coded adaptation of English (or another spoken) language. To write a legitimate summary of such a foundation and its corollaries, one must have intimate knowledge of this history to ensure logical congruence with other accounts previously acknowledged within the mathematics community. As a result of this intimate knowledge, the terms and symbols carefully chosen by the author will appear to carry the intricate meanings as they are written. But the novice reader will not apprehend the richness of the authors' personal linked meanings. As Ernest (1998) argues, "It is a mistake to assume the existence of a unique meaning or 'correct' interpretation of a text" (p. 199); conveyed meaning is fragmented at best.

I realize that, from a practical perspective, people do learn from the writing of others in textbooks. But the high school mathematics student is at a disadvantage when reading a mathematics textbook because of negligible experience with new topics and because disciplinary knowledge consists of socially constructed norms of a culture alien to them (at least for the time being). All these factors make the process of reading texts (including textbooks, lectures, and notes) exceedingly complex. What Cherryholmes (1988) calls the "ferreting out" of meanings from a text is difficult but can be eased with a background of related ideas. However, thoughtful deconstruction, critique, and analysis of a text is uncommon when the students see themselves as knowing little or nothing of the topic and are faced with the perceived task of absorbing and acquiescing to the knowledge and norms being dispensed by the author of a textbook or an instructor.

If readers conceptualize their job as discovering the definitive meaning of words [and symbols] placed before them, [an] asymmetrical relationship between readers and texts is weighted on the side of the latter.

(Cherryholmes, 1988, p. 154)

Here is where I have found new rationales to encourage and use the alternative constructs resulting from my students' open-ended exploration to read the mathematics written by others (see the students' reading of the Product Rule in Chapter 4). I once thought that, when students adopted nonstandard definitions and methods to solve problems like the gas mileage problem, it was an obstacle to teaching for deep understanding. But, through my graduate studies, I came to realize that this phenomenon could play a significant positive role in the pursuit of empowered learning. Having created their own mathematical text, students are in a less subordinate position when reading another text simply because they have well-formulated, prior conceptions of the topic at hand that serve as a comparative foundation. Using this foundation, students can critique and deconstruct presented information. I have observed that when students have an opportunity to analyze situations related to a formal mathematical system before studying the system, their own mathematics increases their cultural capital. Having developed a conceptual framework of related ideas, I see my students more willing to delve into, critically analyze, and attempt to understand the workings of the mathematics written by others.

Completing the circle

In a sense, I have come full circle. I am a constructivist as my initial teacher training sought to make me. But a teacher's mind works via constructive processes also, and I needed experience and reflection in order to reach an understanding of what constructivism can mean in the context of teaching high school mathematics. This may be as much the message of this narrative as the explicit points about the role that philosophical and theoretical study has played in my development as a professional teacher. Constructivism has come to mean how I believe people learn. It describes the social process by which disciplinary knowledge is developed, and it is an approach to curriculum development and instruction that takes the implications of the former two meanings into account.

For me, theory and philosophy have become powerful lenses through which I have learned to view, analyze, and critique many things: my own teaching, new techniques that are proposed, curriculum options, the tasks I give my students, how I assess understanding, and what understanding means. Changes to my classroom practice are the out-growth of philosophical shifts and clarifications, not the result of someone showing me a new manipulative or tricky math problem. It seems only practical to become intimately conscious of the driving forces behind my professional choices. Learning to make deliberate choices and no longer "feel (my) way" into the tasks I assign and the pedagogical tools I select seems more a responsibility to my students than a personal preference for a particular model of professional development.

Views of mathematics and teaching mathematics

Dave Hildebrandt, Kellie Huhn, and Kelly Hodges, Holt High School

DAVE HILDEBRANDT: I think Marty's essay shows how his stance toward teaching has been affected by his experiences inside the classroom with his students and outside the classroom with the readings he has done and the courses he has taken. As he began to observe more of what the students were saying by allowing them the opportunity to have a voice, even if it was a small one at the beginning, he began to think about how *they* thought about mathematics. This forced him to revise how he thought about mathematics, something he has continued to do for the past several years.

KELLIE HUHN: My experience is similar. I began teaching with very different ideas – of mathematical beauty and order and so on, all *a priori*, all given from the outside. But that began to change in response to my teaching; I began to worry about students' conceptions and the connections we have to make.

KELLY HODGES: When I think of what I brought initially to teaching, like Marty, I think about how I grappled with the conceptual change model. I also graduated from the Academic Learning teacher education program at MSU. I remember writing in a journal entry once that I didn't think that the conceptual change model applied to mathematics. Like Marty, I felt that many (although certainly not all) mathematical topics are not already within the experiences of high school students. A model for teaching that revolved around identifying and addressing student misconceptions seemed to fall short of much of what I was charged with as a mathematics teacher.

DAVE: But, even that model is not what most of us had when we were students. Most of us had a traditional learning background as far as our mathematics education went. In our conversations at Wednesday-morning meetings and during prep time, I have heard most of the department express the following sentiment, more or less:

> I always did well in math in grade school and high school – I got As, and for me the math was easy. Numbers and calculations made sense. Then I got to college and realized how little I understood about mathematics. All that stuff I did really didn't teach me much. It just taught me how to solve specific problems in specific ways. When it came to really thinking about mathematics I was unprepared. It wasn't until I started teaching others that I really began to *know* mathematics for myself.

This is where the social constructivism aspects of the conceptual change model come into play. In my pre-college mathematical experience rarely was I ever asked to negotiate aspects of mathematics or to participate in open discussions. I can remember a few exceptions. In Geometry, students would be asked to share proofs with the class, and in Calculus we would be asked to share strategies for solving problems. But both of those instances took place as part of homework review, not as part of the classroom discussion. Back then we were told what to do and how to do it, end of discussion.

KELLY: Some years, I couldn't have been asked to participate in discussion. In two different years during my K–12 education, my mathematics class consisted of only a textbook and me. For me, these experiences raise the question of conventions. During these experiences, I would read the textbook, work on problems in the text and then compare my answers to an answer key. Many times I had the sense that the times when my way didn't match the book's way, the book's methods (like having rationalized denominators, for example) were merely conventional, although I don't know that I would have said it that way at the time. It wasn't until some years in teaching that I realized that these conventions were part of the reason that some people thought math didn't make any sense. In the courses I taught, I began to bring out conversations about the arbitrary, but nonetheless purposeful, nature of some mathematics. For example, in Algebra 1, we talk about whether it makes any difference which variable goes on which axes when graphing a function. We graph in both ways and talk about what one graph tells you that the other doesn't. Students debate about which way "makes more sense." We eventually settle on putting the independent variable on the bottom, and students have a variety of reasons they bring to support the reasonableness of this choice. But they also begin to appreciate that in mathematics many things are only reasonable choices, and not the only way things could be. Other examples of this include the definition of "quadrants" (do they include the axes or not), the convention $a^0 = 1$ (as opposed to leaving a^0 undefined), the "standard form" of functions like polynomials, and a host of other things.

KELLIE: Your examples remind me of the issue of proving in the Geometry course I've worked on with Sandy Callis, and now Kristin Povlitz. In geometry, there is a two-column structure for proofs that has traditionally been used, and that might be used to help students prove their conjectures. But I think that convention is rarely helpful for students in their explorations. As we know from constructivist theories of learning, students come to our classrooms with their own set of experiences and understandings. If we force them to explain using someone else's format, someone else's way of reasoning, the proof process no longer becomes an explanation of the mathematics, but a game. If there is a blank in the two-column proof, students guess what fits or discount the activity as purposeless. I have learned a lot from those students who discount two-column proofs. I'm intrigued by the idea of teaching mathematical proof in a way that is like the writing process. Typically, as I've observed it, writing in an English class, say, includes brainstorming together in groups, writing drafts, proofreading, and preparation of a final draft. This seems to be a useful model. I think this might access an organizational structure that students are familiar with and allow students' proofs to be based on their own thinking and ideas.

DAVE: To my mind, what you are describing, and what Marty articulated in the essay, differ from the conceptual change model and involve one's views about knowledge. It seems like we are imagining that there isn't a right way and misconceptions, but rather different ways of thinking about things. For example, Marty and I have talked about the practice in our department of reversing the traditional "definition-first, problems-second" approach to mathematics. In the conversation with Marty, I quoted, and repeat now, an adage from a text on post-structural thinking. "To know is to kill." If, in the classroom, we tell students what to think, we in essence end any exploration or investigation they might have attempted on their own and, as a consequence, any further learning or discovery they might have made. By their being told that which we wish them to know, we kill their own ability to learn for themselves. Marty brings this point up several times, that he is looking for the students to construct their own knowledge through discourse and deliberation. Another example from the same text on post-structuralism comes to mind. If two individuals (teacher and student or student and student) attempt to engage in a discussion about a specific object, they, by definition, must mediate a mutual understanding of what that object represents. A consequence of this process, for me, is a redefinition of the object in question, be it a parabola, an asymptote, a function, or Bayes's Law. Any conversation I have moves me in some degree toward the other person's conception. And so do they move toward me. Historically, I think the approach has been that the subject of mathematics was immovable, but it seems to me that we are questioning that.

KELLY: I think you are right. Now, when I craft problems for my students I specifically try to bring the need for conventions to light. I want them to highlight some of the reasons why existing mathematical conventions were adopted. In some areas I think I have been quite successful, such as the "which variable on which axis" example above. In other areas I have not been successful. Most notable are the importance of the quadratic formula, of factoring, and of solving equations by applying properties of algebra ("doing the same thing to both sides"). In all of these cases, students consistently come up with other methods for answering the same questions these techniques are designed to answer. When I find myself with no other reason than resorting to the claim that "you'll need to know this later," I stop. I don't try to force students to learn the standard techniques. Why do I stop? Because I never want students to get the message that there are things in mathematics that aren't sensible. It seems to me that I have to respect my students' views and capacities to think for themselves.

Part IV

Stepping back

The perspective of a local "outsider"

Our case study has portrayed a complex and ongoing relationship between Holt High School's mathematics department and Michigan State University. Within the limitations of space and our talents as writers, we have tried to portray the experiences of participants in shared efforts to teach mathematics to a wide range of secondary school students. In order to conclude our case study, we have turned to a local "outsider" to our work. Gary Sykes was a key participant in the development of the Holmes Partnership's notions of Professional Development Schools and is a well-respected observer and commentator on school reform. He is also a long-term member of the MSU faculty. As such, he has watched our efforts over time from the distance of a small number of miles.

Chapter 21

A quiet revolution?

Reflecting on mathematics reform at Holt High School

Gary Sykes, Michigan State University

This essay was developed for this volume.

Why would anyone really care about teaching meaningful mathematics to high school students who are unlikely to attend college?

And if, for some odd reason, you did care, how could you pull it off?

Anyone who's hung around a high school – which is all of us, counting our student years – knows this is an absurd ambition. The non-college-bound show little or no aptitude for math. They arrive at high school with a history of failure and a strong dislike for the subject. And few people, including students themselves, will see much point in supplying more than a smattering of the basics. Why bang your head against this wall?

Most high school math teachers sensibly shun lower-track students. The plum assignments are the honors and AP classes, filled (relatively speaking) with bright, eager novitiates who have aptitude, who like the subject, and who envision careers in engineering, finance, medicine, computer science, and other fields where math matters both as gate-keeper and as a basis for technical competence. So the best and most experienced math teachers work the system to get the best assignments. Imagine being a math teacher. If you like math – maybe even love math – and were good at it in school, why would you want to teach it to a bunch of malcontents who arrive in your class every day bored, alienated, and resistant? How could such teaching possibly be rewarding? The smart move is to enlist at a high school filled with motivated, middle-class kids, or to carve out a niche working with the slice of such students who are available in nearly any high school. Tracking makes this an easy option. Once you've gotten enough seniority, just maneuver your assignments to the academic tracks. Leave the lower-track assignments to the new teachers, who don't have seniority, or to the odd courses that are tacked onto others' loads.

Forget the slogans – "all children can learn" – and be honest for a moment. Isn't this how the American high school has always worked? There is a hierarchy of students, strongly oriented around social class and race; a hierarchy of knowledge that schools dole out according to the student hierarchy; and a seniority-based hierarchy of teachers that matches the other two hierarchies. Despite the democratic and egalitarian rhetoric surrounding this social institution, it is these principles of hierarchy that have dominated the American high school throughout its history.

Try to crack this nut, and you will be punished for your intentions. Dissension will divide teachers into reform advocates and adversaries; parents won't understand what's going on and will object; students who've prospered under the traditional system will chafe as rules for winning the scholastic game change on them; mathematicians in higher ed may complain that the "reform" waters down the rigor of the discipline; and avant-garde teachers will have to confront lots of uncertainty with meager support in learning to teach in new and unproven ways. Not exactly a formula for success. Under such conditions the best prediction is: reform fails. . . .

* * *

There. Do you find this caricature offensive? You should. But do you find it inaccurate? The answer is less clear. There have always been teachers of working-class kids who identify and enjoy working with them. These teachers often come from such backgrounds themselves, were the first members of their families to attend college, and have returned to work with students like themselves. So too are many working-class students terrific learners, thoroughly gratifying to teach. Many career teachers participate at one time or another in reforms that bespeak their deepest ideals, that confirm their commitments to lives in the classroom that make a difference. So it is possible to counter the jaundiced portrait above with a different historical tale about high school teaching. Social mobility through education is the American dream, even if the record reveals its quasi-mythic character.

And yet. Authors of a contemporary history of the American high school summarize their account with these words:

> for the most part, two ideas have guided the professional educators who shaped the development of the public high school in the twentieth century: (1) that equalizing educational opportunity meant offering different courses to different students based on their pro-

bable futures; and (2) that most of the steadily increasing number of high school students were incapable of and had no need for serious academic study.

(Angus and Mirel, 1999, p. 198)

They go on,

> few ideas have been more destructive to equal educational opportunity or to democratic education itself than the[se two]. . . . Despite claims by educators that they were building "democracy's high school," the institutions they created were deeply undemocratic, providing only a small percentage of students with the opportunity to master the knowledge and skills that might lead to power and success in American society.
>
> (ibid.)

The story of the math reforms at Holt High School is an important one against this historical backdrop. Skeptics might demand more hard data – test scores, for example – but the mix of qualitative and quantitative evidence presented here is persuasive. Holt students take more math of an intellectually serious kind. They must now demonstrate their understanding of math in more authentic ways. And the vignettes illustrate some extraordinary intellectual accomplishments on the part of students who would never have had the opportunity without the reforms. This is a success story with big implications.

No less an authority than Ted Sizer has called reform of suburban high schools one of the most difficult tasks in our society. Based on his deep personal experience as a school head and as founder of the Coalition of Essential Schools, a notable effort to improve high schools, he has reckoned the combination of middle-class community resistance and complacency an insidious force to overcome. While everyone understands that urban high schools are in trouble – look no further than their dropout rates – most observers regard suburban high schools as working tolerably well. Students who want to attend college can do so; those who don't can pursue vocational and technical careers. There may be some modest appetite for tinkering with this or that aspect of the suburban high school – maybe introduce block scheduling or a bit of interdisciplinary study – but deep reform is out of the question.

Yet this benign view neglects an existential truth faced by high school teachers every day. Too many of their students show up with meager motivation and minimal interest. They often see little point to what they are expected to learn. They believe they can get along just fine in life without knowing how to solve quadratic equations. Faced with such dispiriting circumstances, teachers must rely on personal charisma, or strike bargains with students that exchange behavioral compliance for reduced academic demands, or desperately invoke extrinsic rewards and sanctions ("this will be on the test, so pay attention"). If anyone asks, most high school teachers are not happy with these expedients, which often rob teaching and learning alike of their pleasures. But they feel that they have little choice. In their bones, teachers believe that students must meet them at least half-way. If they do not, then the responsibility for school failure must rest, at least in part, with the student, not entirely with the teacher. It is the rare teacher, though, who does not experience some sadness, some anger, and some frustration in the face of student indifference to her best efforts.

When John Goodlad (1984) reported on a large-scale, national study of schooling over 20 years ago, one of the most notable findings concerned the emotional tenor of classroom life. He wrote then that

> this relationship between teachers and classes of students was almost completely devoid of outward evidences of affect. Shared laughter, overt enthusiasm, or angry outbursts were rarely observed. Less than 3% of classroom time was devoted to praise, abrasive comments, expressions of joy or humor, or somewhat unbridled outbursts such as "wow" or "great."
>
> (pp. 229–230)

If too much of classroom life is flat, gray, and dull, then it is hard to imagine how the joint efforts of teachers and students could be productive. Many of education's highest ideals such as cultivating a love for the subject, appreciating its beauty and its logic, continuing its study, or discovering diverse, real-world applications, simply shrivel up in ways that standardized tests will never detect.

Attempting, then, to engage lower-track students in lovely, lively, and challenging mathematics goes directly to the satisfactions of teaching itself. The opening question can easily be turned around. Why would anyone want to suffer year after year through a kind of teaching that is routinized, defensive, and mind-numbing? Still, high school teachers might continue to avoid students they find unappealing. Such sinecures – if that is what to call them – will continue to shrink in the face of transformative demographics. Preliminary results from the 2000 census tell the story. Consider:[1]

- Students of color are expected to make up 24 percent of the total school-age population (ages 5–17) by 2012, a 5 percent increase from 1990;
- By 2010, these students will represent more than half the school-age population in seven states, including California, Florida, New York, and Texas;

- The term "minority" is losing its statistical meaning, as a new "student majority" rapidly emerges, composed of African Americans, Latinos, Asians, Native Americans, and Alaskan Natives;
- In 22 of the 25 largest urban school districts, "minorities" are already in the majority;
- Some 35 percent of US children are members of minority groups, a figure that is expected to climb to more than 50 percent by 2040;
- One in five students comes from a household headed by an immigrant;
- One in five students lives in poverty.

As the old teaching collides with the new demographics, something has to give. The traditional hierarchies that have organized the American high school are increasingly likely to rob a sizable number of students of a meaningful education.

These realities, however, are far away in time and space from the contemporary comforts of Holt High School (a claim, however, that teachers at the school might well dispute). More remarkable then that this group of educators pursued the dramatic reforms described in this volume's essays and commentaries. What drove them was not necessity, at least not of the stark, demographic sort, but an idealism that might be called "professional." A local network of school and university mathematics educators seized the opportunity buttressed by the formation of a Professional Development School to work out the practical implications of their commitment to bringing ambitious learning to lower-track students. The teachers saw a chance to work on a central problem in their practice in the company of like-minded educators. What they produced over a ten-year span serves as a model of professionalism in teaching for a number of reasons.

The reform was knowledge-based in significant respects, drawing on advanced disciplinary and pedagogical sources. It took up central issues in the core practices of the profession – curriculum, instruction, and assessment. It placed the practitioner on equal footing with university scholars in working out the program. Consonant with professionalism's ethic of care, the reform put students at the center. And most tellingly, the reform was carried out in a critical spirit that involved frequent testing of assumptions, modifications along the way, and regular attention to evidence of effects. Such a reform stands as the perfect antithesis of externally introduced innovation with its familiar defects – faddish ideas, shallow implementation, administrative careerism.

If the motivation to pursue such a reform over an extended period may be associated with something like professional idealism, this does not yet account for its success. How should we reckon the lessons here, if we believe that this is indeed an important example for American education? The general tendency is to abstract the essential elements, converting them to guiding principles. I suspect, however, that reform of this kind is not easily susceptible to external engineering. It is an organic, emergent process that evolves as participants extend and adjust their ideas in response to evidence and experience. Consequently, we might propose to study such reforms as stories to be shared, to which may be added other stories, all tending toward the general goal of making education an intellectually engaging experience for all students. Cast in such light, we can explore what might be learned from each story, and with a growing collection of such stories we can seek their "family resemblances," to use Wittgenstein's famous metaphor. In this manner, we do not privilege the principles from any one story. The saga of the math reforms at Holt High School uncovers one path, but not the only one, toward the ideal of an education that is at once rigorous and egalitarian. By assembling more stories of this kind, each proceeding from unique, local conditions but sharing certain features, we might build up a knowledge of successful reform under many, varying circumstances. Such knowledge might then fortify similar efforts in an expanding array of American high schools.

* * *

In this spirit, then, here are several conjectures about this case of mathematics reform, identified by the key words, "beliefs," "knowledge," "practices," and "community."

BELIEFS

The first conjecture is that deep instructional reform must break into the circle of seeing and believing. For teachers to genuinely hold high expectations for low-track students, they must come to believe that actions under their control can produce good effects. Research has uncovered a critical link between teacher "sense of efficacy" and student achievement (Ashton & Webb, 1986), but this is the beginning, not the end, of the matter. How to break into the circular relation between expectations and efficacy is the reform puzzle. Teachers must see that a reform "works with this kind of student" in order to believe in it. But to give the reform a real chance, they have to suspend their disbelief in order to try it out – and keep trying in the face of early difficulties and uncertainties – until they achieve the success that offers a "demonstration proof."

Or so it might seem. In truth, though, teachers employ two criteria to judge whether an instructional reform is worth the risk. Teachers tacitly calculate whether a reform helps make the central tasks of teaching more manageable; whether it increases the rewards of teaching relative to the difficulties of making change. And they also ask whether a reform is likely to yield improved learning among more students. Cuban's (1993) history suggests that many teaching reforms failed because they did not meet the first test; numerous first- and third-person accounts of teacher learning testify to the motivating power of the second test. The two tests may not coincide. Reforms that simplify the complexities of teaching may not genuinely improve learning; and reforms with ambitious learning goals may be difficult to carry out. Between these tests the burden of proof differs as well. Teachers can gauge directly and immediately whether a reform benefits the tasks and rewards of teaching. But evidence about effects on students and learning is likely to emerge slowly and ambiguously.

This separation of teaching and learning cannot be hard and fast, of course, but if these observations capture even a partial truth, then teaching reforms that supply more immediate and direct evidence of effects on students and their learning will stand a better chance of prospering. The idea of a "demonstration proof" around student learning takes on particular significance. The results of new teaching must be made public in order that such teaching be validated against the ultimate standard of effects on students. A powerful, even revelatory experience in many teachers' lives comes with the discovery of unimagined student capabilities. Opening up spaces for such encounters may be vital in sustaining teacher faith in the reform.

When Mike Lehman pioneered the assessment reform, he created a space that made both teaching and learning public. The whole community now could witness "performances of meaning" in mathematics. Such demonstrations might reveal that students understood very little beneath their problem-bound grasp of procedural knowledge. Or the community might discover students' increasing conceptual reach along with their capacity to apply mathematical knowledge to new and novel problems. Such performances, and the preparation for them in countless classes, might also open up windows to student thoughts and feelings that teachers previously lacked. And if student performances of meaning began uncovering pleasant surprises concerning what lower-track students were capable of, that would inevitably raise questions about the teaching. What kind of teaching could produce such performances among students who were traditionally written off? So might a widening circle of teachers – and not just math teachers – be intrigued into some reconsideration of their beliefs about student capabilities.

Managing the assessment reform year after year has been onerous. The first time through must have been exciting and scary. No one knew what to expect with public performances whose roles – teacher, student, community member, examiners, and examinees – had never been rehearsed. Gradually, though, the process became familiar, and incremental improvements emerged. Now, with Hawthorne effects worn off, the task is to sustain the vitality of the process and to discover anew the learning possibilities contained within it. The logistics will always be daunting, but the potential for renewal may lie in the annual design of the assessment tasks as these link back to instruction, and in the expanding number of participants brought in to serve as examiners.

The assessment reform, then, did not simplify the core tasks of teaching. It involved more work and increased coordination. But it played a critical role in opening up and making public what students were learning and by extension what new teaching was producing. Deep reform of teaching, I suspect, must operate at least in part through *persuasion*, a point that has not received enough attention in the change literature. As the old saw has it, seeing is believing. The performance assessment allowed the entire school community to see – and to participate in – something extraordinary. The first conjecture, then, is that significant reform in teaching must involve some kind of direct access to student learning that serves several purposes. It reveals what students are capable of. It makes the hard work worthwhile ("we're doing it for the students"). It provides a new basis for continuing work on teaching. And it expands the circle of believers. In short, the assessment reform broke into the expectations–efficacy circle, raising expectations for students and helping to create a context for increased teacher efficacy. Through this reform, the teachers at Holt came to believe more in themselves *and* in their students. The reform was ultimately persuasive because the entire school community could see what students could do if given the chance.

KNOWLEDGE

If one reform puzzle concerns how to influence teacher beliefs, another concerns what kind of knowledge to build instructional reform around. In the Holt math case, one aspect of change looks quite familiar. Chapters describe teachers moving from a teacher-centered, lecturing mode to a problem-based approach, in which teachers "launch" an instructional task; students "explore" individually or in small groups, perhaps with the aid of some technology; the whole class then discusses and evaluates the student inventions; and the lesson culminates with reflection on what has been learned. While this model has a venerable provenance (for one richly detailed, scholarly, and practical exploration of teaching through problems, see Lampert, 2001), the innovation is to employ it in low-track high school math classes, where many would say it could not be effective. Equally prominent in this story, though, is the introduction of a "functions-based" approach to algebra described by the authors as linked to advances in graphing technology. In the algebra made familiar to generations of students, x's and y's are treated as unknowns in equations to be solved. Under the functions-based approach, x's and y's are treated as variables useful in communicating relationships between quantities. Algebra now involves representing change in and accumulation of quantities, and students must learn to work with a variety of representations including Cartesian graphs, symbolic expressions, tables of value, and such informal methods as diagrams, mechanical devices, and the spoken word.

This knowledge transformation seems noteworthy on several counts. First, the reform directed teachers to the core of their practice, which is the teaching and learning of subject matter. Whereas much educational reform takes up matters at one or more removes from the instructional core, this reform operated at the very heart of teaching. The knowledge which teachers had to master centrally involved their subject matter along with the pedagogy of the subject. The reform's knowledge focus directed teachers to the "right stuff," rather than diverting their time and attention to subsidiary matters. Perhaps equally important, though, the reform was grounded deeply in knowledge of subject matter *and* pedagogy, not pedagogy alone. This seems an obvious point, but many instructional reforms – groupwork, for example, or activity-based teaching – have been introduced in content-free ways, leading to predictable shortcomings. When teachers merely change their grouping arrangements or merely begin to use manipulatives in math class, they do not reach deeply into the nature of learning. The outer form of teaching may change, but its inner dynamics remain relatively unaffected.

The power of the reform at Holt High, I believe, stems in part from its concentration at the instructional core and its dual, reinforcing attention to subject matter and pedagogy. The reform simultaneously introduced a new instructional mode – teaching with problems – and a revised conception of algebra that subtly altered student learning experiences.

In this sense, the reform at Holt resembles such other successful and widely cited efforts in mathematics as cognitively guided instruction (CGI) or QUASAR (see, for example, Carpenter *et al.*, 1996; Silver & Stein, 1996). While these projects operate at the elementary and middle levels respectively, there is one important parallel. All three reforms centrally engage teachers in subject-matter-related knowledge. CGI introduced teachers to the research on how children learn particular mathematical operations, supplying a focus on the psychology of learning the subject. QUASAR concentrated on assisting teachers in designing and implementing instructional tasks in middle school mathematics that varied in their cognitive demands. And the algebra reforms at Holt reconceptualized the subject matter itself in conjunction with an innovative pedagogical approach.

The basic conjecture here then is disarmingly simple: the subject matters. Much school reform, however, has begun elsewhere, with governance or school restructuring, for example, or with students, as in efforts to individualize instruction, construct ability groups, or influence motivation. Here, though, the reformers started with the subject in order to reach the students. What opened access to mathematics among students who had been left out was a joint reconceptualization of the subject and its pedagogy. Judging from the character of past reform, starting with the subject must appear counter-intuitive to reformers intent on extending learning to diverse students. Yet this may be a knowledge key of great strategic importance in creating a more inclusive education.

PRACTICES

The Holt case illustrates another conjecture, that it takes practice to change practice. Most change narratives portray teachers as making incremental and partial changes, mixing bits of old and new practice with uncertain effects. But in Jan Simonson's account of Marty Schnepp's teaching, we witness a dramatic change unfolding in three well-rendered acts. This story within the story is interesting in its own right. How was this teacher able to manage this complex shift? Several features stand out.

First, Marty underwent an unusually extensive apprenticeship at Holt High School, beginning as a high school student, then an undergraduate student teacher, then becoming an employed teacher at the school. Jan's account covers the period from 1993 through 1996, but I suspect that Marty worked toward this transformation over an even longer period. He received an unusually long and well-staged induction into an evolving reform practice where master teachers such as Sandy Callis modeled not only the instruction but also the disposition to experiment. Over time, Marty had the opportunity to read about, discuss, observe, and try out new practices in a community that supplied social and technical support. Influences on his teaching included senior teachers in the department and university faculty who shared an interest in exploring progressive approaches to mathematics instruction. In order to translate "theory into practice," Marty needed to see the new practice in action, and he needed the chance to practice it in his own classroom with feedback from others.

The aphorism, "it takes practice to change practice," has this dual meaning. There must *be* a practice to learn from, and there must be a process of induction through which the learner can try out the new practice in the company of other practitioners.

"Practice" in this usage is not simply what's visible in the classroom – grouping arrangements, materials, tasks, discourse – but the assumptions, beliefs, knowledge, and dispositions that inform the more visible aspects. To learn – or to re-learn – a "practice" then is a complex undertaking.

In this case, for example, the practice required a high degree of interactive decision-making as the teacher learned how to design and use mathematics tasks and problems, listen closely to student reasoning, then shape the classroom discourse to gradually build understanding. This new practice involved a major shift in the teacher's role, the development of new skills and knowledge, and deep change in assumptions about the means and ends of teaching. Marty also had to learn to live with the uncertainty and unpredictability entailed by this kind of teaching. He had to embrace the risks involved in opening up the classroom talk to student ideas. And he had to face his own doubts about how well he was managing the process.

To cultivate and sustain teaching of this kind may place particular demands on reform. Given Marty's willingness to undertake transformational change, he still required at least the following supports:

- an extended period of time to work on and work out the new practice;
- other teachers in the department, some with greater experience and expertise, who wanted to work with him on this teaching; and
- periodic access to expertise outside the school that supplied ideas, suggestions, encouragement, and connection to larger currents of professional reform.

These elements were available in this case, and they supported the gradual extension of the reforms to a widening circle of teachers in the department.

Change of this magnitude is a rare event in schools. Evolution, not revolution, is the dominant metaphor for teacher change. This case, however, raises the prospect that change of this far-reaching nature may be needed to realize the goal of engaging lower-track students in meaningful mathematics. If so, then the conditions for teacher learning in schools assume major importance, and the Holt math department may supply important clues about what will be required.

COMMUNITY

A final conjecture reinforces a prominent finding in the school-reform literature about the importance of community among teachers. Along with the profound changes in curriculum, assessment, and instruction, a transformation in social relationships took place as well, and this was integral to the reform.

Several features of the community that coalesced to support this reform seem significant. The community's focus was the discipline of mathematics. The membership extended laterally across organizations rather than being embedded in a single organizational hierarchy. The community encouraged plural, status-equalizing forms of expertise that recognized the importance of knowing students, knowing subject matter, knowing pedagogy, and knowing the larger community being served. And the community included gradations of experience from early novice to master, which stimulated multi-directional professional learning unified around a reform vision of mathematics teaching. Teachers learned about mathematics. Teacher educators learned about high school teaching. Experienced teachers taught novices even as they were learning how to be teacher educators. New teachers learned from veterans and in turn encouraged other veterans to join in.

Communities with these features have been identified as "professional" in the organizational literature (e.g., Weick & McDaniel, 1989), and they serve a number of functions. One is to articulate the values that guide practice. The educators engaged in this reform pursued a very difficult ideal – meaningful mathematics for lower-track students – that cuts against the grain of tradition and societal expectations. They had to work out a vision of mathematics that made connections to core values of democracy, equity, an ethic of care, and ultimately, humanity. Such values and their translation into more particular beliefs and practices are essential and often overlooked aspects of professionalism. Leadership manuals these days brim with references to the importance of "vision" and "mission" but such advice can be maddeningly elusive. Too many teachers can testify to the hollowness of developing a bureaucratically mandated mission statement. This case reveals how a professional community gradually and purposefully developed a values-driven mission that informed all of the work. Without this community, the mission building could not have been accomplished.

Then, the community also served both to *author* and *authorize* the reform. Leadership in this reform was distributed broadly with contributions from many participants. That the whole community authored this reform is reflected in the many voices composing this narrative. To the now-familiar aphorism that it takes a village to raise a child we may add, it takes a community to invent a practice. Moreover, this community lent authority to this reform. The prestige associated with Holt as a Professional Development School, the involvement of university professors, and the commitment of highly respected teachers with connections to the local community combined to authorize the departure that the math department embarked on. Professional knowledge in its several varieties, resident in this community, legitimated the reform.

Finally, this community served two additional functions. When teachers and schools innovate, they face high degrees of uncertainty and unpredictability. The emotional costs are correspondingly high. Teachers may be resolved around their ideals yet still feel uncertain, even conflicted, about whether the new practice will work or whether they can master it. A professional community supplies the social support and the conviviality needed to persevere. Although understated in most of the individual chapters and commentaries (perhaps with the exception of Chapter 14), I believe that such support supplied buoyancy and renewal to this reform work.

The theory of professional organization emphasizes a related point. If practice can be codified in routines, standard procedures, or technologies, then bureaucratic forms of organization may be efficient. But if practice involves non-routine judgment, information use, and decision-making, then the professional form of organization is optimal as it supplies access to expert sources of knowledge that help to mediate complex tasks and problems. Although couched in the abstract language of organizational theory, these observations fit the reforms pursued at Holt High School. A new technology – the graphing calculator – played an important role in the story, but the work on curriculum, instruction, and assessment involved teachers in complex practices that placed heavy demands on skills of interpretation, judgment, and problem-solving. Such work could not be managed via bureaucratic oversight or standard operating procedures. Rather, it required participation in a professional community of the kind that formed at Holt.

* * *

This case of mathematics reform at Holt High School can be glossed in other ways. Indeed, one of the pleasures of reading this case is to reflect on what we might learn from it. Different readers will reach different conclusions, which signifies the richness of the narrative. My point of departure, however, is the conviction that we must reinvent the American high school in some important respects due to its historically conditioned incapacity to serve students outside the middle class, academically able mainstream. Various arguments have been advanced in support, but I find the demographic changes most compelling, coupled with the rising standard for what it means to be educated in our society. High school reform takes many shapes with initiative most often from the outside in, proceeding from structural change to presumed instructional effects. The record of such reform, however, is not promising (see Elmore *et al.*, 1996). Perhaps we need to consider anew how to reform the high school from the inside out, drawing on the best thinking of those currently engaged in working there.

This multi-layered account is one contribution to this difficult and important task. Certain general features of the story are constant companions to any successful school reform. The duration of the effort, the resources that were mobilized (including infusions of PDS funding), and the stability of the leadership were clearly essential. Perhaps, too, a new technology – the graphing calculator – played a greater role than my commentary has suggested. We might hope that technology will enable the transformations that we need. These factors might be regarded as both necessary and extraordinary. They cannot be easily transferred to rurally isolated schools or to impoverished inner-city schools. In this sense, then, high schools must construct reforms out of their own distinctive circumstances. But I propose that the Holt story contains some provocative leads for the needed reforms. These may be expressed in aphoristic form:

- *Seeing Is Believing, and Vice Versa.* Reform must simultaneously raise expectations for students' capabilities, and persuade teachers that they can summon extraordinary learning in students.
- *The Subject Matters.* With students' minds in mind, begin with the subject matter of instruction.
- *It Takes Practice to Change Practice.* Orient reform around new practices that can be shared, studied, emulated, and extended among teachers and with other relevant experts.
- *It Takes a Community to Invent a Practice.* Purposefully build the social and professional relationships that will support reformed practice over the long haul.

This case contains two final implications. The ideal of professionalism in teaching must not be retired. In an era that favors stronger government control of schooling (standards, mandated testing, school accreditation, punishments, and rewards), greater parental choice over schooling (charters, open enrollment plans, vouchers), and increased privatization of educational services (contracting, education management organizations, proprietary school designs), the professional resource has been overlooked. Can we make major changes inside of our schools without enlisting the hearts and minds of the educators who work there? I doubt it. The motivation to engage in reform, the expert knowledge and skill, the organizational form represented in this case all draw on the professional ideal, which must be more vigorously fortified in the mix of grand strategies employed to reform our schools.

And the case brings to mind what the philosopher Tom Green (1983) has called the "equity of excellence." He argued that there is a natural priority among ideals such that, "policies in pursuit of educational excellence are more likely to produce gains in equity than policies in pursuit of equality are likely to produce gains in excellence" (p. 335). The protagonists in this account began with an equity goal in mind, to enhance the learning of students who have traditionally been left out or left behind. But the starting point was not disaggregated test scores or remedial instruction or compensatory strategies or even accelerated learning. It was a fundamental conception of excellence in mathematics teaching and learning that opened the portal to all. The math reforms at Holt High School did realize gains in equity but through the pursuit of excellence. The implications for reform are profound, and this may be the most important lesson of the case. Beginning with visions of intellectual excellence that form the basis for transformed practice may be the surest hope for the egalitarian dream that is education in America.

Epilogue

We began to work on this book in 1999, four years after the external funding for our PDS effort decreased dramatically. Since then, there have been numerous changes. Though the mathematics department at Holt High School has been more stable than those in many schools, teachers have come and gone. And, the university participants have also moved. Some of the MSU graduate students have graduated and gone on to other pursuits. Post-docs and faculty have gone on to other institutions. People have married, had children. The students described in this book completed high school and have gone on to a range of endeavors.

The institutions have also changed. In 2004–2005, Holt High School entered a new building, across the street from the 9th grade that now occupies the old junior high school building. While the two schools still have two separate math departments, over time, this may change. Such a move would bring a number of new teachers into the department, formerly from the grade 8–9 junior high school. The school also affiliated with the Coalition of Essential Schools. MSU has changed some aspects of its teacher education program, but the major features of the five-year program, most crucially the year-long internships, are still in place. And, there continue to be ties between members of the Holt High School mathematics department and mathematics educators and teacher educators at MSU. And, as this book goes to press, the State of Michigan is changing its high school graduation requirements dramatically. The push is to have all students graduate having studied Algebra 2, an ambitious goal given where schools like Holt were in 1990.

From this distance in time, the years of the PDS relationship between the high school and the university were exciting times that shaped us in important ways. Those of us who had the chance to participate in the work during those years miss it terribly.

Those experiences shaped us. We have experienced the impact of instructional activities that value mathematical sense-making for a wide range of individuals. The conviction has stayed with us that, if given the opportunity, students reason in mathematically sensible ways. We continue to believe that mathematical activity is the province of all of us, students and teachers alike, that it is not limited to those who are more likely to find it initially intuitive and sensible, and that we can find better ways to teach mathematics to more of our students.

We continue to consider teaching a challenging, though often rewarding, but insufficiently recognized, professional activity. Our work together has strengthened our convictions about the importance of valuing the expertise of teachers. We hope that one day this expertise will be valued enough to change the working conditions of teachers. We imagine opportunities in teaching that will allow all teachers greater room for reflection and professional autonomy, for example, greater opportunities for mathematics teachers to explore the mathematics that they teach.

That does not mean that we advocate *laissez-faire* policies that leave teachers to their own devices and unaccountable. We embrace the notion that teachers and schools must take responsibility for their work with students and that decisions about what to do with students should be based on evidence that is discussed and debated.

But we find many of the ways that such goals are currently being pursued counterproductive. The goal of improving student achievement for all students often seems to suggest policies that involve restricting teacher autonomy in order to hold teachers accountable for their students' performance. These are not the policies that we seek and which accord with our experience. In our experience, strides were made in educating a wider range of students when a supportive departmental culture and interesting mathematical ideas excited teachers and challenged them to rethink their practices. Such excitement seems hard to generate with policies that, utilizing rhetoric of accountability, leave teachers little room to respond to their students. We seek another way: a profession that challenges itself to address some of its most difficult issues, while recognizing that such work is always local and personal and cannot be scripted from a distance, a country that is interested in education, but also allows educators a degree of professional autonomy.

Initiatives designed in this way wouldn't cut corners, for example, by simply requiring the passing of a cut-point on a single assessment of teachers' knowledge, or requiring certain mathematics or education classes in a teachers' preservice program. The kind of professional, collaborative atmosphere we imagine, and were a part of at Holt High School, requires informed leadership, where teachers are challenged and supported. In such an initiative, teachers are not only held accountable for student learning, but for professionally set expectations of practice. Such expectations would require teachers to work together and with others from outside to continue to learn rigorous mathematics, explore and hone effective instructional strategies, and create useful and reflective assessment practices that give concrete evidence of student outcomes. Such expectations would require shifts from the current organization of the high school teacher's workday.

Moving forward from our experiences together, we seek to bring these insights with us as we tackle new and continuing endeavors.

Cast of characters

Editors

Daniel Chazan is an Ed.D from Harvard Graduate School of Education and a faculty member in Teacher Education at MSU. He taught one period a day at Holt High School for three years in the early 1990s. For two of those years, he and Sandy Callis co-taught one section of Algebra 1. He is an editor of this volume and author of an essay in Part III on teaching a particular view of school algebra and its impact on his understandings of school mathematics. He also co-authored essays in Part I and III. Dan is now a member of the Center for Mathematics Education at the University of Maryland, Baltimore.

Michael Lehman is a graduate of Central Michigan University, has taught at Holt since 1977, and has been department chair at Holt High School since 1992. He is an editor of this volume and author of an essay in the first section on performance exams and one in the third section on the beginnings of the MSU/Holt High School PDS effort.

Sandra Callis, formerly Bethell in print, is a graduate of MSU and holds master's degrees both from Michigan State University and Western Michigan University. She student-taught at Eastern High School and has taught mathematics and Spanish at Holt Junior High School and High School. She has shared Algebra 1 teaching assignments with Dan Chazan and with a number of teachers at Holt. After a stint in the Holt District's curriculum office, she is now principal of Washington Woods Middle School, Holt, Michigan. She is an editor of this volume, co-author on two essays in the first section, and author with her students of two essays in the second section.

Teacher authors and responders

Marty Schnepp grew up in Holt, is a graduate of MSU, student-taught for Bill York at Holt High School (his field instructor was Sandy

Callis!), and has taught at Holt since 1991 after a three-year stint in the San Diego Public Schools. Marty holds an MSU master's degree. He has also been involved in the SimCalc project at TERC in Cambridge, Massachusetts and shared Algebra 1 teaching assignments with four other teachers in the department. He is co-author of an essay in the first section, sole author of an essay about his Calculus class in the first section, and one in the third section on his view of the role of theory in practice.

Craig Huhn is a graduate of MSU, interned together with Adam Kelly at Holt with Mike Lehman as mentor and Whitney Johnson as field instructor, and has taught at Holt since 1999. Craig edited an essay on mathematical conversations among teachers for Part III of this volume.

Kelly Hodges is a graduate of MSU and holds a master's degree in mathematics from Western Michigan University. She student-taught at Holt with Bill York and taught at Holt from 1992 until 1999. She currently works as a teacher educator at MSU. Kelly is co-author of an essay in Part I and sole author of an essay in the third section about being a mentor teacher.

Teacher responders

Dave Hildebrandt is a graduate of the University of Connecticut and holds a master's degree and teaching certification from MSU. He was an intern at Holt with Mike Lehman as mentor and Jan Simonson as field instructor and has taught at Holt since 1994.

Kellie Huhn, nee Bachman, is a graduate of MSU and holds an MSU master's degree. She interned at Holt with Mike Lehman as mentor and Jan Simonson as field instructor and has taught at Holt since 1996.

Sean Carmody is a graduate of MSU, interned at Holt with Mike Lehman as mentor and Gary Lewis as field instructor, and has taught at Holt since 2000.

Laura Kueffner is a graduate of MSU, interned at Holt with Sandy Callis as mentor and Whitney Johnson as field instructor, taught for two years in northern Michigan, and has taught at Holt since 2001.

Adam Kelly is a graduate of MSU, interned together with Craig Huhn at Holt with Mike Lehman as mentor and Whitney Johnson as field instructor, and has taught at Holt since 1999.

Tom Almedia taught for one year at Holt Junior High School and then for two years at Holt High School from 1998 until 2001.

Holt student authors

Nicolas Miller was a student at Holt High School and co-authored an essay with Sandy Callis. Upon graduation from high school, he did not immediately pursue further education.

Ryan Mosley was a student at Holt High School and co-authored an essay with Sandy Callis. After graduating, he studied both at Lansing Community College and Michigan State University and now runs a painting company in the area.

Carolyn Ososkie was a student at Holt High School and co-authored an essay with Sandy Callis. After graduating from high school, she went on to studies at Lansing Community College and Michigan State University. She plans to do postgraduate education in mechanical engineering.

Non-Holt authors

Bill Rosenthal holds a PhD in mathematics from SUNY Stony Brook and is currently a visiting instructor in the Department of Secondary Education at the University of South Florida in Tampa. From 1992 to 1998, he was a mainstay of the secondary mathematics component of MSU's teacher education program. He is author of two essays in this volume, one co-authored with Jan Simonson.

Jan Simonson is a 1998 PhD in Teacher Education from MSU and an associate professor at Calvin College, Grand Rapids, MI. From 1993 to 1998, she participated in PDS work at Holt and in MSU's teacher education program as both field instructor and course instructor. She is sole author of two essays in this volume. She is also co-author on essays in Parts II and III.

Whitney Johnson has her PhD in Teacher Education at MSU and is now a postdoctoral fellow at the University of Maryland. She has participated in the secondary mathematics component of MSU's teacher education program as both field instructor and course instructor. She is the author of an essay in Part III.

Dara Sandow is a PhD candidate in Teacher Education at MSU. She has participated in the secondary mathematics component of MSU's teacher education program as both field instructor and course instructor and contributed to one of the essays in Part III.

Candy Hamilton is a PhD candidate in Counseling, Educational Psychology, and Special Education at MSU. She is the author of an essay in Part II.

Cesar Larriva was a faculty member in Teacher Education at MSU and is now on the faculty of California State Polytechnic University, Pomona. He has participated in the secondary mathematics component of MSU's teacher education program. He is the author of an essay in Part II.

Gary Sykes is a faculty member in Educational Administration and Teacher Education at MSU and author of the concluding essay in this volume. Gary participated in writing *Tomorrow's schools* for the Holmes Group.

David ben-Haim is a faculty member at the University of Haifa in Israel. While on sabbatical in 1994–1995, he participated in PDS efforts at Holt High School. He co-authored one of the essays in Part III.

Notes

Preface

1 As will be illustrated in Part II, a number of students now take more than one math course at the same time. This phenomenon has a small impact on reducing the disparity in percentage of students taught over the last decade.

2 Since the 2000–2001 school year, the number of students in the school has continued to increase. The number of sections of math courses has stayed consistently around 40, while the number of students in each section has increased. Overall, the percentage of students in the school seen by the mathematics department has remained consistently where it was in 2000–2001. And, the size of the mathematics department has not changed substantially.

1 Introduction to our case study

1 Although it is not an explicit focus of any of the essays in this text, Holt High School has also played an important role in the education of doctoral students intending to be teacher educators.

2 Assessment

1 I have noted that students who go through the process more than once have very similar grades. Therefore, there seems to be a certain level of consistency, and I continue to work for ways to increase it. In addition, with a few exceptions, students seem to be comfortable with their scores. I have had only one case where I needed to discuss a grade with the judges after a student raised an issue. In this case, after listening to the judges and having one of them discuss the grade with the student, the grade remained unchanged.

Part II Student experience of the curriculum

1 In the late 1990s, the state began to make this data about student performance available to the public on its website. Starting in the year 2000, Governor John Engler even introduced an award for the high school in each athletic conference to have the largest number of students whose performance on all the high school proficiency exams was either a 1 or 2, making them eligible for a Michigan Merit Award, worth $2,500 towards continued education. Holt High School has won the award in its league each of the years it has been

given. However, since this award is based on absolute numbers of students achieving at this level, it is greatly influenced by the percentage of students taking the MEAP. And, it is unclear what the contribution of the mathematics department is to this school-wide result.

12 Interlude C: student teaching/internship

1 I have also interviewed two other matched pairs of Holt and non-Holt interns, but will limit my discussion here to this one pair.

13 Time and respect

1 In this section, we refer to Perry Lanier as Dr. Lanier to remind readers of the initial distance between teachers in the school and university faculty, and the ongoing power differential between them. In day-to-day work, such references became uncommon.

18 Interlude D: learning math from coursework conversation

1 A proof in class that this sequence $\left\{1 + \dfrac{1}{n}\right\}$ converges to 1 would have gone as follows.

$$\left|1 + \frac{1}{n} - 1\right| = \left|\frac{1}{n}\right| = \frac{1}{n}. \quad Let \ \frac{1}{n} = \varepsilon \Rightarrow n = \frac{1}{\varepsilon}. \ and \ thus \ we \ should \ take \ N = \frac{1}{\varepsilon}.$$

20 Graduate study

1 These statistics come from the Cross City Campaign for Urban School Reform. See their website at www.crosscity.org/pubs/flashfacts.htm.

References

Angus, D. L. & Mirel, J. E. (1999). *The failed promise of the American high school, 1890–1995.* New York: Teachers College Press.

Ashton, P. & Webb, R. (1986). *Making a difference: Teachers' sense of efficacy and student achievement.* New York: Longman.

Barnes, D. (1976). *From communication to curriculum.* London: Penguin.

Ben-Peretz, M. (1990). *The Teacher–curriculum encounter: Freeing teachers from the tyranny of texts.* Albany: State University of New York Press.

Bensman, D. (2000). *Central Park East and its graduates: "Learning by heart."* New York: Teachers College Press.

Bracey, Gerald (1992). If you ask me – Cut out Algebra! Mostly it's a useless, impractical exercise. *Washington Post,* 12 June.

Britton, E. D., Paine, L., Pimm, D., & Raizen, S. (2003). *Comprehensive teacher induction: Systems for early career learning.* Dordrecht: Kluwer.

Britzman, D. (1991). *Practice makes practice: A critical study of learning to teach.* Albany: State University of New York Press.

Calinger, R. (1995). *Classics of mathematics.* Englewood Cliffs, NJ: Prentice Hall.

Carpenter, T. P., Fenema, E., & Franke, M. L. (1996). Cognitively guided instruction: A knowledge base for reform in primary mathematics instruction. *The Elementary School Journal,* 97(1): 3–20.

Chazan, D. (1996). Algebra for all students? *Journal of Mathematical Behavior,* 15(4): 455–477.

Chazan, D. (1999). On teachers' mathematical knowledge and student exploration: A personal story about teaching a technologically supported approach to school algebra. *International Journal of Computers for Mathematical Learning,* 4: 121–149.

Chazan, D. (2000). *Beyond formulas in mathematics and teaching: Dynamics of the high school algebra classroom.* New York: Teachers College Press.

Chazan, D. & Schnepp, M. (2002). Methods, goals, beliefs, commitments, and manner in teaching: Dialogue against a Calculus backdrop. In Brophy, J. (ed.), *Social constructivist teaching* (pp. 171–195). Greenwich, CT: JAI Press.

Chazan, D. & Yerushalmy, M. (2003). On appreciating the cognitive complexity of school algebra: Research on algebra learning and directions of curricular change. In Kilpatrick, J., Schifter, D. & Martin, G. (eds), *A research companion to the principles and standards for school mathematics.* Reston, VA: NCTM.

Chazan, D., Larriva, C., & Sandow, D. (1999). What kind of mathematical knowledge supports teaching for "conceptual understanding?" Preservice teachers and the solving of equations. *Proceedings of the Twenty-third Annual Conference of the International Group for the Psychology of Mathematics Education, 23*(11): 197–200.

Cherryholmes, C. (1988). *Power and criticism: Poststructural investigations in education.* New York: Teachers College Press.

Clandinin, D. J. & Connelly, F. M. (1992). Teacher as curriculum maker. In Jackson, P. W. (ed.), *Handbook of research on curriculum* (pp. 363–401). New York: Macmillan.

Cohen, D. & Ball, D. (1999). Instruction, capacity, and improvement. CPRE Research Report Series RR-43. July, University of Pennsylvania. Downloaded from www.cpre.org on 8 January 2002.

Connelly, E. M. & Clandinin, D. J. (1988). *Teachers as curriculum planners: Narratives of experience.* New York: Teachers College Press.

Cuban, L. (1993). *How teachers taught: Constancy and change in American classrooms, 1880–1990* (2nd edn). New York: Teachers College Press.

Cusick, P. (1983). *The egalitarian ideal and the American high school: Studies of three schools.* New York: Longman.

Davis, B. (1997). Listening for differences: An evolving conception of mathematics teaching. *Journal for Research in Mathematics Education 28*(3): 355–376.

Davis, P. & Hersh, R. (1981). *The mathematical experience.* Boston, MA: Houghton Mifflin.

Davis, P. & Hersh, R. (1986). *Descartes dream: The world according to mathematics.* San Diego, CA: Harcourt, Brace, Jovanovich.

Devlin, K. (2000). *The math gene: how mathematical thinking evolved and why numbers are like gossip.* New York: W. H. Freeman and Company.

Dewey, J. (1902/1990). *The school and society: The child and the curriculum.* Chicago, IL: University of Chicago Press.

Dewey, J. (1904/1964). The relation of theory to practice in education. In Borrowman, M. L. (ed.), *Teacher education in America: A documentary history* (pp. 140–171). New York: Teachers College Press.

Dewey, J. (1990). The relation of theory to practice in education. In Archambault, R. D. (ed.), *John Dewey on education: Selected writings.* New York: Modern Library.

Dolciani, M. & Wooton, W. (1970/1973). *Modern algebra: Structure and method, Book One.* Boston, MA: Houghton-Mifflin.

Dugdale, S. & Kibbey, D. (1986). *Interpreting Graphs.* Pleasantville, NY: Sunburst.

Eckert, P. (1989). *Jocks and burnouts: Social categories and identity in the high school.* New York: Teachers College Press.

Elmore, R., Peterson, P., & McCarthey, S. (1996). *Restructuring in the classroom. Teaching, learning, and school organization.* San Francisco, CA: Jossey Bass.

Erickson, F. & Schultz, J. (1991). Student's experience of the curriculum. In Jackson, P. W. (ed.), *Handbook of research on curriculum* (pp. 465–485). New York: Macmillan.

Ernest, P. (1991). *The philosophy of mathematics education.* Bristol, PA: Falmer Press.

Ernest, P. (1998). *Social constructivism as a philosophy of mathematics.* Albany: State University of New York Press.

Fauvel, J. & Gray, J. (1987). *The history of mathematics: A reader.* Milton Keynes: Open University and Macmillan Press Ltd.

Fawcett, H. P. (1938). *The nature of proof: The thirteenth yearbook of the national council of teachers of mathematics.* New York: Bureau of Publications, Teachers College, Columbia University.

Feiman-Nemser, S. (1983). Learning to teach. In Shulman, L. S. & Sykes, G. (eds), *Handbook of teaching and policy* (pp. 150–170). New York: Longman.

Fey, J. (1989). School algebra for the year 2000. In Wagner, S. & Kieran, C. (eds), *Research issues in the learning and teaching of algebra* (pp. 199–214). Hillsdale, NJ: Erlbaum.

Fey, J. T. & Heid, M. K. (1999). *Concepts in algebra: A technological approach.* Chicago, IL: Everyday Learning.

Gardner, M. (1998). The new new math. *New York Review of Books,* (45): 14.

Geen, A. G. (1985). Team teaching in the secondary schools of England and Wales. *Educational Review,* 37(1): 29–38.

Goldenberg, P. (1988). Mathematics, metaphors, and human factors: Mathematical, technical, and pedagogical challenges in the educational use of graphical representations of functions. *Journal of Mathematical Behavior,* 7: 135–173.

Good, T., Grouws, D., & Ebmeier, H. (1983). *Active mathematics teaching.* New York: Longman.

Goodlad, J. (1984). *A place called school.* New York: McGraw-Hill.

Gore, J. (1993). *The struggle for pedagogies: Critical and feminist discourses as regimes of truth.* New York: Routledge.

Gormas, J. (1998). The centrality of a teacher's professional transformation in the development of mathematical power: A case study of one high school mathematics teacher. Unpublished doctoral dissertation, College of Education, Michigan State University, East Lansing.

Green, T. (1983). Excellence, equity, and equality. In Shulman, L. & Sykes, G. (eds), *Handbook of teaching and policy* (pp. 318–341). New York: Longman.

Gutiérrez, R. (1996). Practices, beliefs, and cultures of high school mathematics departments: Understanding their influences on student advancement. *Journal of Curriculum Studies,* 28(5): 495–530.

Hall, R. (1990). *Making mathematics on paper: Constructing representations of stories about related linear functions.* Irvine: University of California Press.

Hall, R., Kibler, D., Wenger, E., & Truxaw, C. (1989). Exploring the episodic structure of algebra story problem solving. *Cognition and Instruction,* 6(3): 223–283.

Heid, M. K., Choate, J., Sheets, C., & Zbiek, R. M. (1995). *Algebra in a technological world.* Reston, VA: NCTM.

Hill, R. (2004) On the transition in mathematics from high school to Michigan State University, October. Downloaded from www.math.msu.edu/~hill/Transition.pdf on 15 April 2005.

Holmes Group (1986). *Tomorrow's teachers*. East Lansing, MI: Holmes Group.

Holmes Group (1990). *Tomorrow's schools: Principles for the design of Professional Development Schools*. East Lansing, Michigan: Author.

Horn, I. (in press). Fast kids, slow kids, lazy kids: Framing the mismatch problem in mathematics teachers' conversations. *Journal of the Learning Sciences*.

Jackson, A. (1997). The math wars: California battles it out over mathematics education reform (Part I & II). *Notices of the American Mathematical Society, 44*: 695–702, 817–823.

Janvier, C. (1998). The notion of chronicle as an epistemological obstacle to the concept of function. *Journal of Mathematical Behavior, 17*(1): 79–104.

Kaput, J. (1995). Long term algebra reform: Democratizing access to big ideas. *The Algebra Initiative Colloquium* (Vol. I, pp. 33–49). Lacampagne, C., Blair W., & Kaput, J. Washington, DC: US Department of Education.

Karmiloff-Smith, A. & Inhelde, B. (1977). If you want to get ahead, get a theory. In Johnson-Laird, P. N. and Wason, P. C. (eds), *Thinking: Readings in cognitive science*. Cambridge: Cambridge University Press.

Kincaid, J. (1996). *The autobiography of my mother*. New York: Farrar, Straus, and Giroux, p. 132.

Kirsner, S. A. & Bethell, S. (1992). Creating a flexible and responsive learning environment for general mathematics students. East Lansing, Michigan State University, National Center for Research on Teacher Learning.

Koendinger, K. & Tabachneck, H. (1994). *Two strategies are better than one: Multiple strategy use in word problem solving*. New Orleans, LA: American Educational Research Association.

Lacampagne, C., Blair, W., & Kaput, J. (eds) (1995). *The algebra initiative colloquium*. Washington, DC: US Department of Education.

Lakatos, I. (1976). *Proofs and refutations: The logic of mathematical discovery*. Cambridge: Cambridge University Press.

Lakoff, G. & Núñez, R. (2000). *Where mathematics comes from: How the embodied mind brings mathematics into being*. New York: Basic Books.

Lampert, M. (1990). When the problem is not the question and the solution is not the answer: Mathematical knowing and teaching. *American Educational Research Journal, 27*(1): 29–63.

Lampert, M. (2001). *Teaching problems and the problems of teaching*. New Haven, CT: Yale University Press.

Lanier, J. E. & Little, J. W. (1986). Research on teacher education. In Wittrock, M. C. (ed.), *Handbook of research on teaching* (2nd edn) (pp. 527–569). New York: Macmillan.

Lappan, G. (1998). Texts and teachers: Keys to improved mathematics learning, July. www.nctm.org/news/pastpresident/1998_07_lappan.htm Downloaded on Wednesday, 8 May 2002.

Lappan, G., Fey, J., Fitzgerald, W., Friel, S., & Phillips, E. (2002). *Connected mathematics project*. Glenview, IL: Prentice Hall.

Larson, R., Hostetler, R., & Edwards, B. (1997). *Trigonometry: A graphing approach with technology updates*. Boston, MA: Houghton Mifflin.

Lave, J. & Wenger, E. (1991). *Situated learning: Legitimate peripheral participation*. Cambridge: Cambridge University Press.

Lee, L. F. (1996). *Algebraic understanding: The search for a model in the mathematics education community.* Unpublished dissertation. Quebec: Université du Québec A Montréal.

Lester, F. (1994). Musing on problem solving research. *Journal for Research in Mathematics Education, 25*(6): 660–675.

Lial, M. & and Miller, C. (1977). *Trigonometry.* Glenview, IL: Scott, Foresman and Co.

Lindsay, P. & Norman, D. (1977). *Human information processing: An introduction to psychology.* New York: Academic Press.

Little, J. W. (1990). The persistence of privacy: autonomy and initiative in teachers' professional relations. *Teachers College Record, 91*(4): 509–536.

Lortie, D. (1975). *Schoolteacher: A sociological study.* Chicago, IL: University of Chicago Press.

McCarthy, C. (1991). Who needs algebra? *Washington Post,* 20 April.

McConnell, J., Brown, S., Eddins, S., Hackwarth, M., Sachs, L., Woodward., E., Flanders, J., Hirschhorn, D., Hynes, C., Polonsky, L., & Usiskin, Z. (1990). *The University of Chicago school mathematics project: Algebra.* Glenview, IL: Scott, Foresman and Company.

Mitchell, J. H., Hawkins, E. F., Jakweth, P. M., Stancavage, F. B., & Dossey, J. A. (1999). *Student work and teacher practices in mathematics.* Washington D.C., National Center for Education Statistics.

Monk, S. (1992). Students' understanding of a function given by a physical model. In Dubinsky, E. & Harel, G. (eds), *The concept of function: Aspects of epistemology and pedagogy* (pp. 175–195). Washington, DC: Mathematics Association of America.

Moschkovich, J., Schoenfeld, A. H., & Arcavi, A. (1993). Aspects of understanding: On multiple perspectives and representations of linear relations and connections among them. In Romberg, T. A., Fennema, E., & Carpenter, T. P. (eds), *Integrating research on the graphical representation of function* (pp. 69–100). Hillsdale, NJ: Erlbaum.

National Academy of Education (1999). Recommendations regarding research priorities. To the National Educational Research Policy and Priorities Board, March. Downloaded from www.nae.nyu.edu on 8 January 2002.

National Council of Teachers of Mathematics (1989). *Curriculum and evaluation standards for school mathematics.* Reston, VA: Author.

National Council of Teachers of Mathematics (1991). *Professional Standards for Teaching Mathematics.* Reston, VA: Author.

National Council of Teachers of Mathematics (1995). *Assessment Standards,* Reston, VA: Author.

National Council of Teachers of Mathematics (2000). *Principles and standards for school mathematics.* Reston, VA: Author.

National Council of Teachers of Mathematics Algebra Working Group (1998). A framework for constructing a vision of algebra: A discussion document. In National Council of Teachers of Mathematics & Mathematical Sciences Education Board, *The nature and role of algebra in the K–14 curriculum: Proceedings of a national symposium* (pp. 145–190). Washington, DC: National Academy Press.

Nelson, B. S. (1995). *Inquiry and the development of teaching: Issues in the transformation of mathematics teaching*. Newton, MA: Center for the Development of Teaching Paper Series.

Nemirovsky, R. (1994). On ways of symbolizing: The case of Laura and the velocity sign. *Journal of Mathematical Behavior, 13*(4): 389–422.

Nemirovsky, R. (1996). A functional approach to algebra: Two issues that emerge. In Bednarz, N., Kieran, C. & Lee, L. (eds), *Approaches to algebra: Perspectives for research and teaching* (pp. 295–316). Dordrecht: Kluwer Academic Publishers.

Ohanian, S. (1999). *One size fits few*. Portsmouth, NH: Heinemann.

Packer, G. (2000). *Blood of the Liberals*. New York: Farrar, Straus and Giroux.

Piccioto, H. & Wah, A. (1994). *Algebra: Themes, concepts, and tools*. Alpharetta, GA: Creative Publications.

Popkewitz, T. (2004). The alchemy of the mathematics curriculum: Inscriptions and the fabrication of the child. *American Educational Research Journal, 41*(1): 3–34.

Roberts, W. (1991). Algebra is not just math, it's the language of science. *Minneapolis Star Tribune*, 27 April.

Rogoff, B. (1994). Developing understanding of the idea of communities of learners. *Mind, Culture, and Activity*, 1: 209–229.

Romberg, T. A. (1992). Problematic features of the school mathematics curriculum. In Jackson, P. W. (ed.), *Handbook of research on curriculum* (pp. 749–788). New York: Macmillan.

Rosenthal, B. (1989). *The satanic calculus*. Self-published volume used as in-house text for the course Humanistic Calculus at Ursinus College. Available from the author.

Russell, B. (1910). The study of mathematics. In *Mysticism and Logic*. London: Penguin.

Schifter, D. (1995). Teachers' changing conceptions of the nature of mathematics: Enactment in the classroom. In Nelson, B. (ed.), *Inquiry and the development of teaching: Issues in the transformation of mathematics teaching* (pp. 17–26). Newton, MA: Center for the Development of Teaching Paper Series, Education Development Center.

Schmidt, W. H., McKnight, C. C., & Raizen, S. (eds) (1997). *A splintered vision: An investigation of U.S. science and mathematics education*. Dordrecht: Kluwer.

Schmidt, W. H., McKnight, C. C., Cogan, L. S., Jakwerth, P. M., & Houang, R. T. (1999). *Facing the consequences: Using TIMSS for a closer look at US mathematics and science education*. Dordrecht: Kluwer.

Schnepp, M. & Chazan, D. (2004). Incorporating experiences of motion into a Calculus classroom (videopaper). *Educational studies in mathematics, 57*(3): 303–321.

Schnepp, M. & Nemirovsky, R. (2001). Constructing a foundation for the Fundamental Theorem of Calculus. In Cuoco, A. (ed.), *The role of representation in school mathematics* (pp. 90–102). Reston, VA: NCTM.

Schoenfeld, A. (1988). When good teaching leads to bad results: The disasters of "well-taught" mathematics courses. *Educational Psychologist, 32*(2): 146–166.

Schoenfeld, A., Smith, J., & Arcavi, A. (1990). Learning: The microgenetic analysis of one student's understanding of a complex subject matter domain.

In Glaser, R. (ed.), *Advances in instructional psychology* (pp. 55–175). Hillsdale, NJ: Erlbaum.

Schubert, W. (1986). *Curriculum: Perspective, paradigm, and possibility*. New York: Macmillan.

Schwab, J. (1978). Education and the structure of the disciplines. In Westbury, I. & Wilkof, N. (eds), *Science, curriculum, and liberal education: Selected essays* (pp. 229–274). Chicago, IL: University of Chicago Press.

Schwartz, J. (1997). Shuttling between the particular and the general: Reflections on the role of conjecture and hypothesis in the generation of knowledge in science and mathematics. In Perkin, D., Schwartz, J., Katz, M. M., & Wiske, M. S. (eds), *Software goes to school* (pp. 93–105). Oxford: Oxford University Press.

Schwartz, J. & Yerushalmy, M. (1992). Getting students to function in and with algebra. In Dubinsky, E. & Harel, G. (eds), *The concept of function: Aspects of epistemology and pedagogy* (pp. 261–289). Washington, DC: Mathematical Association of America.

Schwartz, J. & Yerushalmy, M. (1995). On the need for a bridging language for mathematical modeling. *For the Learning of Mathematics, 15*(2): 29–35.

Scott, D. B. & Tims, S. R. (1966). *Mathematical analysis: An introduction*. Cambridge: Cambridge University Press.

Sedlak, M., Wheeler, C., Pullin, D., & Cusic, P. (1986). *Selling students short: Classroom bargains and academic reform in the American high school*. New York: Teachers College Press.

Senk, S., Thompson, D., Viktora, S., Rubenstein, R., Halvorson, J., Flanders, J., Jakucyn, N., Pillsbury, G., & Usiskin, Z. (1990). *The University of Chicago school mathematics project: Advanced algebra*. Glenview, IL: Scott, Foresman and Company.

Serres, M. (1982). Mathematics and philosophy: What Thales saw … In Harari, J. & Bell, D. (eds), *Hermes: Literature, science, philosophy*. Baltimore, MD: Johns Hopkins University Press.

Shell Centre (1985). *The language of functions and graphs*. Nottingham, MD: Joint Matriculation Board.

Silver, E. A. & Stein, M. K. (1996). The QUASAR project: The "revolution of the possible" in mathematics instructional reform in urban middle schools. *Urban Education, 30*: 476–521.

Skemp, R. R. (1978). Relational understanding and instrumental understanding. *Arithmetic Teacher, 77*: 9–15.

Thomas, G. & Finney, R. (1992). *Calculus and analytic geometry, Part II* (8th edn). Reading, MA: Addison-Wesley.

Tobias, S. (1993). *Overcoming mathematical anxiety*. New York: W. W. Norton.

Trubowitz, S. & Longo, P. (1997). *How it works: Inside a school–college collaboration*. New York: Teachers College Press.

Usiskin, Z. (1987). Why elementary algebra can, should, and must be an eighth-grade course for average students. *Mathematics Teacher, 80*(6): 428–438.

Usiskin, Z. (2002). The shortage of qualified math teachers: A major problem and some suggested solutions. *UCSMP Newsletter*, no. 30. Chicago, IL: UCSMP.

Usiskin, Z. (2003). In *Next steps in mathematics teacher development, grades 9–12: Proceedings of a workshop* (CD Proceedings). Washington, DC: National Academies Press.

Van Zoest, L. R. & Bohl, J. V. (2000). The role of a reform curriculum in an internship: The case of Alice and Gregory. Paper presented at the Annual Meeting of the American Educational Research Association, April, New Orleans, Louisiana.

Wagner, S. (1981). Conservation of equation and function under transformations of variable. *Journal for Research in Mathematics Education, 12*(2): 107–118.

Watson, B. & Konick, R. (1990). Teaching for conceptual change: Confronting children's experience. *Phi Delta Kapa, 71*(9): 680–685.

Weick, K. & McDaniel, R. (1989). How professional organizations work: Implications for school organization and management. In Sergiovanni, T. & Moore, J. (eds), *Schooling for tomorrow: Directing reform to issues that count* (pp. 330–355). Boston, MA: Allyn & Bacon.

Wenger, E. (1998). *Communities of practice: Learning, meaning, and identity.* Cambridge: Cambridge University Press.

Wigfield, A. & Eccles, J. S. (1992). The development of achievement task values: A theoretical analysis. *Developmental Review, 12*: 265–310.

Wilensky, U. (1991). Abstract meditations on the concrete and concrete implications for mathematics education. In Harel, I. & Papert, S. (eds), *Constructionism.* Norwood, MA: Ablex.

Wilson, S. (2003). *California dreaming: Reforming mathematics education.* New Haven, CT: Yale University Press.

Yerushalmy, M. & Schwartz, J. (1993). Seizing the opportunity to make algebra mathematically and pedagogically interesting. In Romberg, T., Fennema, E., & Carpenter, T. (eds), *Integrating research on the graphical representation of function* (pp. 41–68), Hillsdale, NJ: Lawrence Erlbaum.

Yerushalmy, M., Shternberg, B., & Center for Educational Technology (1992). *The grapher's sketchbook* (computer software). Scotts Valley, CA: Wings for Learning.

Index

Figures are indicated by **bold** page numbers, tables by *italics*.

9 780415 879040